EDUCATION INCORPORATED

Recent Titles from Quorum Books

Forecasting Sales with the Personal Computer:
Guidelines for Marketing and Sales Managers
Dick Berry

Entrepreneurship and Public Policy:
Can Government Stimulate Business Startups?
Benjamin W. Mokry

Handbook of the Money and Capital Markets
Alan Gart

Envisionary Management: A Guide for Human Resource Professionals
in Management Training and Development
William P. Anthony, E. Nick Maddox, and Walter Wheatley, Jr.

Marketing Real Estate Internationally
M. A. Hines

Advertising Self-Regulation and Outside Participation:
A Multinational Comparison
J. J. Boddewyn

The New Environment in International Accounting: Issues and Practices
Ahmed Belkaoui

Legal Structure of International Textile Trade
Henry R. Zheng

Accounting for Data Processing Costs
Robert W. McGee

The Management of Corporate Business Units:
Portfolio Strategies for Turbulent Times
Louis E. V. Nevaer and Steven A. Deck

How to Write for the Professional Journals:
A Guide for Technically Trained Managers
Ryle L. Miller, Jr.

Effective Information Centers: Guidelines for MIS and IC Managers
Robert J. Thierauf

EDUCATION INCORPORATED

SCHOOL-BUSINESS COOPERATION FOR ECONOMIC GROWTH

Edited by Northeast-Midwest Institute

Foreword by William S. Woodside

With Contributions by:

PAULA DUGGAN
CHARLES W. BARTSCH
IAN McNETT
CANDICE BRISSON
PETER H. DOYLE
JACQUELINE MAZZA

QUORUM BOOKS

NEW YORK • WESTPORT, CONNECTICUT • LONDON

Library of Congress Cataloging-in-Publication Data

Education incorporated: school-business cooperation for economic
  growth/edited by Northeast-Midwest Institute; foreword by William
  S. Woodside; with contributions by Paula Duggan . . . [et al].
      p. cm.
    Bibliography: p.
    Includes index.
    ISBN 0-89930-282-3 (lib. bdg. : alk. paper)
    1. Industry and education—United States.   2. Education—Economic
  aspects—United States.   3. Education and state—United States.
  I. Duggan, Paula   II. Northeast-Midwest Institute (U.S.)
  LC1085.2.E38   1988
  370.19—dc19

                                                              87-32591

British Library Cataloguing in Publication Data is available.

Library of Congress Catalog Card Number: 87-32591
ISBN: 0-89930-282-3

First published in 1988 by Quorum Books

Greenwood Press, Inc.
88 Post Road West, Westport, Connecticut 06881

Printed in the United States of America

∞

The paper used in this book complies with the
Permanent Paper Standard issued by the National
Information Standards Organization (Z39.48-1984).

10 9 8 7 6 5 4 3 2 1

Copyright Acknowledgments

Chapters 2 through 7 were published originally by the Northeast-Midwest
Institute in a six-part, education-economic development series with the
generous support of the Primerica Foundation; Charles W. Bartsch, project
director, Deborah Cooney, editor.

Contents

Key Acronyms

ABE   Adult Basic Education. Programs of basic skills instruction for persons over the age of mandatory school attendance, designed to lead to the attainment of a GED (see below).

AACJC   American Association of Community and Junior Colleges. An association of over 1,000 community, junior, and technical colleges, with headquarters in Washington, D.C.

AAU   Association of American Universities. An association of 56 major public and private universities in the U.S. and Canada, with headquarters in Washington, D.C., supporting research and graduate education.

BLS   Bureau of Labor Statistics. The federal statistical agency, part of the U.S. Department of Labor.

CETA   Comprehensive Employment and Training Act. A federal program in effect from 1973 to 1982 providing funds to states and localities for job training and employment of the economically disadvantaged and long-term unemployed; replaced by JTPA (see below).

EDA   Economic Development Administration. Part of the U.S. Department of Commerce offering economic development planning, grants, and technical assistance to alleviate unemployment and to promote investment in distressed communities.

GED   General Educational Development. A measure of educational attainment generally equivalent to a high school diploma.

JTPA   Job Training Partnership Act. The federal program enacted in 1982 that provides funds to states and localities for job training for the economically disadvantaged and dislocated workers.

NASA   National Aeronautics and Space Administration. The government agency that manages the U.S. space program.

NSF   National Science Foundation. A major federal organization that sponsors research, primarily at universities, in a variety of scientific areas, including computer applications and small business innovations.

SBA   Small Business Administration. An independent federal agency that provides loans, loan guarantees, and a variety of technical assistance programs to help launch and nurture small businesses.

SBDC   Small Business Development Centers. Entities supported by SBA to fund counseling series, training programs, and publications for small business owners and operators to help them improve the efficiency and productivity of their firms. SBDCs are usually located at colleges and universities and operated in conjunction with them.

SBI   Small Business Institute. Part of SBA, SBIs provide broad-scale research and technical assistance services to improve business development opportunities.

SBIR   Small Business Innovation Research. A program administered by SBA to promote the establishment and growth of U.S. small businesses because they produce two and one-half times as many technical innovations as large firms.

SDA   Service Delivery Area. A geographically contiguous local area designated by the governor of a state as a planning and administrative district for JTPA.

SESA   State Employment Security Agency. A generic name for the state executive branch agency that administers both the unemployment insurance (UI) program and the Employment Service (ES).

SYETP   Summer Youth Employment and Training Program. A federal program, part of JTPA, of summer jobs and remedial education for economically disadvantaged youth.

PIC   Private Industry Council. The business-dominated local governing board that plans and administers JTPA programs.

UI   Unemployment Insurance Service. The federal-state cooperative program, financed by a payroll tax, providing partial income replacement for eligible laid-off workers.

Acknowledgments

The authors wish to thank several individuals for their contributions to this report. William Woodside, chairman of the Executive Committee, Primerica Corporation; Peter Goldberg, director of the Primerica Foundation; David Harrison, former director of the Northeast-Midwest Institute; and Richard Munson, the Institute's current director; all believed in the value of this project and supported it to completion. Several members of Congress helped review and publicize the original monographs: Senators William Cohen, Christopher Dodd, and Paul Simon; Representatives Sherwood Boehlert, William Clinger, Hamilton Fish, Jr., William Ford, William Goodling, Augustus Hawkins, James Jeffords, Nancy Johnson, Dale Kildee, Henry Nowak, Donald Pease, and Howard Wolpe.

The following people gave advice and comments that improved the content: Pamela Burns, Mary De Gonia, Evelyn Ganzglass, Paul Jurno, Richard Long, Jorie Mark, Steven Pines, Joseph Scherer, and Nevzer Stacy.

Several staff members of the Northeast-Midwest Institute were essential to the success of this project: Deborah Cooney, who edited the original manuscripts, combined them into this report, and revised Chapter 7; Glenn Starnes, Terry Terrien, and James Wise, who typed the original series; and Lilian Koper, who researched higher education issues.

Foreword

The United States is in the midst of a profound economic transformation. While traditional manufacturing continues to play a crucial role in the economy, its profile is changing rapidly. Companies are reorganizing their plans to improve productivity, they are introducing new technologies, and they are diversifying into new, high-growth ventures.

Unlike previous economic transformations, today's changes are occurring with tremendous speed. We once had decades to identify and solve the problems of economic adjustment. Cycles have now been compressed into only a few years. Because we have less time, we have less room for error. We also have more need for cooperation among private- and public-sector leaders.

These rapid economic shifts create tremendous opportunities. But they also can displace workers, disrupt communities, strain state treasuries, and divert attention from more deliberate strategies of long-term economic growth.

How we achieve the needed flexiblity to adapt to new economic and technological conditions is a critical issue facing business executives, labor leaders, educators, and elected officials in the late 1980s. Obviously, there is no simple, grand solution. We need a broad vision of U.S. competitiveness. But perhaps more important, we need a dedication to finding practical solutions to specific problems, and a commitment to the people caught up in the turbulence of economic change.

Education Inc. appropriately argues that we must first identify our people—our human capital, if you will—as the major resource for revitalizing our economy. Economic renewal is a human problem. Technology and management ability are critical factors, but economic growth and renewal ultimately depend upon our work force. They depend on whether we, as a nation, can provide our people with the education, training, and job opportunities that will allow them to reach their full potential and attain security in their personal lives. They depend on whether we can create a climate in which entrepreneurs can flourish.

Perhaps no asset of this nation is more critcal to its revitalization than our public and private educational systems. Yet many of these resources go untapped. For too many years, the corporations of America ignored the public schools. We had contributed generously to colleges and universities, but rarely thought twice about what was happening in the public elementary and secondary schools. Fortunately, that is beginning to change.

The Northeast-Midwest Institute has helped lead efforts to promote stronger ties between the nation's educational institutions and the economic development process. Clearly, public education and a healthy economy need each other to flourish. The educational enterprise must have the support of local citizens to secure funding, while good schools help to create a climate that nurtures business development.

The Primerica Foundation is pleased to have supported the institute's work on these issues. The development and refinement of the proposed business-education partnerships deserve the attention of top policymakers.

William S. Woodside
Chairman, Executive Committee
Primerica Corporation

EDUCATION INCORPORATED

1. Introduction

Sweeping changes in the economic structure of the Northeast-Midwest region—and the nation—call for a realignment of the institutions that undergird the economy. The old boundaries behind which the sectors of society have operated in virtual isolation must now be redrawn to create powerful new economic instruments. To meet the challenges that face the economy, close interaction is needed between education and business, with the support of government and other institutions. Such collaboration has begun.

Six studies by the Northeast-Midwest Institute explore a wide range of these collaborative efforts. Chapters 2 through 7 describe them in detail and provide models of how all sectors of society can work together to foster a vital and healthy economy.

THE NATURE OF THE CHALLENGE

The American economy is on the move. It is shifting from the heavy industry/smokestack model to one that is more oriented toward high technology and service. This transition has seen many low-skill jobs eliminated by machines or moved overseas. The changing economy places a premium on workers who possess strong basic skills and higher level analytical abilities. Industry increasingly requires well-educated employees with flexible skills to fill jobs very different than those performed through repetitive tasks on the assembly line.

Where will these workers come from? In addition to those coming directly from educational institutions, they will come from two sources: disadvantaged youth, and workers dislocated by structural unemployment. Preparing these workers for useful employment is a large educational challenge, but it is only part of the job. Businesses also need help in applying new technologies, developing, management and entrepreneurial expertise, and re-training and upgrading the existing work force. These needs imply new roles for schools.

The economic challenge can be met only by the full mobilization of all sectors of society. Structural changes require new institutional arrangements. This is especially the case in the field of education. To capture the full potential of investments already made and new ones being committed, education must find new uses for its buildings and resources (Chapter 2); develop and expand educational and training services to develop work force potential (Chapters 3 and 4); make use of research capacity and faculty expertise for business applications, and develop flexible funding strategies to support their services to business and industry (Chapters 5, 6, and 7).

. A considerable amount of overlap exists between business and education. Businesses find they must offer basic skills programs to new workers before they can perform satisfactorily on the job. The schools offer a great deal of job-specific training. This book deals with what is happening at the intersection of the two sectors. It describes the needed redefinition of roles and relationships that can bring about cooperation between education and business, rather than allowing each to operate with insufficient knowledge of the needs of the other. It also shows that government can have a positive effect on public/private collaboration. As the chief supporters of education and as regulators of business and industry, governments can remove unnecessary barriers, adopt policies promoting cooperation, and pass legislation where necessary.

WHY COLLABORATE?

Business and education have mutual interests that are better served if they work together. A strong economy benefits both. Such an economy depends on the full use of all resources: the technologies that education can help business apply, the managerial skills that education can help business develop, and the educated work force that schools can provide.

Educational institutions need to be more in tune with the economic life of the community. To flourish, education requires both the political and economic support of the community, of which business and industry are an essential part. A large part of the success of educational institutions is measured through the placement of their graduates and the use of their services by the business community. Through collaboration with employers, schools can develop programs and services that fit the needs of the private sector.

The benefits that business, education, government, and the community can expect from such cooperation are many.
Benefits to business include:

- educated and well-prepared workers:
- training and retraining of existing employees;
- help in applying technology to improve business operations;
- assistance in efforts to attract, retain, and expand business in the community;
- use of the facilities, equipment, and other resources of educational institutions;
- expert assistance for management, planning, marketing, and other business operations;
- direct economic benefits from educational institutions that buy goods and services in their local communities; and
- spreading the tax burden from economic growth.

Benefits to educational institutions include:

- a market for graduates and services;
- a stronger tax base to support their operations;
- increased political support from the community;
- the opportunity to expand to meet the needs of business and industry;
- assistance in terms of contributions, the loan or donation of equipment, and on-site training opportunities at employers' facilities;
- expert assistance from business for policy-making, resource allocation, and planning;
- information about needs of the workplace that will enable educational institutions to develop more effective programs; and
- use of experts from business as part-time or temporary full-time teachers and trainers.

Benefits to the government and community include:

- reduction of the costs of services such as welfare through the fuller employment of citizens;
- increased tax base from a stable and expanding economy;
- more jobs and income for citizens; and
- improved social and economic climate due to reduction of unemployment and underemployment.

NATURE OF THE COLLABORATION

Successful collaboration requires that each sector bring its full range of talents to the effort. Although business and education are the primary collaborators, other sectors play important supporting roles and should be brought together at the outset. Each sector has a particular role to play, but all should strive for a synthesis or synergistic effect, rather than having each simply work its side of the fence.

As the backbone of the economy, business provides the goods, services, job opportunities, development of natural resources, capital, and paychecks on which the economy depends. But employers also depend on educated workers and services provided by schools and colleges. Business leaders should tell education what kinds of skills workers need to succeed in the workplace and what kinds of services enterprises need to succeed in the marketplace.

To ensure that these services and workers are appropriate, business must work directly with schools and colleges to develop curricula and programs. Private-sector leaders should serve on school boards, planning committees, advisory groups, and other bodies that shape educational policies and programs. Also, business executives can develop formal and informal relationships with individual institutions through which information and expertise can be exchanged and particular programs can be developed. Further, industry can support education's efforts to obtain the necessary resources, both through the political process and direct donations of money, equipment, and the services of employees.

Of necessity, business reluctantly has taken on the task of teaching basic skills such as reading, writing, and mathematics to its employees. Working with the schools, employers should shift this task back to where it belongs, the classroom. And to the degree it can, business should guarantee jobs for those who complete school with the necessary basic and higher-level skills.

Generally, employers should be responsible for training their workers for particular jobs. The school's primary task is education. However, companies may want to purchase training from institutions capable of the task—vocational-technical schools, two-year colleges, and four-year institutions.

Educational institutions have the responsibility of finding out from employers what kind and level of skills they require of their employees. Those that provide other services—technology transfer or business assistance, for example—also have to ensure that their programs meet the needs of businesses. Educational institutions should take the initiative in reaching out and inviting business participation in planning and designing programs. This does not mean that business needs should dominate the educational mission at the expense of schools' other social functions--citizenship, public service, social services, culture and the arts, and so on. But education should seek advice, help, and cooperation on those matters that directly involve private-sector interests.

Goverment's role is helping plan, support, and coordinate programs that foster the collaboration of business and education. Because it provides most of the funds that support education, government must ensure that these funds are spent wisely, efficiently, and without duplication.

Local governments can work with companies and schools to make sure that programs fit local conditions. They can gather the information needed to plan the programs--assessing local needs for training and other assistance and resources available for meeting those needs (see Chapter 2). Local governments also have important roles in economic development efforts—the retention of existing industries and the attraction of new ones. They can provide services on their own or hire appropriate educational institutions or business associations, such as chambers of commerce or Private Industry Councils (PICs) (Chapters 3 and 4).

State governments can plan and support unified programs, which can be tailored to fit local conditions through individual schools, two-year colleges, vocational-technical institutions, and adult education programs linked to their statewide systems (Chapters 3, 4, 5, and 6).

The federal government needs to support programs aimed at particular national situations, such as disadvantaged youth (Chapter 3), structural unemployment (Chapters 4 and 6), and research and technology (Chapters 5 and 7). Such programs need not require large new sums of money. Refocusing existing programs can support collaboration between education and business.

FOCUSING ON THE EDUCATIONAL ROLE

The American educational system is large and complex, ranging from elementary and secondary schools through graduate and research institutions. Each segment of the educational system has important work to do in ensuring that the nation maintains and sustains a strong economy. All levels of education should work together to develop an integrated approach to collaborating with business. Considerable overlap exists among the services that various kinds of educational institutions can provide to business. They should aim to blend their interests and use each other's strengths to make the greatest impact and avoid duplication. Educational institutions should not only cooperate with business, but should collaborate with each other.

For example, an Ohio partnership helps companies adapt new technology to commercial applications; twenty-three centers provide start-up training through resource consortia of secondary schools, two-year colleges, vocational-technical centers, and university branches. The program is coordinated at the state level, but provides services locally through the educational institutions.

Generally, each segment of education, by the nature of its mandate, has a particular strength in promoting economic stability and growth. Public schools are concerned primarily with preparing young people for the workplace or further education. They can best serve the needs of the economy by teaching each young person the basic skills required for work, citizenship, and an effective private life. By ensuring that all their students learn to read, write, and compute effectively and to take care of their own economic needs, the public schools will well serve the needs of the private sector. Public schools also can mount adult education programs to teach basic skills to millions of illiterate adults.

Two-year colleges have a dual role. They serve as stepping-stones between high school and four-year colleges, and also offer terminal associate degrees for students who do not want four years of college. However, two-year colleges increasingly are providing job-related training and retraining, business assistance, and other services to companies. As members of statewide systems, two-year colleges offer states an opportunity to develop programs specific to local conditions.

Four-year institutions can offer services that require a massing of resources. They serve as consultants to business; provide extension services to business and industry; and promote technological and other innovations. Both two-year and four-year colleges aid new business start-ups through management training and incubators where enterprises can get a head start before striking out on their own.

Education's role in partnership with business has four dimensions.

1. The most obvious dimension is work force preparation. Each level of education develops intellectual skills. And some, such as two-year colleges and vocational-technical schools and institutes, provide job-specific training, either as part of their ongoing programs or under contract with employers.

2. Many institutions, particularly at the postsecondary level, provide a wide variety of services to companies. These services include helping them adapt new technologies; assisting them with planning, management, marketing, and financing; helping develop overseas markets; and gathering and managing data on local economic conditions.

3. Educational institutions also play a direct role in retaining and attracting businesses to a community. They work with state and local economic development groups in planning strategies, developing services, and directly recruiting companies. Postsecondary institutions, two-year colleges in particular, can bring their resources to bear on economic development

work. They can help groups prepare grant applications, develop and disseminate publicity, and develop business libraries. In some cases, economic development groups locate their offices on the college campuses and share computer, staff, and other resources with the colleges.

4. Schools also can aid their local economies by conducting themselves in a more businesslike way. Schools and colleges buy everything from milk to computers and fuel and heating oil. They help sustain the local economy by purchasing as much as possible from local merchants. Schools also have facilities that can be used in off-school hours for community and business betterment—classes, meeting places, training sites. In periods of declining enrollments, schools often have surplus buildings that could be converted to office space or other economic uses.

COOPERATIVE ARRANGEMENTS

The possiblities for cooperation between education and business are virtually unlimited. They range from informal partnerships to highly structured formal ones. No one model can be adopted to fit all situations, or even situations that are similar. Educational institutions and businesses must work together to develop the kind of relationship that best fits the local situation.

Partnerships between companies and local schools or school systems are one form of collaboration. For example, in Indianapolis, the chamber of commerce works with the city's school board and superintendent to guide policy, establish priorities, provide advice and evaluation about program activities, recruit volunteers, help with fund-raising, and develop a comprehensive communication program.

In other instances, a lead organization takes the initiative. In North Carolina, the Industrial Services Board of State Community Colleges administers a statewide training program, helps the state's department of commerce sell the state as a desirable industrial location, and helps colleges design and put into operation quality training programs.

In Boston, a coalition of groups—the Boston Compact—has established a wide-ranging partnership that includes literacy education among its many activities. Decisions are made by administrators of secondary schools, colleges, and community colleges, and leaders of community groups, and executives of major corporations—who pledge jobs for those who successfully complete programs.

Often, educational institutions provide services under contract with particular businesses and industries. An educational administrator with extensive business experience works with companies to develop training and service programs tailored to meet the companies' needs. In economic development efforts, representatives of business and education sometimes serve on each other's board of directors.

In all of these collaborative arrangements, the important element is the ability of each side to provide the other with immediate information on needs and available services. It must always be a two-way street. Though education provides services to business, educational institutions also have needs that business can fulfill—on-site training facilities, equipment, employees who can serve as trainers and teachers, contacts in the community to generate support for school programs.

In developing viable partnerships, education administrators and business leaders should not lose sight of other institutions that can help the effort. The support and participation of labor should be enlisted. Unions can provide trainers and political support. Financial institutions, though they may not directly benefit from the collaboration, do benefit from a stronger economy. They can provide financial support and introductions to other interested parties. Business organizations can broaden the base of these efforts; chambers of commerce and private industry councils (PICs) often take the lead as the business partner in a project. Community organizations offer opportunities for political support, networking, and even training and employment efforts. Frequently, the nonprofit sector—hospitals, mental health services, public libraries, and charitable organizations—are large employers and sources of influence in a community. And foundations, as well as government, are sources of funding for innovative efforts.

One example of a broad-based collaboration was a program to remodel and revitalize an aging automobile plant in St. Louis. St. Louis Community College, Ford Motor Company, the United Auto Workers, the St. Louis Department of Elementary and Secondary Education, the Governor's Office of Manpower Planning, the St. Louis Regional Commerce and Growth Association, and the Private Industry Council of St. Louis/St. Louis County all work together to save jobs and keep an industrial customer. Such broad-based partnerships can ensure a high-quality program, wide support for the effort, and a variety of funding sources.

OVERCOMING BARRIERS TO COLLABORATION

For many decades, business and education preferred to keep each other at arms' length and viewed each other with mutual distrust. Many educators feared that business would take over the schools if closer involvement were encouraged. And business has looked at the schools with an expectation of failure, and has tended to view education as a purely social issue. These barriers are coming down. Where mistrust persists, each side should work to overcome it. Honest communication and a recognition of mutual interest can begin to breach the barriers. In addition, each side should deliver fully and promptly on what it undertakes in any cooperative project. Nothing builds trust faster than the perception that the other partner delivers the goods.

In collaborating with universities, business has some particular fears— about patent policies and the sanctity of proprietary information. Where this is the case, universities should develop patent policies that satisfy faculty and the industry that may be supporting research. Universities must take steps to ensure that proprietary information remains inviolate.

Beyond the issue of historic distrust, education and business have distinctly different approaches. They differ in terms of tempo, time frames, goals, and tasks. For example, business training needs often do not fit education's term or semester system. University research programs may not focus on the development of products and processes to the degree that business requires, or move as quickly as business would like. Only careful work and planning can ensure that the efforts of each partner mesh in the programs they undertake together.

In establishing relationships with business, postsecondary institutions may confront problems with faculty members. First, faculty members may be jealous of colleagues who earn consulting fees and prestige from business programs. The reverse of this issue is that some faculty may regard practical programs to serve business and corporations as unworthy of their institution's academic image. Further, faculty may resist efforts to hire business employees as part-time or temporary faculty. In addressing all of these issues, colleges and universities must establish specific policies and procedures for faculty participation in programs with corporate or industry ties. Affirming that such programs contribute to the strength and growth of the institution also could help diminish opposition.

Finally, the partners should establish clear and measurable goals for the project. Each side should know from the beginning exactly what to expect from the other. Mechanisms should be established to evaluate the project periodically to determine if goals are being met, and to identify and correct problems before they get out of hand.

INGREDIENTS OF SUCCESS

The success of a partnership depends on many elements. Some strengths arise from the effort to overcome initial barriers to cooperation. However, participants of successful collaborations stress the need for commitment and participation by top executives, whether the university president or a senior vice president, a top business executive, the mayor's or governor's office, senior union officials, school superintendents, school board members, and principals. The visible involvement of top executives ensures that subordinates take the collaboration seriously. Without it, lower-level staff may fail to mobilize suficient resources or allow deadlines to slide. If that occurs, carefully built trust can be eroded, and one partner or another will abandon the effort.

Given such commitment, all partners need patience and careful building of programs to establish the opportunity for success to occur and for mutual trust to develop. In some cases, such as a contract for services, expectations are obvious; fulfillment of obligations can be measured with a great deal of precision. In other programs, however, success occurs over a longer term and is harder to measure precisely. A partnership designed to improve basic skills may take a year or two to prove itself, for example, or a university research effort for a corporation may require several years before benefits begin to flow. In such cases, benchmarks of progress may be established to gauge progress before the final product is delivered or the desired outcome is achieved.

Each partner must make good on its promises. That means a business employee assigned to teach a course must be in the classroom every time, well-prepared to teach the course. If a company contracts for the training of existing or new employees, the instruction must give them the necessary skills in time to meet the company's production schedule. If an educational institution offers its facilities for training, they must always be available for the scheduled training; and if a company provides on-site facilities for training, they must be available as scheduled. A university that promises to provide quarterly reports on sponsored research must submit those reports on the agreed-upon date. These are only a few of the myriad obligations of a successful collaboration.

Another essential for success is adapting programs to fit particular needs. It is rare that a program can be adopted entirely from one situation to another. Each business, educational institution or system, and economic challenge has its own character and peculiarities. For example, a literacy program that works for Puerto Rican Hispanics in New York City may very well not be suitable for Mexican immigrants in San Antonio. A program for youth employment in Appalachia will certainly be different from one in Los Angeles. Not only are the participants different, but the local economic conditions are different. Prospective partners may wish to examine models that worked in other areas, but planning and development are always required to tailor the programs to fit the local situation.

Adequate funding is another obvious essential for a successful program. Some state and local jurisdictions recognize the importance of education for economic development. They provide funds for training, business assistance, and programs to help business adapt technology to their operations. The federal government also provides money for training through the Job Training

Partnership Act, and other funds for small business development, research, and other programs of interest to education/business partnerships.

Many partnerships have shown flexibility and creativity in putting together a combination of resources from various funding sources to mount collaborative efforts. For example, an Ohio technology transfer program receives support from business and industry, local foundations, state and federal programs, and services contributed locally. Funds for the development of new facilities or economic development centers may also come from the federal Economic Development Administration and the Department of Housing and Urban Development. The federal/state unemployment insurance program may also offer possibilities for supporting training and self-employment.

EVIDENCE OF SUCCESS

Several public-private partnerships have established substantial track records by now. Many programs are in place—some for decades. The very longevity of some of the older programs shows that business, state officials, and legislators are convinced that cooperation between business and education is a highly productive venture.

Success can be measured more precisely, however. Numerous documented cases exist that have data on numbers of people trained; job placements; businesses created, attracted, and retained; and so forth. Here are a handful of brief examples of success that are documented more fully in the following chapters.

- The Columbus, Ohio, school system has mounted a program to improve its curriculum and benefit the local economy. The sixth largest employer in Columbus, the school system seeks to spend its resources with local businesses. In addition, it has contracted to assess the aptitudes and skills of prospective employees, provide specialized training programs, set up vocational education for adults and vocational work-study opportunities for students, and provide after-school care for the children of working parents.

- The Boston Compact's collaborative effort provides business assistance for raising literacy levels in the schools. In return for educational improvements, the corporations promise to recruit new employees from city schools before looking elsewhere.

- The South Carolina Technical Education System is credited with helping generate $17.6 billion in business investment and 330,000 new jobs in the state during its 25 years of existence. Two-year colleges in North Carolina have provided training for more than 400 companies during the past 15 years.

- A collaboration between the University of Alabama at Tuscaloosa and General Motors saved a carburetor plant that was losing money; more than 200 jobs were saved, plus an important element in the local economy. In addition, the university, which rented the facility as a research location, provided its students with a laboratory and established a reputation as an institution that can work with business and deliver on its commitments. Incidents of faculty consulting with other businesses have increased. General Motors, pleased with the venture, is strengthening its relationship with other universities around the country.

- Thirty-eight business assistance centers established by the Illinois Community College Board are credited with creating 6,240 new jobs and retaining another 3,560 during fiscal 1985 alone. During the same year, the state's two-year colleges offered workshops and seminars in entrepreneurship and technical training attended by 19,034 small business owners and operators.

- Polaroid Corporation's Inner City, Inc., program to provide disadvantaged youth with training in employment competencies and work maturity found that of the first group of trainees who graduated to full employment with the corporation, 80 percent stayed more than nine years.

These programs represent a sample of a sample; they are selected from the programs the Northeast-Midwest Institute discovered in its studies of partnerships between business and education. A fuller description of that collaboration is offered in the chapters that follow.

PART I
EXTENDING
SCHOOL RESOURCES

2. School Service to the Community

SCHOOL SPENDING AND ECONOMIC GROWTH

Providing all children the opportunity for a good public education is one of this country's most important social and political goals. Its stature is reflected by the fact that school expenditures are one of the largest budget items of most states and localities. States in the Northwest and Midwest especially have a long tradition of striving for excellence in public education. Generally they have funded education from kindergarten to graduate school through times of surplus and austerity. Fourteen of the states in the region rank above the national average in student-teacher ratios and in expenditures per student.[1]

Schools do more than produce educated students; in their capacity as significant local businesses, they sometimes employ hundreds of people, consume a variety of goods, and require a broad range of services. Benefits flow both ways between a community and a school system. The community invests public tax dollars in the system. Schools repay this investment by preparing students for the working world, providing a range of job opportunities, and generating economic activities.

Education contributes to the public good much the same way as local businesses. In fact, public education and a healthy economy need each other to flourish. The educational enterprise must have the support of local citizens to secure funding, while good schools help create a climate that nurtures business development. The availability of high-quality education keeps families in an area and attracts new ones to maintain and increase the tax base. Good schools also contribute to the kind of living environment companies look for in choosing locations.

Businesses depend on schools for literate, well-rounded employees. The Bureau of Labor Statistics projects both a shortage of workers in several occupational fields and higher entry-level skill requirements for even more jobs by the 1990s.[2] Business will need high-quality public schools to prepare people for these positions. Businesses know that educational preparedness is vital for maintaining U.S. competitiveness in international markets.

Many states and localities in the Northeast and Midwest have grasped the importance of supporting the educational process and involving it in economic development. They understand the manifold relationships among a school system, the community, and the local economy. In a time of tight budgets, declining school enrollments, and heightened competition among public agencies for funding, school systems can champion increased educational budgets on grounds of benefits to students and contributions to community economic viability. Educators must show the public that schools are a resource serving broader business and community goals. Until they do, many taxpayers may conclude that school spending simply is a major burden that, if anything, inhibits economic growth. Ronald Everett, a professor of educational administration, urges administrators to counter this assumption and to make the case publicly for schools' contribution to economic growth.

Educational leaders need to develop an awareness and a visibility in the area of economic development because the educational agency they lead or direct, whether a local board of education or a community college, will benefit through higher property values, increased community support for education and the schools, greater economic stability, enhanced educational and employment opportunities for students, and a stablilized or growing student population.[3]

State legislatures are feeling new pressures to compensate for reduced federal funding for some educational programs. States now provide about 49 percent of public education funds,[4] but will have to bear either a larger proportion of the costs or pass responsibility on to local governments. Therefore, school administrators have to build more local support and appreciation for education budgets.

School operations should be placed in a larger economic context. The school system frequently is one of the largest employers in the community. It may have the area's largest payroll, which circulates throughout local commercial and service establishments. The system may operate the largest fleet of motor vehicles. It may have extensive real estate holdings and function as the largest building manager in the area. It probably is the largest food service operator. Clearly, public educational systems are economic entities that play substantial roles in generating and supporting jobs in the local community.

In this analogy, the superintendent of schools is the chief executive officer of a major local corporation with the opportunity to lead the school system in achieving its full economic potential. Successful school administrators are both good managers and effective school program advocates. Discussion and examples in the following sections guide administrators toward reviewing their roles in economic development. Toward this end, they are encouraged to reconsider traditional school system spending and its effects on the local economy. Next, they are asked to think more creatively about educational resources in a less familiar context—as economic and social development tools.

The discussion poses a variety of questions. How can the community realize a greater return on its investment through reduced costs or increased services? How can the dollars-and-cents value of the system to the local economy be maximized? Are there ways to target procurement to local businesses? Are economies of scale achievable in specific programs through cooperative programs with other schools? Do the transportation and food service operations offer possible training opportunities for students? What steps can the superintendent take to strengthen ties to the business community and to the neighborhood groups?

Adminstrators are asked to consider the effectiveness of the examples presented in light of their own local circumstances and needs. The efforts of the Columbus, Ohio, school system to maintain quality teaching and help the local economy are presented in a case study.

Superintendents have the resources at hand and authority to initiate changes based on the ideas presented in the following discussion. However, they should not bear sole responsibility for taking the necessary action. Business executives, government officials, and other community leaders should join in and contribute their talents and support to linking public education with community development. These two sectors may have conflicting interests at times, but their long-term goals are similar. Both want their community to prosper. With this in mind, every attempt should be made to resolve any apparent differences.

The following sections are designed to help school administrators and other interested readers analyze their systems' many contributions to their local economies and identify new growth opportunities. Administrators who strengthen these connections prove the contention that school spending is directly and inextricably linked to a community's development and long-term vitality.

REASSESSING TRADITIONAL SCHOOL EXPENDITURES

Administrators' assessments of the economic impact of the school district on the community should begin with an understanding of the numbers. Local governments spend almost twice as much on education as any other category. The school system usually is one of the largest employers in the local community, if not the largest. It also is a significant consumer of goods and services. Public school expenditures for basic needs—office and classroom supplies, transportation, food—exceeded $100 billion nationally ever since the 1986-1987 academic year.[5] The school system also may have the community's largest payroll, generating local and state taxes, thereby recycling revenues that support education. In addition to paying taxes, school system employees help create significant demand for local business products and services, such as housing, health care, financial services, and consumer goods. In short, a school system's overall effect on the local economy is more pervasive than administrators may realize. Therefore, school system CEOs must develop a new understanding of the dollar value of the school system in the community.

To be effective players in the local economy, educators must recognize that school districts cannot be viewed in isolation from the rest of the community. They should reevaluate traditional expenditures in the context of the local development climate, analyzing them as contributions to its ecomonic health. **Specifically, adminstrators should reexamine three aspects of traditional school outlays:**

- how purchase and contract awards generate direct and subsequent benefits to the local economy;
- how school expenditures can be justified in a manner that builds business, citizen, and government support for school budgets; and
- how more economic advantages can accrue the community when school systems stretch resources and increase the spending power of each education dollar.

Econometric models have been developed to measure the impacts of industries and universities on a community. Some elements of these models are applicable to elementary and secondary school systems. With local business and employment data and some common sense calculations, administrators can develop economic impact estimates that are appropriate for local use. These include the amount of employee salaries likely to be spent locally on food, housing, and other consumer items; the extent of school system funds spent locally on supplies such as paper products and classroom materials; and services such as accounting, legal assistance, and maintenance. Such statistics, in turn, can provide the basis for discussions with the local chamber of commerce, city development planners, and community leaders, who can provide further "real life" information on the multiplier effects of these expenditures on new jobs, business development, and increased tax revenues.

Viewing school systems as major local economic forces and thinking of school superintendents as corporate executives triggers a host of related questions. How can administrators improve the public perception of the district as an economic entity in its own right? How can the schools generate a greater return to the community through increased services to students, businesses, local development organizations, and residents? How can standard services be delivered at lower cost? How can the schools help improve the area's quality of life, making it more attractive to potential businesses and residents? Administrators who respond effectively to these questions will promote greater appreciation for school expenditures and expand political support in the process.

School System Purchasing

School systems contribute greatly to community business activities through purchases of goods and services. Administrators should orient procurement policies toward local merchants because increased sales volume translates into additional jobs and tax revenues—and more business support of education. It may not be practical or possible to acquire items locally that are purchased in large quantities or through national wholesalers, such as textbooks. But administrators should examine local businesses and identify procurement opportunities from this market. School districts have varying amounts of discretion in purchasing goods and services. Small communities may have only one appropriate manufacturer or distributor or none at all. In such cases, a large portion of goods and services have to come from nonlocal sources. Large city systems, however, have greater opportunities to solicit competitive bids from local companies.

The power of school purchasing becomes apparent when the yearly totals for supplies are compiled. For example, Florida school districts each spent an average of $4.6 million for materials and supplies, $4 million for food services, and $308,500 for acquisition and construction of school facilities in the 1982-1983 school year.[6] Even a relatively small item can become a major purchase. The Columbus, Ohio, school system spends more than $1 million each year just for milk (see the case study). Taken together, these expenditures can increase a community's production of goods and services significantly—a boost to the local equivalent of the gross national product. Properly targeted and orchestrated, local purchases can play a vital role in business development and growth and help recycle funds within the community.

This type of activity has important secondary or multiplier effects in the local economy. Schools are comparable to businesses in that purchases of goods or services translate into income for those who have provided the products or services. Some of this income will be spent on additional goods and services. These new expenditures, in turn, generate more economic activity, which may continue for several cycles. Thus, each dollar spent by the system will create additional economic benefits, sometimes as much as four times the original expenditure. School administrators need to recognize how this multiplier effect works; they can then establish locally targeted procurement policies that, in effect, "multiply" the impact of school purchases.

Procurement should always be carried out in a fiscally prudent manner to ensure that school district funds are used efficiently. At the same time, administrators should make every effort to purchase supplies from capable local dealers. Otherwise, the school system loses an opportunity to contribute to the local economy and deprives itself of a natural budget ally. Some school procurements policies may limit the ability of local merchants to bid on contracts. For example, small businesses may find bonding requirements prohibitive. Others may find the paperwork requirements burdensome or payment schedules too slow. Administrators should evaluate procurement procedures to identify and, if possible, remove impediments that inhibit local bidding unnecessarily.

School district purchasing policies can be shaped to target an area as large as a state or as small as a neighborhood. School business may be channeled to distressed neighborhoods as part of local economic development programs. Sometimes "local" boundaries are difficult to define; for example, northern Virginia, southern Maryland, and the District of Columbia are considered part of the Washington, D.C., metropolitan area. Therefore, school officials must decide whether they should restrict their market to the home city or state or should purchase from merchants in another jurisdiction where goods are cheaper or more readily available. Again, there are no standard answers. Local factors will influence administrators' decisions on these purchasing issues.

Local procurement can be used in conjunction with federal and state business development programs to stimulate growth. School officials can work with regional officers of the U.S. Small Business Administration (SBA) and state and municipal development agencies to identify viable businesses to provide supplies and services to schools. Many states and cities have selected certain types of businesses or geographic areas for development assistance. School systems may want to channel business to competent companies in these categories. These and other links formed among school, government, and business officials foster business success and cost savings for the schools.

To alert firms to possible business opportunities, school officials could produce a brochure describing a system's procurement policies and encouraging the firms to seek school business. The brochure should explain how bidding procedures are carried out, the laws governing school purchasing, and a list of people to contact in the system. Copies can be distributed through the chamber of commerce, professional organizations, and direct mailings. A comprehensive and clear procurement brochure can help avoid misunderstandings often associated with purchasing, such as procedural peculiarities and accusations of favoritism.

Some communities already have this type of brochure for federal procurement; a version for local purchasing would be useful. School administrators can draw on the experience of city and state officials involved in procurement when composing guidelines for their school system. Designating one staff person as a contact can simplify the answering of procurement inquiries and the bidding and negotiations process. This person could coordinate publicity, oversee preparation and distribution of a brochure, and serve as liaison between businesses and school officials.

In some cases, "buy local" efforts may conflict with low-bid purchasing policies. State and local laws also may limit discretion. Administrators have to maintain a balance between local preference policies and the need to buy at the lowest price no matter what the origin. Administrators possessing some flexibility should consider the degree of price differences and the amount of local business generated, as well as product quality. Even if local goods and services are more expensive than nonlocal ones, the benefits of patronizing local firms, from better service to goodwill, may offset the higher prices. Administrators should, to the extent possible, include these factors as they make their spending decisions. Economists term this as "cost-benefit analysis," an approach that weighs estimates of relevant variables, relationships, and benefits against costs.[7]

Finally, administrators should not discount a related procurement issue—transportation. Schools spend substantial amounts for the purchase, maintenance, and support of vehicles to transport students and administrative personnel. These buses, cars, and trucks affect the local economy through contracts for drivers, repairs, insurance, and fuel. Depending on the district's arrangement, vehicles may be stored at a central location, incurring additional spending for rent. Transportation expenditures should be considered in the same policy light as purchases described above.

Administrators should increase the school system's purchases in the local economy. They could do the following:

- Establish a "buy local" policy whenever possible.
- Identify businesses capable of providing services or supplies, and solicit bids from them.
- Find a knowledgeable contact person to handle business inquiries.
- Identify those policies, such as bonding requirements, that shut out local business bids and change them. The chamber of commerce and other business groups can provide ideas, suggest alternatives, and notify businesses of contract opportunities.

- Produce a brochure or find other means of informing businesses of school policies and regulations affecting purchasing processes.

- Contact appropriate program officials to tie into local, state, or federal business assistance programs such as SBA loan programs, state enterprise zones, or local programs that target specific neighborhoods.

- Establish, to the extent possible, "buy local" policies for purchasing such items as new vehicles and insurance, service and maintenance contracts, and school uniforms, from local businesses.

Payroll and Staff

Expenditures for payroll and staff place a school system in the mainstream of a community's economic operations, even though they may have less obvious paybacks than direct purchases. Quite simply, the larger the staff, the larger the school "corporation" and the greater its local economic impact.

A major hurdle for many school administrators to overcome is convincing local businesses and taxpayers that payroll increases are worthwhile. The fact is that money for additional staff positions creates a return on investment. It increases a school's ability to educate young people and provide services that build up the local business environment, perhaps making the difference between entrepreneurial survival and failure. Using the same argument presented earlier, administrators can illustrate how salaries are put back into the community through purchases made and taxes paid, and thus are not a drain on the economy. School officials should develop a formula that measures the approximate net cost of hiring personnel. Such a formula would factor in salaries paid, local taxes generated, spending per staff person, administrative costs to the system, and other items.

Administrators usually have little short-term flexibility to stimulate the payroll and or the local economy in hard dollar terms. Tight budgets frequently prevent hiring additional personnel. As a way of working around budget constraints, some school systems have hired staff jointly with other geographically close school districts or with government agencies. For example, different districts may have common needs for part-time special education, art, administrative, or other personnel. Joint hiring is a cost-effective way to recruit and fill similar positions in different offices or districts. It allows schools to offer a broader range of services that produce economic advantages and community benefits—all of which improve the overall "quality of life" for present and prospective companies and residents.

Over half the states have set up educational service agencies to expand their educational programs. These agencies are cooperative groups supported by member districts that pool resources to purchase and share the

the services of counselors, librarians, foreign language teachers, and school psychologists. Pooling resources enables these districts to hire personnel that few could afford on their own. In Minnesota, Education Cooperative Service Units (ECSUs) were authorized in 1976 to help school systems meet specific educational needs of students and provide educational planning on a regional basis. In addition to aiding secondary schools, ECSUs allow districts to establish postsecondary, vocational, adult, and community education courses.[8]

Ideally, the effective delivery of services by these cooperative agencies raises the educational level in the community. These gains, in turn, improve both the work readiness of the labor force and its adaptability to new businesses. Students receive a better and more diverse education and are prepared for the work world. Adults get the chance to sharpen their skills. Businesses can count on better educated high school graduates and working adults, who are likely to be more productive and require less training. The community's investment saves companies money and makes them more likely to hire additional employees. Again, the economic advantage of these services and programs, while less obvious, nonetheless is important in stimulating growth.

Another way to expand staff at little or no cost is to use trainees, especially for clerical and other nonteaching functions. Depending on local policies and program rules, some federal Job Training Partnership Act (JTPA) programs reimburse a portion of the wages of the on-the-job trainees. Private training centers may welcome opportunities to place participants in real-world settings as part of their curricula. Local universities may have programs in which students can serve internships or work part-time in schools to gain experience in their chosen fields—librarianship, computer technology, accounting, and so on.

Drawing on volunteers can expand a district's ability to provide services. Parent associations, senior citizen groups, and similar organizations are likely sources of volunteer help. However, some districts have met with objections from labor unions over their use. School officials should be sensitive to this issue and deal with it as needed. The purpose of volunteers is to perform services for which the district can not afford to pay, not to displace workers.

Both trainees and volunteers can be especially valuable in expanding a school system's overall breadth of services. By tapping these resources, school administrators can reach beyond their main mission of educating students to offer technical assistance and provide social and cultural programs to enrich the community.

Administrators should redefine their staffing policies, and their effects on the local economy. They could do the following:

- Develop an income model or formula to assess the primary, secondary, and multiplier effects of the school system payroll on the local economy.
- Build support for more staff positions by determining what percentage of new income will be spent on local products, services, and taxes.
- Initiate cooperative hiring arrangements, such as Minnesota's ECSUs, with nearby districts and perhaps the state department of education.
- Stretch the personnel budget by pooling resources with other districts, creating on-the-job training opportunities through professional and technical internships, and using volunteers from local citizens organizations or parent groups to fill in personnel gaps.

Real Estate

Real estate holdings, including both land and improvements, are undoubtedly any school district's largest asset. They represent an enormous investment of public education funds and, in most places, untapped economic development resources that can be developed in many ways.

All school systems, especially those with older buildings, have large maintenance and repair budgets. Although in-house staff do much of the work, numerous projects require outside contractors. Like supply purchases, this capital plant investment can be targeted to local businesses. Repair, renovation, and construction activities promote the same economic multipliers and spin-off benefits as other types of school system investments and contribute to local job creation and retention. Equally important, they generate good will and greater appreciation of the school system by the area's small business owners and employees.

Expenditures for buildings and grounds in this context have more relevance to the community as a whole. Administrators should create local contractor preference policies similar to those for procurement. Administrators again would have to make judgments on bids and their relative benefits to the local community. As with procurement, a service-provider brochure would be a valuable tool to explain and promote this policy.

A decline in enrollments has left some areas with empty school rooms and closed buildings. Empty buildings are a drain on the local economy; they incur costs for maintenance, security, and insurance that should go to productive uses. Maintenance of an empty school building in New York City can cost from $20,000 to $85,000 per year.[9] Ironically, these situations thrust upon school officials another way to realize the economic potential of school real estate: turning these facilities to other uses. They should not be allowed to stand empty; this is a waste of prime space that could be used by a community group or rented to a government agency. Administrators can boost the local "return" on real estate investments by using space in school buildings creatively.

This prescription is particularly relevant to the Northeast and Midwest sections of the country, where numerous communities have suffered drops in school populations over the last ten years.[10] Areas already characterized as "declining" cannot afford to carry the visible and symbolic burden of closed, underused school buildings. Productive reuses of surplus real estate for shops, offices, or community centers can help counter an image of economic stagnation and encourage new development. (The next section contains a more detailed discussion of alternative uses for school property.)

Administrators should integrate their real estate policies into local development strategies. They could do the following:

- Conduct an annual survey of the district's real estate holdings (both buildings and land), calculate their worth, annual maintenance costs, and related expenses.

- Solicit opinions on the relative value of holdings from local planning officials and realty boards.

- Identify local contractors for repair and modernization projects.

- Consider a local preference policy for such activities.

- Prepare a contractor-building brochure or fact sheet that includes a sample school system contact.

- Identify uses by the private sector or public sector for the unneeded buildings.

Utilities

Schools usually have little choice in purchasing their fuel, electricity, water, and sewer services even though they are large-volume customers. Except in larger metropolitan areas, only one utility exists for each service, allowing no competitive pricing. In most instances, utilities bill each school individually, rather than treating the system as one customer. Administrators could negotiate with utilities for discounts based on the high volume consumed throughout the system. Few school systems have the ability to shift consumption to off-peak periods. In this case, savings and efficient uses should be introduced in other ways. As major businesses, school systems can exert more clout than they imagine.

Some school districts have made great strides in reducing their utility costs through innovative conservation programs and negotiating agreements with various utility companies. These efforts merit consideration because substantial savings free up resources to expand other school services. Also, as major consumers, schools are excellent candidates for conservation efforts. Many utilities are willing to help schools save energy, which helps them with more efficient load management. For example, the Tennessee Valley Authority (TVA) helps schools in its area find ways to conserve energy through its Solar Technology Outreach Program. Schools can reduce energy

costs associated with new construction, renovations, and additions by requesting TVA's computer modeling services, thermal performance calculations, recommendations for energy-saving devices, and cost-effectiveness
studies. Schools participating in this program have reported estimated consumption reductions of up to 52 percent for heating, cooling, and lighting.[11]

Schools can serve as public testing sites for innovative energy designs or
programs. The appropriate school office can arrange with a utility to be a
model or participant in an experiment in exchange for discounted services.
In return, utilities can try out their designs or equipment inexpensively in
easily accessible and often-visited sites. Such projects encourage the community to adopt new ideas, and both schools and utilities benefit from the
good publicity. Local buildings suppliers also may be receptive to using
schools as models for new and innovative products in exchange for discounts.

Schools can realize energy savings through the use of energy-efficient
designs even without the help of a utility. The Fort Stewart Elementary
School in Hinesville, Georgia, cut its air-conditioning requirements by 65
percent and reduced overall energy consumption (in its late 1960s buildings)
by two-thirds, using passive solar heating, active solar hot water, and
various other means of energy conservation. Abrams Elementary School in
Bessemer, Alabama, installed passive solar collectors and now uses approximately one-third as much energy as the average area elementary school.[12]
School officials should check with local design firms to see if they will
donate time and advice on how to incorporate energy conservation measures.
Some conservation improvements might be added by the school's shop students
in exchange for course credit or pay.

The Philadelphia public school system saved $3 million over ten months
during 1984 through a conservation campaign involving all 250 schools.
With the promise that saved energy dollars would be converted into education dollars, a committee of maintenance, administration, and teaching representatives formulated a low-cost conservation plan. Each school was responsible for cutting its energy consumption. As an incentive, the system
returned 40 percent of each school's annual savings for its discretionary use.
Schools channeled their savings to educational programs, thus expanding
their abilities to meet students' needs and provide a broader range of community services. Public recognition of conservation programs has helped to
improve public confidence in the management of the school system.[13]

The Philadelphia program, like other examples, did not require extensive
investments or costly staff time. It simply required each school to do its best
to save energy. All school districts should investigate conservation measures
such as those suggested here. The potential is there to save a significant
amount of scarce school dollars.

Administrators should look for savings through efficient energy use. They could do the following:

* Explore with utility companies the possibility of considering the entire school system as one customer so it can receive discounts for quantity use.

* Adopt energy conservation programs, such as weatherization of older buildings, and use shop students and maintenance staff to help where possible.

* Allow schools to be used as sites for testing new conservation designs or equipment in exchange for discounts.

* Incorporate energy efficiency into daily school operations.

* Seek donated time and advice from a local design firm.

WIDENING SCHOOL RESOURCES FOR BUSINESS AND COMMUNITY

The preceding discussion called on administrators to reexamine the role of the school system, and their own roles, in terms usually applied to private-sector enterprises. By virtue of their assets and spending power, school systems are economic units. As such, they stimulate the local economy directly, a fact that many educators believe should be better understood by the public.

School administrators and school board members are in a position to make wider use of their influence, physical plants, and financial resources to help local businesses and the entire community. Increasingly they see this kind of service as part of their duties as educators; a growing number view their classrooms as having more dimensions. Individual administrators and their staffs must decide how active a role they and their systems will play. A strong presence can bring a school system to the forefront of a community's economic activities, with resulting benefits for community groups and the educational system.

School systems can promote local development prospects, strengthen local businesses, enhance educational and recreational opportunities for residents, and build up community services. These elements must be present for a jurisdiction to nurture a healthy environment for private investment and growth. Economists acknowledge that the rate of economic growth is closely related to numerous physical and social conditions in addition to private investment decisions.[14] Levels of educational achievement, poverty, or public services, for example, can add to or constrict local growth. Therefore, to understand the economic function of a school system, factors affecting the "quality of life" in a community must be considered.

Research in educational literature and recent interviews show that administrators are leading their districts toward participating in substantial, if less traditional, business and community activities. Specifically, many have recognized the importance of good schools to economic development. Some school systems are even putting their underused facilities to more profitable use. Others have seized opportunities to run cooperative programs with businesses and government agencies, including community planning agencies, the city councils, and mayor's offices. Many systems have expanded the school's basic function of educating young people to include work force training and adult education. Others have found school involvement in health care issues important for their areas. These kinds of activities build and sustain a school district's involvement with community affairs. They can play an important part in creating a strong economy and improving a community's livability.

Education as a Development Incentive

A recognition of schools' importance in developing the economy should be a major element of school-community cooperative ventures. The quality of the local school system is an important factor in businesses' selection of locations. Administrators should work closely with the local chamber of commerce and city officials to publicize this asset. They may want to prepare a synopsis of educational services and attributes that includes a discussion of school facilities, teaching staff, rank of students' test scores, and other positive features. This document can be part of a larger, community marketing strategy. School officials should make the initial contact with local officials, if necessary, in order to get started.

The quality of the local educational system is especially important to businesses for two reasons. Studies have found that employees' satisfaction with their jobs is affected by their perception of their children's education. Also, businesses have found that their success in attracting and retaining a skilled and motivated work force is grounded in effective local elementary and secondary schools.

A 1979 report of the Joint Economic Committee of Congress found that quality of schooling is one of the principal elements of a favorable business climate in central cities. It concluded that people perceive the business climate as roughly parallel to a city's livability; if one is good, so is the other. Many of the executives interviewed stated that no financial offer could persuade them to move to an undesirable location.[15] Areas with low ratings for schools and other quality-of-life factors may find that tax breaks and financing packages are not enough to attract new businesses. In short, favorable public perception of local school quality is crucial to a community's fashioning a positive image and assuring long-term economic health. High per capita student spending levels and the rich variety of school-related services found in Northeastern and Midwestern states should be viewed in this light—as important business development inducements.

Cooperation between school administrators and other public officials can lead to a pooling of educational and community resources. These two groups can undertake activities that the school system or the community would be unable to sponsor individually. The combination of personnel, funds, and facilities can add to a location's range of services, including business assistance, that make an area more attractive for development.

Cooperation of school and business leaders is equally important. Administrators should become well acquainted with local businesspersons through the chamber of commerce, private industry council, and other groups. Parent-teacher groups and neighborhood organizations also are allies for school officials. Administrators can organize and lead regular discussions of school-community marketing plans for all parties involved. These groups should receive reports of the school board's and individual schools' work on educational goals such as teaching staff improvements and student retention rates.

Administrators should find ways to work with other local officials in promoting the quality of schooling as an economic development incentive. They could do the following:

- Initiate or improve working relationships with representatives from business groups, the planning department, city or county council, and the mayor's office.

- Make these representatives aware of the role of school quality in business location decisions.

- Prepare a synopsis of educational services for them, and brief them on the interrelationship of business development and education quality.

- Help attract business to the area by presenting the synopsis in meetings with corporate leaders or by conducting tours of education facilities.

- Identify any community groups or government offices with which the school district can undertake cooperative projects.

- Promote regular discussions to update all participating groups about activities underway.

Surplus Resources

Many school districts with declining enrollments or shifting residence patterns have "surplus" facilities. Some studies have shown that communities with closed schools are perceived as declining overall. They also show that the value of nearby real estate tends to decrease when a school is closed.[16] A closed school not only fosters a negative image, it burdens the local system with very real maintenance and security costs.

School officials must know the number and value of all facilities and sites under their jurisdiction. This information can be gathered most efficiently by conducting a comprehensive survey and updating it periodically. It should note characteristics such as location and condition, and marketable features such as auditoriums, food service facilities, gyms, labs, and parking. With this knowledge, administrators can work with local development, government, and social service agencies to find other uses for empty buildings.

One option is to sell, loan, or convert the buildings for use by other government agencies or private businesses. If officials are hesitant to sell outright, they can negotiate multiyear leases for the property. This way buildings can generate revenues for the school system now but can be returned to classroom use if needed later. Sale-lease-back options, while not commonly used for schools, might be considered.

In Medina, Ohio, an outdated junior high was sold to the county for conversion to office space. The school district used the proceeds to build a new school in a high-growth area and the county obtained an administrative building for less than the cost of constructing a new one.[17] The city of Ann Arbor, Michigan, and its board of education worked out a creative alternative-use arrangement. A multipurpose center, owned jointly by the city and school board, was added to an existing elementary school. When a new elementary school was constructed, the city purchased the old building for a small fee in order to house a variety of community activities and a new public swimming pool. The school board still owns the gym, which the city uses in off hours; the locker rooms are owned cooperatively.[18]

School buildings are ideal for some specialized educational and public purposes, especially those with auditoriums, parking lots, and food service facilities. They can serve as sites for small business incubators or technical centers, adult education classes, job training programs, or community meeting space. A local university or community college may wish to lease this space for off-campus programs.

The Downriver Community Conference (DCC), a sixteen-city, public service consortium headquartered in Southgate, Michigan, converted the unused Schafer High School into a comprehensive business and training center. The DCC complex includes a small business incubator, a job clearinghouse, and a Small Business Assistance Center. The layout of the old school was suitable for the assistance center, whose staff members offer counseling to individual business owners and managers as well as sponsor larger workshops and forums. A Michigan venture capital company has opened an office in a former classroom. The DCC operation, which has received national acclaim, has trained and placed hundreds of persons. It also has provided information and technical and financial assistance to over 500 small companies.[19]

Horizon Middle School became a focal point of Aurora, Colorado, when it was refurbished as a multipurpose community center. In addition to seventh- and eighth-grade classrooms, Horizon houses a branch of the public library, a community recreation center, a Boy Scout troop, soccer teams, home-owners associations, and two Sunday church groups. The result is that many more people are involved with Horizon than if it had remained as only a middle school. Even people without children in school now take an interest in educational issues and support schooling as vital to their community.[20]

The purchase and conversion of surplus school buildings by private developers can be attractive propositions for school boards and tax assessors. Unused schools with sound structures and convenient locations have high potential for conversion. Renovations of abandoned schools in central city areas for housing, offices, and other commercial use are among the most common rehabilitation and historic preservation activities. Such projects help further local economic development activities and generate considerable tax revenues. The Franklin Square School 100 in an older section of Baltimore, Maryland, now contains sixty-five apartments for the elderly. The project, coordinated by a local businessman, was financed with tax-exempt bonds and a grant from the U.S. Department of Housing and Urban Development. A historic school in downtown Dallas was restored and refitted as the offices of an oil pipeline and drilling firm.[21] In Ithaca, New York, a high school once slated for demolition now houses shops, offices, and apartments.[22]

In many cases, restoration or renovation is less expensive than new construction. Older buildings are eligible for rehabilitation tax credits, which can be incorporated into a project in two ways. The cash value of the credit can permit investors to raise additional funds; with less due in federal taxes, they can devote more cash to financing project debt. Secondly, the additional cash flow stemming from a reduced federal tax burden can provide developers with a suitable return on investment, which may mean lower rents for tenants. In either case, rehabilitation tax credits add to a property's real estate value while preserving its historical or architectural features.

Conversion of schools may face citizen opposition and restrictions from local laws. Some are located in residential areas where zoning laws do not permit commercial or office uses. Local supporters may be able to lobby for a zoning variance if the project will benefit the community. For example, they could argue that the neighborhood economy will profit or local residents will have access to needed services. Proposed uses deemed controversial or incompatible with the surrounding area may require revamping to blend better with the character of the community.

Fairfield, California, incorporated the site of an obsolete elementary school into a 54-acre parcel assembled for a large shopping mall complex, which it planned for development in increments. The school structure was outdated for contemporary student needs and located far from areas with school-aged children. The city sold off portions of the site as development progressed and made substantial profits on the transactions. In the final phases of development, Fairfield gained an equity position in the mall's leasable space. Some of the proceeds were earmarked to replace the old school, which was demolished, with a modern facility nearer residential areas.[23]

Administrators should consider innovative uses of surplus school property that would benefit the local economy. They could do the following:

- List attractive characteristics such as location, historic value, parking, and recreational facilities in annual real estate surveys.
- Find out if any local community groups, colleges, training providers, or businesses need facilities for meetings, classes, training programs, or business incubation space.
- Define the pros and cons of selling property rather than keeping it in the school inventory.
- Determine how sale proceeds will be used, such as improving other facilities or expanding business outreach efforts to build community support.
- Explore the economic and tax feasibility of leasing space or sale-lease-back arrangements of the property.
- Identify the community's particular economic development needs and preferences for school neighborhoods: shops and other small businesses, housing, offices, or social service centers.
- Investigate any legal restrictions on selling, leasing, or renting school property.

Administrators may allow other organizations to conduct their activities in underused classrooms in their schools. These arrangements would help expand existing community services. A community saves when it can run programs at existing facilities with vacant or underused space rather than constructing new ones. The following are examples of services carried out at schools that benefit the entire community.

School-Business-Community Service Partnerships

School systems are uniquely suited to help overburdened local governments provide community services more efficiently or expand their range of services. These efforts can help a community enhance its image with prospective businesses, while freeing up resources for other needs. For example, schools can extend normal school cafeteria operations to provide meals for elderly and indigent persons. The East Meadow school district on Long Island, New York, has operated a program for several years that allows senior citizens to buy meals in school cafeterias. This popular program is self-supporting. Senior citizens get well-balanced, hot meals for a fraction of the cost in a restaurant. School and local officials believe that bringing together senior citizens and youths is beneficial to the community.[24]

After the regular school day, schools also can open language labs for bilingual education classes or cooperate in orientation programs for recent immigrants. Large numbers of Southeast Asian refugees have settled in Arlington County, Virginia. The local government opened a specially staffed center in a public school were they learn English, American customs, and get help finding jobs. The program reduces their dependency on public assistance and welfare, and eases their transition into the community's economic mainstream. The Arlington program's federal funding allows it to provide services free of charge to most of the 400 participants.[25] School administrators in areas with concentrations of immigrants do a special service for the community with such nontraditional programs. In using existing facilities and resources, programs like Arlington's permit more targeted and effective help. Graduates of such programs undoubtedly will become better employees and business owners as a result of the smoother assimilation process. Those who start businesses will repay community efforts by creating jobs and generating tax revenues.

Other possibilities exist for innovative programs to further specific community growth objectives or address certain citizen needs. Promoting such programs is an important but usually overlooked role the school system can play in economic development. Adopting the right approach is a matter of matching a school system's strengths with the needs of the community, including the business sector. For instance, in some communities, budget restraints have limited library hours and services. School systems could open their libraries to the public after school hours or combine operations with the local public library systems. A pooling of school and community funds may be enough to expand a school's library to partially fill community needs, if only for an interim period. Small business owners or prospective entrepreneurs will welcome the availability of the technical materials that many school collections contain.

In Aurora, Colorado, public and school officials collaborated on a project to provide better library services by locating a branch of the public library at Horizon Middle School, as mentioned previously. The school district provides space, furniture, shelving, and audiovisual equipment. The school and library buy their books and materials through separate budgets, but items are ordered by one person and computerized on a single system to avoid duplication. Both parties contribute to staff salaries and share the benefits. Students have a larger library, open longer than a typical school library, and can order books from any public library branch via the computer network. The expanded library receives free space and pays less for staff salaries and materials.

Besides these immediate gains, this collaborative approach yields two intangible benefits. It attracts people to the school who would not ordinarily think about educational issues. More importantly, it expands the library's capacity to serve the needs of the neighborhood residents and those seeking local business information.[26]

Most schools have equipment and personnel that could help area businesses greatly if they were more accessible. Offering services free to businesses in need of help might be best, providing the system could afford it. However, charging minimal prices for services might be more practical; the fees would cover the educational costs, thus saving public dollars, while still providing business services at less than market rate. For example, schools could invite small businesses to use the school's computers after classroom hours for a nominal fee. Proceeds could be applied to maintaining existing computers, purchasing new equipment and software, or diverted to other uses. Businesses unable to afford their own computers or training would benefit most. This type of service could be an important part of an economic development incentive package if properly structured and marketed to the business sector.

The St. Louis Park, Minnesota, school system became involved actively in the local business community out of a conviction that schools should provide lifelong learning. Several years ago, administrators commissioned a survey of fifty local businesses to determine their needs and what services they could offer the community. School officials analyzed the survey results carefully to determine what role the school system could play in assisting local businesses. They decided to develop training courses in word processing and computing, assertiveness training, listening skills, creative problem solving, and use of video equipment. The program also taught local doctors, accountants, and city employees how to use automated business equipment. Businesses, in turn, provided schools with needed services, such as specialized training for teachers and administrative staff, and set up student internships.[27]

The St. Louis Park system has developed a close relationship with Honeywell, Inc., over the last three years. Honeywell expressed a need for both staff development and counseling seminars to help employees advance within the company and reduce the chances of job dissatisfaction and low productivity. The school system responded by loaning staff to write and conduct a training program. Since then, Honeywell specialists have trained one of the school system's job counselors in interviewing techniques, and the counselor, in turn, trains Honeywell's job counselors. Other cooperative projects have examined employee effectiveness, shared teaching techniques, and developed seminars for technical employees on presentation skills.

So far, these projects have taken place mainly in summer months; now both partners are considering the possibility of exchanging staff for an entire semester. No fees are charged because school officials believe the services traded and benefits of cooperating with businesses are more valuable than money. With each proposal, representatives from the schools and businesses meet, then decide how they can help each other. The resulting arrangement always includes mutual commitments and exchanges of resources. The school system undertook an extensive curriculum review and training project for Honeywell; in return, the company introduced teachers to its latest technology and gave internships to students. This cooperation helps the schools prepare students to deal with the kinds of technologies they will be expected to handle in future jobs.

The school system markets the program to ensure that as many businesses as possible know what the schools can offer them. The St. Louis Park Chamber of Commerce created a staff position, funded by several local school districts, to coordinate these arrangements. The schools now have established such a reputation that many businesses approach them to establish programs.[28]

Schools also can use their facilities and staff to assist unemployed and displaced workers. Many schools already help their students with job placement and career counseling, which also could be offered to unemployed workers in the community. Some schools have set up interviews for workers with school counselors, provided telephones for job searches, helped with resume preparation, and contacted potential employers. This cooperation increases the quality of services for the unemployed—which neither community nor worker might be able to afford otherwise. When school, municipal, and business resources are combined, the sponsoring organization can offer better standard services and try more innovative approaches at lower cost.

These programs improve the quality of the local work force and help people adapt to changing economic circumstances. This is particularly important to communities where workers have been displaced by slack demand and plant closings. School-sponsored special programs for unemployed or dislocated workers, as well as first-time job seekers, improve their chances of finding suitable jobs and their job skills in general. A continuing process of worker training is a must for areas pursuing economic growth.

Administrators should offer the school system's services and resources to improve the community's economic development potential and quality of life. They could do the following:

- Identify school resources, such as computers, audiovisual equipment, or library collections, that would improve services to local businesses, neighborhood associations, and senior citizens groups.

- Consider offering special summer or evening classes for small business owners and their staffs.

- Explore the feasibility of trading school services for business or individual resources, as the St. Louis Park, Minnesota, system has done.

• Identify segments of the population, such as recent immigrants and displaced workers, needing special services that schools can provide.

Training and Adult Education Programs

School systems are natural partners for business groups and nonprofit organizations involved in adult training and education. A system can work jointly with employers and community officials to plan training programs and adult education classes, open school facilities for after-hours sessions, and distribute information on education and training options to the community.

Labor is the most important production factor in nearly all businesses and industries. The presence of skilled and appropriately trained workers is a key consideration for investors or business owners who want to launch a new enterprise or expand an existing one. Therefore, school administrators should work with local businesses to adapt their schools' employment-oriented courses to the local job market. They also could look for opportunities to improve the existing work force and thus strengthen their community's economic viablility.

Many school districts are helping to train local residents through the federal Job Training Partnership Act. JTPA specifically encourages cooperative efforts among local business, training, and education groups to design suitable training programs. A Private Industry Council (PIC) in each local area determines JTPA training program priorities. By law, the majority of PIC members must be owners, managers, or executives of local businesses. The remaining members must represent educational institutions and other local organizations with interest and expertise in employment and training, such as economic development agencies and community service groups.

PICs and local officials determine jointly how federal training funds will be spent. Acceptable options include job counseling, remedial education and basic skills instruction, General Educational Development (GED) test preparation, classroom-based occupational education, on-the-job training, bilingual education, and education-to-work transition activities for youths and adults. The school system can contribute personnel and space to these programs or become a contractor to run programs for the PIC. Whether through donations or by contract, administrators can broaden the school's regular offerings and the community's human resources base with their involvement in PIC-sponsored training activities.

School systems also can provide on-the-job training opportunities in the schools themselves. Using PIC trainees in school-related jobs produces benefits for both. Trainees receive "hands on" experience while the PIC partially reimburses the schools for their wages. For example, when the school system has openings on its clerical, maintenance, or food service staffs, it could fill them with PIC trainees who would learn the job while doing it and eventually become permanent employees. Also, the school system can hire graduates of other training programs in the community for its entry-level positions. As one of the community's principal employers, schools should take steps such as these to promote a healthy local labor market.

Schools can improve work force skills and raise literacy rates through special courses for adults. The St. Paul, Minnesota, system developed an unusual basic education program that is highly responsive to the special needs and circumstances of adults. Established jointly by the school system and several area foundations, the Technology for Literacy Center (TLC) opened in May 1985. Located at an inner-city shopping center, TLC offers convenient walk-in services from 9 a.m. to 9 p.m. daily to accommodate adults' diverse schedules in an unintimidating atmosphere. Its target audience is persons 18 years and older with reading, writing, or mathematical skills measuring below an eighth-grade level.

TLC is a technology-based teaching operation using computers, video cassette recorders, and slides to encourage students to learn at their own pace. Its staff set up individualized learning programs based on packaged software specially designed to teach basic skills. TLC's major goal is to raise St. Paul's literacy level. But it also intends to train operators of educational programs in the use of advanced technology, carry out joint research with the University of Minnesota and Carnegie-Mellon University on teaching with technology, and raise matching funds for similar programs. TLC hopes to serve 1,300 participants over the next three years, 300 the first year and 500 in each of the next two.

The strong support given to the project by the St. Paul community promises to make it a vehicle for attacking local literacy problems.[29] Before its opening, TLC invited various community groups to the center for an introduction to its purpose and methods of teaching. An advertising agency donated time and advice to TLC to help attract adult learners. The contributing foundations are all located in the St. Paul area, and community representatives sit on the center's advisory council. The project recruited volunteer tutors from the community to help students get started and solve problems that arise.

Many areas have high rates of adult illiteracy that limit individuals' opportunities and hinder the long-term development prospects of the entire community. Recommendations for businesses and public policymakers concerned with this issue are contained in Chapter 4, "Developing Adult Basic Skills for Employment."

Schools also can strengthen their communities and their own educational offerings by adopting innovative work-and-learning programs. For example, trainees in auto mechanics courses may be available for maintenance work on school vehicles. School settings also might offer opportunities for training vocational education students and technical degree candidates. Students in nutrition courses or those interested in food service careers might work as interns in the school's food service operation.

Administrators in Montgomery County, Maryland, outside Washington D.C., arrange for their students to participate in school-based businesses through the postsecondary Regional Vocational-Technical Center. Students in auto mechanics and body repair programs run two automobile dealerships where they repair, then advertise and sell used cars. They have sold almost 400 cars since the program began in 1978. The dealerships are managed by a nonprofit corporation established cooperatively by the Montgomery County Public Schools and local businesses. Participation by the American Automobile Association, local accountants, bankers, lawyers, realtors, rotary clubs, and the county government indicates a high level of community support for this program. Students also run a flower shop and a home construction business, act as volunteers in small businesses, and serve internships with local fire and emergency medical services, among other programs.[30] The school system has expanded traditional educational approaches for students to gain experience with real-life working situations. Employers can hire graduates attuned to the operation of a business. In turn, the community benefits from increased services.

School-based enterprises have taken root in rural areas as well. In Arkansas, five towns now benefit from businesses made possible by foundation grants and local school contributions. In one town, students publish the town's only newspaper; in another, students run a maintenance shop. Other projects in Arkansas and Georgia include renovation and conversion of a historic building into apartments, and the operation of a day-care center, a roller skating rink, and a movie theater. The local schools coordinate the operation of these programs and provide services that bolster the local economy.[31]

Administrators should plan school system participation in work force training to help retain local businesses and make the community more attractive to new enterprises. They could do the following:

- Assess school-run education and training programs to see that they supply the types of skills needed by local businesses.

- Learn who represents local educational agencies on the PIC, and explore with local business and public officials the possibility of an appointment to the PIC.

- Work with the local PIC and the Job Service office to coordinate efforts with other training and employment programs.

- Give training-program participants internships or jobs in the school system and look first to local training programs to fill job openings in the schools.

- Familiarize themselves with all state and federal training programs in which they have a role to play and develop a systematic method for keeping in contact, e.g., by designating a liaison person for each of these programs.

- Reach out to the broader constituency of adult learners by involving the schools with local adult literacy training efforts.

- Develop work-and-learning programs that increase services in the community while offering opportunities for students to learn the real world of work.

- Be an active partner in community efforts to produce a fully prepared work force as the base for its economic growth.

Health Care Services

Finally, schools have an unusual opportunity to help the entire community by contributing to local health care services in a cost-efficient manner. School-sponsored health care has several advantages. Healthy students learn more readily and businesses lose fewer work days to the illnesses of their employees' children. Local governments also can extend and concentrate their health care resources on those most in need. The availability of a satisfactory and convenient health care network sustains the local quality of life; it is another piece of an attractive business environment package that local development officials can include in their marketing strategies. For these reasons, this service contribution is worthy of administrators' consideration. Not every community needs school-assisted health care, but it is a good example of cooperation to fill area-specific needs.

Students usually receive some physical and mental health care and learn preventive measures through their schools. In cooperation with community officials, school administrators may choose to invest money, staff time, and/or school facilities in more complete health care and information programs. Such programs may reduce health care expenses for the local government. Students from low-income families, who often do not receive regular or adequate medical attention, are more likely to need public medical services in the future. If they receive preventive or early care in their school, medical costs later may be trimmed or avoided.

School administrators and public officials should treat these health and welfare expenditures as investments with significant payoffs now and in the future. A five-year study completed recently by Johns Hopkins University Hospital found that more use of nurse practitioners in schools greatly improved students' health, especially in minority and low-income populations. These improvements meant fewer student absences from school and fewer missed work days for their parents.[32]

Some school systems have extended their health care services beyond basic examinations and immunizations. For example, four high schools in St. Paul, Minnesota, serve as sites for clinics emphasizing teenage maternal health and infant care. One of the centers also provides day care for students' children. Run cooperatively by the school district and the St. Paul-Ramsey Medical Center, the St. Paul Maternity and Health Care Project began in 1973 in response to students' exceptionally high pregnancy rates. It has helped to cut the birthrate from 59 per 1,000 students in the 1976-1977 school year to 26 per 1,000 in the 1983-1984 school year.[33] These dramatic decreases lowered both school dropout rates and dependency on public aid associated with teenage births. St. Paul's clinics and many of the 35 similar school health projects find that most of their patients seek help unrelated to birth control. But their success in lowering student pregnancy rates prompted school officials in Los Angeles and Washington, D.C., to set up clinics on a trial basis in 1986.[34]

School administrators should also consider lending medical personnel and equipment to community groups. A district could purchase cardio-pulmonary resuscitation (CPR) equipment for training in schools and lend it to community groups for CPR courses. In addition, school health staff members could speak outside the schools on a wide variety of health topics. A local economy cannot be truly "healthy" if large numbers of residents are unable to fill jobs due to poor health.

Administrators should offer more health care services through the schools. They could do the following:

- Identify those school health care resources that can be extended to the community.
- Set up school-community cooperative programs to meet specific needs, such as lower student pregnancy rates.
- Identify personnel or medical equipment (such as CPR equipment or school nurses to teach first aid or prenatal care) that the school system can lend or share with other groups in the community.

Most school systems are facing lean budgets, which may limit the introduction of new or expanded programs. Some argue that increasing school system funding is a less effective investment than traditional economic development programs. Publicizing the positive effects of a school system in the community is the best way to defuse that criticism. If citizens and businesses are aware of these issues, they will be much stronger allies.

Instituting new programs may mean choices between spending public funds for school budgets or business development. Money spent for business development can increase employment and the local tax base. Money allocated for school programs can provide a well-trained work force, more services for businesses and residents, and a more livable community—all of which attract business. Cooperation among school officials, planning officials, elected officials, the business community, and citizens is the only way to reach agreement on balancing the needs of both. In fact, school and business needs are more complementary than many policymakers and school administrators realize. One need not exclude the other.

MAKING THESE IDEAS WORK

School administrators face the challenge of translating the vision of a school system as a multiple contributor to local economic and social vitality into policies and programs. The potential gains are great: stronger ties to businesses, greater community appreciation of and support for educational funding, and a more livable environment. Combined, these elements improve a locality's appeal to new commercial enterprises and prospective residents. Administrators' most difficult task is finding support for their ideas and putting them into practice. However, they cannot institute programs singlehandedly that affect the entire community. Linus Wright, superintendent of the Dallas Independent School District said, "The bottom line: if it's going to get done, educators can't do it alone."[35]

The fundamental responsibility of any school system is to meet the educational needs of its students. Administrators thus have limited time and resources to devote to these "external" goals. New or expanded school-based programs require the cooperation and involvement of businesspersons, economic development groups, neighborhood associations, parent-teacher groups, and service organizations. Administrators should develop strong networks of appropriate public and private-sector leaders in the community. Close ties will help them build strong foundations for more ambitious activities. Forming stronger links within the community, however, is more than a precondition for program development; it is an important goal in its own right.

"Selling" the school system is the necessary prerequisite for putting the mechanisms and strategies thus far described into place. While a public relations role may seem foreign to many administrators, it is a necessary one. Publicizing the accomplishments and potential of the school system is one of the best ways to gather support and bring about joint efforts. Administrators should keep their networks of government officials, businesses, and community leaders informed and involved in their use of school resources to improve the community's economic climate. Public confidence in a school system is an important factor in delivering quality education.

The South Orange-Maplewood, New Jersey, public school system plans to start a public relations program to explain the complexity of managing a $25 million organization to the public. The district's public relations advisory committee emphasized that such an informational program was important in maintaining financial and moral support for the school system. Like many other districts, South Orange-Maplewood is struggling to maintain high-quality programs in spite of a decline in funding.[36]

Positive Parents of Dallas was formed in 1982 to build support for that city's school system. It combined interested members of the PTA and the local business community to bring the schools' accomplishments to public attention. The Positive Parents program increased public school enrollment, changed public perception of the quality of local schools, and brought new recognition to noteworthy school programs and staff.[37]

The Decatur, Illinois, school district's Partners in Education program also aims to raise the community's confidence in its school system. The program had a new graphic image designed for the system, sponsors programs at individual schools to give their character and achievements more visibility, and publishes a guide for improving school relations with other sectors. This project is supported partially by the Public Education Fund (PEF), a nonprofit organization based in Pittsburgh, Pennsylvania, that provides technical assistance and developmental grant support to schools in urban communities.[38]

PEF also helps the four school districts covering Wilmington, Delaware, to remind the community of the value of schools. Wilmington's Public Awareness Campaign and Volunteer Program publishes newsletters and develops radio spots and programs on public education. It has established a telephone information line and computerized volunteer information system. Program members conduct school tours for local corporate executives and real estate brokers—the people who can promote the schools' role in economic development and social service to potential businesses and residents.

Wilmington's marketing campaign has been a notable success. Other school systems should consider adopting this kind of promotional approach. It can include media advertisements, brochures on the system, booths at local fairs, and talks to service organizations. Everyone knows the school system exists, but probably few have considered its varied roles. Marketing can remind citizens and taxpayers of their contributions.

The Arlington County, Virginia, school system recently found its enrollments declining because of the large numbers of single adults and childless couples moving to the area. County officials grew concerned that this demographic trend would erode the schools' support base. They have begun to publicize the importance of good schools, specifically, how they raise real estate values. By tailoring the message for childless taxpaying adults, the county hopes to gain their backing for the school system.[39]

Many of these activities—school tours, radio spots, speaking engagements—are virtually free and can be designed and put into practice quickly. Administrators also can arrange for real estate brokers to bring prospective homebuyers to tour schools with just a few phone calls. Chambers of commerce and businesspersons can do the same. Administrators should look for small but important projects like these to show their allies in business and government and the public that school officials are committed to the community's prosperity.

Steps to Take

To be fully effective, administrators should make themselves experts on the functioning of schools as economic entities within a local jurisdiction. They should have facts and figures ready to quote. Identifying unique features of their systems or districts is also important. They should undertake an assessment of their schools' strengths and advantages and write them up formally.

Administrators should find opportunities to publicize the results in appropriate forums, which will vary with individual community traditions. They could sponsor workshops for selected area representatives or community meetings open to any interested persons. They could design a brochure to explain how school expenditures and programs stimulate the economic development process and lead to community betterment. School officials also may want to consider appearing on local talk shows or writing newspaper editorials to discuss school involvment in the community and what it means. Other opportunities include making presentations to local business and training groups and to parent-teacher associations.

Administrators should gear publicity strategies toward the entire community—especially groups that are not normally involved with schools. They should try to involve senior citizens, families with children in private schools, and single adults in school-community programs and seek their ideas on school-related issues. The case should be made to these groups that their property taxes support public schools whether or not they have children enrolled; they benefit from school-based services to the community in addition to their educating children. Administrators also might find ways to remind these groups that good schools give property owners some return. According to G. Donald Jud, professor of economics at the University of North Carolina at Greensboro,

Public schooling, like other public services, enhances the value of urban property. Changes in the quality of the schools in different neighborhoods affect the desirability of those neighborhoods as places to live and, thus, the market demand for property in those areas.[40]

School boards should designate someone as a liaison to community and business groups—perhaps a senior administrator or other top-level staff person.

This contact person would be responsible for circulating information and responding to inquiries. Routing community contacts through one person or one office will make them simpler to handle.

Administrators also might recruit a prominent local businessperson as a school advocate to the public. Having a well-known and respected person outside the system touting the schools' accomplishments makes the case even stronger. Other local businesspersons may be easier to reach if the liaison is one of their peers. For example, the Memphis, New Orleans, and Cincinnati school systems have enlisted business allies to help them build support for tax increases for local educational purposes.

To promote and develop school system contributions further, administrators should consider starting an education/economic-development committee that includes representatives from business and community groups, elected officials, and school officials. These committees can advise administrators on improving their own efforts to purchase locally, increase the schools' role in development incentive policies, improve community services and quality of life, and connect school activities with other community initiatives. In districts where school-community relations are already strong, administrators' informal networks should provide a catalyst for increasing community support and launching cooperative development projects.

School systems should strive to gain recognition as a major employer in the community and get the kind of support community officials give other businesses of that stature. This support might include facility planning assistance, development of a model to measure economic impacts, or forecasts on commercial and demographic trends. Obviously, school system planning should be integrated into a community's comprehensive planning efforts.

School officials also should seek support for their programs at the state level. Minnesota recently passed a community school law that qualifies districts with cooperative community and school programs to state financial assistance.[41] Even though many state education budgets have been stretched thin in recent years, some funds still may be available for school system improvements. Since states appropriate three to five times as much as aid as the federal government, school officials should maintain their relationships with state officials. Closer contact will keep them abreast of programs at the state level. State staff also can apprise local school officials of innovative and workable projects undertaken by other districts.

In sum, schools do not operate in isolation from the community. Administrators should seek opportunities to demonstrate to the public that school systems can use their resources to strengthen the local economy. The important tie between a successful school system and long-term community economic well-being ought to be better known. However, those recognizing the importance of educational quality to economic competitiveness are growing steadily.

A successful development strategy strengthens and builds on these natural bonds between a school system and its environment. Working with other officials, the business community, and citizens' groups, school administrators can strengthen these connections and build wider support for school systems. Professor Dale Mann of Teacher's College, Columbia University, states this idea well: "The most helpful outcomes of business-school partnerships are those sorts of political coalitions aimed at major, permanent increases in financial support for public schools."[42] As the examples and suggestions in this discussion demonstrate, school systems have great potential to become even stronger influences on the economic evolution of local communities.

CASE STUDY: THE COLUMBUS, OHIO, SCHOOL SYSTEM

The Columbus, Ohio, school system has begun to assess the effect of its activities on the local economy. The school system is the sixth largest employer in the community, with an annual expenditure of over $176 million for salaries and fringe benefits for approximately 7,000 employees. The total annual school budget is over $220 million, more than Columbus's municipal government budget. In 1984, the district's net worth was $3.9 billion. Close to 69,000 students attended classes at 123 sites in the 121-square mile school district.

Much of the education budget flows back directly into the local economy in the form of school purchases and community services. Obviously, a significant portion of the payroll goes to local businesses for consumer goods and services. The system spends millions of dollars each year for supplies. Its food services operation spends more than $1 million a year just for milk. Even this amount is only part of the money spent locally in preparing and serving nine million meals each year. The district also supports 500 buses for student transportation. Expenses for running this fleet include drivers' salaries, maintenance, and fuel for the 37,000 miles the buses travel each day. These are only a fraction of the many and complex ways the school system helps to support the local economy.[43]

The school system is careful to use its funds and resources efficiently. For example, more than $700,000 was saved in 1983 through an energy management program. Savings are expected to top $1 million per year when the program is fully established. These funds can be devoted to other educational uses that benefit both the school system and the community.

The Columbus school system merits attention because it has channeled its resources not only to improve its curriculum and student activities but to benefit the community more broadly. Through its support of Columbus's economy, partnerships with businesses, training and educational programs for citizens, and additions to overall quality of life, this school system has improved the economic health of the area.

Columbus schools offer many services in conjunction with and in support of business. Companies have contracted with the district to assess the aptitudes and skills of current and prospective employees. It also set up specialized training programs for which a group or business selects the location, timing, and training objectives. For example, a major high-technology firm, Rockwell International, hired the district to train job applicants with potential but whose skills were deficient. On completion of their training, Rockwell hired those trainees who met its standards. The benefits of this program went beyond those selected: trainees not hired by Rockwell still received instruction to be applied to other jobs. Local businesses continue to benefit from the larger pool of trained job applicants available through the Rockwell program.[44]

Columbus schools also participate in a vocational cooperative-education program in which students work part-time in local businesses. This program promotes smooth school-to-work transitions and gives businesses a larger number of qualified graduates from which to draw. Through the co-op program, more than 5,000 students have worked toward careers in business, health care, construction, day care, and the performing arts. The program is popular with students, who earn money while still in school. In 1983-1984 academic year, co-op students earned more than $2.6 million. Most of these wages were spent locally.

The system has extended vocational education to adults in the community as well. In 1983, more than 23,000 persons were enrolled in adult training programs. The schools offered them job placement services along with counseling and career assessment. These kinds of adult programs increase the availability of trained workers and make people less dependent on public assistance. Eighty percent of the graduates found jobs upon completion of their programs, and over 1,100 found jobs and no longer require public help. The system also runs the North Education Center, which offers dropouts and potential dropouts another opportunity for career training, high school degrees, and help with job searches.[45]

Columbus's community education program is popular because of its diverse course offerings. Residents can take low-cost courses for high school credit, pursue full- and part-time career training, enroll in a two-year program in small business management practices, learn computer skills, or develop special interests. A partnership formed recently among the Columbus public schools, Ohio State University's (OSU's) Office of Continuing

Education, and Ohio unions allowed the program to expand. Noncredit university courses now are located conveniently at local schools. Columbus schools and OSU also have worked together in two computer training programs, Compu-Tech and Summer Tech. Both have provided low-cost computer training to 17,000 Ohio residents, ranging from preschool aged children to businesspersons. These courses also are held at public schools, but are staffed by OSU personnel.

The Columbus system's involvement does not stop at academic programs and business assistance; it includes social service programs that help people with day-to-day life as well. For example, a latchkey program offers low-cost day care before and after school to children of working parents. Children are well supervised, eliminating problems for both parents and their employers. Local citizens benefit further from home and family-life workshops that discuss parenting, nutrition, child development, homemaking, and consumer education. Workshops are offered free of charge at public housing developments, churches, schools, and community centers. Typically these programs are provided by municipal governments, but in this case the school system uses its resources to deliver them more efficiently.[46]

Much of Columbus school administrators' success with cooperative programs is due to the strong, mutual commitment of the school system and the community. It is reflected in the thousands of hours devoted by 3,500 volunteers annually to the schools and the school system's commitment to a broad range of community needs. A volunteer-staffed telephone information line and a brochure entitled ''Columbus: A Great Place to Go to School,'' published by the system, help publicize school contributions to the local community. School officials also are actively involved with the Columbus Chamber of Commerce and with the economic development initiatives of city and state officials.

School administrators base their commitment of resources to the community on the premise that making Columbus a better place to live makes it more attractive for business. Like many cities in the region, Columbus was hit hard by the recession of 1981-82. It is recovering by building a strong work force and creating an environment in which development can flourish. Local officials also realize that the school system is an integral component of an economic development strategy and are using the knowledge effectively. The school system's work is recognized and appreciated by the general community as well.

3. Improving Youth Employability Through "Learning to Work" Programs

YOUTH AND EMPLOYMENT: A LOOK AT THE PROBLEM

A quiet crisis is building throughout our nation, one destined to worsen if steps are not taken to do something about it. Millions of our young people are out of work—cannot get work—because they lack the education and proper skills to qualify for jobs. For every unemployed adult, two young people are out of work; among Hispanic youth, that number climbs to three, and for blacks, it is five.

Estranged from the schools where they performed poorly, often unable to enter the work force because they cannot satisfy minimum requirements of even simple jobs, today's unemployed youth face a bleak future unless someone intervenes. These youth are not in a position to help themselves escape this dilemma. Policymakers and the public are concerned about adult unemployment, but few realize the scope of the predicament for jobless youth.

The Committee for Economic Development termed the situation "not only an economic tragedy, but a human tragedy of dire dimensions."[1] The National Commission on Excellence in Education warns that the United States is becoming "a nation at risk" because of a youth population unprepared to meet the changing job requirements imposed by technological advancement and international competition.

According to the Commission, the skills of most sixteen- to nineteen-year-olds are deficient.[2] The problem involves all young people to some extent, but is particularly concentrated among the "disadvantaged"—youth from poor families and from racial and ethnic minority groups. Many of these young people have severe educational deficiencies and face nearly insurmountable barriers to employment. Often, they lack the basic skills needed to find and hold even a first job.

And things generally are not getting better. Young people did not gain their share of the jobs brought back or created in the recovery from the 1981-82 recession. A distressing trend has emerged: the proportion of youth in the general population is decreasing, but the number with employment problems is growing. In other words, even as fewer young people are available to take jobs, more are unfit to fill them.

The ranks of youth increasingly are made up of the very groups—the poor and minorities—who experience the greatest difficulties with school and work. These youth in general complete fewer years of school, suffer from lower levels of educational attainment, and have minimal or nonexistent experience with work. A recent National Alliance of Business report found that "the most rapidly growing, yet most vulnerable, of the nation's labor pool is concentrated where schools are inferior, work experience opportunities are poorest, and available full-time jobs are declining."[3]

The youth unemployment rate consistently is double that of adults. Rates are even higher for poor and minority youth. In 1985, the unemployment rate for white sixteen- to nineteen-year-olds was 16 percent, but it was 23.7 percent for Hispanics and 42.7 percent for blacks.[4] Even more disadvantaged youth have given up looking for work altogether. These numbers do not show up in unemployment calculations, thus masking the full extent of youth joblessness.

Many of today's unprepared youth are on the road to becoming tomorrow's hardcore unemployed. Their difficulties start early, often before reaching grade school, and extend beyond the teenage years. Early labor market troubles are good predictors of problems in adulthood; initial joblessness results in a higher probability of unemployment over the years and lower lifetime wages. These long-term effects carry high costs for society: lost productivity and earnings, unemployment and welfare payments, prosecution and incarceration of those resorting to crime, and costly remedial programs to compensate for the original failures.

The private sector knows that a labor force with skills fully developed to meet work demands is essential for economic growth. Businesses invest billions annually in training. They see the development of employees' skills as the key to improving productivity and profitability. But employers' programs are geared to workers already on the job who demonstrate a good capacity for learning. These in-house programs are not intended for those who lack a firm grasp on the eduational fundamentals.

For these reasons, public funding to equip people with the skills they need to work is important. Investments in basic skills instruction, counseling, job-search training, and work preparation pay off in the future. They benefit the individual, and also help promote a healthy climate for business growth and expanded employment opportunities. Unfortunately, existing public and private programs are a fraction of what is needed for young people at risk.

Regional Dimensions

High rates of youth dropping out of school and facing unemployment are occurring throughout the country. Nationwide, 28 percent of students may not graduate from high school.[5] The problem in many cities is even more severe. More than 55 percent of all public school students in Chicago do not graduate; in New York City, 45 percent fail.[6]

A key economic asset for the Northeast and Midwest has been a large number of well-trained workers. In the past, population increase was a dynamic source of growth for the region's economy, providing a steady stream of workers for industry. However, lower birthrates in the 1960s resulted in a decline in young entrants to the labor force in the 1980s. In keeping with overall demographic trends, the fall-off in the youth part of the population has been greater in the Northeast-Midwest region than in the rest of the country. From 1980 to 1984, its youth population fell 11.5 percent compared with a 7.3-percent drop in the South and West.

In addition, the aging of the general population due to slower population growth and longer life spans has been more pronounced in the Northeast-Midwest region than elsewhere. Taken together, minimal population growth plus fewer youth and more elderly persons mean that economic expansion in the Northeast and Midwest will depend on more productive use of existing labor resources. No region can afford idle or underused youth if it wants to maintain a healthy economy.

Another source of economic strength in the Northeast-Midwest region has been the skill level of its workers. Traditionally these states have spent more on education than other states—with good results. Secondary school graduation rates are highest in the Northeast-Midwest region—80.1 percent overall. The region has more college graduates and generally higher levels of academic achievement than other areas. Now, however, state governments are mounting a new drive for educational reform,[7] with the South taking the lead in many areas. While these states strive to ''catch up,'' northeastern and midwestern states seek to maintain their edge in education and training in the face of competing claims for funding.

The region's work force has developed a third advantage over the years that complements sheer numbers and good education: experience. In general, the Northeast-Midwest region has a greater percentage of young people working than other regions. Six of the region's states, Maine, Massachusetts, New Hampshire, Rhode Island, Delaware, and New Jersey, have enjoyed recent healthy trends of reduced youth unemployment rates even as more youth entered the labor force. Other states are not faring as well. Michigan's youth unemployment rate, at 24.5 percent, is the sixth highest in the nation.

Some of the statistical "improvement" in the overall unemployment rate has resulted from young people dropping out of the labor market altogether. In Illinois, Michigan, Ohio, and ·Wisconsin, unemployment rates among youth still actively looking for work have risen at the same time that large numbers are giving up in their search for work. In New York, the employment/ population ratio, a comparison of persons employed to total population, shows only 34 percent of the state's youth working, one of the lowest rates in the nation.

Statewide data mask the high incidence of unemployment in major cities and many rural areas, particularly for minority populations. Youth unemployment in New York City was over 40 percent in 1984, while it was 19.4 percent for the state as a whole. The Northeast-Midwest region has many areas where teenage labor market problems are among the worst in the country. Of the top ten metropolitan areas with the highest youth unemployment in 1984, seven were in the Northeast and Midwest: Chicago, Cincinnati, Cleveland, Detroit, Milwaukee, New York, and Pittsburgh.[8] This combination of high unemployment and declining proportions of youth in the general work force signal an escalating problem in many northeastern and midwestern states.

Jobs in the teenage years lead to adult employment by providing experience and personal contacts for later on; early jobs are a chance to form "working capital." When youth remain unemployed or drop out of the labor force altogether, they lose invaluable opportunities to learn about working. Unemployed youth mean real losses to today's economy. More importantly, youth joblessness portends a greater problem in the future, when employers will be unable to find experienced adult workers to fill job openings. Policymakers in both the public and private sectors should make programs to prepare young people for work a top priority. Otherwise, these youth may be lost to the U.S. economy of the future.

What Is Employability?

Despite its severity, the youth unemployment problem does not defy solution. Major federal investments in research in the 1970s identified successful strategies for intervening in the lives of young people to develop the characteristics of employability. "Employability" means the capacity and willingness to do the job. Basic skills, such as reading and math, and rudimentary occupational skills form the foundation. But employability encompasses a wider range of skills needed for work, including the appropriate attitudes and motivation, behavior, and interpersonal skills. Youth program practitioners generally agree that employability has four components: basic skills, pre-employment competency, work maturity, and occupational skills. This broad vision guides youth programs run under the auspices of the Job Training Partnership Act (JTPA), the federal government's current youth preparation strategy.[9]

1. *Basic Skills*: These include the fundamentals of reading, writing, and arithmetic; they also include speaking standard English and listening to and understanding instructions. Mastery of the basics translates into an ability to apply them to work situations and to learn new aspects of a job.

2. *Pre-employment Competency*: This is a large range of skills a person uses in searching for a job. It icnludes a general knowledge of the working world, an understanding of the local job market, and a realistic assessment of one's place in it. Job-search techniques such as filling out applications, preparing resumes, and handling interviews are necessary skills. An understanding of career ladders, work histories, and credentials also is important in making connections with work.

3. *Work Maturity*: These skills signal that an individual is ready to perform in a job. They include behavioral qualities such as punctuality, consistent attendance, personal neatness, working well with others, following instructions, and completing tasks. Work maturity also means the ability to take initiative, accept constructive criticism, and be flexible.

4. *Occupational Skills*: Occupational skills are the most job-specific of all the components of employability. They include technical proficiency in a given job and specific occupational knowledge.

Programs to develop these four clusters of skills have evolved over the past twenty years and commonly are called "employability development" programs. They seek to improve the capacity of individuals to compete in the job market, that is, to improve the labor supply. Such programs do not address the demand-side problem of too few jobs.[10] Nor do they redress other social and economic conditions that may work against youth, such as word-of-mouth hiring practices, racial discrimination, or household demands that keep many young people—especially teenaged mothers—out of the job market.

Programs to develop the employment potential of young people do improve their chances of success in the labor market. Experience shows that such learning-to-work activities raise employment levels and earnings of youth and have the greatest impact on the disadvantaged. The most effective programs are comprehensive, include all aspects of employability, and consist of a planned sequence of activities in which youth achieve small successes step by step. Today's best youth programs in both the public and private sector incorporate this knowledge about targeting and sequencing, gained through careful research in youth programs since the 1960s. The youth problem persists and grows not because of lack of knowledge about how to solve it, but lack of commitment to do so.

Today, business, education, and government leaders are stepping up efforts to prepare youth for work. For some, new attention at the secondary level comes too late. For many others, special programs make the difference. The next three sections describe some of these activities, presenting "real world" examples of business-education partnerships and drawing on current research to provide recommendations for action.

Suggestions are made to policymakers in education, business, and government on contributions they can make in each of the four areas of employability development: basic skills, pre-employment competency, work maturity, and occupational skills. Activities to promote pre-employment competency and work maturity are combined in the discussion as they are in many youth programs.

BASIC SKILLS

Basic skills—reading, writing, and mathematics—are the fundamental tools for work. Lacking them, young people stand little chance of getting a job. Andrew Hahn and Robert Lerman, research associates at Brandeis University, recently conducted a thorough review of past programs that prepare youth for work. Their findings show that the most important factor in persistent youth unemployment is lack of basic educational skills.[11]

Basic skills deficiencies among today's youth are alarming by any standards. The National Assessment of Educational Progress, the ongoing study of student achievement, finds that 13 percent of all seventeen-year-olds fail to attain reading and writing competence beyond the sixth-grade level. Only one-third of all seventeen-year-olds are able to solve mathematical problems requiring several steps; nearly 49 percent cannot draw inferences from written material.[12]

The U.S. Department of Education estimates that one million teenagers leave school each year functionally illiterate—unable to read, write, or compute with the proficiency needed to function in society. The Center for Public Resources, a private research organization established by the life and health insurance industries, found serious inadequacies in the basic skills of employees in these industries. In the center's 1982 survey, companies reported significant problems in reading, writing, math, and science, plus reasoning, speaking, and listening among the majority of their employees in clerical, blue-collar, management, and supervisory positions.[13]

The rising number of teenagers dropping out of high school compounds the nationwide weakness in basic skills preparation.The National Center for Education Statistics estimates that 28 percent of those entering the ninth grade may not graduate. Frustration with their inability to read, write, and compute up to the level of their peers usually prompts the decision to leave school. The dropout problem is severe among minorities and the poor, who make up an increasingly large percentage of the current school-age population and the future work force. Having left school, these young people are unlikely to get the remedial education they need to perform in the workplace.

Definition of the constituents of basic skills has evolved as the demands of the economy have changed. Today's requirements include mastery of reading, writing, and mathematics, plus the ability to learn new information, analyze, and draw inferences. Employers, educators, and youth themselves have different perceptions of which skills are most important for finding and holding a job.

A task force of the Committee for Economic Development, a business-led policy group, declared recently that employers required two "absolute essentials" for job readiness: good character and fluency in English.[14] However, the 1982 Center for Public Resources study found that line supervisors, personnel officers, and youth themselves tended to see occupational skills and "technological literacy" as the prerequisites for employment. Yet, company executives and youth program operators stressed the importance of basic skills in reading and math plus good work attitudes and behavior.[15] William Grady, president of Albuquerque National Bank, agreed with this latter view. "Send me a kid who can read and write and add a little, and [one] who has the right attitude. The company will train him. We'll do the rest," he stated.[16]

In general, the private sector has taken the stance that basic skills are the responsibility of the educational system. The study by the Center for Public Resources came to this conclusion. "What business decidely indicated it did not want to do, but is in fact doing, is to educate its employees in ninth- and tenth-grade skills."[17]

Employees acquire specific occupational skills most readily in company-provided training on the job. Sponsors used to assume that trainees had mastered the basics in school. Increasingly, howver, businesses are finding that employees need remedial help with basic skills before they are ready to begin more technical training. The military services have dealt with these deficiencies with a massive rewriting of training manuals to bring them down to the level of new recruits.

In response to the basic skills problem among both school graduates and dropouts, many businesses have paid for or provided basic skills training themselves to improve productivity among workers. (The next chapter recommends steps that schools and businesses can take to combat illiteracy in the labor force.) However, many businesses want to change their role in basic skills training. The cost of remedial education and the number needing help have caused businesses to turn away from exclusively in-house solutions to such problems.

Several industry-related groups, through various committees and task force reports, have recommended that companies gear their efforts toward preparation at the school site rather than remedial training on the job. Many business leaders seem to agree with the Task Force on Education for Economic Growth of the Education Commission of the States. Its report, *Action for Excellence*, states, "It should be our long-range goal to end remedial courses wherever possible: to make them unnecessary—because our schools will have done their work effectively the first time."[18]

Business leaders must continue to stress to school administrators the importance of basic skills in readying youth for jobs. Business leaders should tell school officials what levels of verbal and mathematical proficiency they expect from youth entering the marketplace. School officials should solicit this information and enlist business help in the planning of basic skills curricula.

Many businesses have committed time and money helping school systems fulfill their mission of teaching basic skills. An early example of business-education collaboration is the Boston Compact. Several of the city's firms and unions, acknowledging the direct connection between quality education and employee performance, joined with the educational system to promote the link between schooling and work.

Business leaders and school officials jointly established goals for the education system. Businesses agreed to give hiring preference to local graduates in return for educational improvements such as better attendance and higher test scores. City officials gave strong political support, which contributed to the project's success. The Boston schools exceeded nearly all goals for better educational performance in the first year of the project. Impressed by the success of the Boston Compact, Cleveland, Ohio, and Oakland, California, have launched similar efforts. More are in the planning stage.

Collaborations between businesses and schools often begin with a focus on the other components of employability, despite mutual concern over basic educational attainment. The Boston Compact shows that the goal of gains in basic skills can be the basis for productive school-business partnerships. School adminstrators can draw on business executives' knowledge of work demands to determine basic competency standards.

The two groups can work together to plan a basic skills program promoting agreed-upon levels of student achievement. Business can reciprocate by pledging jobs for students who perform up to companies' expectations. **Both school and business officials should make gains in basic skills the basis for new partnerships. In addition, school officials should seek business participation on educational planning and advisory boards to define** the improvements needed in the schools' product. Businesses should make hiring commitments in return for better student performance.

Emphasis on basic skills training may be a top-level policy decision involving the leadership of an area's business, labor, educational, and political communities—as in the case of the Boston Compact. The effort also might start smaller, with companies and schools working together one-to-one. In such partnerships, called "Adopt-a-School" or "Join-a-School," a company pairs itself with a specific school. Company employees tutor individual students in a remedial education program or work with them in other education-related activities. For example, employees of Time, Inc. tutor high school students in Queens, N.Y., in reading, writing, and math. Other companies use their organizations' strengths more directly. In New York, Columbia Broadcasting System (CBS) brings its communications expertise to adopted schools by lending video and television equipment, arranging site visits, and offering internships.

"Adopt-a-School" partnerships can take other forms as well. In Dallas, over 1,000 businesses have adopted virtually all of the city's 200 public schools. Some companies loan equipment to their schools to ensure up-to-date instruction; others work with school administrators to improve management techniques. The Adopt-a-School concept is flexible enough to allow companies whose primary concern is with basic skills to focus their efforts in that area. The adopted school on the other hand can use offers of business help to suit the school's and students' needs.

Company officials should examine what resources—equipment, management expertise, release time for employee volunteers—they can bring to an adoptive relationship, committing them to the goal of school and student improvement. Organizing employees for tutoring programs is a concrete way for companies to help upgrade basic skills.

Successful partnerships to improve basic skills must fit the needs of the particular youth population. The New Bedford-Hyannis (Massachusetts) Private Industry Council (PIC) used a highly flexible model for two different youth problems in its service area. In New Bedford, where educational problems are severe, the PIC emphasizes basic skills to bring youth up to a level where job-oriented training can be successful. The skills and aptitude levels of each youth "client" are measured with a formal test and a face-to-face interview. Students then use an individualized, competency-based curriculum, the Comprehensive Competencies Program (CCP), to teach themselves with help from the instructor. This program allows students to proceed at their own pace, enjoying small successes along the way.

In Hyannis, where the overall youth skill level is higher, CCP instruction is geared to helping young people earn a high school diploma or GED. This instruction is combined with pre-employment seminars and an occupational training program. About 150 sites around the country use CCP. By matching basic skills instruction to the needs of each youth, the program allows the PIC and its clients to get the maximum advantage.

Youth programs work best when they are tailored to individual needs. For many youth, this means focusing on basic skills and emphasizing the importance of a high school diploma or GED. Research repeatedly has shown that the higher the level of education achieved, the more likely a person is to find and hold a job. A high school diploma or its equivalent is an important job credential, recognized by employers and used widely as an employment screening device. The job market is virtually closed to those without one.

Programs operated by the 70001 Training and Employment Institute, a nonprofit training organization, base their instruction on the essential need for a diploma or GED. The 70001 programs are designed to help youth whose educational deficiencies create severe barriers to employment. In 1984, the organization helped over 3,600 youth, many of them hard-to-employ dropouts, in over fifty locations nationwide. Most 70001 participants have significant hardships to contend with. Many read at a sixth-grade level, many are functionally illiterate, and one-third have dependent children.

The programs have four components: educational instruction, work-readiness training, motivational activities, and job placement with follow-up. The educational component is designed to improve participants' reading, writing, and mathematical skills through one-to-one tutoring, individual study, and ongoing assessment, with earning a GED as the focus of their energies. In Jamestown, New York, 70001 forged a partnership with the Boys Club of America. The two groups created a "full-service" program that included educational instruction, work-readiness training, motivational activities, job placement, and recreation. Funding comes from all sectors of the community: corporations, education, welfare, employment and training agencies, and private donors.

In the current spate of broad-based educational reforms, disadvantaged youth with serious employability problems may be overlooked. When youth programs target their efforts on those most in need, such as those served by 70001, the payoff in the long run is greatest. **Schools and businesses should reexamine school reform efforts in light of the problems of the disadvantaged. They should invest in programs to help these youth reach the educational level necessary for employment.** Without this attention, well-meaning efforts of schools to raise achievement levels alone may not help the disadvantaged. Imposition of higher standards, longer school days, and other reforms may produce more frustration, failure, and dropping out among those students who are already finding it difficult to keep pace.[19]

One way to raise the skill level of youth who fall behind in the regular school year is to provide them with instruction during the summer. Studies show that more fortunate youth continue to learn during the summer break, while their disadvantaged peers lose ground. One study estimates that up to 80 percent of the difference in the retention of knowledge from year to year occurs during the summer.[20] Evidence of this summer learning gap suggests that a "summer strategy" may be useful in increasing the long-term employability of disadvantaged youth.

Public/Private Ventures (P/PV), a Philadelphia-based research and demonstration organization, developed a summer training and remediation program targeted to fourteen- and fifteen-year-olds. With financial support from the Ford Foundation and the federal Job Training Partnership Act, P/PV tested the program in Boston, Baltimore, and Pinellas County, Florida, in 1984. It selected as participants young people who were at least two grade levels behind their peers. Nearly 10 percent were on public assistance. All were disadvantaged.

The program consisted of a half-day of work experience and a half-day of remedial education and life-planning. Youth in the first summer's demonstration made gains, relative to a control group, in both mathematics and English. The P/PV project placed participants in their half-day jobs through the Summer Youth Employment and Training Program (SYETP), a federal program under JTPA that provides summer jobs for approximately 700,000 disadvantaged youth each year.

Including remedial activities in the summer jobs program also has become a priority of the U.S. Department of Labor. The department encourages PICs to use JTPA funds for more literacy training, a move that will prompt more PIC activities in this area. **Federal policymakers should agressively promote the combination of jobs and remedial education to provide youth with basic skills training in the summer months.**

More severely disadvantaged youth require longer-term and more intensive strategies than a summer program can offer. The Job Corps is a comprehensive federal program devoted exclusively to education and job training for the most disadvantaged. With over twenty years experience, Job Corps has demonstrated its ability to improve employment and earnings for youth who face the most difficult barriers to success in the labor market.[21]

Many factors contribute to the effectiveness of Job Corps: a greater range and intensity of services than found in other programs, and a combination of remedial education, work, and skills training. In addition, the residential nature of the program allows for around-the-clock supervision and exposure to positive values, attitudes, and behaviors sometimes missing from their home environments. **Federal policymakers should continue full support for the Job Corps as a worthwhile investment in the future of youth who otherwise will remain unemployable.**

Widespread concern over basic skills calls for cooperative action by school administrators, business leaders, and government officials. Special intensive efforts are called for to assure young people the basic education required for work. This is true especially for disadvantaged youth, where the problem is concentrated. Only when those youth unlikely to make it on their own are ready for productive employment will these school-business collaborations be termed successful.

PRE-EMPLOYMENT COMPETENCY AND WORK MATURITY

Newcomers to the job market need more than basic education to succeed in the working world. They also must learn the techniques of job-hunting and develop appropriate attitudes and behaviors for the workplace. Youth program operators call these skills pre-employment competency and work maturity. They do not substitute for basic education, but they are necessary for putting educational achievements to use. Young people can acquire these skills partly from books or in classrooms; however, they are developed and assimilated most effectively through imitation of adult behavior and experience in the outside world.

The majority of American youth acquire pre-employment competency and work maturity from a combination of three sources: their home environments; informal exposure to work through chores, odd jobs, and community activities; and schooling. For many disadvantaged youth, however, the immediate family is fractured, and support from an extended family or friends and neighbors is weak. Impoverished environments are poor sources of workplace information and values. Few employed people are on hand to act as role models, provide work connections, or give guidance and information on careers. Actual jobs, another source of learning, are virtually nonexistent in many areas. The third source—schools—also may fail to convey the knowledge or produce the socialization necessary for the disadvantaged to find their way into the work force. The probable result is a lifetime of intermittent, low-level employment and poverty.

Schools always have played a role in imparting the skills used in work. In recent years that role has expanded to include access to the working world itself. School systems have instituted guidance and counseling services and given them an important place in educational programs.

For many students, schools now serve as the main avenue of contact with the working world. Teaching young people how to search out job openings and plan careers has become a necessary and accepted function of secondary schools. However, guidance counselors often are swamped by caseloads in the hundreds, preventing them from giving adequate help to those needing it most. In many systems, counselors direct most of their attention to the college-bound; "placement" offices frequently are little more than repositories for college catalogs. Fewer resources and less expertise are available to students who plan to go to work directly after high school.

The skills of pre-employment competency and work maturity are bridges between the worlds of education and work. Programs to impart these skills are a natural starting point for educational systems and private employers to work together. Both have their own particular kind of expertise and resources to contribute, as well as sharing a mutual, commonsense understanding of what pre-employment competency and work maturity mean.

The federal Job Training Partnership Act also encourages collaborative efforts in these skill areas and has given impetus to the development of joint programs. Thanks to this coincidence of understanding and interest, pre-employment competency and work maturity programs have formed the basis for many flourishing alliances between business and education around the country. Schools and businesses should take advantage of their mutual interests and develop programs for pre-employment competency and work maturity as first steps in building more comprehensive school-to-work partnerships.

A person's knowledge of the working world and adaptability to its routines make a big difference to employers in deciding whom to hire, promote, or fire. Programs developing the skills of pre-employment competency and work maturity help young people become employable and promote their chances for successful careers. Some of the programs discussed in this section are classroom-based; others use jobs themselves as the primary learning vehicle. The best combine both approaches. Especially for the disadvantaged, whose living environments may convey scant learning for work, special programs provide the best opportunities for developing the traits needed for employment.

Pre-employment competency programs begin with the recognition that youth often are unaware of their own assets or liabilities as potential employees. Frequently they do not understand how their accomplishments relate to demands on the job or how best to present themselves and their abilities to employers. Many have unrealistically high expectations for their first jobs, thinking that some types of work are beneath them. Others' expectations of themselves are too low.

A lack of knowledge about how to look for work or market themselves to employers greatly handicaps many youth in their job search. On the other side, employers find it impossible to distinguish among job candidates whose identical credentials say little about the special contributions each might make to a job.

One program to overcome difficulties is the Career Passport, designed by the Institute for Work and Learning in Washington, D.C. The Career Passport program helps teenagers identify their assets and translate them into selling points to use in job-hunting. In the program, youth develop an experience-based resume, or "passport," which describes their academic work, previous jobs, and outside activities in terms relevant to employers.

The passport is both a process and a product. Youth work through a series of exercises to discover their strengths and weaknesses, explore career options, plan next steps for education and work, and learn about job-hunting techniques. They use resulting document in the course of actual job searching. Employer panels in Worcester, Massachusetts, and Santa Clara, California, contributed to the relevance of the passport process by giving advice on how employers evaluate job applicants and how youth can match their life experiences to local employer needs.

The Institute for Work and Learning recognizes the central role of the classroom teacher in employability development and trains them in the "how-tos" of creating a Career Passport. The institute encourages school districts to start the passport exercises early, preferably in the ninth grade. Typically, the process is integrated into the curriculum through English or social studies classes or into guidance and counseling activities. Instructors can grade students' workbook exercises as part of English classes or assign research projects that involve learning about career fields. For example, students might interview staff of local companies as part of a survey project.[22]

Incorporating work concepts into the curriculum does not present teachers with a burden but with a new tool for instruction. **Educational administrators should relate schooling to the world of work and provide training for teachers in how best to integrate work concepts into the high school curricula. Businesses should advise school officials on ways to help young people recognize and develop their job-relevant experience and present it to potential employers in meaningful terms.**

Job Readiness Training (JRT) is another program that promotes both pre-employment competency and work maturity through a special course of classroom-based exercises. JRT, developed by MDC Inc., a North Carolina research and demonstration organization, operates in over fifty schools in that state. Participants, selected mostly from economically disadvantaged groups, often have negative self-images and poor academic records. They spend the first half of the full-year, ungraded course completing personal growth and development exercises. They encompass building positive attitudes and self-image, improving family and peer relationships, and increasing their decision-making skills. The second half of the course emphasizes the job hunt, application, and interview processes. The program limits class size to ten to fifteen students and stresses active participation in discussions and field trips to company premises.

The JRT program gives students an opportunity to develop their understanding of the working world and improve their options before plunging directly into a job search. The motivational and self-improvement aspects of the program contribute to students' work maturity. The attention to job-search training complements the school's academic program. It motivates underachieving students and gives them self-confidence in present schooling and for their future working lives.

School administrators became enthusiastic supporters of this program from the beginning. They touted its long-term advantages to classroom teachers and made the necessary contacts with the business community. Local employers contributed to the program by acting as project advisors, designing actual program components, and participating with students and school faculty in evaluating its strengths and weaknesses. The success of the program in North Carolina prompted Florida school officials to adopt it statewide, with the help of JTPA funds and foundation support.

School officials should offer programs to help students develop self-awareness and job-market skills, especially to help those likely to encounter the greatest obstacles to employment. Employers can advise schools on how best to prepare students for the job-search process and working life. They also can help plan programs geared to local labor markets.

The Philadelphia school district recently launched a training program with yet another design for developing pre-employment competency and work maturity. It includes business support during the actual training, plus an innovative follow-up component. Marion B.W. Holmes, executive director of the district's Career and Vocational Education Center, considers the follow-up a large factor in the program's success. "[In this program] the teacher-coordinator develops the jobs, places the students in the jobs, and then follows up with visitations on site." She said, "We call that 'brokering jobs' for the young person."[23]

The program's one-year curriculum was designed by the Work in America Institute of Scarsdale, N.Y., and now operates in eleven Philadelphia schools. Students first learn a broad range of job-hunting and employment skills. the classroom becomes a "career laboratory" modeled and equipped like an office with video-recording and playback equipment, telephones, and copiers. Nearly fifty small and large business have supported the program by donating equipment and services. Honeywell Corporation of Minneapolis contributed twenty-one computers, allowing students to learn appropriate skills using the latest technology.

More important than equipment is the connection businesses set up between the working world and student performance. Business volunteers conduct mock interviews, explain career options, and in many cases, provide students with jobs. At the job site, the program's teachers act as mentors, helping students to work out problems and adjust to their work situations. This support on the job can be a crucial factor in developing a positive employer-employee relationship. The presence of business volunteers in schools and teachers in the workplace connects the two worlds for students. Businesses can support job search/job-holding programs with financial contributions or in-kind volunteer services. Businesses can work with school guidance counselors to identify local employment openings appropriate for "mentoring" situations.

The Jobs for America's Graduates (JAG) program exphazises job placement as the way to help high school seniors make the transition from school to work. Begun in Delaware, the program now operates at sites in several states, including Tennessee and Arizona. It provides pre-employment skills development, career exploration, and job-search assistance to students unlikely to succeed in the workplace on their own.

"Job specialists" under contract with JAG work in the schools with JAG participant "clients" individually and in groups. They help students put together academic curricula, choose occupational training appropriate to their interests and background, and identify employment opportunities. After placing the young people in jobs, these specialists work with their newly employed clients throughout the next year, helping them adjust to workplace demands.

JAG also organizes complementary "career associations" with club-type activities to attract students to the program, develop their leadership qualities and sense of responsibility, and motivate them. Similar to vocational education-based clubs such as Future Farmers of America, these associations have local, state, and national offices and meet at a national convention every year. In holding competitions, sponsoring social outings, and organizing elective offices, JAG associations give disadvantaged students, who often are left out of regular "student government" activities, opportunities for development important to success in jobs and in life.

Studies of the effectiveness of JAG and other transition programs show substantial employment and earnings gains for disadvantaged youth in the first year out of school. However, most of the improvement is attributable to participants' steadier work rather than any substantial improvement in their skills or wage levels. Without attention to basic skills deficiencies, first-year gains can disappear in the second year. These findings reveal more about the need for comprehensive programs in addressing the special problems of the disadvantaged than they discredit other, more limited types of programs.

The goals of pre-employment competency and work maturity programs are narrow: they aim specifically to improve youths' chances for finding and holding jobs. Evaluations suggest strongly that programs of job search and placement should not stand alone. In general, long-term, more intense and comprehensive programs encompassing all four aspects of employability have the greatest impact on youths' future employment prospects. Fostering work skills among the disadvantaged especially requires long-term attention. **School and business officials should continue and even expand their joint school-to-work transition programs. However, they also should concentrate on improving basic educational levels of students in employability development programs.**

The Polaroid Corporation created an independent subsidiary, Inner City Inc., to involve itself directly in training disadvantaged youth. Although the program aims to develop pre-employment skills and work maturity, basic skills instruction plays a large part in its activities. It lasts a minimum of sixteen weeks and is organized into phases through which trainee employees move. The purpose is to orient employees to manufacturing, but emphasis is on those qualities that make an individual more eligible to obtain and retain a job: attendance, productivity, attitudes, personal habits, and basic educational skills. According to Richard Lawson, president and chairman of the board of Inner City: "We provide counseling at every stage of the program. And, we believe very strongly that training is meaningless without a job at the end."[24] A study of the first group of trainees who "graduated" to full-time positions with the Polaroid Corporation found that 80 percent stayed nine years or more.

Other companies have seen the advantages in tying pre-employment and work maturity programs with basic skills and work experience. The New Horizons Project, a local business-education alliance in Richmond, Virginia, works with the school system to assist economically disadvantaged students identified as potential dropouts. The year-round project begins in the months before the eleventh grade. In the summer, youth work in paid employment for half the day and attend regular classes the other half.

During the regular school term, students attend basic education classes in reading, writing, and speech. They also learn life skills such as personal budgeting and consumer awareness, and receive some computer training. Participants must maintain good attendance and make reasonable grades (generally a C average). They receive weekly reports on their progress from the instructors. With the aid of a job counselor, youth also work on improving workplace behavior and attitudes. Job counselors have become instrumental in solving work-related problems, such as aversion to criticism and correction. Program operators acknowledge that the academic criteria tend to exclude the most difficult-to-employ youth. But those meeting program requirements are placed in entry-level clerical and sales positions in local corporations.

The New Horizons Project enjoys strong corporate ties. Several business leaders designed and implemented the program working through the local

Private Industry Council. Businesses found that the project gave them opportunities to try out potential employees; many hired New Horizons trainees after graduation. Several made multiyear commitments to earmark entry-level positions for trainees completing the program. This kind of stability allows the program's directors and businesses themselves to plan the program's future carefully; it also improves the quality of the experience for youth. **Business leaders should expand their efforts to hire youth from programs emphasizing preemployment skills, work-readiness training, and academic study. Business commitments should be multiyear to assure stable, well-planned programs.**

The Job Training Partnership Act (JTPA) offers tangible incentives for business involvement in these kinds of programs through its exemplary youth program called "try-out employment." This program, which the local PIC may choose to operate, provides compensation to participants in lieu of wages for up to 250 hours of employment in the private sector, which may include part-time work for up to 20 hours per week during the school term and full-time jobs in the summer. Businesses pledge to hire participants at the end of the tryout period. Meanwhile, the company receives the benefits of their labor without the payroll costs, while students learn firsthand about the demands of working life. The law emphasizes the learning nature of "try-out employment" by stating that disadvantaged youth usually would not be hired for these positions because of their lack of experience and other barriers to employment.

School officials also have a direct interest in this program, since the law limits participation to youth enrolled in secondary schools or GED programs who meet academic and attendance requirements. **Private Industry Councils (PICs) should fully use JTPA's provisions for tryout employment to give disadvantaged youth the experience of working in the private sector. Schools should ask PICs to organize try-out employment positions for their disadvantaged students. Businesses should create slots where these youth can be put to work.**

The Smokey House Project in Danby, Vermont, is another program that gives disadvantaged youth the chance to learn to work through actual work experience. Targeted to potential dropouts, it involves work projects in carpentry, agriculture, forestry, and appropriate technology. Participants and their supervisors, or "crew leaders," draw up a "work plan agreement" that lays out goals and tracks individual progress in mastering tasks. This process is a practical example of what JTPA envisions for youth programs: formulation of an individual employability development plan for every person—one that measures achievements leading to a positive goal.

Youths work at Smokey House four hours a day during the school year earning minimum wages; they attend school the other half-day. The project maintains a strict "no school, no work" policy. In the eight-week summer session, the youth work at Smokey House all day. In addition to "hands-on'' experience, crew leaders emphasize the specific math, language, and science skills used in the work projects, encouraging participants to develop or improve these skills to solve practical work problems. Crew leaders also talk with teachers about their weekly lesson plans to coordinate youths' work programs with their schooling.

The Smokey House Project uses experience itself to foster work maturity. Its designers saw that while jobs are important for the income they produce in the short term, their real value lies in how they lay the groundwork for the future. With the potential to convey learning in the present, employment also puts young people on the path to further occupational training and development. **Those who hire youth, whether in publicly funded jobs such as the federal summer youth program or in private-sector jobs, should structure work to maximize its potential to teach as well as to show the way to future employment.**

Employers should view wage costs not just as the purchase of today's labor but as investment in building capacity in tomorrow's work force. From this perspective, the rationale for private-sector "hire a youth" campaigns is not corporate charity but corporate self-interest. Similarly, the rationale for public jobs programs is not merely to "keep kids off the streets," but to develop their work potential. Albert Brown of IBM, chairman of the New York City Cooperative Education Commission, explains how jobs can reinforce schooling, especially in teenagers lacking other avenues to learn:

At the job site, students learn that excellent attendance is a prerequisite for job success. This important work ethic transfers directly to the school situation. The stimulation of the job renews their interest in academics as they begin to understand the relationship between job requirements and courses.[25]

State governments are playing an increasingly active role in designing and funding youth programs. In addition to their already dominant role in financing secondary education, states are sponsoring programs specifically oriented to developing the employment potential of young people by putting them to work. The most popular model of state involvement to date is the conservation corps; in the last three years over one-third have adopted legislation to establish these programs.

The oldest and largest is the California Conservation Corps (CCC), founded in 1976. With an annual budget of $44 million, the CCC operates 18 residential centers and 22 nonresidential satellites enrolling approximately 2,000 participants statewide. Its program includes mandatory literacy training and GED preparation, critical elements to balance the "jobs" emphasis. Participants work in conservation activities on public lands and in emergency and disaster assistance efforts, blending public service with hard work.

Other state programs have their own unique features. In Michigan, the state conservation corps is targeted to young people receiving state general assistance payments. In Iowa, participation is limited to the disadvantaged. Local public and private agencies using corpsmembers' services provide 30 percent of the funding for the program. In New Jersey, the corps is targeted to high school dropouts who must return to school or an alternative educational program to participate. The job thus is made contingent on education.

Many local jurisdictions around the country also have established service corps programs. J. Anthony Kline, presiding justice of the California State Court of Appeals and cofounder of the San Francisco Conservation Corps, summed up the experience of these programs:

Those kids need life skills—how to show up on time, how to take care of tools, how to be self-disciplined. They need discipline and structure in their lives and that's what the conservation and service corps are giving them.[26]

States should continue and, where possible, expand these service-work programs to give disadvantaged youth the experience they need to move into private-sector employment.

State programs have emerged in part to fill the gap left by expiration of several federal youth programs since 1980. Current federal involvement in youth employment issues is carried on, at a much reduced level, through the Job Training Partnership Act. JTPA emphasizes placement in private-sector jobs as an important criterion for evaluating program performance. Because of this emphasis, much of the 40 percent of JTPA funds for youth programs is devoted to short-term world of work instruction, job-search assistance, and placement for in-school youth. This stress on placement and the desire to limit program costs creates a disincentive to providing disadvantaged youth with the long-term, comprehensive, and more expensive employability development programs they need.

However, JTPA also uses a performance measure called "youth competencies attained" to evaluate youth programs. These skills correspond to the four aspects of employability outlined in this chapter. Private Industry Councils are already developing these competency measures; all states are collecting data to evaluate youth programs by these standards, appropriately reserving placement-related judgments for adult programs.

As PICs begin to accept youth competencies to measure program accomplishments, they will be more disposed to offer an appropriate range of developmental activities that serves those youth most in need and increases their long-term employment potential. **Federal Department of Labor officials should emphasize use of "youth competencies attained" to measure the success of employability development programs. This policy would allow more comprehensive programs better focused on youth at risk.**

The federal government also funds, as part of JTPA, the largest public jobs program, the Summer Youth Employment and Training Program (SYETP). It provides work experience for approximately 700,000 disadvantaged youth each summer at a cost of $825 million. (The potential for adding a remedial education component to this program was discussed in the previous section.) Funding is a perennial question mark as successive budget proposals have threatened to halve the program or change the distribution of funds in other ways. **Federal officials should continue their support for the federal summer jobs programs to give disadvantaged youth the chance to work.**

While pre-employment competency and work maturity are essential ingredients for finding and holding jobs, they may seem "second nature" to adults with successful careers. The public should come to realize that for many inexperienced youth, these skills must be learned. Disadvantaged youth in particular benefit from special programs that explicitly teach what working is all about. Schools and businesses should cooperate fully in these programs. Businesses and government should provide jobs that give youth a chance to experience the working world first hand. The result will be a better prepared youth labor force for the nation's economy.

OCCUPATIONAL SKILLS

The fourth aspect of employability, occupational skills, encompasses the technical knowledge and ability to do a specific job. A variety of agencies provide training in skills in many different forms, from classroom-based activities in vocational schools supported by public funds, to hands-on training at the work site as part of an employer's cost of doing business. Preparing youth for jobs, however, is a broader enterprise than occupational training, an activity that lies at the end of the school-to-work continuum. This part of youth employability development is best left to employers, rather than educational systems.

Most people acquire their work skills on the job; jobs lead to training, rather than vice versa. When the President's Commission on Automation recently asked workers where they learned the actual skills they used in their work, only 40 percent reported learning them in formal education and training programs. The rest learned on the job, either informally by trial and error, or in company-sponsored training.[27]

The private sector spends an estimated $30 to $40 billion annually training its employees. For this reason, youth development programs should focus on the areas of basic skills, pre-employment skills, and work maturity that help young people secure employment, thus putting them in line for company training.

Business leaders appear to agree with this approach. Economist Anthony Carnevale stated the business position in an article for the private-sector-based American Society for Training and Development:

The learning of broad occupational or professional skills should be left to postsecondary institutions and job-specific training should be left to employer-provided workplace training. A more general curriculum for all students that emphasizes basic academic and vocational skills, including career planning and job search skills, would seem more appropriate.[28]

School administrators have not always welcomed this approach. The 1982 Center for Public Resources survey found that

while school respondees often cited vocational skills as the most important factor in youth employability, the business view was that if schools provided adequately educated youth, business would provide, indeed, overwhelmingly does provide technical training.[29]

Educators and business leaders should talk directly about their respective roles, and their expectations of each other's systems, in preparing young people for work.

Schools do best imparting basic skills; businesses do best generating jobs and training people to do them. Many opportunities exist for the two sectors to work together. Neither should have to play the other's role. Schools should keep vocational courses broad and orientational, and use them to motivate students for the task of learning basic skills. Employers, on the other hand, can provide jobs that impart learning and demonstrate the connection of education to work. Making jobs and classrooms more relevant to one another is a key to successful youth programs.

Educators must be realistic about what school-based occupational training can achieve. It can be an important part of overall employability development. Aside from introducing young people to occupational skills, vocational training helps motivate them, demonstrates the importance of academic skills, and helps keep potential dropouts in school. These effects on employability can be as important as any direct gains in occupational skills.

Schools err, however, when they try to make vocational education courses too occupationally specific. Federal and state governments have advocated vocational programs for over seventy years. Many are criticized today for their shortcomings on two fronts: failure to improve the basic education or improve earnings and length of employment. Narrow, job-specific skills training at the secondary level, for example, results in immediate labor market gains for only two groups: males in the seasonal construction trades and females entering clerical occupations. Even these gains disappear within five years, however, as youth with more broad-based educations gain experience and training in the workplace.

The biggest problem with vocational education is that secondary schools cannot possibly keep pace with industry in state-of-the-art equipment to train students, nor can they compete successfully with the private sector for trainers with up-to-date knowledge of the content of jobs. School-based vocational training all too often fails to relate to emerging opportunities in the local labor market. To have access to the equipment, instructors, and up-to-date job information students need, administrators of vocational programs must join forces with employers. **Schools should seek opportunities for students to use company equipment and work with private-sector trainers. Companies could "release" employees to teach a course or work**

for a semester in a vocational school, thus bringing their current experience of the workplace into vocational curricula.

In general, vocational education programs should concentrate on developing the employability of students and leave occupational training to employers. Several types of programs have developed, with varieties of business support, that capture the employability effects of this broader definition of vocational education. "Magnet," or career schools, pioneered in the 1970s, have become common, especially in larger cities. They provide specialized study and training directed toward specific professions as part of the general high school curriculum.

Magnet school programs usually center on one particular occupational theme. They prepare youth for immediate job entry, postsecondary training, or college enrollment, depending on location and orientation. Magnet schools have a number of strengths: they draw and motivate students, forge greater business and education ties, and can help attract new businesses to the area. Companies have taken a leading role in developing these schools because they provide a pool of motivated potential workers already oriented toward a professional field.

The Wall Street business community, through the Downtown Lower Manhattan Association, helped design one of the New York City's successful magnet schools—the Murry Bergtraum High School for Business Careers. Many Wall Street firms believe that a business-oriented high school attracts students into the financial industry. Now, after several years of operation, the school still benefits from business assistance in planning the general curriculum, updating courses, soliciting equipment donations, and providing internships and jobs. Professional educators translate business priorities into specific courses and requirements.

A variation on the magnet school model exists at New York's Academy of Finance, which combines five high schools and a community college in offering a business-oriented curriculum developed by Shearson Lehman Brothers, Inc. Students take special courses in finance and economics in their junior year and more advanced courses the next. Summer jobs with Wall Street firms give students an opportunity to put classroom learning into effect. Their teachers join them in this summer experience, thus sharpening their own knowledge of job requirements in the financial community.

The Atlanta school district established an extensive system of magnet schools, four of which make up what school officials call their "technology quadrangle." Each of the units offers specialized courses in technology application, communications, science and mathematics, information processing, and decision making. All four emphasize basic course work in languages, science, and mathematics. The private sector supports the program financially and with many services, including one-semester internships for students.

Upon completion of their internships, students receive an "experience certificate" recognized by local employers as proof of employability. This certificate is an important selling point for students looking for their first "real jobs" because it attests to their readiness for work in terms that employers have agreed on. Strong ties to employers in a particular field of business, such as those developed in Atlanta, keep magnet schools relevant to the occupations they focus on. **Business can help schools stay up-to-date with labor market demand by working closely with them to design curricula, supply equipment, and offer internships and part-time jobs to students.**

Cooperative education is experiencing renewed interest as a program that connects vocational education directly to the working world. While in magnet schools the curriculum centers on one career field, cooperative education offers students many occupational choices in one school setting. As in magnet schools, "co-op ed" students combine learning with working in their field of interest, while maintaining the focus on education. Cooperative education differs from the more familiar "work-study" in that schooling and job placement are linked directly.

The New York City school system has the oldest and largest program of this type in the country, monitored by an advisory board of over 40 city business, education, and labor leaders. This board advises school staff on emerging job trends and recruits employers to give students jobs in their chosen occupational fields. Close contact with these local employers continually provides school officials with information about local labor market needs.

The state of New Jersey is expanding its cooperative education programs using JTPA education funds and its provisions for "try-out employment" (described in the previous chapter). With this help, companies create additional job slots, giving disadvantaged youth a chance to strengthen their vocational preparation by working.

In cooperative education programs, the business "constituency" is more varied than is the case with magnet schools. These schools' placement counselors must develop relationships with many different employers to find appropriate slots for students. Despite the extra effort involved, many school systems are expanding cooperative education. Its appeal is due largely to the fact that the content of the job reinforces the importance of education. **Schools can expand the use of cooperative education by contacting more employers and securing jobs that relate directly to each student's vocational interest. Employers should contact schools to offer placement opportunities for cooperative education students.**

Schools can strengthen the link between vocational education and the job market by instituting intensive placement services for graduates. School officials in Pittsburgh improved the entire system's vocational education program by organizing student job placements systematically under one "umbrella"—the Student Job Placement Section. As a result, job counselors do not duplicate efforts contacting employers, and this way all students, including the educationally and economically disadvantaged, are assured a chance at the most appropriate jobs. A combination of federal, state, and local monies support the program. Over 800 private-sector employers—from U.S. Steel to small grocery stores—and 250 public-sector employers are involved each year. **School officials should organize job-placement services carefully and work with other placement agencies, such as the Employment Service, to improve the match of students to jobs, ensuring use of classroom-based learning on the job.**

Making sure that occupational training is relevant to the job market is a critical issue for schools and other training providers. The state of Vermont assures a close fit between its training programs and job opportunities through careful development and application of information about the occupational structure of the state's labor markets. The state Department of Employment and Training uses an extensive competency-based system for its JTPA training programs. They cover all four aspects of employability, thus ensuring a complete work preparation system.

To implement JTPA, Vermont, like many other states, conducted an employer survey that identified thirty-six growth occupations with upcoming needs for additional workers. The department uses this information to decide what sort of training programs to fund. It scrutinizes these programs carefully, insisting that they provide young people with the skills that local employers have indicated they need. Funds for training in other occupations are not denied out-of-hand, but the department has asked for program revisions based on this local employment information.[30]

School and local officials should assess local labor market needs carefully. Before offering occupational training, they should be certain that it corresponds to demand in the local economy.

Local business organizations, such as the Chamber of Commerce or the Private Industry Council, are closer than schools to knowledge of developments in the job market. They can assist the education system by providing up-to-date information to school guidance counselors, curriculum planners, and other school officials responsible for employment outcomes of education.

In contrast to training provided by schools and other public agencies, employer-based occupational training can be specific to a particular job in a particular company. This employment tie is its strength. However, for public investments in preparing youth for work, this specificity can present problems. It may lead to "tracking" youth into specific job categories at too early an age, compounding problems for minorities and the economically disadvantaged. For some youth, however, specific occupational training may be appropriate. Two of the best employer-based approaches to occupational training that retain a role for public agencies are the apprentice system and publicly funded on-the-job training.

Apprenticeship is a time-honored model of occupational skill training with a specific employer. Apprenticeship involves the employer, current jobholders and relevant unions, and classroom-based educators in a formal program of hands-on training and related instruction to prepare young people for jobs. Many northern European countries base their work preparation system on the apprentice model, but it is not used widely in the United States. Limited access to such programs has prompted efforts in recent years to open apprenticeships to more women and minorities. Movement has begun to broaden the list of occupations accepting apprentices to include more jobs, especially in the health care and food service industries.

Apprentices are trainees in the employ of a firm. Employers and current employees (frequently through their unions) decide which jobs will have apprentices, how many there will be, and what kind of workplace training and related classroom instruction is appropriate. Because this method of training is concentrated in highly skilled, well-paid trades, apprenticeship programs generally require several years to complete. Apprentices become journeymen and "graduate" to full wages with the firm when the training period is over. Journeyman status is a portable credential, recognized by all employers with jobs in the particular occupational field.

Businesses support these programs to ensure themselves of a supply of well-trained workers. School officials are gratified to see their graduates enter well-regarded occupational training, assume jobs, and enjoy the prospect of steady careers. As apprentice opportunities expand, more disadvantaged youth will benefit as well.

Businesses with apprenticeship programs or apprenticeable occupations can work with their current employees and school officials to expand existing apprenticeship opportunities. In whatever occupational training programs they undertake, business-education collaborations should strive to reach the correspondence between training and labor market demands that the apprentice system exemplifies.

In the past decade, school officials and administrators of public job-training programs have developed pre-apprenticeship programs to put disadvantaged youth in line for full participation. The Ventures in Community Improvement (VICI) program is a successful pre-apprenticeship model designed by Public/Private Ventures. VICI projects teach occupational skills and make physical improvements to communities in six- to twelve-month training programs. Each project involves crews of six or seven disadvantaged youth enrollees in on-site training under the supervision of experienced craftspersons. Trainees earn at least the minimum wage and meet demanding production schedules to fill commitments to contracting organizations.

In New York City, two six-woman crews are trained each year by journeymen from the painters' union; they repaint fire-bombed, water-damaged school buildings under contract to the Board of Education. Craftsperson-supervisors teach the skills required to do the work, demand good work habits, and provide their trainees with entree into related jobs and union apprenticeships. In each VICI site, local private and public money is committed to supplement federal or foundation funds.

Evaluations of VICI projects show that disadvantaged participants, upon completion of training, are twice as likely to find employment and three times as likely to be apprenticed as similar teenagers in a control group. **School officials and administrators of public job-training programs should work with unions and private companies to explore the possibility of developing preapprenticeship programs as "feeders" for apprentice training.**

On-the-job training (OJT) is another skills-training approach based on existing jobs in the labor market. Like apprentices, participants in OJT are employees of the firm from the beginning of training. Their wages are partially reimbursed from federal funds through the Job Training Partnership Act. The local Private Industry Council contracts with an employer to provide the training and oversees its design and implementation. In most cases, trainees must meet JTPA eligibility requirements regarding income, i.e., they must be economically disadvantaged. The PIC expects that trainees will become permanent employees.

In 1967, Consolidated Edison (Con Ed), the New York utility company, launched an OJT program to hire and train teenaged dropouts. The program places equal emphasis on remedial education and job-related skills. "Trainees are actually trial employees," according to Regina Frederickson, director of employment services for Con Ed. "They're on salary and are clocking vacation and pension time from the moment they enter training and do not have to go through a probationary period when they move into the job."[31]

The academic component, consisting of 200 hours of half-day sessions averaging fifteen hours a week, emphasizes job-relevant math and reading skills. Training groups are small, allowing extensive student-teacher interaction and weekly counseling. Because of this individual attention, job-retention rates are higher than with Con Ed's regular hires. Today, the program is supported by the New York City PIC, with Con Ed contributing 20 to 25 percent of the training costs.

OJT operates on the basis of contracts between a company and the Private Industry Council. In New York City the PIC deals with companies and potential trainees one at a time. The PIC focuses on the small and medium-sized businesses that comprise 92 percent of the city's 190,000 employers. In some years, the PIC has signed OJT contracts with over 100 companies. At the present time, few programs concentrate on youth because employers are reluctant to offer them the hiring commitment that implicitly or explicitly is part of OJT contracts.

As a practical matter, OJT contracts generally reimburse the employer for up to 50 percent of wage costs for a specified time period. Payments are not intended to subsidize trainees' wages. Instead, the OJT process gives workers time to learn how to do a job, and gives employers a financial incentive to provide this learning time. The reimbursement feature of OJT is an explicit recognition that jobs themselves are learning experiences.

Schools and businesses can work together to identify job possibilities within a firm where reimbursement for training would be an appropriate hiring incentive. They also can identify graduates for whom this type of training would be useful. If JTPA funds are involved, OJT slots can be developed for a school's disadvantaged students.

In making decisions on which job applicants to hire and which employees to train, employers choose those most likely to succeed. For this reason, whatever additional efforts the public and private sector mount should concentrate on those least likely to make it on their own. **Public investments in learning to work should focus on the needs of disadvantaged and minority youth, those least likely to find their own way in the job market.** This is a difficult standard to maintain. Policymakers and the public judge programs such as JTPA and vocational education on their ability to place people in jobs, creating the inclination to "choose the best" for public programs. This is the very tendency that helps exclude the disadvantaged from employers' in-house training. Too great an emphasis on job placement can cause public programs to enroll only those who would have been hired anyway. This danger is very strong in OJT.

All those involved in youth preparation efforts, school officials, business leaders, and public policymakers, should be aware that rapid job placement may not always be appropriate for youth, advantaged or disadvantaged. When scarce public funds are involved, schools and other youth-serving agencies should spend them on broad developmental activities, such as programs of basic skills, pre-employment competency and work maturity, to prepare youth for jobs and training in the private sector.

Schools, businesses, and government agencies already have invested heavily in the enterprise of preparing youth for work. Still, millions remain unemployed because they lack the essential skills for today's job market. For poor and minority youth especially, the problem is becoming chronic; it threatens to become acute for the U.S. economy as these young people make up ever larger proportions of the available labor pool.

The answer may lie in a reexamination of the existing "portfolio." Schools, businesses, and all levels of government bring different expertise and resources to the effort. Each must recognized and draw on the other's strengths, joining their activities to nurture the difficult passage of student to productive citizen. For the disadvantaged, that passage is arduous and tenuous.

The best means of preparing youth is a chain of assistance from basic skills instruction in schools to the training employers provide at work. In this system of shared responsibility, youth who are at risk of failure could progress in a logical sequence to productive employment.

Planning this continuum of services requires all partners to act together to find their mutual interests, define common goals, and discover the contributions each can make. Preparing youth for work demands the best efforts of all.

4. Developing Adult Basic Skills for Employment

THE ILLITERACY PROBLEM IN THE UNITED STATES

Dimensions of the Problem

The connection of literacy to the demands of the modern workplace has become a major concern for employers and public policymakers. A person has difficulty acquiring necessary job skills or even looking for employment in the absence of literacy. Yet evidence continues to mount that illiteracy is pervasive in some segments of the population. The director of one skill training program believes that "illiteracy is the hidden shame in this community."[1] The Northeast-Midwest region of the country has long been noted for having a well-educated and adaptable work force, an asset that has served as an attractive inducement in business location and expansion decisions. Maintaining and enhancing this "edge" is an important part of the effort to build the foundations of economic stability. Literacy is crucial to that effort.

Recent statistics indicate that up to one-third of the adult population—perhaps 60 million men and women—cannot read the front page of a newspaper. The Adult Performance Level study has shown for the past several years that perhaps 20 percent of adults are functionally illiterate—unable to read, write, or compute with the proficiency needed to function in society. Among adults, 16 percent of whites, 44 percent of blacks, and 56 percent of Hispanics are either total, functional, or marginal nonreaders. The National Assessment of Educational Progress, the ongoing study of student achievement, finds that 13 percent of U.S. high school graduates fail to reach reading and writing competence beyond the sixth-grade level. The U.S. Department of Education estimates that 2.3 million people are added each year to the ranks of the functionally illiterate: 1 million teenagers who leave school without elementary skills and 1.3 million non-English-speaking arrivals.

In 1982 Navy officials told the National Commission on Excellence in Education that one-quarter of recent recruits did not read at the minimum level (ninth grade) needed to understand written safety instructions. Without remedial courses they could not even begin the sophisticated training necessary for modern military service.

This literacy gap exists at a time when changes in the labor market are increasing the premium on communications skills. Employers in service industries expect employees to be able to read and write well—in many occupations these abilities comprise the major part of the job. Many companies are moving to involve employees more fully in planning and organizing work; this kind of worker participation in decision making calls for good verbal skills. Even in more traditional manufacturing companies, the content of many jobs is changing; higher levels of reading and writing ability are becoming necessary. One adult illiterate describes the situation aptly:

Today, even if you're a janitor, there's still reading and writing involved. Like if they leave a note saying, "Go to room so-and-so, this and that." You can't do it. You can't read it. You don't know. And they ain't going to hire somebody to run along and tell people what to do.[2]

Research confirms these recent increases in literacy needs. The Business Council for Effective Literacy found that literacy standards are higher today than they were ten years ago. In the face of these changing standards, 11 percent of today's professional and managerial workers are functionally illiterate, as are 30 percent of semiskilled and unskilled workers. Workers face more difficult literacy demands on the job than students encounter in high schools; today even blue-collar job manuals and directions average a tenth-grade level of reading difficulty. The requirements of Army job printed materials, for example, range from a tenth- to a twelfth-grade level. While estimates of necessary reading levels for specific occupations are imprecise, several studies have concluded that a twelfth-grade reading level generally defines essential literacy for today. Studies also have found that workers who perform better on reading tests are rated higher in job proficiency and productivity as well.

The link between competitiveness and a literate work force is a compelling reason for concern over the current state of basic skills. Business losses attributable to basic skills deficiencies run into the hundreds of millions of dollars annually because of low productivity, errors and accidents, and lost management and supervisory time. Jonathon Kozol, whose *Death at an Early Age* examined the effects of poor schooling on children, writes in his recent book *Illiterate America*:

The dollar cost to our society for our neglect of this injustice is intolerably high—$20 billion yearly to support unemployable, imprisoned or disheartened people, and in losses caused by workplace accidents and damage to military equipment, billions more lost in lowered G.N.P. The Federal Government budgets something like $1.65 a year to reach each illiterate adult in our society.[3]

Critical as the problem is for adults of working age, it has intergenerational effects as well. Children's participation in the learning process is related to the educational attainment of their parents; illiteracy thus can be "handed down." The Commission on Excellence in Education exhorted parents to read to their children, help them with homework, and act as role models by reading themselves for both knowledge and pleasure. The commission saw this as one way in which parents could support the work of the schools and improve the educational enterprise. However, many of the people to whom the recommendation was addressed could not read it. One illiterate young mother expressed frustration with the effects of her situation on her children. She said:

I can't read to them, of course that's leaving them out of something they should have. Oh, it matters. You believe it matters! . . . Donny wanted me to read a book to him . . . . I tried it one day, reading from the pictures. Donny looked at me. He said, "Mommy that's not right." He's only 5. He knew I couldn't read.[4]

A current public service announcement on television promotes the national literacy campaign by picturing a father trying to read a story to his young daughter . . . and failing.

The result is a cycle of illiteracy and poverty in which children repeat the life experiences of their parents. Kozol summarizes the problem:

Illiterate adults are crippled . . . in at least three ways. They cannot find employment, which, today more than ever in the past, depends upon a competence that eludes them. They cannot voice their grievances in press releases or in other forms of discourse that might win political attention and response. They cannot help their children escape a comparable fate.[5]

A Particular Case: Dislocated Workers

The situation of many dislocated workers—out of work and with slim prospects of reemployment—illustrates the relationship between literacy and jobs. Dislocated workers typically have been on the job and out of school for many years. Most went to work directly from high school, before or after graduating, for a firm (usually manufacturing) at which one of their parents was employed, and expected to say there until retirement.

Now, however, many of their jobs have disappeared because of international competition, plant relocation, or technological obsolescence. Where new jobs exist, they frequently have different, often higher, literacy requirements. Workers may have to review (or learn for the first time) reading, writing, and basic mathematics in order to *start* the training for more complex jobs. Recognizing and adjusting to this need for competence in basic skills is difficult for dislocated workers who typically complain, "I didn't need it before—why do I need it now?" However, remedial education and basic skills instruction can help reemploy some of these workers, thereby strengthening the economy.

Dislocation affects a large number of the unemployed. An ongoing study by the Bureau of Labor Statistics (BLS) found that over five million workers were dislocated from 1979 to 1984. The high incidence of long-term unemployment in the Northeast-Midwest region signals the existence of disproportionate numbers of dislocated workers in these states. In 1983, 44 percent of the unemployed in the region were out of work for fifteen weeks or more. Also, dislocation has been especially pronounced in industries historically central to the region's economy, such as manufacturing and mining. Plant shutdowns and mass layoffs have become frequent occurrences.

According to the BLS study, many dislocated workers had been in their jobs for relatively long periods, nearly one-third for ten years or more. By January 1984, 60 percent of these workers had found new employment and about 25 percent were looking for work; the remainder had dropped out of the labor force. The BLS survey found that the higher the skill level of the worker, the greater the chance of reemployment. However, of the 60 percent who were reeemployed, almost one-half were earning less than in previous jobs; over 600,000 had taken pay cuts of 20 percent or more.

Prolonged unemployment and underemployment are expensive; economists estimate that each 1 percent of unemployment costs the federal government $30 billion in outlays for assistance and in forgone revenue. Idled physical plant capacity creates costs for businesses: production is affected adversely by the changed ratio of investment capital and labor, and profits fall. Increased outlays for unemployment benefits translate into higher unemployment insurance taxes for employers. Unemployment and underemployment drain state and local treasuries and reduce revenues. Tight budgets force cutbacks in services, including cutbacks in education.

Beyond the personal suffering of dislocated workers and their families, these costs heighten the urgency of getting people reemployed as quickly as possible in well-paying jobs. Employers, educators, and governments all have a stake in this effort. Producing a more literate work force is one key to its success.

Some dislocated workers find new jobs on their own; others need training in new skills before they can be reemployed. However, employers, unions, and training program operators have found that many dislocated workers lack the basic literacy skills required for their courses. One assistance center, Downriver Community Conference in Southgate, Michigan, estimates that 20 percent of its dislocated worker clients read at or below the sixth-grade level and need remedial education before they can be retrained. The Career Development Institute at Cuyahoga Community College in Cleveland, Ohio, found that 25 percent of its clients tested between seventh- and ninth-grade levels in reading and math, with another 35 percent at the fifth- and seventh-grade levels.

Some journalistic accounts of dislocated workers contain discussions of exciting training programs to prepare people for the jobs of tomorrow. An article in *High Technology* magazine described the successful robotics repair program operated by the Community College of Allegheny County in Erie, Pennsylvania. Thirty workers were selected from 200 applicants for this program. Most had gone to vocational high schools and 18 had received training in electronics in their military service. Participants averaged ten years of experience in electromechanical repair. The program's director acknowledged that the program intends to train "more or less the cream of the crop of the U.S. blue-collar work force."[6] Workers with functional literacy deficiencies would not be chosen for such a demanding program. Press reports have paid scant attention to the needs of a significant number of laid-off workers for remedial instruction to raise the level of their basic educational attainment. Even trainers in private companies and public programs are just beginning to recognize the need.

Costs to the private sector of basic skills deficiencies and the benefits of remediation are not precisely quantifiable. However, there is a growing awareness that the United States is falling short of the goal of a fully literate work force. This awareness must now be translated into action. Business leaders and public policymakers alike acknowledge the positive relationship between literacy and a growing economy.

EMPLOYERS' RESPONSES TO ILLITERACY

Employers recognize that the lack of basic skills among Americans is of crisis proportions in many parts of the employment market. And the problem can only worsen, if, as some economists predict, the United States faces impending labor shortages in the coming decade. Businesses must mobilize their resources to increase employee literacy in ways that are consistent with their own needs for productivity in increasingly competitive world markets.

The Center for Public Resources, a private, nonprofit organization, surveyed employers nationally in 1982 to determine the extent of basic skill deficiencies among their employees.

- More than one-half the responding companies identified writing deficiencies among their secretarial, skilled labor, managerial, supervisory, and bookkeeping personnel. The most frequently cited problems were poor grammar, spelling, and punctuation.

- Over one-half found inadequacies in mathematics in a wide range of employees, from semiskilled laborers to bookkeepers.

- More than one-half identified deficiencies in speaking and listening skills among secretarial, clerical, service, supervisory, and managerial personnel.

- Over two-thirds noted that basic skills deficiencies limit the company's ability to promote employees, both high school graduates and nongraduates.

The study concluded:

While school respondees often cited vocational skills as the most important factor in youth employability, the business view was that if schools provided adequately educated youth, business would provide, indeed overwhelmingly does provide, technical training. What business decidedly indicated it did not want to do, but is in fact doing, is to educate its employees in ninth- and tenth-grade skills.[7]

Companies can provide programs to upgrade their employees' basic skills. For example, the Planters Peanuts factory in Suffolk, Virginia, offers its workers four hours of elementary-level instruction per week on company time, with additional classes available after hours. Employees can work on basic skills in grade levels 1-4 and 5-8, as well as prepare for the General Educational Development exam which leads to the GED certificate of high school equivalency. Instruction is individualized and the curriculum is designed to meet each person's needs. Planters runs the program with the public schools and the United Auto Workers. Standard Oil Company of Indiana hired a teacher to give courses in grammar and spelling for new secretaries. Polaroid Corporation enrolls 500 to 750 employees annually in remedial programs. In 1983, the Gillette Company in St. Paul, Minnesota, offered remedial instruction to 30 employees. The company renewed the program in 1984 when it discovered that one in six production workers needed the instruction.

The Conference Board, a network of business leaders that conducts research on the economy and public policy, reported that 20 percent of the nation's banks and insurance companies provide remedial and basic literacy courses to employees lacking the necessary skills. Travelers Insurance Company has had a remedial education program for the past sixteen years. By December 1982, 616 Travelers employees had completed the program successfully. Participants receive eight weeks of full-time classroom training, studying math and English as well as basic office skills. Successful completers then spend ten weeks in a combination work-study component, with mornings devoted to classroom instruction and afternoons to on-the-job training. Company officials attribute the program's success to several factors:

- Trainees are Travelers employees from the outset. Therefore, the relationship between completing the training and doing well in the job is clear.
- The physical environment simulates real work situation rather than a classroom.
- Everything taught, including English and math, is shown to be directly relevant to the job. There is a concrete purpose for the learning.
- Participants have access to individual counseling to improve skills for coping with real-life problems. This service is particularly important to persons with low levels of reading comprehension because they have difficulty processing written information.[8]

Although examples can be found, company-sponsored in-house programs focused solely on remediation account for only a small fraction of private-sector training investments. One recent study found that only 8 percent of courses offered by employers during working hours are basic remedial courses. The American Society for Training and Development, an association of private-sector human resources managers, estimates that less than 1 percent of company training funds are spent on remedial education. Even so, corporate participants in a recent series of forums on business and education felt that business is spending too much time and money on remedial training in communications and other basic skills. Typical company programs, such as Travelers, are geared to new entry-level employees and are combined with training in the company's operations. Often they are partially supported by federal job training funds aimed at the disadvantaged. Only very large corporations with major in-house training capacities are likely to find it efficient to cover the entire cost of their own basic literacy training.

The American Telephone and Telegraph Company (AT&T) offers its employees courses in basic reading, writing, and mathematics at an annual cost of $6 million. However, the company's policy shows the cautious approach of most corporations. It calls for a review of the cost and benefits of alternative methods of providing remedial education, such as contracting with community institutions or providing tuition aid. It also calls for assurances that graduates can be placed in jobs before undertaking such training. "In most companies, efforts are constantly being made even to reduce the cost of specifically job-related training, so it is small wonder that employers are generally conservative about literacy training for which the cost-benefits are less clear," said a company official.[9]

Company policy also calls for the definition and measurement of program objectives beforehand. Standards should be set for measuring success in terms of participants' job behavior, not merely their ability to pass tests.

Any program should have realistic goals tied to practical business needs—the development and maintenance of a proficient and motivated work force. The program also should be evaluated systematically.

Companies therefore may do well to contract with educational institutions or community-based organizations for their employees' remedial needs. Several Maryland companies, including Baltimore Gas and Electric, Marriott Corporation, and Singer-Link Simulations Systems, contract with the adult education branch of the state department of education for basic skills classes conducted at company sites. Costs are shared by the companies and the adult basic education program.

This approach can be used by companies planning to shut down or relocate. Carter Carburetor Company in St. Louis contracted with the local school system to have adult basic education instructors hold classes in the plant prior to its closing in 1984. In this way the company made a major commitment to helping its employees make the transition to new jobs. In 1983 the Levi Strauss Company helped relieve the potential for dislocation among its laid-off workers in Charleston, South Carolina, by purchasing needed educational services. The company arranged with Trident Technical College for a program of assistance as lay-offs began.

The program prepared workers for retraining by helping them develop coping skills. They were then given instruction in math, English, and reading. Exercises were designed in individualized units so participants could work at their own pace, even completing them at home. All participants received counseling on career decisions using peer role models. They reported that the basic skills instruction increased their confidence and self-esteem. Only when they overcame their fear of learning and began to feel comfortable with the basics did participants feel ready for skill retraining.

Perhaps the best-known of the dislocated workers programs are the ongoing efforts sponsored by the United Auto Workers (UAW) in cooperation with Ford and General Motors. The Ford-UAW model emphasizes the necessity of combining community resources to help the newly unemployed. In the Milpitas plant closing in San Jose, for example, Ford and the UAW contracted with the local adult education office to provide courses at the plant, including remedial math and reading. Eight hundred persons altogether participated in adult education, and 183 received high school diplomas or GEDs.

The UAW-Ford program recognizes remedial education as an important, sometimes crucial, component in an overall worker-readjustment strategy. It is this new mastery of the basics that increases workers' self-confidence and opportunities for reemployment. Other dislocated worker programs have duplicated the UAW-Ford approach.

The Kelly Springfield Tire Company realized that an alternative to closing its Tyler, Texas, plant was to convert it and upgrade the basic skills of employees so they could run the new facility. Presently 230 employees take part in the remedial progarm, which operates during regular working hours and gives full pay for the first 100 hours of participation.

In addition to working on specific literacy needs of their own employees, both current and former, companies contribute to the solution of the national illiteracy crisis by forming partnerships with educational institutions and community-based groups to improve basic skills. The attitude of AT&T toward cooperative projects is typical of many forward-looking businesses:

Communication between business and education must be greatly expanded. This must take place on a national level, but it is even more important on a local level. There must be a combined effort of business and education to provide the literacy skills necessary for productive employment.[10]

Several models already exist which businesses could adapt to fit their own needs and the particular circumstances of their local communities.

Companies can commit themselves one-to-one with a particular secondary school. "Adopt-a-School" programs pair schools and businesses to work on jointly identified problems (see the discussion in Chapter 3). While they generally concentrate on schools-to-work transition activities, some Adopt-a-School programs focus on basic skills. Some companies provide useful advice to schools on the literacy expectations of the local business community. Corporations with active outreach policies such as IBM and Hewlett-Packard pair company employees with individual students as tutors in reading, writing, and mathematics. B. Dalton Bookseller and McGraw-Hill Publishing Company, both active school adopters, have a special interest in the broad goal of a literate society.

Adoptive relationships have other outcomes as well. In some programs one company and one school work together to improve curricula. In other places company employees visit "their" school to counsel students and provide role models to encourage them to further achievement. Some loan equipment to their schools to ensure up-to-date vocational instruction. Company officials also work with school administrators to improve management.

The Adopt-a-School movement is growing. In Nashville, for example, thirty area businesses have allied themselves with specific schools. In Dallas, more than 1,000 businesses have adopted virtually all of the city's more than 200 public schools. In Milwaukee, the Chamber of Commerce manages the process of teaming companies with schools. All activities undertaken in these collaborations are arrived at jointly.

Companies also must become more broadly involved in policymaking, resource allocation, and planning for their local secondary school systems as a whole. Business leaders are joining top-echelon educational administrators and contributing their resources, time, and expertise to designing system improvements. Many of these efforts focus on basic skills. The goal is to improve the quality of literacy training in the community's secondary school system so as to raise the average skill levels of new entrants into the work force.

Financial investment is one type of system involvement for business. Many corporations have instituted social responsibility programs that include making direct grants to school systems. The John Hancock Mutual Life Insurance Company established a $1 million endowment for the Boston school system in 1985 that will generate $100,000 annually in interest. The system will use some of the income to improve the reading program in the city's middle schools, which enroll 10,000 students.

Companies also can become partners with the education system in planning and policy-making. The Boston Compact (discussed in Chapter 3) is an example of such a community-wide partnership. Executives of major corporations in the city, the administrators of secondary schools, colleges and community colleges, and leaders of community groups make decisions on how best to use all available resources to raise the skill levels of high school students. In return for educational system improvements, the corporations pledge to look first to the city's schools as a potential source of new employees.

The Boston Compact is a true partnership in that responsibility and accountability exist on both sides of the business-education equation. Improvements in the school system translate into jobs for its graduates. Also, cooperation is more than financial; the time and expertise of top executives on both sides are thoroughly engaged. The compact can command this level of involvement because it is a locally generated agreement arising from mutual needs for better performance and because it has the sustained interest and support of the city's political leadership. Other system-wide partnership efforts, including the Oakland Alliance in California and the Portland Partnership in Oregon, have these same characteristics.

These industry-education collaborations concentrate on secondary schools and youth just entering the work force. Many were spurred by the well-publicized critiques of the nation's school systems, especially *A Nation at Risk*, the report of the National Commission on Excellence in Education in 1983. However, the Commission on Higher Education and the Adult Learner pointed out that the excellence commission limited its recommendations to reforms in the education of youth, reinforcing the idea that learning is only for the young and that adults have completed their schooling.

Yet adults' education needs are at least as great as those of the young and constitute an equivalent obligation for policy and societal action. Clearly, a major effort is required to raise the level of awareness among education providers, government, prospective adult learners, and the general public.[11]

Companies should target their concern and activities on adult illiterates in the wider community beyond the schools. Businesses should involve

themselves in community-based adult literacy efforts and programs in adult basic education. Company actions are wide ranging. Numerous corporations are contributing funds to public literacy-awareness efforts at national, state, and local levels. The Ashland Oil Corporation provided a major grant through its charitable foundation to the Kentucky educational television network for a campaign encouraging adults to earn their GED certificates. Viewers will be directed to a variety of programs designed to suit their individual needs—school-based instruction, on-site courses provided by employers, or study-at-home programs.

IBM Corporation makes grants to community-based organizations as part of its commitment to the literacy movement. In 1984, IBM joined with other companies in Washington, D.C., to give financial support to Push Literacy Action Now (PLAN), a community-based program to help city residents with basic skills. It also contributed funds to Philadelphia's Center for Literacy to expand adult basic skills services at several tutorial sites around the city.

Companies can encourage their employees to participate in community-based volunteer programs. B. Dalton Bookseller, already involved in many adult education strategies in the 500 communities where its outlets are located, recently undertook a campaign to enlist employees on all levels to tutor adults in basic skills. It hopes to recruit 10 percent of the company's 8,500 employees. A recent company survey showed that more than one-half of its regional managers serve on boards and advisory committees of local and state literacy organizations. Recently Time, Inc. expanded its remedial education strategies beyond direct funding for literacy programs to include organizing employee volunteers. Pacific Gas and Electric Company gives release time to employees who tutor students in the basic skills program of the San Francisco Community College District.

Some companies have opened their in-house remedial programs to the larger community. In Winston-Salem, North Carolina, R.J. Reynolds Tobacco Company uses the services of Forsyth Technical Institute to provide an in-plant adult basic education program. The program is open to dislocated workers in the community as well. Classes meet four days a week at times chosen to accommodate day, evening, and midnight shifts and unemployed persons. Treasure Isle, Inc., a Florida shrimp company, set up a small training center on company grounds to upgrade its workers' skills. Now the center is open to all adults in the community. The company pays custodial and utility costs, the county school system provides teachers, and the adult education program furnishes money for supplies and equipment. Since the program began, 300 learners have advanced from functional illiteracy to eighth-grade reading levels.

Companies can contribute to public awareness of the literacy problem by documenting its scope and impact. At the national level, several blue-ribbon groups of corporate leaders have announced their concern over basic educational attainment. This national perspective must be brought home to the local level. For example, Standard Oil of Ohio currently is sponsoring a project in the Cleveland area to clarify the extent and nature of the illiteracy problem there and determine what action is needed. In other areas, local Chambers of Commerce could take the lead to study the literacy needs in their communities from a business perspective. Trade associations could assess the occupational structures in their member companies and the literacy requirements of various job categories. This research contribution would be invaluable in raising the level of public debate and suggesting directions for educational improvement to meet business demands in basic skills. AT&T, in fact, believes that

obtaining worthwhile data on abilities needed in jobs is not an impossible task but it is, indeed, a complicated one. Unless jobs can be described accurately in a language which is useful for curriculum development, it may well be useless to discuss adult literacy training.[12]

Companies also can use their political power and connections to influence decisions on funds and priorities for public institutions. Business groups already have formed in Memphis, New Orleans, and Cincinnati to work for the passage of tax levies to benefit education. Efforts of individual companies to ease the literacy crisis are important, but in the long run, success will depend on collective efforts to influence policy in state capitals and in Washington. Companies must organize themselves into highly focused coalitions to provide sustained support to the public institutions whose job it is to equip people with the basic skills required by the labor market.

Some employers already have decried basic skills deficiencies in their workers and in job applicants. Others are concerned that employees facing termination lack the elementary skills to find new jobs or take advantage of retraining. At the present time, most companies have ample choices in a slack labor market. Yet in the next decade demographic changes—an aging work force and a pool of younger applicants increasingly composed of the educationally and economically disadvantaged—could reduce the range of choice. "Literacy for all" is becoming as much an economic imperative as it is a social and cultural one.

WHAT SCHOOLS AND PUBLIC AGENCIES CAN DO

Improve the Assessment Capacity

The first step in a comprehensive attack on the problem of illiteracy is identifying who needs help. Many states now require that students pass minimum competency tests in order to graduate from high school. However, many of these tests are "subminimum" in relation to the literacy needs of the workplace or further schooling. Testing in the twelfth grade is too late:

literacy problems have their roots in early grades. Alaska, Connecticut, Arizona, Ohio, and Mississippi are among the states that use basic skills testing programs at various levels below the twelfth grade to catch deficiencies soon enough to make a difference.

The National Center for Education Statistics estimates that 25 percent of those entering high school eventually will drop out. A major cause of this phenomenon is the inability of students to read, write, and compute up to grade level. Many of these people will show up later on as adult illiterates. **Early identification and action on the problem of illiteracy is a major unfulfilled responsibility of public elementary and secondary education systems.** It is a sad reflection on these school systems that 25 percent of all college mathematics courses today are remedial. Courses offered most frequently at community colleges are those in remedial reading, writing, and arithmetic. The Task Force on Education for Economic Growth pointed out that

the United States no longer teaches the three R's, but the six R's: remedial reading, remedial 'riting and remedial 'rithmetic. It should be our long-range goal to end remedial courses wherever possible: to make them unnecessary—because our schools will have done their work effectively the first time.[13]

The Florida legislature declared in the 1983-1984 session that its public secondary schools, not postsecondary institutions, bear responsibility for remediation. California law proscribes remedial education courses in the state's community colleges.

Identifying adult illiterates is more difficult than testing and offering remedial courses to behind-grade students. Adults find ways to cope. They stick to familiar neighborhoods where reading street signs is unnecessary; they buy groceries by looking at pictures on labels. They get through the work day (if they have jobs) by imitating and copying what others do. Often they ask friends to fill out forms, applications, and tax returns for them.

Employers have difficulty in identifying the marginally literate. Based on the Supreme Court's interpretation of Title VII of the Civil Rights Act, employers cannot give reading tests as part of an employment-screening process unless they can prove that such tests measure the kinds of reading needed for the job. Courts have been stringent in their application of this rule, even though few job-specific reading tests have been developed. Thus people reading at substandard levels find their way into the workplace.

Public agencies can be enlisted to identify illiteracy and contribute to the effort to overcome it. Senator Paul Simon (D-Ill.) has suggested that the welfare office and the unemployment insurance office could be used effectively to establish who needs help:

In the area of welfare, we have to take a look at who signs up. You don't have to ask them if they can read or write. If they can't fill out the form, that ought to be noted. We ought to get help for them. We shouldn't simply be saying we're going to give you a check. A check, yes, but let's give people some help on their problems. Unemployment compensation—the same. A huge number of people are involved and we ought to find the illiterates among them.[14]

Every state has Employment Service offices that also could provide assistance. When the federal government reduced this agency's budget in the early 1980s, the Employment Service (ES) cut back on testing and assessment activities in favor of keeping local offices open. Now, however, these priorities should be reviewed. Those involved in the new (since 1982) ES planning process—especially local elected officials and private-sector business leaders—could explore ways to reprogram available resources to strengthen and expand testing and assessment services. They could, for example, convince state policymakers to target these functions as a priority for discretionary state ES funds.

Adequate assessment is essential to placing adults with basic skills problems, including many dislocated workers, in skill-training programs that match their abilities or into jobs appropriate to their capabilities. When a mismatch occurs, the person is frustrated and the productivity of companies and economic goals of the community are impaired. Corporations such as Digital Equipment have recognized the value of the assessment function in designing skills development programs. Digital uses extensive diagnostic testing to design programs to help their employees realize their full potential in the workplace.

Community colleges, vocational-technical schools, and other training program operators also must assess more carefully the basic skill levels of incoming students and trainees. They should give new entrants into training programs and remedial activities corresponding to their proficiencies.

Educators also should recognize the implicit expectations in these courses of the level of basic skills needed for success. Recently, two parallel studies funded by the National Institute of Education reached the joint conclusion "that teachers in community colleges rarely talk with each other about the literacy requirements of their individual courses and programs."[15] Thus public resources may be wasted as those people seeking to improve their employment potential through training and education fail and drop out. Better assessment of basic skills on both sides of the equation—individual attainment and program assumptions—is one key to harnessing the nation's education resources to economic development needs.

Increase the Flexibility of Educational Institutions

As the literacy requirements of the workplace mount and the need for adult education grows, businesses look increasingly to educational institutions and expect them to respond. To meet these demands, schools and colleges must develop more flexible programs and calendars. Traditional classroom models with rigid semester-based schedules and "seat-time" measures of success do not serve illiterate adults, dropouts, or behind-grade youth well. The Commission on Higher Education and the Adult Learner concluded in a 1984 report that

much about postsecondary education is inappropriate for adult learners; within the present system, there is excessive standardization, insufficient individualization, needless repetition, and inadequate recognition of prior learning. State funding formulas are too frequently obsolete, ignoring part-time faculty and off-campus locations, and anxiety about new partnerships hampers collaboration with business, industry, and others with educational needs. What appears to be a golden opportunity for cooperation among education providers is very slow in coming; the higher education establishment must change if it is to be an effective partner.[16]

Community colleges and vocational-technical schools generally adapt to marketplace realities more quickly than traditional four-year institutions. Yet employment specialists fault even community colleges for offering programs that extend over too long a time period, given the daily economic pressures the unemployed face, and that demand reading and mathematical proficiences beyond their present capabilities.

Illiterate adults have radically different educational backgrounds and life situations, which makes it impossible to design one program for all. For example, a plant closing may mean layoffs and dislocation for hundreds of people at once. But they do not arrive at the training institution at once, nor do they have the same needs or require the same amount of time to acquire new skills. These people make up a large constituency for educational services if the necessary changes are made. **Officials of secondary and appropriate postsecondary schools should adapt their institutions to adult learners.**

Several courses of action lie open for the education community. Educational administrators—academic deans and curriculum planners—can iniiate the sorts of changes that will benefit adult learners.

Educational administrators should structure remedial efforts to relate to possible future jobs, rather than providing basic skills instruction by itself. For years the Army has defined basic skills as "the academic competencies essential to learning and performing a military job." To achieve this end, the Army has attempted to mesh basic skills instruction with job training. It started a major program in 1980 to improve job performance through a refined approach to basic skill competencies. The program seeks to identify the basic skill levels needed for training in ninety-four military service occupations. Competency levels are defined by desired performance on the job, not by reference to years completed in school. New diagnostic tests were developed to analyze tasks, and new curricula currently are being developed to teach basic skills in each job context. According to the Army, these products may be transferable to civilian training and education in related vocational skill areas.

The Boston Private Industry Council favors programs that develop basic competencies and job skills simultaneously. The previously mentioned programs of the Travelers Insurance Company and Downriver Community Conference also use this approach, which recognizes that adult learning occurs more readily on the job or in other practical situations. When remedial instruction is delivered in tandem with skill training, attention is focused on the particular kind of reading or math needed. Remedial efforts become more relevant to trainees, who otherwise may not be aware of basic skills deficiencies. Workers also have greater incentive to learn when there may be a direct payoff in a new job.

The Career Development Institute at Cuyahoga Community College in Cleveland structures its program to guide participants toward making these informational and motivational connections between remedial education and training. Its director insists, "This is not an abstract program."[17] In 1982, Portland Community College in Oregon provided instruction in remedial mathematics or math upgrading plus job skills training to a selected number of the city's unemployed residents. A German company, Wacker Siltronic Corporation, helped the college design the program and select the instructors. This guarantee of specially trained workers was a major factor in convincing the company to build its new $60-million plant in Portland. The first 460 production jobs were filled by workers who developed or upgraded their basic and technical skills through the Portland-Wacker partnership. This is a prime example of what an investment in adult learning can contribute to a community's development.

Administrators should use self-paced, individualized, competency-based methods of instruction and institute open entry-open exit programming. Participants in self-paced programs begin at their own convenience as soon as they have decided on a course of action. Each person devotes the needed time, but only that, to mastering the course content. For this kind of program to operate successfully, the curriculum should be modular—constructed in discrete units —so that different people can work on different parts at the same time. Ideally, it should be computerized in an interactive mode so students can learn from their mistakes without fear of embarrassment before their peers. In this program design, the teacher is a manager of the learning process rather than an instructor.

Flexible, nonthreatening programs are particularly important for adults, many of whom must overcome psychological barriers and an aversion to schooling caused by earlier failures. Adult workers dislocated from their jobs, who worked for years and never anticipated a return to school, find the freedom and self-reliance permitted by this program design attractive. The Job Corps, a work preparation program for very disadvantaged youth, is the most systematic user of this type of educational programming. While the Levi Strauss-Trident program previously cited trained dislocated workers this way, too few Job Corps instructional methods have been adopted in mainstream educational institutions.

The city of Cleveland operates a successful remedial reading program developed when it found in 1982 that 50 percent of the disadvantaged unemployed population over the age of 25 was functionally illiterate. Cleveland's program, budgeted at $1.2 million for 1985, uses Control Data Corporation's computerized "PLATO" system to prepare the disadvantaged for jobs requiring a high school education. The program proceeds in three stages. Those with skills below the sixth-grade level go through a remedial program that aims to move them up two grade levels in ten weeks. Participants then are ready for training and job-directed remediation. After 12 weeks, they prepare for the GED examination and high school equivalency status. The state of Ohio currently is planning to spend $3 million of its federal job training funds to replicate this program in other cities.

Educational administrators should seek the expertise and support of the business community regularly to solve basic skills problems. The current patchwork quilt of adult education programs needs a focal point to capture business attention. Employers may need a new institutional structure around which to frame their involvement in adult literacy efforts. Schools should organize the existing piecemeal efforts in remedial and adult basic education into a coherent system. With a more clearly defined structure, the business community would have a more direct avenue for its views, recommendations, and assistance.

Educational administrators also can obtain private-sector help through their local Private Industry Councils—organizations of leading community employers. These councils decide on appropriate uses of federal job training funds for disadvantaged youth and adults and, in some cases, for dislocated worker programs as well. Involvement with a PIC offers educators the opportunity to understand local employers' expectations and problems with basic skill levels. They also can get advice on how schools could improve their product and better tap into the hiring process. Cooperation also gives educational administrators a chance to market education services to employers. In demonstrating how schools can fill the training and remedial education needs identified by the PIC, schools can become "delivery agents of first resort" for PIC-sponsored programs.

St. Louis Community College and the Private Industry Council designed the Metropolitan Re-Employment Project to help dislocated workers find new jobs. It started with private-sector contributions and funding from the Job Training Partnership Act and the Fund for the Improvement of Post-Secondary Education in 1981. In its first year of operation, the project found that less than 2 percent of laid-off workers were seeking retraining or further education on their own. Each dislocated worker believed, "I'm not the sort of person who needs that sort of thing." But assessment showed that nearly 20 percent of its potential clients were reading at only a fifth-grade level. The project expanded its activities to provide testing, assessment, and counseling and made referrals to adult basic education courses in community colleges and high schools (as well as to retraining programs and new jobs). The college-PIC collaboration has provided a myriad of services to 5,000 workers in the last four years. Funding for the project continues with the help of Civic Progress, an organization of the chief executive officers of the largest corporations in St. Louis.

The public response to the literacy crisis involves numerous institutions and individuals in the education and training communities: the Employment Service, community colleges, secondary schools, training programs, Private Industry Councils, and so on. The success of their activities has an effect on the ability of local businesses to fill their labor needs and compete successfully. Companies have a stake in literacy levels and must be enlisted in the basic skills battle. Public institutions have their own mandate for action as well.

STATE AND FEDERAL REPONSES TO THE PROBLEM

State policymakers must play their part in strengthening the basic skills of their citizens to ensure a strong work force base for economic growth. They set the context for local action even though actual services—literacy training and remedial programs in reading, writing, and math—are delivered locally. **State policymakers can promote greater recognition of and commitment to solving the literacy problem. They can combine state and federal aid to maximize resources available for the effort.** The national call for educational reform has led every state to take some steps for change. More than 250 state task forces have sprung up to date to study every aspect of education. Most have focused on the achievement of youth in secondary schools: few have devoted attention to the issue of adult literacy and the remedial efforts necessary to achieve it.

Governors should take the lead by establishing as state policy the goal of a fully literate work force. Business recognizes a literate work force as an essential part of a favorable climate for economic growth. Robert Orr, governor of Indiana, recently signaled his understanding of this connection. "I see the Indiana Literacy Initiative as helping us not only with our fight against illiteracy, but with our overall economic development strategies as well," he said.[18] Governors could engage the state's business and educational leaders in examining the extent of literacy needs and recommending action. These leaders might be charged with developing a resource inventory of literacy programs, both company-sponsored and publicly funded, around the state. Communities and companies then could use this information to locate program models appropriate to their own circumstances and share ideas and experiences with other program managers. Such a network of data and people could become an important service to business from the state's economic development arsenal.

State legislatures should assure adequate appropriations for adult literacy programs. States now provide over one-half the funding for local education. State legislators are in constant communication with local business and educational leaders. Legislatures thus are well positioned to champion the cause of adult literacy. Business leaders should make known to the appropriate legislative committees their views on the soundness of the educational enterprise and its products, and the extent to which they match workplace needs.

Federal policymakers in Congress and the executive branch should sort out competing claims for scarce federal education funds and focus them on true national priorities. Congress should direct federal spending in vocational and adult education to leverage improvements in program design and services for population groups in particular need, such as illiterate adults. Federal aid-to-education acts should enable state and local efforts to meet the important national goal of a fully literate work force, rather than dictating and specifying minutely how this goal is to be accomplished.

State education officials should examine how federal education resources, such as vocational education and adult education funds, are spent. These officials—state school officers and members of state boards of education—can work for the integration of these resources with state and local spending to produce a comprehensive system of work force preparation programs. They should analyze how effective those federal funds are in enhancing and improving ongoing state efforts, and how they might better be used to improve adult literacy. They should look particularly at how these education-oriented funds can be used to complement job training programs.

State officials responsible for the Job Training Partnership Act (JTPA) should look for the most effective uses of this law's various sections. Title III of JTPA directs funds to states for the establishment of programs of training and reemployment assistance for dislocated workers. State JTPA administrators can make sure their state's JTPA-funded dislocated workers projects contain sufficient education components. They should direct more of these funds to remedial efforts, if appropriate. Title III officials also could tap educational sources to complement job training programs. If federal Title III funds must be matched with state contributions, remedial education activities might provide the source. Another section of JTPA provides that 8 percent of the state's allocation for Title II should be used for educational services and coordination. State officials responsible for this set aside could use the 8 percent funds for more adult remedial education and encourage similar efforts in the education community.

The Carl D. Perkins Vocational Education Act of 1984 contains provisions that commend it to state education and training officials. It authorizes funds for coordinated services and activities between vocational education and the JTPA dislocated workers program. It also allows the use of funds for upgrading the skills of workers threatened with dislocation. Joint programs focused on improving basic skills in the course of vocational training would be a practical way to implement these legislative priorities.

A third part of the Job Training Partnership Act establishes a special fund of 10 percent of a state's allocation for the Employment Service. This set aside, aimed at local program improvements, could provide the means for strengthening the assessment and testing capacity of the Employment Service. The special needs of illiterate adults and the dislocated workers among them would be well served by this use of funds.

State employment and training officials can tap the expertise of business leaders on the State Job Training Coordinating Council, the governor's advisory committee for the Job Training Partnership Act. These private-sector members know the work force needs of the state's employers and any literacy problems that may exist. They can take the lead in achieving the kind of education and training system that the state's economy requires for growth.

State and federal policy can spur local action to benefit the efforts of employers and educators. By enlisting the state's business leaders in making literacy an essential part of state development goals, governors can rally local companies. Legislators can highlight the need as they design and oversee state aid-to-education budgets. Congress can do the same as it sets priorities for federal spending. Those who administer federal categorical funds in education and training can work jointly to make their programs complementary to each other and to state, local, and private-sector remedial activities.

The three chapters in Part I of this text have examined ways that elementary and secondary schools, vocational education programs, and job-training programs can work with business to help the community at large, as well as disadvantaged youth and those whose jobs are threatened or gone. Educational resources often are overlooked by elected officials and community leaders when they plan for future economic and human resource development. If joined by government and local business, schools and other educational programs can multiply the benefits any one sector could achieve alone.

Part II will emphasize the economic development and job-creation potential of two-year colleges, technical institutes, and four-year institutions. Community and junior colleges, with their more local focus, are ideal partners for business and industry to collaborate in carrying out various phases of local and statewide economic growth strategies. Four-year colleges and universities often have the faculty expertise, funding, and physical capacity to undertake more ambitious and comprehensive projects, which can have a great impact on local and regional economic vitality. Postsecondary schools and businesses can become partners in growth. The two sectors, with the help of government, must use and build upon each other's strengths.

PART II
BUSINESS
AND POSTSECONDARY
EDUCATION: PARTNERS
IN GROWTH

5. Community College Assistance to the Development Process

THE ECONOMIC DEVELOPMENT TRIANGLE

Economic development has been defined in various ways over the years. Basically it is the process by which interested individuals and organizations are inspired to invest capital in an area. The resulting economic activity generates or expands industrial, commercial, or service enterprises, creates new jobs, and retains others. Economic development is not a spontaneous process; optimum sequence of events occurs only within the proper "environment," one conducive to investment. Several elements are necessary, including a suitably educated and trained work force, a public-sector capacity to help development, and support services such as technical advice and management counsel.

Increasingly, this process requires time, resources, and work from three diverse participants in several sectors—private-sector businesses and financiers, public and private economic development agencies and groups, and resource institutions and organizations such as colleges and professional associations. Together, they form an "economic development triangle" that serves as a catalyst for local and regional economic expansion.

Economic development is not a one-way street for any of the partners. Every member of the triangle contributes to and reaps benefits from their collaboration. Economic development groups—state and local agencies, private industry councils, chambers of commerce, and other organizations—are one side of the triangle. They are responsible for marshaling the resources and establishing the alliances needed to mount a successful economic development effort. To create the strategy and plan for a strong program, these groups use all the resources available in their communities to create an attractive climate for the retention and attraction of business and industry.

By cooperating with two-year colleges, economic development groups draw on, yet strengthen, an important source of support. At the same time, they increase their own capacity to encourage business to remain, expand, or relocate in their areas. Joint efforts boost the overall economic health of their regions.

Business and industry comprise another side of the development triangle. Businesses work individually and collectively with economic development groups. They collaborate on their own with two-year colleges, contributing information about local markets, labor pools, and the kinds of services they need. They also may donate funds, equipment, and personnel to the overall effort. Business and industry have an interest in both the economic stability and growth of their community. They need a strong two-year college system to train personnel and offer more direct assistance.

Two-year colleges comprise the third side of the triangle. As a major component of the country's resource institutions, community colleges have a stake in the economic vitality of the regions they serve. These colleges furnish training and other services to business and industry, and provide assistance and information to economic development groups. In return, they garner a stronger tax base to support their operations, more students and clients, a market for their students and services, and increased general support in the community.

Evolution of Community Colleges

Two-year colleges are an integral part of the nation's educational system. They began as stepping-stones to four-year institutions. The role of two-year colleges, however, has evolved in the face of expanding and changing student enrollments and demands.

In 1960, fewer than 700,000 students were enrolled in about 600 community, technical, and junior colleges in the United States. Today, more than 5 million students attend more than 1,200 two-year institutions.[1] These colleges have developed more diversified programs to serve the increased number of students, particularly adult learners and part-time and full-time students who want occupational training but not necessarily a degree from a four-year institution.

External economic forces have brought changes as sweeping as those wrought by enrollment increases. Together they have resulted in demands from local communities for an expanded range of services. The shift from primarily a manufacturing economy toward an information and service-based economy, the spread of technology, and foreign competition have made today's students and colleges more aware than they were a decade ago of the need for occupational as well as academic education. As a result, two-year colleges now offer a much wider array of vocational and educational services to students and the surrounding communities.

Two-year colleges now find they have an opportunity to assist the business community. Their traditional role as providers of training has expanded to include a wide range of services from helping with contract applications to expediting foreign trade opportunities. Colleges' participation in the economic development process may become even more important in the future, due to changing demographics. The New England Board of Higher Education estimates that community college enrollment will decline 19 percent between 1985 and 1995, with a 35 percent decline in the Northeastern states.[2] Community colleges may have to diversify resources now devoted to standard courses to other development activities, such as technical and management assistance to companies, specialized training, small business incubators,and similar ventures.

Increasingly, two-year colleges recognize that they can serve an important function in cooperation with the business community as well as public and private economic development groups. Most of the colleges have experience providing services to business and industry. Nearly three-fourths offer employee training programs for private-sector enterprises; 83 percent report some involvement with state and local community development offices and various economic growth alliances.[3] Many instances exist of one-to-one ventures between two-year colleges and businesses. These projects are often substantial and offer significant contributions to economic growth.

An important payoff may result for the community, the colleges, business, and economic development groups from a comprehensive joint economic development strategy. Such a strategy aims at attracting new businesses or retaining and expanding existing ones to provide jobs and economic benefits to their areas.

Economic Development Capabilities

Despite a growing record, however, two-year colleges are not perceived as development partners by some business executives and local, state, and federal policymakers. Many factors account for this lack of visibility. Four-year institutions have a long history of assistance to the private sector through extension services, industrial parks, research laboratories, and consulting services. The size and prestige of many four-year institutions also gives them an edge in this arena.

Where their economic development capabilities are recognized, two-year colleges usually are perceived as providers of training. Most do offer an array of occupationally specific training programs that culminate in the award of an Associate of Arts degree. Two-year colleges are more than education and training mills, however. They deliver many of the same economic development-oriented services as four-year institutions.

Many state and local economic development groups and business associations have tapped the colleges' capacity to provide other kinds of services—foreign trade assistance, economic surveys, data base maintenance, and support services such as use of facilities, equipment, consulting, and data management systems. Moreover, they have found that community colleges possess some advantages that four-year institutions do not.

First, nearly every community in the United States is served by a nearby two-year, junior, or technical college. Illinois, Iowa, Wisconsin, and North and South Carolina have found that the practical orientation of two-year colleges offers a way to focus economic development efforts at the local level, across the state.

Second, two-year colleges tend to be more flexible than their four-year counterparts. They operate on shorter time frames for curriculum and service development and are more adept at shifting resources to meet the emerging needs of their communities. Their faculty and governance structures usually are less rigid than those of four-year institutions,[4] which encourages greater use of practitioners as instructors and of community situations as laboratories and case studies.

Finally, two-year colleges can assemble a critical mass of resources that is often the largest in any given community. Faculty and staff, who are accustomed to working with the local community, can offer expertise in the whole range of areas required to put together an effective economic development campaign. These colleges maintain equipment and facilities to promote economic growth and increased productivity. These resources, including libraries and data processing equipment useful to businesses of all kinds and sizes, can support training and other business development activities.

The following sections describe the major types of business aid, including strategic planning, one-stop assistance, technology transfer, and training. Each offers illustrative cases and makes recommendations for increasing the roles of two-year colleges in economic development. Examples from across the country and from various types of schools will illustrate the importance of their participation.

COMMUNITY COLLEGE ROLE IN THE PROCESS

Economic development efforts should encompass all who can contribute to or who will benefit from attracting or retaining business and industry, including banks, civic organizations, state and municipal governments, business groups, labor unions, and educational institutions.

As indicated earlier, economic development is the systematic promotion of economic growth through increased business and employment activity of all kinds. Successful development requires strategic planning, which is undertaken by public or private agencies and organizations that strive to improve local, regional, or state economies. Community colleges should be called upon early in the strategic planning process and made active partners.[5] They can offer planning expertise to the process, and inform the private developers and local agencies what services they can provide to help businesses start and grow.[6] All parties should work together to sort out the contributions each can make and to mobilize those resources at the point where they can exert maximum impact.

In many instances, North Carolina and the Quad Cities area in Iowa, for example, college representatives sit on the economic development boards; in North Carolina, economic development officials sit on the community college board. Arrangements vary among programs; some have written contracts, and others have verbal agreements. In Illinois, the Carolinas, Wisconsin, and Iowa, the role of two-year colleges is spelled out in legislation.

For example, St. Louis Community College in Missouri was part of an economic development effort to remodel and revitalize an aging Ford Motor Company plant. The college provided training and worked with Ford and United Auto Workers representatives to develop training modules and to monitor the training. A coordinator from the campus worked closely with instructors and union representatives to refine the various training components to ensure specific needs were met and the variety of learning levels was accommodated. Ford, the state Department of Elementary and Secondary Education, and the Governor's Office of Manpower Planning provided $583,000 for the 11-month project—a total that included Job Training Partnership Act (JTPA) funds. Also providing support and coordination for the effort were the St. Louis Regional Commerce and Growth Association, and the Private Industry Council of St. Louis/St. Louis County.[7]

Such broad-based collaboration ensures not only the mobilization of resources but the active support of groups essential to the success of the process. The St. Louis program supported the training of 270 skilled workers and supervisors in the new technologies needed to revitalize the auto plant. More importantly, the St. Louis area retained a major employer and economic contributor.[8]

Developing the Plan

An important aspect of economic development is gathering the information needed to draft and implement a plan. In small communities and rural areas particularly, the colleges may be the only institutions with the necessary staff and expertise to conduct surveys of markets, employment pools, and other local economic conditions. Such surveys are essential grist for the economic development mill. **Economic development groups should use the survey expertise and background data resources of two-year colleges to gather the economic information necessary for successful planning.**

Daytona Beach, Florida, Community College conducts ongoing surveys of economic conditions in Volusia and Flagler counties and maintains a data base from which local economic development efforts can draw. Evelyn Fine, director of the college's Mid-Florida Research and Business Center, says information is gathered regularly about taxes, new business starts, growth trends, labor market conditions, and available training. Such data are made available to public-sector development offices and businesses through publications. Studies include a comparison of the business climates in sixteen Florida counties, a survey of employers of their short- and long-range hiring needs for the Volusia Council for Employment and Economic Development, and an ongoing tourism study for the local Tourism Advertising Tax Authority.[9]

Fine says the center answers around 750 requests a year for demographic and economic information. Referrals come from the Volusia county Business Development Center, six local chambers of commerce, business owners and managers, state officials, bankers, accountants, and lawyers.

Once the necessary data are gathered, the economic development team can put together a strategic plan. Many two-year colleges have planning experts on their staff and faculty with experience in grantsmanship and contract negotiation. Development groups should draw on the expertise of two-year colleges in drafting economic development plans. In Wisconsin, the North Central Vocational, Technical, and Adult Education (VTAE) District in Wausau works with local government agencies and chambers of commerce to identify economic development priorities and to help establish committees to carry out the organizations' goals. The Southwest Wisconsin VTAE District in Fennimore participates in meetings of the Southwest Wisconsin Economic Development Group, which analyzes the economic climate and seeks to avoid duplication of effort. Other participants in these meetings include the Southwest Wisconsin Regional Planning Commission, the private industry council, a Wisconsin utility company, and representatives of the University of Wisconsin campus at Platteville and the university's extension division.[10]

Marketing and Implementing the Plan

Once an economic development plan is drafted, it must be "sold" to various constituencies and implemented. Again, community colleges, which must market their own programs, can help economic development groups carry out marketing campaigns. They may include television and radio spots, newspaper advertisements and articles, brochures, fact sheets, and other materials. The Mercer County Community College in New Jersey develops marketing packages and publishes a quarterly newsletter to assist the marketing efforts of local development officials.[11] The college's efforts also include printing mailing labels, hosting breakfasts and seminars for business people, and hosting conferences. The San Diego Community College District has developed an elaborate brochure of the economic resources in the San Diego area that would be attractive to relocating businesses and industries. **Economic development groups should make use of the marketing expertise and facilities of two-year colleges, including printing and video resources.**

In addition to the use of print and broadcast media, economic development depends on personal contacts. Development groups should include two-year college representatives on the teams that talk to business owners and investors about the advantages and resources of state and local areas. The college representatives can provide business executives with clear and accurate information about the services the colleges can provide and personify their commitment.

Recognizing this, Illinois community colleges are increasingly involved in helping companies locate, remain, or expand in their district. The colleges cooperate regularly with local chambers of commerce, economic development commissions, local governments and the Illinois Department of Commerce and Industry to attract new companies and key existing ones.[12] Statewide programs in Iowa and North Carolina also have two-year college representatives on their business attraction and retention teams. The representatives join economic development officials, local businessmen, officers of financial institutions and others making on-site presentations to explain the advantages of expansion or relocation in those states.

In Monmouth County, New Jersey, and in South Carolina, two-year colleges are on the regular tour for business executives exploring the possibilities of establishing new operations or relocating existing ones. During such college visits, the executives can examine the facilities and resources, meet with faculty and other service providers to discuss ways to meet training and other needs, and learn about the local business climate and resources. **High-ranking college representatives should be included on economic development recruitment teams, and the colleges should be regular stops for visiting business executives.**

Development groups, particularly non-governmental organizations, should explore with colleges the possibility of locating offices on the campuses, where appropriate. The colleges offer some very practical, day-to-day resources. The Economic Development Group for Volusia/Flagler Counties,

Florida, has an office at the Daytona Beach Community College's Research and Business Center.[13] The location provides the group officials with easy access to college representatives, the ability to monitor programs, an opportunity to use the center's computer system and library, and instant access to economic data.

Finally, local developmnent efforts can tap into college expertise in grant and contract procurement. In addition to state and local appropriations and leveraged funds from the private sector, economic development programs are funded via grants and contracts from government and from private foundations. **Economic development groups should draw on the funding expertise of two-year colleges.** The two-year colleges participating in the statewide economic development efforts of the Illinois Community College Board provide assistance in grant and contract procurement. Such assistance may include everything from the identification of funding agencies and organizations to developing proposals and putting together grant applications.[14]

Clearly, two-year colleges can make important contributions to the crafting and implementation of economic development plans. In calling upon the collges for assistance, however, the partners in the economic development triangle need to keep in mind that the colleges' primary role is education. The colleges need to balance social, personal, and general education programs along with technical development activities. Their primary purpose remains the education of students to be both employable and well-rounded, not narrowly trained in one skill. This applies to courses offered to local businesspersons, customized training programs, and projects that teach businesses how to apply new technology.

Understanding the logistics, advantages, and disadvantages of two-year college collaborations gives planning officials a foundation for applying these resources to the economic development process in the most effective way. Well-informed officials are also better equipped to advise those involved in development-assistance programs on how to take best advantage of local business opportunities and labor markets. As a result, trainees have a better chance at employment and businesses have more hope of success. The involvement of colleges in economic development throughout the process helps build a climate of trust between them and the other partners, and, over time, should contribute to the economic strength of the region.

ONE-STOP ASSISTANCE

Two-year colleges are becoming "convenience stores" for business assistance. They can provide, in one location, many varieties of services that all types of businesses, but particularly small and medium-sized ones, need in order to flourish. In addition to employee training and technology analysis and integration, these firms need help with management, planning, data processing, marketing, contract procurement, and other activities. Many of the same capabilities colleges offer the economic development process are applicable to the specific needs of businesses themselves. In this regard, the development triangle can become a tightly knit cooperative arrangement.

As noted, two-year colleges can mobilize a critical mass of resources to further a development strategy focusing on local problems and accessible to local clients. Through curriculum offerings and administrative practices, colleges routinely engage in many of the same kinds of activities as those needed to spur investment in development projects and encourage successful business practices. Thus, the colleges have developed the faculty and staff expertise to help businesses with many of their problems. And because of their local orientation, the two-year colleges often are more accessible and less intimidating to small business people than four-year institutions. Large universities may be more remote or aloof psychologically and seem more overwhelming because of their size and complexity.

Entrepreneurship and Technical Training

Programs of entrepreneurship training for budding business owners and technical training for more experienced company managers now are vital community college offerings. Businesses often fail because of poor management, and such training can help the managers and owners solve problems before they lead to failure. Courses and training modules run the gamut from beginning a business through management skills, computer applications, and financing.

At the direction of the Illinois Community College Board, the state's community colleges have become providers of entrepreneurship training and many other kinds of business services. Community colleges there are experienced in working with public and private sectors, and can serve as neutral coordinating entities to bring all parties in the economic development process together.[15]

Illinois colleges offer workshops and seminars on a variety of topics of interest to nascent entrepreneurs, such as starting and operating a small business, business applications of computers, fundamental accounting practices, and government financing programs. The workshops and seminars frequently are cosponsored with the U.S. Small Business Administration (SBA), the state Department of Commerce and Community Affairs, or local chambers of commerce. The colleges also provide technical instruction to thousands of business founders and operators through regular course offerings in business administration, business law, business financing, accounting, and personnel administration. These courses often are available during evening hours, a boon to small business operators unable to attend daytime courses.

These courses are offered at both urban and rural campuses. Because the state's business training program is run primarily through local colleges, it can be shaped to meet any special needs of businesses in rural, urban, or suburban areas. During fiscal 1985, Illinois's 38 community college districts offered workshops and seminars attended by 19,034 small business owners and operators.

Stark Technical College in Canton, Ohio, has created the "Thursday College for Small Business Owners." The college offers several courses weekly, most of which are taught by small business owners. They include "How to Start and Manage a Successful Small Business" and "What Managers Do." Specialized courses are also offered in restaurant management and getting results from a tiny advertising budget. "Like many community colleges, Stark uses experts and resource materials from the nearby SBA field office and the local chamber of commerce," says a report in *Nation's Business*.[16]

State and local agencies and economic development groups should support entrepreneurship and technical training tailored to local needs at two-year colleges, and steer business operators to such courses.

Business Assistance Centers

The cornerstone of the Illinois colleges' economic development program is a network of business assistance centers in all 38 community college districts. These centers are like department stores. They provide industrial attraction, retention, and expansion services to economic development groups; customized job training for area business and industry; entrepreneurship training; contract procurement assistance; small business incubators; and employment, training, and job-search services for unemployed and underemployed workers. The centers' contributions to all businesses are credited with creating 6,240 jobs and retaining another 3,560 in fiscal 1985, due largely to the colleges' industrial attraction activities, customized job training, and individual counseling and management advice to small businesses.[17]

Experts from the colleges help businesses in a variety of situations. For example, an accountant will help the business set up its books, or a computer expert will give advice and information on how to automate bookkeeping, accounting, and inventories. Such assistance could range from how to conduct an advertising campaign to how to lay out a business facility.

In fiscal 1985, Illinois provided $2.7 million for the operation of the centers and planned to provide another $4 million in fiscal 1986. The colleges generated another $17 million from a variety of sources—the Job Training

Partnership Act, revenues for training and services, the colleges' own operating funds, private-sector and local government donations, federal small business development center funds, and foundation grants.

The Illinois model is an outstanding example of the advantages of clustering a variety of economic development resources and services in one organization. Businesses do not have to shop around to find employee training one place, management assistance in another, and technological assistance in still another. In addition, economic development groups can point to one source of assistance, delivered locally, when seeking to attract new industries or persuading existing ones to remain in the area and expand. Economic development agencies should identify likely components of a one-stop approach and evaluate its potential advantages to the business community.

Another example of comprehensive business assistance and services is the Daytona Beach Community College, which has established two centers for small business in collaboration with the Volusia County Private Industry Council.[18] The college also advises businesses seeking foreign trade opportunities, conducts economic surveys, maintains a data base on the local economy, and provides customized training.

State and local governments should authorize and fund business development centers at two-year colleges, where businesses of all sizes, but particularly smaller ones, can receive a variety of services at one location.

Small Business Centers

The Illinois and Daytona business centers were created to serve all applicants whatever their size. However, community colleges' most important contribution to economic development may be the help offered to small businesses. Recent studies show that most new jobs and innovations come from businesses with eight or fewer employees. Few can afford expensive training and consulting. In league with their triangle partners, two-year colleges are filling the gap between small business needs and required resources by providing flexible, accessible, and locally available assistance.

Some states locate small business development centers (SBDCs) at two-year colleges. SBDCs receive financial and technical support from the Small Business Administration. This agency supports business advisory services through a cooperative agreement between the federal government and a statewide network set up within a university system. Two-year colleges have participated in the SBDC program as subcontractors to four-year institutions; some have established similar small business centers on their own. SBA provides half the funding for each center, and the other half is arranged by a lead agency—a government unit, university, or private organization.

Two-year college systems or networks can muster the same level and magnitude of resources as four-year institutions. But so far only two colleges systems, in Oregon and Alaska, have been designated as lead institutions in the SBDC program.[19] **Two-year colleges should be considered as lead organizations in the SBDC program on an equal basis with other types of organizations.**

According to Rose Ninni, dean of continuing education, the Mercer County Community College SBDC offers low-cost workshops and many other services gratis to small businesses.[20] The center offers management assistance to companies in all industries, including high-tech, manufacturing, retail, service, and wholesale. Its small business consultants use the latest techniques of management analysis to help business operators identify options and strategies and select the best alternatives, Ninni says.

The consultants range from accountants to zoning specialists. The college draws on more than seventy-five professionals from the local community who have volunteered to serve as small business advisors. Consultation is available in a wide variety of areas, including accounting, advertising, computerized services, financial planning, licenses, graphics and printing, and stress management. In addition, the center offers training in business planning, financial management, real estate, and tax analysis for small business, among other options.

Oregon's Lane Community College was the first two-year institution to operate an SBA-supported SBDC. "The college combined existing programs and resources and devised new ones to offer a wide range of management services," according to James McKenney of the American Association of Community and Junior Colleges.[21] Offerings include long-term educational programs, short-term workshops and seminars, business consulting, and supporting physical resources. In some cases Lane acted as liaison with economic development organizations offering other programs and services.

During its first year of operation, 1983, Lane's SBDC served hundreds of businesses, which reported increased sales, higher employment, and increased ability to obtain financing. The Oregon legislature has provided $530,000 to expand the SBDC concept to other state two-year colleges. **Community colleges and economic development groups should explore the establishment of SBDC centers on campus.**

Other Small Business Help

With or without SBA support, many states and local communities are conducting small business assistance programs through the community colleges. Small business is particularly important in rural areas that lack large employers and access to sufficient amounts of either public or private investment capital. In such areas, the two-year college may be the only institution that can package the resources required for business development. **State** and local policymakers should identify ways in which the needs of rural communities can be served through two-year colleges.

Niagara County Community College in New York is active in promoting development in its rural service area through industrial training and assistance to small business. The college funnels its support through a Technical Assistance Center (TAC) funded by special state appropriations.[22] The center provides management advice, a small business incubator, small business "survival training," revolving loan fund management, and help in implementing regional economic development plans.

The center's management assistance counselors help its clients gather, present, and organize financial reports and loan packages. TAC can produce studies and evaluations of new business proposals and expansion plans, start-up cash requirements, marketing strategies, calculation of break-even points, and cash-flow analyses. The small business incubator is designed to nourish small businesses until they can get on their own feet. Incubators provide businesses with facilities, telephone and secretarial services, access to computers, and other help. Tenants at the TAC are considered students and use college facilities and staff at cost to improve their chances of survival. State and local agencies and private economic development groups should establish small business incubators linked to two-year colleges.

TAC survival training counsels about 200 potential entrepreneurs annually. Depending on program design, JTPA funds can be used to finance this kind of training. Many dislocated workers have skills that could be used for self-employment; TAC had developed a 120-hour course to help dislocated workers build the managerial skills necessary to run their own businesses. **State and local governments and economic development agencies should promote managerial and survival training. Community colleges should set up or expand appropriate training courses, seeking state and federal support.**

In its revolving loan fund management effort, TAC contracts with individual economic development agencies. Businesses can borrow money from the fund if they are judged eligible but are unable to obtain conventional loans from ordinary lenders. Repayments are channeled back into the fund for loans to other businesses. The TAC currently manages $1.2 million in revolving loan monies for an eight-county region. Revolving funds can play a crucial role in rural areas, where often they are the only financial resource for small business development other than branch banks. The funds are flexible in use, can be targeted to diverse or specific industries, and capitalized from a variety of public and private sources.

State and local governments, economic development groups, and private financial organizations should explore establishment of revolving loan funds in collaboration with two-year colleges to help small and medium-sized businesses, especially in rural areas, get started or expand operations.

Kirtland Community College in Roscommon, Michigan, also has taken a comprehensive approach to economic development in its rural service area, which covers more than 2,300 square miles.[23] Kirtland's Business Development Center provides local development groups with help to develop business leads, promote development opportunities, conduct trade shows, and maintain local business and industrial files. The center's functions include microcomputer networking, access to local and regional economic data systems, and help in tapping state and national systems.

Foreign Trade and Contract Help

Small and medium-sized businesses often are not regarded as candidates for competition in the international trade arena. Yet their sales of goods and services to foreign customers strengthen local economies and affect the nation's overall balance of trade. Community colleges can become involved in activities that help businesses enter the international marketplace.

Mercer County Community College in New Jersey helps businesses develop foreign trade contacts and assess opportunities in foreign markets. The college supplies much of the information and training that businesses need to compete effectively. For example, the college recently offered an "international business over breakfast" workshop. Experts from business and government explored the mechanisms and stumbling blocks of dealing with foreign governments' import and export regulations and procedures. Participants were led step-by-step through a process that helped one company succeed in the international marketplace. The process dealt with research, capital, regulations, and sales techniques. Agents in international trade addressed other topics, such as cultural factors that affect trade and basic exporting techniques.

The college also offers workshops on the fundamentals of exporting, international transportation, freight forwarding, letters of credit, and tax benefits of exporting. The college sponsored a China Roundtable for businesses and hosts monthly international business luncheon workshops.[24] **Community colleges, in conjunction with state, local, and federal economic development policymakers, should create practical programs that help businesses expand their foreign trade potential.** Business executives with foreign trade experience should be urged to work with the colleges as expert consultants or adjunct faculty members to help emerging exporters overcome foreign trade hurdles.

Contract procurement is another area in which small businesses face a disadvantage in the marketplace; they cannot afford to maintain full-time procurement staffs needed to obtain contracts from the federal and state governments or larger firms. Community colleges have developed expertise in procuring funds from such sources. Some colleges offer this expertise to small businesses.

In Illinois, the Department of Commerce and Community Affairs cooperates with the Illinois Procurement Outreach Program to enlist community colleges statewide in procurement assistance to business.[25] Currently, twenty-two community college districts are involved with area businesses and industries seeking state and federal contracts. Some colleges have incorporated contract procurement assistance into other services. In fiscal 1985, these colleges served 2,255 firms through workshops, bidder list applications, bid preparations, and counseling. These services helped obtain nearly $6.3 million in contracts for Illinois businesses. The effort resulted in the start-up or expansion of 14 companies and the retention of 6, creating 15 jobs and retaining 511. **Community colleges should establish procurement outreach programs to serve local, small business interests.**

LABORATORY TO WORKPLACE

New technologies are permeating every aspect of business and industry. Their use creates new business development and prospective new jobs. Technology transfer—the application of new technologies to industry operations and processes—provides extraordinary opportunities for the partners in the development triangle.

However, all the partners should be aware of the realities of "high technology" in the economy. High-technology industries currently represent only 3 to 13 percent of total U.S. employment.[26] While high technology is the fastest-growing segment of the economy, it will not provide the greatest number of jobs through the end of the century.[27] A recent report by the Office of Technology Assessment on the role of technology in regional development states:

While the conditions that led to concentrations of microelectronics firms in Silicon Valley and Route 128 are unlikely to be replicated in other areas, new opportunities are being created elsewhere by advances in microelectronics and other technologies and in the application of new products and processes to existing industries.[28]

Two-year colleges can help business and industry incorporate these technologies into their operations through training, applied research, education, and demonstrations. By establishing and nourishing the technological capabilities of two-year colleges, policymakers add an important incentive to companies to remain or relocate in their areas of responsibility.

Community colleges, in conjunction with development groups, should define the role they can play in introducing new technologies to existing industry. In this regard, economic development agencies can help the colleges acquire the funds and state-of-the-art equipment and guide industry to their high-technology programs. In addition to using the services offered by the colleges, businesses can donate equipment and work with colleges to create the programs that industry needs.

One of the nation's largest corporations, General Motors (GM), has recognized that two-year colleges have the experience to help the company adapt technology to manufacturing processes. GM has called on two-year colleges to provide technological training for its workers in Michigan, in Delaware, and at its new Saturn plant in Tennessee.[29]

Ohio's Advanced Technology Centers

Ohio has gone to great lengths to equip its two-year college system with technology-transfer mechanisms. The state has created and funded high-technology centers at the colleges to introduce Ohio industry to the most up-to-date technological processes, and to help make companies more efficient, cost-effective, and competitive. The state's program addresses such problems as obsolescent manufacturing plants, a decrease in manufacturing jobs, and the migration of jobs and industries to other states.

To further the technological development of its industry, the state has established advanced technology centers, hired technology transfer agents, and organized a network of vocational/technological resource consortia that include two-year colleges. Advanced Technology Centers have been established at Lorain County Community College (LCCC) in Elyria and Cuyahoga County Community College in Cleveland.[30] The state created the centers to promote technological advancement by encouraging industrial applications of the latest technical research and innovation. The legislature voted $5.4 million to construct the first center, which also provides technology transfer, print and nonprint information libraries, and an industrial data base. Different sections house robotics, a computer-integrated manufacturing laboratory, microelectronics, and computer-aided design and manufacturing (CAD/CAM).

Regional industries have responded well to the new center. Manufacturers have been eager to loan and donate equipment to the center because it helps market their products. For example, LCCC students and industrial trainees can learn to use the latest robots for assembly, machine-to-loading, and welding. Students and faculty benefit from opportunities to use the equipment for "real life" applications. This hands-on experience makes them better manufacturing workers or advisors.

An example of LCCC's cooperation with industry is a technology-sharing relationship it has developed with Cincinnati Milicron. Recognizing the advantages of an affiliation, the large machine-tool producer has donated more than $1 million in robotic equipment to the center. Cincinnati Milicron uses LCCC facilities to demonstrate equipment to customers, and to train company sales and service representatives and purchasers of its products. The collaboration is an excellent example of the way industry can help establish and support such centers while benefiting from the services the college can offer in return.[31]

Economic development officials should outline mutual advantages to encourage industry to make contributions of equipment to two-year colleges for training and demonstrations of new technologies. Business executives should explore with the colleges the best ways such partnerships can be carried out.

Cuyahoga County Community College's (CCCC) Unified Technology Center is a second effort by the state to bring the advantages of high technology to industry. The legislature provided $8.5 million to the college in 1983 in line with the state's strategic plan for economic development. A steering committee of senior executives from area firms guides the center's programs and products. The center provides business with the most sophisticated and cost-effective mechanism for advanced multi-technologies training. The center features a telecommunications center with satellite link, a media resources library and learning center, and laboratories designed for fields ranging from manufacturing to laser electro-optics.[32]

In cooperation with the Cleveland Advanced Manufacturing Program, a coalition of six Advanced Technology Application Centers throughout the state, CCCC focuses on three major activities:

• conducting annual manufacturing surveys of target businesses in order to measure the impact of high technology on businesses and help determine the need for employee retraining;

• designing an efficient model for competency-based customized training in advanced manufacturing technologies; and

• acquiring and producing customized education and training packages in specific advanced technology fields.

State policymakers should identify two-year colleges with the capability to develop high-technology centers and provide the necessary funding and support to establish such centers. Of course, not every community college can or should be developed into an advanced technology center. States should locate such centers in areas with industries that can take advantage of their services.

An Advanced Technology Training Consortium

CCCC also participates in the Mid-America Training Group, which is establishing high-technology centers at ten community college campuses in the Midwest. The colleges, in addition to CCCC, are LCCC; Kellogg Community College, Battle Creek, Michigan; Macomb Community College, Warren, Michigan; Rock Valley Community College, Rockford, Illinois; Sinclair Community College, Dayton, Ohio; Triton Community College, River Gorge, Illinois; Des Moines Area Community College, Ankeny, Iowa; Eastern Iowa Community College, Davenport, Iowa; and North Central Technical Institute, Wausau, Wisconsin.

Triton Community College provides an example of the services supplied by members of the consortium. The college sends its faculty to the nearby Japanese-owned Matsushita Industrial Corporation to teach courses in electronic shop techniques, quality-control fundamentals, and robotics. Matsushita components for its television, microwave oven, and video cassette recorder products are used in the courses. Kellogg Community College helped C.A. Picard, metal fabricating company, retrain workers so that the company could introduce a new welding process into its operation.[33] **Economic development officials should, where conditions permit, establish interactive and regional consortia to provide for technology transfer to business and industry.**

Technology Transfer Agents

Ohio's development agencies recently added another tool to the state's economic development inventory. The Ohio Technology Transfer Organization (OTTO) operates through twenty-four community colleges in cooperation with Ohio State University. The network provides technical assistance, technology information, and training to Ohio businesses by connecting research to the marketplace. The network transmits new techniques from laboratories and classrooms to businesses that can put the results to practical use.[34]

Community colleges deliver the services through full-time technology transfer agents on each campus. The agents link businesses with technology experts at the local college, or, if necessary, with Ohio State. The network serves mostly small businesses. For example, if a small business wanted to automate its office, the transfer agent would put it in touch with experts in that field. The system provides the businesses with technical expertise they otherwise could not afford. State and local governments should assess the feasibility of establishing technology transfer agents at local community colleges.

OTTO is funded as a $1 million line item in the state budget. It also receives funds from business and industry, local foundations, and state and federal programs, as well as services contributed locally. The funding illustrates how economic development groups and two-year colleges can draw on a variety of resources to mount creative programs.

State and local economic development groups, the colleges, and other partners should examine all potential funding sources to put together packages for technology transfer and related economic development programs. Such efforts can go a long way toward enhancing the climate needed for small-business development and growth.

Ohio's Vocational/Technical Consortia

Ohio's third program shows how other educational institutions can be drawn into partnership with two-year colleges to foster economic development through technology transfer. The state gives the start-up training industries need through twenty-three vocational/technical resource consortia of secondary schools, two-year colleges, vocational/technical centers, and university branches. This program, linked to OTTO, is coordinated at the state level but provides direct services locally via the two-year colleges and other educational institutions.[35] The program shows that schools and colleges can cooperate among themselves, as well as with economic development agencies and businesses, to further an area's overall economic potential. States and communities should explore and devise ways that educational institutions at all levels and of all kinds can cooperate to promote economic development.

An Industrial Park in Wisconsin

Two-year colleges also can play a role in industrial development through the creation of advanced technology industrial parks. Such facilities usually are associated with research universities. States have long recognized the value of such efforts to their industrial and economic development strategies. Industrial parks of the this type offer extraordinary opportunities for economic development by clustering resources, including the technological expertise of educational systems.

Wisconsin's sixteen Vocational, Technical, and Adult Education districts and their associated technical institutes offer industry a wide array of services to improve productivity and quality in the workplace. The districts have developed an applied technology center, business incubators, a high-technology laboratory, multiple funding contracts, teleconferencing, computerized instruction, technical assistance, and participation in the recruiting of new industries.

A notable example is the Fox Valley Technical-Research Incubator Park (Tri-Park), developed at the campus of the Fox Valley Technical Institute (FVTI). The 290-acre park, now under development, surrounds the institute's campus northeast of Appleton in Outagamie County. The corporation governing Tri-Park seeks to recruit high-growth industries compatible with the technological, educational, and business support services it offers.[36] The tenants are interested in product research and development operations, highly technical and service-oriented firms, and light industries that have an interest in expanding or developing new-technology businesses.

One of the facilities to be located in the park is FTVI's D.J. Bordini Technical Innovation Center. The 30,000-square-foot technology building will house a technical library, economic development center, large group conference area, product development service center, flexography laboratory, demonstration area, customized concepts laboratory, and numerous classrooms. The center, the park, and other facets of the development will aid industry through research, training, technology transfer, and other services.

Tri-Park is an outstanding example of two-year college cooperation with other groups, organizations, and agencies for economic development. An educational consortium—composed of FTVI, the University of Wisconsin Center-Fox Valley, Lawrence University, the Institute of Paper Chemistry, area high school districts, and local agents for the Job Training Partnership Act—helps future tenants-owners develop an educational and training plan for their firms and employees.

Funding also is cooperative. The total estimated cost of development is $1.65 million, with funds contributed by the federal Economic Development Administration, the state VTAE Board, FVTI, and private and business-sector donations. The park is being planned and developed by a nonprofit development corporation formed by the Fox Cities Chamber of Commerce and Industry, FVTI, and Outagamie County. Future tenants automatically will become members of the board and eventually take over full management of the park.

The Fox Valley effort show that two-year colleges, as well as four-year institutions, have the ability to develop industrial parks. **State and local economic development groups should determine if community colleges in their areas have the capabilities to develop advanced technology industrial parks.** Two-year colleges may offer unique opportunities for industrial park development in small communities, rural areas, and other areas without four-year institutions.

Technology Transfer to Small Business

In a venture to assist small business, the North Central VTAE District is creating an Applied Technology Center at the North Central Technical Institute in Wausau, Wisconsin. The center will bring small businesses and industries together to buy special equipment too costly to purchase individually.[37] In this way, the institute acquires highly technical equipment and can transfer the technology to participating small businesses, which then can use it during off-hours. One part of the center's efforts is a laser technology program to transfer this technology to cooperating businesses. Business and industry should explore cooperative purchase, lease, or loan arrangements with the colleges for equipment shared in technology transfer programs.

Such partnerships can do more than secure equipent. Ronald Schubert, economic development coordinator at the institute, says the center will provide small businesses with consulting services, problem-solving expertise, new technological systems, and analyses of their needs for training.[38] "We're not dealing with bricks and mortar, " he said. "We deal with concepts for reorganization, the allocation of resources to make the systems work." For example, the institute might help small companies develop the capability to use laser technology, which then could be applied to a product line in an emerging company housed in a small business incubator at the institute.

In short, more than high-technology leaders or the giant corporations can benefit from high technology. Small and medium-sized businesses can apply the technology of computers, teleconferencing, lasers, and even robotics to their operations. Two-year colleges provide an ideal local setting for transferring such technology, showing small business how to adapt through training, demonstrations, and resources such as incubator facilities. **Policymakers should explore all types of programs to help small businesses to adapt high-technology breakthroughs and processes and findings. They should cooperate with two-year colleges possessing the capability and resources to mount such programs.**

TRAINING: THE BACKBONE OF THE ECONOMY

State legislation spells out in general terms the role of two-year colleges in the overall economic development process. However, cooperation grows through informal interaction, and the partners learn to understand their respective roles through meeting, serving on each other's governing boards, and working together on specific projects.[39]

Collaboration between two-year colleges and economic development groups is most prominent in the area of occupational skills training. Several states have made two-year colleges central to their development efforts through the delivery of training services for relocating and expanding industries. These states have integrated the colleges into their long-range plans as full partners in the economic development triangle. Such states recognize the advantages that community colleges possess over four-year institutions. They can redirect their resources rapidly to meet the changing needs of industry, and deliver customized training on campus or at the work site.

Training is the most common type of business assistance these colleges supply. A 1985 survey of 770 two-year colleges by the American Association of Community and Junior Colleges found almost 75 percent provided some type of training for large businesses as well as for labor unions, small firms, and public-sector employers.[40] There are three basic types of training—general, customized, and entrepreneurial (discussed earlier under "One-Stop Assistance"). Trainees may be employed by a company or be potential employees.

Collaborating on training is important for several reasons. Companies need competent, skilled workers to remain competitive. Without them, modern technology cannot be used effectively, and production and profits fall. Technology changes rapidly, so businesses must update their techniques constantly. This translates into the need for continuing education and re-education of present workers. If all members of the triangle work together, business can avoid duplicating what colleges are already able to deliver and take advantage of the resulting economies of scale.

Colleges benefit from this collaboration by ensuring that their training is applicable to "real world" working situations. An important consideration here is that training costs can be prohibitive. Companies rarely find it economically feasible to set up and operate their own training programs. Many two-year colleges already have trainers on staff and appropriate curricula in place. They can adapt readily to changing business needs. Employers can work with the colleges to develop high-quality, flexible training progarms and lend their own experts to serve as part-time faculty where appropriate.

Community colleges offer workers a chance to update obsolete skills and learn new occupations as a way of guarding against dislocation and unemployment. In slow economic times, two-year college enrollments rise as people seek to master new skills and improve their employment prospects. Older workers, who have been out of school and in the work force for several years, often need retraining, particularly when long-held jobs disappear. Most businesses do not provide any reemployment assistance for workers who must be let go. By joining forces with the two-year colleges, however, a company can begin to provide for the training its workers need for lifetime employment.

Statewide Industrial Training

The availability of training is one of the most important factors businesses weigh in their location decisions. States can help defray employers' costs for worker education through their community college systems. Programs can provide funds to recruit, screen, train, and pay part of the wages of the trainees. Businesses find such arrangements difficult to resist.[41] Economic development officials have found that low-cost training is one of the most compelling incentives to attract new businesses and retain existing firms and encourage them to expand.[42]

State legislators and executives should recognize the role of training in the economic development process and explore the part that two-year colleges can play. They should create and support a flexible training capacity where none exists. The payoff from two-year college training can be very high. Several states have incorporated their two-year college training capacity into their economic development strategies. Both North Carolina and South Carolina have established and maintained programs involving two-year colleges as a central element in their development efforts since the early 1960s.[43]

In North Carolina, fifty-eight community colleges, technical colleges, and technical institutes provide state-sponsored customized industrial training services to all new and expanding businesses. The programs are tailored to meet the specific needs of each company. For example, Norton Simon, Inc., a Fortune 500 firm, established its Max Factor cosmetic manufacturing operation in the state. Vance-Granville Community College trained 280 Max Factor employees in skills ranging from chemical compounding to set-up mechanics—the art of modifying machinery to accommodate an ever-changing product line.[44]

Other training programs are tailored to meet the specific production needs of each company. Industries receive the services as long as they continue to create new jobs. Many of the nation's largest companies now have at least one manufacturing plant in North Carolina; two-year colleges and institutes have provided training for more than 400 companies over the last fifteen years.[45]

The Industrial Services Division of the North Carolina Board of State Community Colleges administers the training programs and helps the Department of Commerce sell the state as a desirable industrial location. The division also helps the colleges design quality training programs and put them in operation. Seven full-time regional training specialists work on various projects.[46]

South Carolina delivers training through sixteen special schools created by an act of the legislature. The program is called the Technical Education System. "The keystone of the program is a partnership for economic development between the statehouse, the courthouse, the schoolhouse, and industry," according to the *Economic Development and the Community College*,[47] a report of the National Postsecondary Alliance. Training is offered at no cost to employers. Since the program began, industries have invested $17.6 billion in South Carolina and created 330,000 new jobs. State officials give most of the credit for this economic growth to the Technical Education System. According to the report, South Carolina economic development officials believe that for a community or state to attract new industry and business in the 1980s and thereafter, it will be necessary to ensure that their two-year colleges can provide a solid supply of trained technicians.[48]

In North Carolina, former Governor James B. Hunt, Jr. said that the two-year colleges are "the backbone of the economy and the single most important element in the state's program of economic development."[49] During the almost twenty-five-year life of these programs, both states have taken long strides in moving from poor, agrarian economies to ones that provide a more affluent, balanced economic structure of industry, services, and agriculture.

State policymakers should conduct a comprehensive assessment of the training capacity in the variety of educational institutions around the state. Where gaps exist, the state should make increased investments so that training for new and expanding businesses can enhance economic growth potential.

Innovative Funding Approaches

The North and South Carolina programs are funded primarily from state appropriations. Iowa uses its two-year colleges in much the same way, but has developed a unique funding plan. The state provides no up-front grants or current resources for its two-year college economic development program. Rather, the financing is generated by the new jobs that are created. The colleges issue "training certificates" for sale in financial markets, patterned after instruments used in more prevalent tax increment financing (TIF) mechanisms. Funds from the sales are used to set up training programs at the colleges and to reimburse new and expanding companies for costs incurred if they choose to conduct training in-house.

Repayment of the certificates occurs in two ways through the businesses that benefit, but at no cost to them. First, 1.5 percent of the withholding tax from the trainee's wages goes to the company to pay the colleges for the training. The second source is an incremental property tax assignment paid directly to the college by the county treasurer after the new or expanding business pays its taxes. This earmarket revenue comes from the employer's existing tax liabilities; no additional taxes are paid by the firm that uses the training program.[50]

This funding mechanism gives the community colleges the ability to raise money, a large portion of which is used to reimburse employers for on-the-job training. It also obviates questions usually raised regarding publicly supported training—such as whether programs are serving people most in need of help or whether businesses would have provided the training anyway in the absence of public funds. To date, businesses and the colleges appear to have achieved a mutually satisfactory arrangement of interests.

In Massachusetts, two-year colleges participate in the Bay State Skills Corporation (BSSC), which also uses an innovative funding mechanism. The BSSC is a quasi-public corporation created in 1981 to respond to the rapidly changing nature of the state's economy. Its basic purpose is to award grants to educational institutions that link up with one or more private companies to train people for jobs in high-growth fields. Every dollar BSSC awards to a training institution must be matched with a dollar from the corporations participating in the training.

BSSC funds programs in a wide variety of occupational areas: machine operation, precision machining, nuclear medicine technology, respiratory therapy, word processing, data entry, microwave engineering, computer-aided drafting and design, electronics, and advanced automation and robotics. The training spans entry-level, retraining, and employee upgrade training, as well as advanced-level college and university education. These programs foster BSSC's goal of expanding the number of skilled workers available for Massachusetts companies. An outside evaluation of the funding method declared, "BSSC's 50/50 matching program is an innovative and important model for achieving economic development and employment objectives. . . . Most employers judge the program a success thus far and would recommend it to others."[51] Its funding model is efficient as well; most BSSC programs achieve a much higher match from industry than the 50 percent required.

The state of California devised an innovative method for financing training when it created the Employment Training Panel. Funds for the panel's programs are provided from a state payroll-based tax that was instituted in the wake of a reduction in the state's unemployment tax. Employers' tax liabilities stayed even in this tax trade-off arrangement, and the state gained a large fund for training. Since its inception, the Employment Training Panel has been involved in many cooperative ventures.

Los Angeles Valley College, Los Angeles Southwest College, and East Los Angeles College joined state and local groups to provide training to laid-off aerospace workers and those likely to be displaced.[52] Partners in the effort were Lockheed California Company, the International Association of Machinists and Aerospace Workers, the Engineers and Scientists Guild, and the California Employment Training Panel.

The program consisted of two initiatives. The first trained 144 machinists and machine operators in computer numerical control. The effort was spread geographically over 50 miles of training sites and employers. To overcome this, a $200,000 computer numerical control lab was mounted in a tractor trailer so that training could be brought to the places where the need existed. The Employment Training Panel was so pleased with the operation that it supported an additional mobile lab and added another $711,360 to continue the program.[53]

The second initiative was a computer-assisted design program. In addition to $485,000 from the training panel, the colleges received $185,000 in software contributions from Lockheed. The industry and the unions helped develop Valley College's CAD curriculum, helped specify the equipment needed, recruited trainees, and supplied instructors who had the required credentials.[54] As a result of this program, a plant faced with the possibility of closing was able to retrain its work force and remain a viable and valuable contributor to the local economy.

This investment in employee retraining was a major effort involving industry employers, organized labor, the state of California, and the Los Angeles Community College District, according to James McKenney of the American Association of Community and Junior Colleges:

The threat of imminent job loss, human resource loss, and tax revenue loss got everyone's attention. Equally important was the investment in the long-term future. The area economy just simply cannot keep up with the demand for highly skilled technicians. Therefore, not only is Lockheed anxious to retrain its present employees, but it is similarly interested in cultivating the vineyards of the future.[55]

State policymakers should explore innovative mechanisms to tap and package new sources of financing or training as an economic development activity. Local and state economic development groups should encourage cooperation among two-year colleges, industry, labor unions, and state and local agencies to mount training programs to retain local industries and the jobs they provide.

Job Training Partnership Act (JTPA)

The Job Training Partnership Act (JTPA) is an important source of federal funding for state and local training efforts, including those launched by two-year colleges. Generally, the colleges participate in JTPA as contractors to the local Private Industry Councils (PICs), JTPA's business-dominated planning bodies. Two-year colleges nationwide have been heavily involved in JTPA since its passage in 1982. Because the Act encourages occupational training with assured placement potential, community colleges are an obvious service provider. Their quick response capability is attractive to the PICs and to employers. At the same time they have much to offer to the disadvantaged clients targeted by JTPA.

The state of Tennessee took a unique approach in implementing the JTPA program. The state chose its existing community college districts as the basis for establishing the boundaries of JTPA service delivery areas (SDAs) in the rural parts of the state. According to David Bedford, the state's assistant commissioner of labor, the choice was fortunate in that the state was able to take advantage of the expertise of proven program administrators in the community college system.[56]

The arrangement also gave JTPA quick access to readily available training in the area vocational/technical schools, which are organized within the community college system. Tennessee also uses the community college system to administer the specially designated education funds (8 percent of a state's JTPA allocation) that provide basic skills training and GED preparation. By maintaining an identity for these funds apart from other state and federal money in the state Department of Education, the Labor Department has been able to boost their impact.

Many persons eligible for JTPA cannot read, or they lack good work skills; these deficiencies often place special demands on the community. Instead of contributing taxes, these people require tax-supported social and income maintenance services. Therefore, efforts to train them for the work force provide a double economic benefit: adding them to the tax rolls, and removing them from dependence on tax-supported services.

In 1979, Chemeketa Community College in Woodburn, Oregon, and the Mid-Willamette Jobs Council in Salem joined forces to provide classroom and hands-on training in production skills for light industry and manufacturing, as well as literacy and work-skills training. In addition to JTPA funds for instructional costs, tuition, and tools, the program used in-kind contributions of materials and equipment from local industries.[57]

This open-entry, open-exit program trains people eligible for JTPA whose limited skills, lack of job experience, and personal histories have kept them from finding permanent, full-time employment. Some participants cannot read, write, or speak English. Some are preparing to reenter the community upon release from prison or the state mental hospital. They need not only job-specific training, but also have to learn good work habits, develop a sense of responsibility and a spirit of cooperation on the job, and improve their basic skills. Because the area lacks major industries, most graduates of the program must find jobs in small firms such as lumberyards, furniture companies, and mobile home manufacturers. By mounting a comprehensive program, the college and the job council enrolled 367 in the program, trained 226 of them, and placed 199.

The program provides for the recruitment, assessment, and selection of the people who will receive training. It includes skill development in which trainees must demonstrate ability to use the full range of tools, understand how they are used in different industries, and complete several building projects. In addition, the program emphasizes the development of interpersonal skills and good work habits such as self-motivation, responsibility, and communication skills. The program also addresses basic skills deficiencies. Trainees who want to earn a high school equivalency diploma or to work on basic mathematics and reading skills attend classes at the Woodburn Outreach Center, a branch campus of the college.

Industry is heavily involved in the project. Company representatives advise the program on job market conditions, placement opportunities, and the skills needed for entry-level jobs. Employers also have been active in informing other business leaders about the program. The industries provide constant feedback on the effectiveness of the training and the individual trainees' needs.

The Oregon partnership demonstrates how economic development efforts can mobilize two-year colleges to provide a wide spectrum of education and training for people who are otherwise unemployable. Such programs contribute not only to the economic health of the community through increased jobs and revenues, but also aid people who otherwise would need an array of social services at the taxpayers' expense. Two-year colleges are ideal settings for providing the mix of training and education needed by people who lack work experience or basic academic and work skills. The involvement of the firms that eventually will employ such people is critical to the success of the program.

JTPA program administrators and economic development officials should continue to use JTPA funds to provide training and education via two-year colleges. Economic development efforts should incorporate training for people whose lack of basic skills, work skills, and work habits hinders their employability.

THE TRIANGLE BENEFITS ALL

Clearly, as part of the vital economic development triangle, two-year colleges have a proven track record in promoting economic investment and generating job opportunities. The number of program examples cited here could be multiplied many times. The colleges can offer comprehensive assistance and services that business and industry need to remain strong and to grow. Obviously, different areas need different types of programs. Through the locally focused two-year colleges, programs can be developed to fit local needs precisely. Local economic development groups can and should develop recovery and growth strategies and plans that include two-year colleges that can serve local needs.

Statewide efforts can use the local colleges in statewide systems to deliver economic development resources targeted to local needs. Such programs can tap the resources of all kinds of educational institutions. Collaboration among two-year colleges, high schools, four-year institutions, and special purpose institutions can provide the whole array of services required for a comprehensive economic growth strategy; all of these institutions and noneducational organizations have very important roles to play in these efforts.

MUTUAL EFFORT/MUTUAL BENEFIT

The economic-development triangle requires the effort of all the partners to create a successful program. But the collaboration also brings major benefits to each of the partners, and the communities they serve.

For public and private economic development agencies and organizations, the benefits include:

- adding an important resource to their economic-development efforts;
- providing additional incentives for businesses to expand existing operations or open new ones;
- adding to the tax base through new or expanding businesses and the employment of more workers;
- increasing jobs and incomes in the state or community;
- receiving assistance to encourage entrepreneurship and the development of small business;
- obtaining survey information and a data base on which to build an economic development strategy; and
- gaining an opportunity to attract new and revamp existing businesses and industries that rely on new technologies.

Business and industry benefit by:

- receiving high-quality, low-cost training and other services;
- obtaining a work force trained to fill their particular needs;
- taking advantage of a local resource for business information, support services, marketing, and consulting;
- expanding the small business base in the community;
- strengthening the overall local economy and business community; and
- gaining access to technology that otherwise would not be available at the local level and having employees and managers trained in the use of that technology.

The benefits to two-year colleges include:

- contributing to an expanded tax base;
- providing jobs at the college;
- placing graduates in jobs;
- developing training and re-training opportunities;
- gaining an ongoing continuing education opportunity;
- finding other sources of equipment needed to maintain up-to-date training programs;
- developing entrepreneurial/consulting opportunities for faculty;
- gaining a new source of corporate gifts and contributions;
- creating a source of new full-time and part-time students; and
- bolstering the overall strength of the institution.

6. Training and Job Creation for the Unemployed

Postsecondary institutions have a distrinct role to play in helping unemployed workers find new jobs. Unemployment insurance (UI), the basic federal-state program that supports workers, is only a temporary measure—generally lasting twenty-six weeks—and is not a solution to their plight. Many workers, among them the dislocated, have characteristics that call into question the usefulness of the UI program in getting them back to work. Obviously, when a plant closes or a mass layoff occurs, some of the unemployed find new jobs quickly. Others need some help—assessment of their skills, occupational counseling, a refresher briefing on job-search skills, resume writing, and interviewing techniques—plus UI income while they look for work. The Employment Service provides some of this needed help in searching for jobs, but dislocated workers often require much greater levels of assistance, such as remedial education and training in new skills, before they can be reemployed. (See the discussion in Chapter 4.) Community, vocational and technical colleges are especially suited to provide this help.

Another option for unemployed workers might be starting a small business. Occupational skills they gained in previous jobs could be a basis for a service firm, or a hobby might have potential for product development and sales. With the right advice and support, which is often available from local colleges and universities, workers might create their own way out of unemployment.

The question for public policymakers in addressing unemployment is whether to continue simply to support those unemployed or to institute new policies to get them reemployed. The next two sections explore ways that public and private-sector leaders can help to turn unemployment insurance from a passive income-maintenance program into an active tool for economic adjustment. The discussion includes recommendations on how educational institutions as well as federal and state policymakers can participate in this new adjustment approach and contribute to the self-sufficiency of individuals and the economic health of their communities.

TRAINING

Training is the key to reemployment for many of those out of jobs. Workers must be flexible and adaptable, ready to learn new skills, and open to the prospect of retraining to meet workplace needs. The growth of the service sector relative to manufacturing has increased the demand for higher-level analytical and reasoning skills. Similarly, in manufacturing, both the changing skill content of jobs and the move to more participatory forms of management require workers to think critically and apply knowledge to a greater degree than in the past.

Some workers facing the prospect of long-term unemployment can benefit from immediate retraining. Some find it through training offered by new employers on the job. Others gain new skills by returning to school.

Educational institutions, particularly community colleges and vocational-technical schools, have experience in the training field. Most offer courses in a variety of occupations. Frequently, they set up training programs under contract for companies wanting courses tailored to their specific needs. They also provide training for clients of public programs, such as welfare or the Job Training Partnership Act (JTPA).

Other workers require help with basic education before they can begin training for new occupations. Employers, unions, training program operators, and educational institutions have found that many dislocated workers seeking retraining lack the basic skills needed for their courses. Educational institutions conduct remedial courses in basic skills: reading, writing, and mathematics. Remedial instruction often is integrated into skill training so that students can see the relevance of basic education for their future work.

Remedial education and occupational skill training have been the route out of unemployment and dependency for hundreds of thousands of people. Educational institutions have a record of success that holds promise for UI recipients. For them to have access assured to these resources, however, federal and state policymakers must make some changes in the UI program.

Approving Training for UI Recipients

Congress has recognized that training can be valuable in the reemployment of UI recipients. In 1970 it amended the UI statute to prohibit states from denying UI eligibility to persons who are in "training with the approval of the state." In essence this provision waives the UI requirement that recipients, for the duration of training, be "available and looking for work." Congress has reaffirmed several times its support for combining UI and training, most recently when it passed the Job Training Partnership Act in 1982; the law states that all training conducted under Title III, the dislocated workers' program, is to be considered "training with the approval of the state."

State agencies differ, however, in their administration of these provisions to encourage training. While all states approve JTPA Title III programs, many have cumbersome procedures for approving other programs or for allowing UI recipients not eligible for Title III to enroll in job-related educational programs.

These difficulties are due in part to the complexity of state approval processes. State agencies must determine what training programs or courses are approved, and which persons are approved. State Employement Security agencies (SESA) are entrusted with this approval process. Few, however, have any particular expertise in deciding what training should be approved. Presumably, questions of the quality and relevance of instruction must come into consideration—questions familiar to state education agencies and accrediting boards, but not so routine for Employment Security personnel.

Some members of Congress have introduced legislation that would require governors to designate an agency to approve training. This would allow governors to choose the agency best equipped to make determinations about the quality of training. Short of congressional action, governors should review which agency in the state is handling the approval process for UI training programs. They should assign this function to the most appropriate body.

Massachusetts has dealt with this part of the approval process by giving automatic approval to courses funded under a variety of employment-related programs, including JTPA Title IIA (training for the disadvantaged), Adult Basic Education (ABE), English as a second language (ESL), GED preparation, Bay State Skills Corporation, and other Massachusetts-specific programs. Other courses must meet the following criteria:

• be conducted on a full-time basis—20 hours per week;

• consist of vocational or industrial training;

• provide intensive training of short duration (1 year or less);

• be designed not primarily to meet the requirements of a degree program; and

• achieve an average "placement rate" of 70 percent during the most recent 12-month period for which such data are available.[1]

Local UI office claims adjudicators have the responsibility for making determinations in the course-approval process.

All states should specify which programs and/or institutions are approved automatically for providing training to UI recipients and should develop clear criteria for prompt approval of additional training programs. Educational administrators should find out if their programs are approved for training UI recipients, and seek approval if it is not granted automatically.

The second part of the approval process deals with a determination of which individuals should be approved to enroll in training. Here, the practical problem in administration is not only whether training will help a person's reemployment prospects but also whether enrollment in a training program will prolong an individual's receipt of UI benefits. Some evidence from the state of California indicates that participation of unemployed workers in training while receiving UI may increase the duration of benefits, and thus increases UI costs.[2]

Massachusetts specifies who may be approved quite strictly because the state will pay additional UI benefits past the 26-week regular program while a person is in attendance at the training facility. The total of these additional benefits may not exceed 18 times the weekly UI benefit amount to which the person was entitled. Automatic approval is granted to JTPA Title IIA participants, those who meet state definitions of "dislocated worker," and "long-term claimants who have been in total unemployment for 15 consecutive weeks or longer and have been permanently separated from their last employer."[3] For individuals who do not qualify for automatic approval, the state has an application process.

The option of enrolling in training while collecting UI is advertised widely to claimants. The Division of Employment Security's policy states: "This opportunity to obtain training and education while unemployed is to be brought to the attention of all claimants. Claimants are to be encouraged and assisted in their consideration of the training option."[4]

All states should adopt clear policies on who may enroll in training while continuing to receive UI and make these determinations promptly in each case. State policies should encourage training for UI claimants who will have difficulty finding new jobs without improved skills.

The Massachusetts criteria for long-term claimants (15 weeks unemployed and permanently separated from an employer) suggest that states can develop objective measures to define automatic eligibility in a way that limits additional costs to the UI system while claimants enroll in training. States already use UI data to study broad questions of occupational growth and decline; these data also could be used to help make determinations of individuals' reemployment prospects and the potential benefits of retraining. States should study historical UI data to see whether patterns of UI exhaustion exist in particular occupations and industries. New UI claimants from these sectors could be made eligible for retraining automatically.

State Employment Service (ES) agencies sometimes administer aptitude tests for UI recipients. They could make these assessments in conjunction with administering the UI work availability test. Using various tests, Employment Service job counselors could judge whether an applicant's basic skills are adequate for the literacy demands of today's jobs. The counselor also could determine if a person's job skills might be suitable for an entirely different occupation. This process might open up possibilities for placing the person in immediate new employment. It also might indicate that a person's skills are so specific to an obsolete job that retraining is the best route to re-employment. States should use assessment of the UI recipient's existing skills to help decide if retraining would be useful.

Federal budget reductions for the Employment Service in the early 1980s led states to cut back drastically on testing and assessment activities. As a result, the number of individuals receiving ES counseling dropped by 40 percent between 1981 and 1983, and the number tested declined by 30 percent. However, accurate assessment is essential to the efficient use of UI and limited training funds available under the Job Training Partnership Act. States should reexamine their use of Employment Service funds and reemphasize testing and assessment to conserve scarce income-support and training dollars.

In 1982, Congress passed the amendments to the Wagner-Peyser Act (the authorizing legislation for the Employment Service) returning a substantial amount of discretion to the states to set their own ES priorities. The amendments also changed the ES planning process to give local Private Industry Councils a say in how ES funds could be used best in conjunction with job-training funds. The legislation directed that each state dedicate 10 percent of its funds to improving performance, including providing services to groups with special needs.

The 10 percent set aside should be used to strengthen the assessment and testing capacity of the Employment Service and to improve the process of determining whether UI recipients would benefit from retraining. Private Industry Councils should emphasize this activity in their consideration of ES plans for local service.

The UI-retraining connection is significant for the providers of skills programs—community colleges, vocational-technical schools, four-year institutions, and others—because it bears on recipients' means for supporting themselves while in training. The Job Training Partnership Act offers scant help; it places emphasis on training rather than income support, and prohibits the payment of allowances, stipends, or wages. Many program operators cite this absence of funds for basic support as an impediment to training. Under JTPA's predecessor, the Comprehensive Employment and Training Act (CETA), a large percentage of funds went to providing stipends for persons enrolled in various educational and training activities. JTPA's ban on support payments, however, has forced training providers to make alliances with existing income maintenance systems, such as welfare and UI, to help trainees in their programs.

Educational institutions clearly have made the necessary connections. Community colleges and vocational-technical schools are major providers of training for JTPA's dislocated workers program (Title III). However, school administrators should look beyond JTPA and make their services available for other UI recipients. Educational administrators should talk with state Employment Security administrators to determine what policies the state has adopted for increasing the enrollment of UI claimants in training and educational programs. They should emphasize the logic of training people while they have some income to support themselves.

The Employment Security system, composed of UI and the Employment Service, is a federal-state partnership. The federal government has a responsibility for promoting the best practices in this system, including the option of training, if they lead to the reemployment of UI recipients. Despite the 1970 congressional prohibition on denial of UI eligibility to persons in training, federal agencies have given the states little help in sorting out the components of "approval" or assessing the costs and benefits of training.

The Department of Labor should provide technical assistance on the training issue to the states, helping them to share information about processes for approving training for UI recipients. In particular, the department should develop optional methodologies for using historical data and assessment tools to help states anticipate who may exhaust UI and who may benefit from retraining.

The Department of Labor also can upgrade and expand existing data collection systems to gather and publish better information on training activities. The Department currently collects only limited information about participants in the JTPA programs for dislocated workers. States are required to report whether participants were receiving UI at the time of enrollment and whether they were long-term unemployed. The reporting system could be expanded to offer more insight on the issue of costs and benefits of training UI recipients.

The Department of Labor should include information in the JTPA reporting system on the number of weeks of UI received by Title III trainees, and data on their exhaustion of UI benefits before or during participation in Title III. The Department also should collect information about the training experiences of non-JTPA UI recipients, including data on occupations and wages before and after training, to evaluate its contribution to their reemployment.

Congress can take other steps to encourage states to use training as an option for UI recipients. For example, states are allowed to count UI payments made to dislocated workers in training programs (Title III) as part of the required state match for federal funds. This precedent could be expanded to other required state spending. Since the potential of training to extend the duration of UI benefits causes concern about UI debt, Congress could offer an incentive to states by allowing them to offset UI payments made to training-program participants against interest owed on loans to cover UI obligations. It could allow other offset-type encouragements for states with no outstanding loans. Congress should develop positive incentives for states to combine UI and training using the offset precedent of Title III of JTPA.

Congress also could "approve" of more training than JTPA Title III. For instance, although few UI recipients are eligible for JTPA Title IIA because of its income restrictions, granting blanket approval to these programs could set an example for states on how to establish automatically what is "approved." Some training programs for veterans also might be treated this way. Congress should explore whether additional federal training programs could be considered "training with the approval of the state."

Work-Sharing

Work-sharing is an innovation in the UI system adopted by several states. Also called part-time compensation, the program provides partial UI payments to workers to compensate for reduced work hours. It serves as an alternative to layoffs when an employer faces slack demand. Rather than laying off 20 percent of the firm's work force, for example, the company could ask employees to work four days a week and receive unemployment payments as partial compensation for the fifth day's wages. The program helps employers by allowing them to retain a skilled work force; it also helps the employees, who share the hardship of unemployment but keep their jobs.

Work-sharing has the subsidiary effect of giving workers time to upgrade their skills or train for new occupations where permanent work force reductions are inevitable. On their day off, workers might enroll in courses at a community college or vocational-technical school. Since people on work-sharing have jobs already, the regular UI rules about "available and looking for work" do not apply. Therefore, state approval for training is unnecessary.

Institution of a work-sharing policy in the UI system requires state legislation. California has run such a program for several years. Arizona, Oregon, Washington, Florida, and Maryland have authorized its operation, and others are considering it. As with training UI recipients, work-sharing may increase costs to the state's UI program. In California, the program has small negative financial impact on state government revenues. Each state would have to analyze potential costs against benefits in work-sharing programs.[5] Where permanent layoffs are anticipated, the program does give workers lead time to prepare for new employment opportunities.

Administrators of education and training programs should find out if work-sharing is authorized in their state. They can work with Employment Security administrators to determine whether training would be a useful option in particular work-sharing situations.

State-Initiated Training Funds

Federal law limits the use of UI funds solely to the provision of benefit payments. Congress could change the law to allow the Federal Unemployment Tax Act (FUTA) tax revenues to fund training directly. Recognizing that such action is unlikely in the near future, states are creating training funds that use the UI tax-gathering capacity in new ways. As discussed, various factors have kept the combination of UI and training from flourishing. However, a general lack of funds to support training also has slowed progress. JTPA Title III is the only readily available financing, but funds for this program nationwide will amount ot $200 million for fiscal 1987. At this level, the program probably serves only about 4 percent of those eligible.

States are increasingly recognizing the value of training to make their economies competitive. A skilled work force is a prime asset for businesses seeking to expand or relocate. States used the opportunity presented by Title III to enlist their educational institutions in helping dislocated workers. They quickly engaged their community college and vocational-technical systems to provide remedial education, skills upgrading, and occupational retraining for those with small chances for reemployment. Now, states are developing innovative ways to fund more training and put their entire educational systems to work for the unemployed.

In 1982, the California UI system had a $2.7 billion surplus. The legislature reduced the overall UI tax rate by 0.1 percent and instituted the Employment Training Tax on employers at the same level. The tax supports programs to help people in the work force learn skills that either put them back to work or keep them from losing their jobs. Thus, workers are eligible for training if they are UI claimants, likely to become claimants, or have exhausted their benefits. About 2 million California workers were eligible in 1982. The new tax can generate $55 million per year for training. Collections in excess of the $55 million limit revert to the state's UI fund.

The California fund is administered by the Employment Training Panel. It relies on the state's extensive community college network to develop programs that meet the needs of specific companies or provide skills in occupations in demand. The community colleges and the state strive to ensure that all training will lead directly to jobs. Colleges are allowed to train workers only for jobs that promise long-term security and reasonable wages. Training does not begin until employers agree to participate and hire those completing these programs.

In addition to the primary mission of training the unemployed, the California legislature wanted the training panel to support two related economic development goals: giving employers an incentive to locate or expand their companies, and improving the business climate by reducing employers' UI costs in the long run. As newly trained persons secure steady employment, all employers are expected to benefit.

A state-owned training fund has the advantage of allowing the state to set its own eligibility rules and establish its own priorities for training participants. Because California's program is an offshoot of the UI system, UI recipients are primary choices for service. States with UI systems generating healthy surpluses should consider lowering their UI tax rates and substituting an equivalent tax to create a training fund.

Delaware recently established a Permanent Training Fund by substituting a training tax for a UI-related tax. A unique opportunity arose when the state's 0.6 percent FUTA penalty tax expired in 1984. (The federal government imposed this penalty tax on all states to pay off the debt created by the Extended Benefits program in past recessions.) Delaware's legislature continued to collect 0.1 percent after 1984 to create the training fund. The new tax represented a lowered burden for employers while generating a 32 percent increase in training funds for the state. Funds collected are used for any of the following activities:

- counseling, training, and placement of dislocated workers;
- providing industrial training; and
- assisting with vocational guidance, training, and job development.[6]

The FUTA penalty tax that allowed Delaware to create its training fund expires at a different time in each state as its purpose is completed. States should retain portions of expiring FUTA penalty taxes to create new training funds.

The Massachusetts legislature is considering a major package of legislation to tie several education, employment, and related activities into a comprehensive, labor market-based training delivery system. The state already has redrawn its employment security system's service boundaries so that UI and Employment Service operations correspond geographically to the JTPA service delivery system. The legislature is considering the creation of a state training fund supported by a small excise tax on employers. This 0.1 percent tax on the first $7,000 of every employee's wages (the same base used for the UI tax) would go into a "skills investment fund" used for skills upgrading, training and retraining, and adult literacy programs. The bill before the legislature envisions that 25 percent of agencies targeting their services to UI recipients, exhaustees, persons about to be laid off, and dislocated workers would receive training contracts.

These state initiatives highlight the efficiency of the UI tax-gathering system and its effectiveness in generating large amounts of revenue. Obviously, its coverage delines during recessions when the payroll base for the tax shrinks and claims for UI grow. All systems must accumulate substantial surpluses to guard against insolvency during economic slowdowns. States also must be zealous in guarding the financial stability of their programs.

However, while unemployment increases the need for temporary UI income, it also makes imperative the need for retraining workers whose jobs will be lost permanently. These state training funds can be a significant factor—perhaps more effective than UI in the long run—in helping workers into more secure employment futures. Quality training, provided through the state's networks of two-year colleges and technical schools, will show profits for individual workers and state economies after temporary income has run out.

Education administrators obviously are concerned about financial resources to operate training programs. They are called upon to speak publicly about the adequacy of budgets for this purpose. Educational administrators should work with Employment Security administrators to examine the feasibility of creating state training funds based on payroll taxes. They could become important allies in presenting this concept to the legislature.

USING UI TO PROMOTE SELF-EMPLOYMENT

Congress and the states have allowed the UI system, in limited circumstances, to support workers in training programs. States are getting up training funds using innovative taxing schemes.

Another course of action taps the potential of UI for creating new jobs: helping people to start their own businesses while collecting UI. Use of public money to underwrite private enterprise usually is reserved for large undertakings; the mechanism, however, can work well for the individual entrepreneur.

Self-employment is growing faster than salaried employment. Its growth accelerated following recent economic swings as some of the unemployed became "entrepreneurs of necessity." Independent small businesses are important contributors to local economies because they often create job opportunities for others. During the 1980-82 recession, small firms with fewer than twenty employees produced a total of 2.6 million new jobs, more than offsetting the 1.7 million positions lost by large businesses.

Starting a new business requires capital investment. The amount varies from enterprise to enterprise, but often it is smaller than people realize. A recent survey of 155 new firms by the National Federation of Independent Businesses showed that 18 percent had started with less than $5,000 in capital, another 13 percent with $5,000 to $10,000, and nearly half had begun with less than $20,000.[7] Start-up investment money usually is in short supply for the unemployed, however. Workers' unemployment insurance could go a long way toward meeting these capital needs.

The amount of UI paid per week depends on the person's wages over several previous quarters. In mid-1986 the average weekly UI benefit nationwide was more than $129. This ranged from $89.52 in Mississippi to $155.60 in Minnesota. Assuming that a person collects UI for a full twenty-six weeks, UI provides sums ranging from $2,328 to $4,046. Budding entrepreneurs could use this money to finance part of their start-up costs.

European Self-Employment Programs

The United States has no experience in using UI to promote entrepreneurship and new business creation. Several European countries, however, have launched programs to help the long-term unemployed create jobs for themselves by founding their own firms. Foreign program designs include loans or grants, lump-sum payments, and periodic installments. Some programs require personal capital and formal business plans, but others do not.

Great Britain and France have had programs in place for several years, and report encouraging results. The British estimate that for each 100 participants in its Enterprise Allowance Scheme (EAS), unemployment falls by 33 persons. France attributes one-third of all business starts in the past three years to its self-employment program.[8] These programs involve between 2 and 3 percent of the unemployed in these countries annually.[9] Both suggest options for experiments in the U.S. to test the feasibility of using UI to create jobs through small business start-ups. In fact, the first of these, the Self-Employment Investment Demonstration, began in 1987. This four-year project sponsored by the Corporation for Enterprise Development will promote self-employment as an option in welfare-to-work programs in seven states in the Northeast and Midwest.

The British Enterprise Allowance Scheme helps those unemployed thirteen weeks or longer start businesses by paying them a flat allowance of 40 pounds (about $60 in 1986) a week for a year in place of their regular unemployment benefits. Prospective entrepreneurs must have at least 1,000 pounds (approximately $1,500) of their own money available to invest in their businesses. Applications are not screened for the viability of the business proposal or likelihood of success. However, applicants must attend an introductory training session. They may attend additional business counseling sessions in which business plans and other necessary management tools are discussed. Training services also are available to EAS participants upon request, but are not mandatory.

Begun as a pilot program in 1982, the EAS proved so popular that it was expanded and made available throughout Britain in 1984. The program, administered by specialist teams located in seventy job centers nationwide, is open to 50,000 potential entrepreneurs each year. By the end of 1985, 139,000 had enrolled.[10] British labor officials estimate that one-third of the participants succeed in staying off the unemployment rolls. A preliminary assessment of business survival rate is encouraging; 52 percent were still in operation three years after their launching.[11] This is comparable to the average success rate of small business in Great Britain.

The weekly allowance under EAS is funded from general revenues. The British government estimates the net cost the first year is approximately 2,690 pounds (about $4,050) for each person admitted. As these new companies begin to generate tax revenues and create additional jobs, their relative cost decreases. In fact, their net cost to the unemployment system drops to about 650 pounds (around $975) per participant at the end of twenty-four months.[12] More than a quarter of these new companies add at least one new employee in addition to the entrepreneur. The British government estimates that each 100 EAS businesses surviving three years creates an additional ninety-nine jobs.[13]

The Department of Labor, together with the states, should establish a pilot program redefining the "available and looking for work" requirement to allow UI recipients to collect their benefits for a limited period of time while starting new businesses. The program could be limited to persons with a certain amount of their own money to invest in the enterprise, be targeted to those with certain education or skills levels, or could have other conditions attached that would help promote the commitment necessary for a positive outcome.

France started an Unemployed Entrepreneurs Program in 1979 as a demonstration project, and made it a national policy in 1980. Since April 1984, French citizens entitled to unemployment compensation or welfare could collect up to 43,000 francs (about $5,500) in a lump sum to help them start a business or buy an existing one; 78 percent opt to start new companies.[14] The average French payment is $2,466. Additional grants are made for each worker the new company hires during the first six months. By the end of 1985, nearly 235,000 unemployed persons had taken advantage of the program.[15]

In a recent survey, the French government found that 51 percent of the new entrepreneurs would not have tried self-employment without the lump sum; another 26 percent indicated they probably would have foregone the attempt. More important, that same survey discovered that between 60 and

80 percent of the new firms survived for three years or more.[16] This is consistent with business success trends in France.

French officials credit entrepreneur program participants with one-third of all new business starts in France in 1984. Many of these enterprises are helping more than just the founder; they have created an average of two jobs each. About 2.7 percent now employ more than ten persons.[17]

The Department of Labor could join with states to design a pilot program offering lump sum UI payments to recipients with viable small business ideas. Like the allowance idea, certain conditions, such as structuring an acceptable business plan or attending entrepreneur counseling sessions, could be included to enhance participants' likelihood of success. Colleges and universities can work with state and local governments and economic development agencies in establishing such thresholds and helping prospective entrepreneurs acquire the expertise to meet them. With their management and technical assistance capacity, business course offerings, training experience, and staff expertise, they are ideally suited to lend a hand to improve the survival odds for small companies started under this type of program.

Belgium has had a program since 1984 to provide loans of up to 500,000 Belgian francs (about $11,500) to persons currently on unemployment who wish to establish a business and are willing to risk up to three years of future benefits. Interest rates on the loans are low, and the notes themselves carry generous repayment terms. The typical entrepreneur participating in this program uses the loan to leverage an additional $19,000 in commercial loans. Belgian officials indicate that about 1 percent of the unemployed on its rolls obtained help through this program during its first year.[18]

A recent study by Marc Bendick, Jr., and Mary Lou Egan examined the nature of the businesses and jobs created under transfer payment programs. In France, for example, they found that 30 percent of the businesses assisted under the entrepreneur program were service-oriented, 28 percent devoted to retail, and 22 percent in construction trades. Nearly 72 percent of these firms started with less than $7,500 in owner's equity.[19]

According to Britain's Manpower Services Commission, 66 percent of the new businesses launched under EAS auspices are service-sector firms, 15 percent construction, and 14 percent manufacturing. More than one-third of the service-sector firms are retail or business-service concerns.[20] Bendick and Egan reported that more than 90 percent of the EAS-assisted firms were started with an owner's investment of less than $7,500.[21]

The experience in these nations suggests that if the program is well targeted to the long-term unemployed, use of UI funds to help launch new business ventures could be successful in removing workers from the ranks of the unemployed. Reporting results similar to those in France, a survey of the British program found that 36 percent of the participants would not have gone into business without the government support, and another 31 percent had accelerated their start because of the assistance.[22] Thus, only one-third used their UI benefits for what they probably would have done anyway.

So far, entrepreneurial assistance has been most successful for skilled workers. The majority of those participating in France's program, some 71 percent, were managers, technicians, and the like. However, the idea can also be applied to disadvantaged workers who may not be considered skilled, and it can succeed with the proper nurturing. For example, more than 100 low-income women enrolled in a business development program in St. Paul, Minnesota, have started successful businesses. These women make clothes, candies, jewelry, and toys. Their success suggests that entrepreneurship for less-skilled, disadvantaged persons can be made a feasible alternative.[23]

The European experience provides some important lessons for U.S. policy-makers:

- **UI can provide entrepreneurs with a significant portion of needed capital to undertake a new business venture, if they obtain it in a lump sum, as in France.**

- **A lump sum UI payment could serve as collateral to leverage additional money in loans, as in Belgium.**

- **The entrepreneurial assistance programs can be designed so they add no new costs to the existing UI program. Both the British and the French programs finance self-employment assistance from funds that the eligible person would have received anyway.**

- **Those businesses that do survive probably will generate important spinoff benefits in the form of additional jobs.**

The UI system has provided an important service to the nation's unemployed since it began. Its explicit objective of providing income in the short-term to cover involuntary unemployment is important and must be maintained. Policy changes must not impair the capability of the UI trust fund to ensure against temporary earnings losses. However, alternatives to the basic payment function could make the system more responsive to changing labor market conditions. Maintaining persons in unemployment is not an answer to structural dislocation. When options for retraining and reemployment are available, UI recipients must be allowed to pursue them.

TRAINING AND JOB CREATION STRATEGIES

The UI system was designed to provide workers with a temporary financial cushion during times of economic downturn. It was conceived fifty years ago as a bridge between periods of "normalcy" in the workplace.

Since the severe economic dislocations of the mid-1970s, though, this idea of UI as a bridge has come under sharp scrutiny. Many of the jobs for which laid-off workers claimed these temporary benefits simply disappeared, as company divisions, subsidiaries, and entire firms succumbed to changes in the economic base. Many of these jobs were in traditional manufacturing industries, long an economic staple in the Northeast and Midwest. Moreover, many of the workers who found themselves displaced were not young newcomers to the work force, but middle-aged with many years of service—and facing dim prospects for retraining and reemployment.

The UI system can address the new reality of the nation's unemployment situation and become an important force in retraining and job-generating activities. Potential changes to UI range from better use of existing data for state and local program modifications to federally authorized pilot programs in entrepreneurship based on similar European experiments. These recommendations are summarized below.

Educational administrators should:

- determine whether training programs offered by their institutions are approved for UI recipients, and seek automatic approval where it is not granted already;
- determine what policies the state has adopted for allowing UI recipients to enroll in training, and emphasize the importance of training people while they still have some means of support available through UI;
- find out if work-sharing is authorized in their state and determine whether training would be a useful option in particular work-sharing situations; and
- work with Employment Security administrators to create state training funds where feasible.

State policy makers should:

- review which agency in the state is assigned the responsibility of approving training programs for UI recipients and assign this function to the most appropriate body;
- specify which training programs and/or institutions are approved automatically for providing training to UI recipients and develop clear criteria for approving other programs;
- adopt policies governing who may enroll in training while continuing to receive UI and encourage the enrollment of UI claimants who face reemployment problems;
- study historical UI data to establish whether patterns of UI exhaustion exist to help identify at earlier stages those claimants who might benefit from retraining;
- reemphasize testing and assessment activities in the Employment Service to identify UI claimants likely to need remedial education or occupational training for reemployment;
- use the ES 10 percent set aside to strengthen the testing and assessment functions of the Employment Service;

- consider creating state training funds by substituting levies for UI taxes where UI surpluses exist; and
- take advantage of expiring FUTA penalty taxes to create state training funds where feasible.

Congress should:

- direct the Department of Labor to provide technical assistance to the states on UI and training by sharing information on state approval processes and by developing models to help states determine which UI recipients may benefit from retraining;
- direct the Department of Labor to expand its data collection activities to include more information on the training experiences of UI recipients, both in JTPA and other programs, and the results of these activities;
- develop positive incentives for states to combine UI and training using the offset precedent of Title III of the Job Training Partnership Act;
- explore whether other federal training programs could be considered "training with the approval of the state"; and
- authorized pilot programs to explore alternative uses of UI to promote self-employment opportunities, and earmark training and technical assistance resources for such efforts.

7. Business-Higher Education Development Strategies

DEVELOPING INFORMAL UNIVERSITY-INDUSTRY NETWORKS

The search for better cooperative relationships between business and postsecondary educational institutions has become a dominant theme in contemporary university management. Sputtering productivity gains and declining national competitiveness in world markets have made government officials rethink the role of academic research in enhancing technological innovation and business development. Officials now expect to derive economic benefits from university research and from the collection of talent and resources made possible at these institutions through public funding. Even private institutions increasingly view their own viability and prestige as closely linked with their local economies.

Businesses are responding to these changes, sponsoring research and relying on postsecondary institutions to meet their training and management-assistance needs. The historic dynamic between academic and entrepreneurial "cultures"—with conflicting ideals, orientations,and goals—is giving way to a search for accommodation and collaboration. The adversarial posture is now considered artificial and based on an exaggeration of differences.

However, several circumstances have kept industry-higher education relations from attaining their full potential. Strong antibusiness attitudes on many campuses in the 1960s and 1970s discouraged interaction. Even internal university discussions about institutional roles and responsibilities in local development were stifled. Post-World War II federal policy and spending patterns also contributed to the divergence.[1] The rapid growth of federal support made industry investments in basic research almost irrelevant. To this day, national laboratories and federal mission-oriented research agencies are seen as vehicles to increase the flow of new scientific knowledge and to aid in the development of scientific talent. A few agencies, such as the National Aeronautics and Space Administration (NASA), do show keen interest in new product development. The National Science Foundation (NSF) views basic research as its primary mission.

In fact, the federal government has a strong role in shaping university research policies. It is a major source of university research funds, contributing $6.5 billion of the $14.2 billion spent annually by federal, state, and private sources for academic research.[2] As a result, universities have been slow to promote the development side of the research and development equation. Many universities, like their federal funders, have been satisfied with whatever indirect benefits accrued. Until recently, few embraced information and technology transfer as a university research responsibility. Tenure and publication requirements, which provide incentives for advances in basic knowledge as judged by one's peers in the scientific community, reinforce the bias against applied research. **Policymakers should confront the research-development issue directly.**

High-visibility initiatives such as technology research parks or state-supported centers of excellence are often emphasized. This narrow view overlooks the resources available to institutions that lack nationally recognized research specializations. It also gives short shrift to the learning process in which partners must share to establish a working relationship—one based on a mutual vision and a belief that the effort will benefit both. A key element of this learning process involves resolving the difficult policy questions that arise inevitably from closer university relationships with the business community. Another crucial aspect of initial collaborations is the development of strong personal ties that can serve as the foundation for new and more ambitious arrangements. **University administrators can promote within institutions the kinds of organizational reforms that encourage communication and problem solving between higher education and industry.**

Carefully conceived individual faculty initiatives can also strengthen ties. This informal "networking" requires no formal commitments from business. It can, however, provide a low- or no-risk opportunity for each side to learn more about the needs, resources, and limitations that the other can bring to more formalized associations. Successful collaborations show that these partners can create mutually beneficial relationships while building greater confidence in the university community and among local business leaders.

Officials on both sides should analyze what, if any, contacts have occurred previously. Universities should reexamine what types of businesses were dealt with, what needs they expressed, the extent of the contacts, and the results. In addition, they should undertake a survey of current businesses to determine what types of industry or business should be targeted for informal relations. These may be the businesses concentrated near the university or those needing the most assistance.

Universities also should develop an inventory of resources that may be of value to businesses. A frank assessment identifying what an institution has to offer could discourage poor matches that advance neither party's interests and detract from the initiative's overall effectiveness. Not surprisingly, small and medium-sized businesses with scant resources need the most help. Even though large corporations tend to have strong independent contacts and the resources to obtain any help they need, they still can benefit from association with universities. Businesses of all sizes can benefit from the political connections acquired through contact with a public university system, from closer ties to research efforts with a national scope, and from opportunities to influence the educational process. Universities can benefit from businesses' feedback on the impact of their educational programs. For example, they can give their curricula a more practical orientation and thus attract more students. Business contacts can produce higher rates of employment for graduates. Closer ties can lead to increased business-community participation in fund-raising, cultural affairs, and joint community efforts.

Universities should consider the nature and extent of the contact they wish to have with businesses. It may range from simple faculty and personnel exchanges to directories of university resources for businesses to complete offices for industry relations. These contacts often are intended to involve businesses in the university's affairs and to display the university's assets. Administrators should tailor their outreach plans to make contacts in which university resources best match business needs.

While individual circumstances will shape every relationship, some factors promote or impede success. First, universities and businesses must acknowledge that both have institutional differences to overcome. These differences are likely to involve management philosophies, research objectives, organizational structures, compensation levels, and timing. Informal relations built little-by-little seem to have greater chances of success; they create a sense of trust, which often inspires the level of confidence required to develop more formal and profitable arrangements.

Vital to the relationship is strong and highly visible support from top echelons of both university and industry. This support will help build confidence at all levels of business, the university, and the local community. Faculty and businesspersons must open their doors to one another, respect the other's objectives, be flexible in their expectations, and align their strengths and resources with the other's carefully.

At the institutional level, university administrators have encouraged types of cooperation that do not require "formal" business agreements. These programs include those that identify research endeavors of mutual interest to academia and industry; set up offices matching the needs and capacities of the industrial sector with those of the educational community; develop directories for business and industry that list the specialities of university departments, research centers, counseling facilities, faculty, and classes or seminars of interest to the business community.

Universities across the country have begun to examine their economic environments to analyze what their role can be in solving business problems. For example, business students at the University of South Carolina at Spartanburg (USC) have surveyed local businesses to determine if the school's business program is meeting their needs. One concern expressed by the Spartanburg business sector was that graduates were not adequately skilled in communications. The university responded by incorporating stronger communications elements in their program. Nevertheless, USC has encountered one problem common to many schools attempting to foster economic development: the reluctance of the private sector to contribute funds and other resources to the effort.[3] The business community often believes that a public university has the responsibility to carry out any program needed. Yet the costs of these programs often are too high for universities to absorb with no assistance, thus they must look to private and federal sources.

The University of Illinois at Champaign has established a business advisory council, composed of senior business executives from the local community, which evaluates components of the university's curriculum. The business program has expanded to include seminars instructing junior college and community college professors on how to teach courses in entrepreneurship. The university also conducts seminars for entrepreneurs, funded by a grant from the state.[4] Such business advisory councils are a common means of incorporating business opinions into university life. They are usually relaxed arrangements, with meeting schedules ranging from once a month to twice a year. Their advice is reviewed by university officials who adopt viable suggestions.

Beyond the institutional level, some state agencies are coordinating efforts to further university-business communication. For instance, Minnesota Wellspring, a joint effort of education, agriculture, government, labor, and business was founded in 1981 to build support for business growth and technological innovation. Its task forces prepare recommendations to the state legislature on technology, education, small business, and rural development issues.

The 1987 recommendations fell into five main categories: the value of technology and innovation to increase productivity and efficiency; the importance of education and training; the need for seed and venture capital to help businesses; a community-based strategy that relies on local strengths and resources; and the collaboration of business, government, labor, and education in the economic development process.[5]

In 1986, Michigan's four major research universities completed an extensive study of industry-university relations in the state, in hopes of determining what types of linkages existed between businesses and universities, what barriers to cooperation were present, and the ways these ties could be strengthened. The goal was to encourage regional economic development through industrial innovation. Three groups were examined: businesses in Michigan; university officials; and university-connected units and programs that promote linkages. Seven basic aspects of joint relations were examined: the nature and extent of contact; benefits or payoffs for businesses; shortcomings of contacts; how existing contacts developed; impediments to relations; unanswered business needs; and changes in policy by businesses, universities, and government. This survey helped to establish the Technology Transfer Network with an office at each of the universities—University of Michigan, Michigan State University, Wayne State, and Michigan Tech. These offices "broker" faculty expertise with the technological needs of individual companies.[6]

The results of building sound relationships between universities and industry are hard to quantify, but their long-term benefits can be well worth the time and effort. What begins as a simple faculty-personnel exchange may well lead to a successful, profitable research project or consulting relationship further down the road. Involvement of business representatives in university cultural affairs and curriculum committees may culminate in a corporate-sponsored program. Both universities and businesses are looking for ways to influence economic development positively and to expand their own capabilities and reputations without increasing expenditures. To accomplish these goals, each partner's resources must be exploited efficiently. This task can be accomplished over time by resolving the range of problems that arise in the development of closer ties between very different entities.

As discussed in Chapter 5, community and junior colleges are at the forefront of the business-education partnership movement. Many have shown tremendous receptivity to assisting businesses and a willingness to respond to particular business problems. Four-year colleges and universities generally have lagged behind these smaller institutions in developing such cooperative relationships. They need to devote more time and resources to these efforts when they will be most fruitful.

UNIVERSITIES AS BUSINESS CONSULTANTS

A host of difficult technical and financial problems confront the entrepreneur in moving from idea to prototype to production. Crafting and polishing a business plan, identifying a market, and obtaining first- and second-stage financing can require costly investments in consulting services for companies without significant working capital or income. Similarly, existing businesses may face major financial, technological, or management difficulties and may lack the resources for the kind of high-caliber, professional consulting services that would ensure their competitive posture and profitability.

Cash-poor businesses often have nowhere to turn for help with consulting services but to universities. Federal, state, and local governments are beginning to develop business-assistance roles, but there are still many areas where help is not readily available. States and localities certainly can do more to bring about the coordinated delivery of all kinds of resoruces. Individual universities can initiate their own programs to assist businesses. These institutions can function both as brokers of services available from all governmental levels and as providers, drawing on their internal expertise.

Universities offer often-underused faculty and student management and technological expertise. A number of schools have developed mechanisms to match business requirements with their own resources. The experience of these universities pinpoints factors that must be considered in setting up and running successful business consulting services in an academic setting. The following is a discussion of goals, policy issues, implementation steps, potential outcomes, and examples of consulting arrangements.

It is vitally important for both parties to set well-defined goals for a program; goals provide benchmarks for measuring a program's effectiveness. The main goals of university-business consulting programs are to help businesses acquire and apply specialized advice to enhance long-term viability and competitiveness, to give students and faculty experience in dealing with real, rather than textbook, problems, and to strengthen trust and respect between the two.

Great potential exists for universities to influence the business community positively. However, the risks are equally great. An official involved in developing a consulting program should consider the following:

- the state of existing relations between the university and the company or business community;
- strengths of the university;
- implications of targeting a certain type or size of business;
- degree of community support;
- provisions for identifying and handling an unproductive relationship;
- justification of university or public spending;
- use of student and faculty time;

- business needs and necessary compromises;
- congruity between program goals and priorities and the state's overall development efforts;
- preference for an active or passive strategy; and
- experience of other universities with similar arrangements.

If both sides have identified common goals and agreed on overall policies, the program can be put in place more quickly. The university's strengths play the greatest role in determining what department of the school will house the consulting service. Business, law, or engineering departments most often serve as the consulting base.

The consulting service may be a separate entity from the school. Under this arrangement, it may use all the resources of the university but still retain a degree of independence. However, physical separation may also result in removal from the mainstream of university life, and interaction may be more difficult to initiate.[7] **University officials should work with the business community to analyze how consulting services should be provided.**

Services may be run out of a center, with clients coming to the school for help, or through on-site consultations. The nature of business problems and the limit the university places on resources available to any single client will have a major impact on the selection of consultants. Cases that will extend for long periods have faculty as the main consultants, with new students working on specific subtasks each semester. Students may also act as primary consultants in more limited projects, with the proper faculty supervision. Students can act either individually or in teams, or would work with a faculty-staff team. Students usually receive course credit for their work; faculty and staff sometimes are paid for their time. Whatever the arrangement, care should be taken to assign faculty and students to cases according to their ability, interest, experience, and reputation.

A major step in the implementation of a successful consulting program is to draft the agreement between the university and businesses. Each party should lay out clearly what it expects the other party to do, what end products will be produced, and how the consultants will be paid, if at all. Both parties should strive to be as flexible and as open as possible, and patient during the negotiations.

Financing and timing appear to be the areas most vulnerable to problems. Program staff often have difficulty securing adequate financing for the consulting services. They seek funding from the university; business contributions; chambers of commerce; local, state, and federal programs such as a Small Business Development Center or Small Business Institute program; or service fees. However, arrangements can be made for the university to receive a portion of cost savings or increased profits. For instance, the University of

Alabama at Tuscaloosa has an arrangement with a metals fabricating company in which the firm reimburses the university for operating costs incurred during the consultation period only, but the two share any cost savings or increased profits accruing from the consultations. This program is discussed more fully below.

Timing can pose difficulties because universities and businesses do not normally work on the same schedule or at the same pace. If students are consulting for course credit, it may be difficult to fit problem solving into a semester-oriented framework. Businesses also are accustomed to working at quicker paces with shorter turnaround times than university bureaucracies.

An evaluation body, such as a board or council, should be included in any consulting arrangement. It should be composed of university, business, and community representatives. Checking the program against the established goals, policy considerations, and feedback from clients and consultants, the review panel should analyze a program's short- and long-term results.

A range of outcomes may result from a university serving as a business consultant. Positive ones include better mutual relations, which may lead to other types of joint undertakings; savings for the business; experience and professional reputations for the students and faculty; and adaptation of the university to area business needs. Unfortunately, there may be some negative results, such as conflicts among faculty over who participates in a program and overburdened students who cannot keep up with their course loads. Widely varying student skills may limit the project. Assessing the impact of consulting may be difficult because the contact may end after a relatively short period, and there may be no systematic contact following completion of the arrangement. The university also faces the prospect of budget overruns. Both sides must accept the fact that problems may arise and should address foreseeable problems in the program's early stages.

Another problem may be competition among professors. Some universities deal with this by setting guidelines on levels of expertise each project requires and how consultants will be chosen. Inadequate students should be detected through project reviews and replaced. Excessive assignments can be modified. Universities that have trouble following up on cases can take on fewer new cases, or attempt to secure more funding to ease the process. They should attempt to avoid cost overruns by constructing and following more realistic budgets.

Looking at how two universities have handled consulting arrangements with industries can help administrators plan for their own programs. The examples presented here reflect exceptionally innovative ways of using university resources to affect businesses directly and positively.

The University of Alabama at Tuscaloosa (UA) has one of the best-known university-business consulting services: an arrangement between the UA and the local General Motors carburetor plant. The plant was losing money and was scheduled to close, despite a great deal of effort by GM to keep it open. As a last hope, GM appealed to the university for creative financing advice. After extensive negotiations, UA decided to rent the plant as an applied research facility for three years. The cost was $500,000 per year minus any cost savings UA found. Gambling $1.5 million of the university's money was a large risk, but thanks to the leadership of both groups and to the hard work of the students and faculty involved, the needed cost savings were found in less than a year with no disruption of plant operations. The plant remained open and now has some prospects for new product lines.

Participants attribute their success to open communication, mutual trust and respect, strong commitment, and dogged persistence. The most significant problems were the financing, meeting the degree of flexibility and speed required by GM, and convincing faculty that this project fit into the university's mission and purpose. Financing barriers were overcome by use of university funds, as well as community support. Both UA and GM officials worked hard at increasing their institutional flexibility and their receptivity to the other's needs and operations. Faculty support solidified as it became clear that the cooperative arrangement would provide students with an actual laboratory and would strengthen the local economy by saving over 200 jobs.

Both GM and the University of Alabama have benefited from this arrangement in ways that extend far beyond the original project. UA has earned a reputation as an institution that can respond to the realities of the marketplace and deliver services that improve profitability. Increasingly, faculty are involved in consulting for other businesses. GM is working to strengthen its relationships with other universities across the country through a university-affiliate program. GM and UA also are working together on other projects.[8]

The University of Wisconsin at Eau Claire (UW) has combined a great deal of initiative, plus funds from the Small Business Administration's (SBA) Small Business Institute (SBI), to create a comprehensive consulting program. UW uses SBA funds to work with businesses in particular economically depressed communities. Begun in 1983 by Professor Richard Lorentz, this program aims to achieve long-term impact on communities with in-depth consulting services.

Teams of seniors or graduate students majoring in business are matched with companies in the targeted area requesting help. Students meet with the client, analyze the problems, and formulate solutions. At the end of the semester, students write up the case and present it to the client and the SBA. If the work is satisfactory to everyone, the school is reimbursed $400 for each case by the SBI (the standard rate) and the students receive course credit.

Covering costs and making sure that students complete their cases were the two biggest problems the program encountered. The university is considering charging the communities a small amount for the consulting work to supplement case fees. Faculty now monitor student time as closely as possible to prevent overloads.[9]

Over 500 universities now participate in the SBI program, a $3-million line item in the annual SBA budget. Most SBI programs use their funding to provide short-term consulting services for small businesses that request help and have the support of their communities.

UW adapted its program from the usual SBI arrangement in order to concentrate on overall community economic patterns rather than scattered individual business problems. In addition to working with individual firms, the university pools the SBA case funds to conduct a broad economic survey of targeted communities, analyzing businesses' needs and the number and types of businesses the area can support.

One of the original communities, Thorp, Wisconsin, requested a follow-up to the original study. Local officials believed that the businesses helped during the first study were at the point where further consultation would take them to a higher level of business development. In addition, new businesses established since the first study have indicated the need for help and have requested participation in the program. Local developers give the program credit as a tremendous aid in helping revitalize the downtown business area.

Other communities that have received consultations believe they have developed a stronger business environment. Typically, the short-term nature of the SBI-funded work does not allow the university to incorporate mechanisms to ensure continuing feedback from all clients. This weakens UW's ability to maintain relationships with these localities and to assess its program. However, because of budget limitations, follow-up consulting is not an option for SBI-funded efforts. UW is looking to other federal funding sources, such as the Economic Development Administration (EDA), for support in longer-term business consulting.

UW's program shows the positive effects of a federal role in supporting university-business consulting programs. The SBA's Small Business Development Center (SBDC) program is another kind of federal support of business outreach effort. SBDCs provide business consulting training, specialized, and information services through a cooperative agreement between the federal government and a lead organization that manages a state-wide network of resources composed of academic institutions, state and local government agencies, associations, and other organizations. The SBA provides half the funding and the other half is arranged by a lead organization—a government unit, a university, or a private concern. Funds are distributed according to a formula based on the population served by the SBDC or $200,000, whichever is greater. The program began in 1980 and is authorized through 1990. There are forty-nine SBDCs in forty-two states plus the District of Columbia, Puerto Rico, and the Virgin Islands. Efforts are now underway in the eight remaining states to organize an SBDC. Its fiscal 1987 federal appropriation is $35 million.

To be eligible for SBA funding, SBDCs must meet several requirements. There must be a designated lead organization responsible for securing matching funds, setting up the actual center, running the program, and reporting to the SBA. Each program must have full-time state director and facilities must be located to serve the entire state. The center must be open forty hours per week (or during the normal business hours of the host organization) and provide both short- and long-term assistance. The governor's written approval fulfills the legislative requirements for state endorsement of an SBDC.[10]

State policymakers should support the creation or expansion of a small business development center system. Several state actions are necessary to leverage federal SBDC resources: the designation of a lead institution, the appropriation of funds to meet match requirements and necessary program expenditures such as the salary of a director and administrative costs.

SBDC goals are to offer consulting, training, research, and a range of other services to small enterprises that cannot afford private consulting services. The services are free to eligible businesses and are normally provided by a variety of resources including SBDC staff, SCORE counselors, graduate students and faculty, volunteers, and private-sector consultants. SBDC goals are more extensive than the SBI program, focusing on developing a network of resources for statewide delivery of comprehensive small-business services. If structured properly, an SBDC program can link the resources of universities and other organizations throughout the state with participating businesses rather than just one business department in a university.

SBDCs frequently encounter problems in selecting the lead organization and in arranging financing. In some cases the choice of the lead institution has become highly politicized, suggesting that SBDC participants should set out goals and requirements to ensure a degree of objectivity in the selection process.

Illinois designated a state agency, the Department of Commerce and Community Affairs (DCCA), as the lead SBDC organization. DCCA and the six university subcenters form a unique partnership between the state and the academic community. Consequently, the SBDC network is well integrated into the state's development plans and has the advantage of direct access to university and governmental resources. Similar state leads exist in West Virginia and Ohio, although most SBDCs have universities as the lead institution.[11]

Pennsylvania's SBDC network is coordinated through the University of Pennsylvania's Wharton School of Business, with subcenters throughout the state. This program's early success can be attributed to its close ties with the Ben Franklin Partnership, discussed below. In fact, the four universities that house the partnership's four advanced technology centers also house SBDCs. The result is that the SBDCs enjoy strong state support and are an integral part of Pennsylvania's overall economic development efforts.[12]

Clearly, state governments have tremendous potential to develop state-wide higher-education networks to provide consulting services to businesses and industries. Many programs are too young to be judged properly, but their comprehensive approach assuredly is a step in the right direction. The federal support that supplements these programs should be continued and increased to help states strengthen their own economies.

UNIVERSITY-RUN INDUSTRIAL EXTENSION SERVICES

Many manufacturing firms and most small businesses have negligible or nonexistent research budgets. In addition to considerations of expense and economy of scale, the lack of contact with, and physical separation from, university technology-development programs inhibits the transfer of technology to these businesses.

Industrial extension services operating from public university settings help to lower barriers to technology transfer and application. Based on the agricultural extension service model, industrial programs respond to individual business problems and promote new technology for businesses. In a departure from most agricultural programs, university staff generally emphasize technology transfer rather than new research advances. This approach can be applied to established firms with growth potential or to needy firms.

State governments are key players in creating or increasing industrial extension service programs. **Initially, policymakers must carefully define state economic development goals and match them with resources available at the state's technically oriented universities.** Goals can include identifying target industries that are or have the potential to become important producers of jobs and revenue in the state.

State legislators must identify funding sources or appropriate new monies for extension services. Such expenditures will provide not only direct benefits to businesses but also promote the better use of the state's educational resources for economic development. University-based extension services reach out to businesses to increase their access to technology and information by opening university resources to the private sector. This diffusion of knowledge and technology can solve business problems, increase productivity, and strengthen university-industry links. Closer ties also will enable universities to identify research problems relevant to businesses, and provide universities with direct feedback on research applicability.

Governmental and university policymakers must confront a number of important design issues. Industrial extension services usually are based at technically oriented universities with both technical and management-assistance capabilities. The extension agents may be faculty working directly out of departments, or affiliated with free-standing offices that use faculty and students for consulting. The agents may offer technical and management assistance, or only the former. Services may be provided to clients for a nominal fee or free of charge. Operating funds for the services may come from the state, the university, or research contract fees.

In setting up extension services, state policymakers must consider carefully whether to establish field offices. Typically extension services are provided anywhere within state boundaries. Some programs choose to have only one main office in order to simplify operations and limit costs. However, this option also may limit the contact and service provided to outlying regions. Programs with field offices may offer service continuity while promoting long-term contacts.

Industrial extension programs adopt either a standard or aggressive approach to service provision. Standard programs often operate as clearinghouses for information and as referral mechanisms to other agencies. Typically, services are provided in response to client requests for information or help. These programs are less expensive to carry out, but may be less effective, over time. **Implementation of an aggressive model requires policymakers to seek out target industries that could benefit from the exposure to emerging technologies.**

In some states, limited funding has hampered the development of extension services. Agricultural extension programs had less difficulty because they offered one comprehensive service that elicited tremendous support. The mix of industries involved in industrial extension services often lacks such community of purpose and the same broad political support enjoyed by the agricultural community, although the economic impact may be as great. One shortcoming of many industrial extension services is that they must cover a broad range of industries and consequently may not be equipped to deal with complicated technical problems.

State legislators and university officials knowledgeable about the numerous positive results of university-based extension services are critical for nurturing the political support necessary to sustain these programs. Potential benefits are great. For example, communities may come to depend on the assistance and information provided by the university, giving each a source of support for future efforts. The links formed by the extension program may lead to economic growth beyond the original arrangement, which benefits every sector. Initial favorable extension contacts also may promote participation in continuing education classes held throughout the state. Universities could decide to develop more specific extension programs, such as those described below, in such specialties as energy conservation, environmental health and safety, and productivity.

The Georgia Institute of Technology Industrial Extension Division strives to address specific problems of small and medium-sized manufacturing firms by helping them achieve innovative technology transfer and traditional technology, and by sponsoring research and extension education. Based at the Georgia Tech Research Institute (GTRI), the division has twelve field offices, each with one to three engineers. Each year more than 1,000 companies without the financial resources for private consulting turn to one of these offices for help, which can range from a simple information request to five days of on-site technical assistance. Businesses requiring more extensive services are matched with other programs in the division, or elsewhere in the university.

Georgia's extension service was established in 1960 by the state, from which it still receives 60 percent of its funding. The rest comes from research contracts in which the extension center consults on specific problems for private industry or programs sponsored by other state or federal agencies. The program is now well established, depending mainly on its reputation to draw clients. Division officials feel that strong state support and cooperation between the universtiy and the state give the extension division credibility with the private sector.

While the Georgia Tech Industrial Extension Division is based at a university, it uses mainly full-time employees as extension agents rather than faculty members. Few students work with the program, and faculty are seldom brought in as paid consultants because Georgia chose to build up an extension staff, which numbers eighty-five. But the university serves as more than just a base for the center. As specific problems arise that are outside the extension division's ability to address, staff from other units of GTRI or the university are brought in to help.[13]

North Carolina State University Industrial Extension Service was created in 1956 by the North Carolina legislature. This service is more closely integrated into the university than is Georgia Tech's program. Faculty serve as extension agents, along with some full-time agents; there are no field offices. Four regional offices maintained previously were eliminated in the expectation that contacts could be continued without them. As a result, extension agents find themselves continually struggling to update and maintain industrial contacts, according to an extension official.

The extension's efforts mainly involve the referral of business problems to appropriate state agencies or to individual faculty members who do private consulting. Extension agents only deal with problems that require less than one day's work. These services are provided free if the business has shown that it cannot afford private consulting. The program emphasizes the integration of computers into manufacturing and factory expansion and design needs. Extension agents mainly serve firms that are stable enough to take the risks associated with technological innovation. This eliminates needier, cash-poor businesses, which are referred to state agencies for help.[14]

State roles in industrial extension services have expanded and show every indication of continuing to grow. State participation is reflected by support from state legislatures and cooperation between state agencies and extension offices. For example, Michigan has developed several kinds of manufacturing extension services to bridge the gap between university research and small and medium-sized businesses. The idea originated in a task force commissioned by former Michigan state commerce director Ralph Gerson. In its far-reaching 1984 study, *The Path to Prosperity*, the task force concluded that the state, as part of its economic strategy, should move innovation into existing small and medium-sized firms on a continuing and systematic basis.[15]

The first extension service was the Technology Transfer Network described earlier. The second, a more technical variety, is the Michigan Modernization Service. It helps small and mid-sized firms adopt computer-based manufacturing tools and methods. Staff members review a firm's current operations and technology, then send a field representative with private industry and manufacturing technology background to visit the plant. The field and office staff can then design a customized employee training program, locate grants to fund it, and recommend private consultants with specialized skills in the appropriate technologies.[16]

Like the programs of other states, Michigan's extension services take advantage of its universities and community colleges. In contrast to others, the services target three specific industries that make up much of the state's critical base of small manufacturers: auto supply firms, food processing, and forest products industries.

Financial support of industrial extension services from the federal government has been minimal and sporadic. According to the terms of the Morrill Act of 1862, land grant colleges were intended to tie higher education to the industrial economic sector. This act established both agricultural and engineering extension services, but the latter never succeeded in the manner of agricultural programs.

By the late 1930s, almost forty state- and university-sponsored engineering experiment stations had been set up without assistance from the federal government. From 1965 to 1968, the State Technical Services program provided a total of $20 million for all fifty states to promote economic growth through industrial modernization. Critics deemed the program a failure after only three years, but some sources, such as the General Accounting Office, concluded that this was not sufficient time to establish stable extension programs and produce concrete results.[17]

Currently, extension services are supported by the federal government through various economic development programs. These include the SBDC and SBI programs, the Economic Development Administration technical assistance services, and the Occupational Safety and Health Administration (OSHA) programs that identify and solve environmental health and safety problems of businesses. More specific information on federal funding can be obtained from these agencies' regional or central offices.

UNIVERSITY-INDUSTRY COOPERATIVE RESEARCH

Industry sponsorship of academic research is on the increase. It rose from $194 million in 1979 to $370 million in 1983, and accounted for 5 percent of total university research budgets by 1987.[18] Total federal support for research and development (R&D) grew 56 percent between fiscal 1981 and 1984, but most went to military research rather than the biological, engineering, or physical sciences.[19] The military R&D component of total federal R&D grew from 51 percent to 71 percent between 1981 and 1987. The other 29 percent devoted to health, energy, and basic scientific research actually declined 6 percent in constant dollars. Virtually the entire growth in the fiscal 1987 military R&D budget went to the manufacture, testing, and evaluation of specific weapons systems. Only 13 percent was tagged for basic research, applied research, and advanced technology.[20]

Bridging the Policy and Culture Gaps

University administrators increasingly perceive business as a source of funds to offset static or shrinking federal grants and contracts, and view the establishment of one-to-one, university-industry research relationships as an important way to achieve this goal. **For university-industry projects to run smoothly, all parties must acknowledge the goals and benefits of enhanced relations as well as the potential problems.** This kind of cooperation raises a host of ethical and legal issues that must be confronted as a precondition to university participation in collaborative arrangements. These issues can be especially difficult for public universities, which are chartered with broad service missions and operate with public funding. **Successful collaboration also requires the development of guidelines in cooperation with potential business partners to ensure that policies are mutually acceptable.**[21]

Business expects a quid for its quo. Business leaders expect to influence the course of sponsored research and feel that they have bought ownership rights to the fruits of the collaboration. Understandably, private-sector investors insist that universities establish procedures to protect proprietary information. University research, in contrast, is founded on the free flow of information. The "right to publish" is frequently a mandate to publish, and publish first, in order to gain stature and security in the university community.[22] Open disclosure policies are particularly defensible when years of government support have made possible commercially valuable research. Therefore, the cooperative agreement must accommodate the divergent interests of each partner. Restrictions on foreign corporation sponsorship may be necessary. **Universities must develop patent and licensing policies before entering into collaborations.**

Companies are not willing to invest in joint research unless the resulting discoveries are protected by patents. Universities are loath to give up the income that flows from a resourceful and creative research faculty. For example, Niels Reimers, head of the Office of Technology Licensing at Stanford University, estimates that within five years the 80 licenses on the university's DNA patent will be worth over $10 million per year in revenues.[23]

Universities should develop conflict-of-interest policies for business-sponsored research. A university may want to restrict its scientists from holding equity positions or serving as officers in companies from whom they also receive research funds. It also must ensure that graduate student research is guided by the principles of open scholarly inquiry and that the system develops skilled scientists. Some institutions simply restrict graduate students from projects that have strong commercial potential to avoid conflicts that could inhibit corporate sponsorships or harm students' professional reputations.

University officials must consider the fact that corporate research sponsorship may affect the direction of research within the university. The choice of topics and the balance between basic and applied research could change as a consequence of private-sector funding. The university must have a clear grasp on these academic freedom issues. However, the record of the past few years demonstrates that these issues can be resolved and successful alliances forged. A 1986 report of the National Academy of Sciences found "a virtual explosion over the past several years in the number and variety of university-industry alliances."[24] Those most involved in collaborations see few, if any drawbacks. The number of abuses and ill-advised associations has been small.

In 1981 the U.S. House of Representatives Committee on Science and Technology requested that the American Association of Universities develop guidelines to govern university-industry associations. Several other organizations exist within which universities and industry representatives can meet to consider common issues and problems. The National Academy of Sciences sponsors the Government-University-Industry Research Round-table, which has developed a model for collaborative agreements between universities and the scientific and technological communities. The Business-Higher Education Forum also exists to give top university policymakers and their counterparts in business and industry the opportunity to meet and confer.[25]

Universities must confront the major "cultural" differences that divide the academic and corporate research enterprises. Research collaboration start-up hurdles are similar to those faced by schools that desire informal relations (described in the first section), but the scope of the endeavor magnifies these difficulties.[26] At the outset, corporations may question the ability of academic researchers at smaller or less well-known institutions to perform industrially sponsored research effectively. Extensive interaction between businesses and universities is the soundest foundation on which to establish ambitious long-term arrangements. Each partner must acquire confidence in the other's talents and an appreciation of the other's operations and limitations. The challenge is to devise coupling mechanisms to strengthen communication and understanding between academic and business communities.

The dimensions of this gap should not be underemphasized. Many universities lack a basic understanding of marketplace demands. University administrators must learn and convey to their research faculty the particular needs, goals, and limitations of their potential corporate partners. They also must educate themselves on the very different ways that federal agencies and corporations budget and operate external research programs. They must develop outreach programs to identify companies whose interests are parallel with those of university research strengths. Perhaps most importantly, scientists must expand the traditional reward system based on peer review and contribution in one's field to one that values corporate resource efficiency and commercial success. University adminstrators are critical facilitators of this transition. They must restructure academic incentives to promote commercially relevant research.

Several universities have developed complex ties to major corporations and international markets. Harvard, MIT, Stanford, Carnegie-Mellon, and Rensselaer Polytechnic Institute (RPI), among others, dispensed with the notion that service to industry violated academic traditions. Other universities have promoted greater business-university interaction by compiling directories or establishing on-line databases that provide detailed information on resources. The University of Wisconsin system and the state's county extension offices have produced a directory listing department research center specialties, small business development centers, and outreach offices.

The Illinois Resource Network provides business with a computerized information file on research interests, current projects, publications, and other details on over 6,500 faculty members and research scientist across the state. Coordinated by the University of Illinois, the network can locate experts for a broad range of purposes.[27]

Affiliate Programs

University-industry affiliate and technology-transfer programs are two models of industry-university interaction that bring a university and the local business community together to exchange information, increase personal contacts, and speed the technology innovation process. They provide opportunities over time to reduce these "cultural" impediments to collaboration.

University-industry affiliate programs provide industry with timely and efficient access to research expertise in exchange for annual participation fees. Members usually receive consultation rights, access to formal conferences, and notice of planned research activities.[28] This interaction can attune universities to industry research needs. **University administrators should use affiliate programs to show that their institutions possess the personnel and equipment to commercialize products and meet other specific research needs more quickly and efficiently than the business partner.** Conversely, business collaborations will help universities identify personnel and equipment investments necessary to develop a technological niche to meet local industry needs. Affiliate programs can generate substantial revenues.

Scores of industrial affiliate programs now operate throughout the country. MIT's Industrial Liaison Program, founded in 1948, is the oldest and one of the largest. With about 300 member companies and an operating budget over $3 million, MIT's program offers seminars, early notice of scientific advances, and faculty consultation privileges. Affiliates pay $10,000 to $100,000 per year in fees, depending on their size.

Carnegie-Mellon University's Magnetics Technology Center charges affiliates $250,000 per year; Cornell's Theory Center charges $100,000. RPI will undertake proprietary research for affiliates, such as a recent project for Norelco. Stanford University has created thirty-two decentralized affiliate programs that provide a broad spectrum of services and levels of participation under a flexible member-fee system.[29]

Smaller universities have established successful programs as well. The Center for Composite Materials at the University of Delaware has attracted thirty-eight industrial sponsors for its research and trainig programs in the areas of aerospace, auto, electronic, general industrial, and consumer products. The center has two major federally supported programs. With backing from NSF and a partnership with Rutgers University, it conducts research on the manufacture of ceramic matrix composites. An award from the Defense Department enables the center to conduct research and testing for the Army. A third discrete center is in the planning stages.

Also at the University of Delaware, the Center for Catalytic Science and Technology supplements its funding through grants and contracts from both federal and industrial sponsors. It undertakes projects sponsored by individual corporations and the State Research Partnership, which provides grants for new industrial high-technology projects.[30]

In one of the largest partnerships ever devised, Amoco Corporation agreed to join the University of Illinois's industrial supercomputer applications program for $3 million over three years. Amoco will receive an office with the latest equipment and up to 1,000 hours of supercomputer time per year. Eastman Kodak was the center's first industrial partner; it uses the supercomputer to help its scientists develop new manufacturing processes. Centers such as Illinois's are attractive to large corporations because they provide opportunities to conduct R&D on the most sophisticated systems available and train their employees in the latest technologies. "This area is explosive," according to the center's director Larry Smarr. "The ability of supercomputers to simulate new product designs and the use of visualization techniques is almost like giving engineers and scientists new eyes to see inside old manufacturing processes." He believes that three-year partnerships will encourage long-range planning among U.S. corporations and will have an impact on the nation's global competitiveness.[31]

Technology Transfer

Technology-transfer programs promote the commercialization of research discoveries. These services generally are supported by the collection of royalties on the new products or processes. Some universities have established internal offices while others use external entities legally distinct from the university.

The Wisconsin Alumni Research Foundation (WARF) is the oldest and perhaps best-known external technology-transfer program. WARF licenses patents derived from university research, redirects most of the royalties back to the university to fund new scientific investigation, and retains a small portion to support its operations. Inventors whose work is supported by WARF funding are not required to assign their work to the foundation. However, voluntary assignment entitles them to receive 15 percent of net royalties and the corporation's services for securing patents and licensing arrangments.[32] Similar foundations are affiliated with Cornell University, the University of Maryland, the University of Michigan, the University of Pittsburgh, and the state of Washington university system. Universities that use external offices, which are sometimes established as for-profit entities, should consider carefully whether the office's reward structure coincides with the institution's long-term faculty, research, industrial sponsorship, and revenue goals.

The Stanford University Office of Technology Licensing is an example of an internal office that also operates on a royalty-sharing arrangement: the office takes 15 percent of the royalty revenues with the remainder split equally among the university, the department, and the faculty inventor.[33] Most universities with patent offices require professors to assign rights to their inventories to the university, unless the government funded the work. The inventor and the institution share any income.[34]

Both models provide valuable patent protection and licensing assistance. Securing worldwide patents involves strict application procedures; the process can take two years and costs can exceed $60,000. It is difficult to find investors to underwrite this process since it may take seven to ten years to move from idea to product. A potential investor can expect to realize a positive cash flow on only one out of twenty or thirty research ideas. Entities such as WARF are able to identify innovations more efficiently. They provide individual and institutional incentives for technology transfer while positioning local businesses to obtain crucial faculty expertise. The state and region benefit as the likely locus of innovation-based economic growth.

Development links were first viewed as an industrial recruitment tool, essentially as a strategy to redistribute the national economic pie. However, the success of technology-transfer programs and other outreach efforts that give business a "window" on research results, demonstrate that these models are contributing to national economic growth. The Washington Research Foundation produced a dramatic jump in the number of invention disclosures and more than doubled patent application filings in its first year of operation.[35] Technology-driven development requires many elements, but fundamentally it takes ideas with commercial potential. The success of innovation-transfer mechanisms shows that these ideas are abundant and argues for strong and federal and state support of these efforts.

Another traditional mechanism to promote closer business-university ties is sponsored-program offices, which can operate either at the department or university-wide level. They are particularly appropriate for large research universities. Typical functions include: promotion of research projects; identification of projects for potential collaboration; and negotiation of contracts and conflicts. These arrangements provide an easily identifiable access point through which business contacts can be channeled.

It is essential that all parties are aware of the complex process that technological innovation represents. It begins with the creation of new technologies, but application of this knowledge will lead to economic improvements.

There are several intermediate steps: development of the basic findings; technology transfer; marketing of the new technology; a whole subprocess of decision making, adoption, and implementation within the company; and finally the dissemination of the innovation throughout the economy. It is more than "a simple capital investment problem."[36] If any of these channels is blocked, the process is not complete, and the positive economic outcomes cannot be guaranteed. It is the responsibility of all the participants to perform their roles effectively in each of the stages.

So far, the evaluations conducted by NSF and other organizations reveal limited commercial outcomes in terms of new products or processes, and a low level of industrial involvement.[37] On the other hand, experts have said repeatedly that the more complex the technology is, the more implementation is resisted.[38] Therefore, the major efforts must be directed to avoiding breakdowns at crucial junctures that could easily halt the process of technological innovation.

Although economists estimate that technological advances or increases in knowledge produce 40 to 90 percent of U.S. economic growth, no coordinated program exists, at the federal level or elsewhere, to channel innovation to the marketplace. Prospects for federal leadership in this area appear slim. The policy of the present administration, only slightly modified by concern over the large U.S. trade deficit, is to leave the sponsorship and development of technological advances to the private sector.

However, the administration supported passage of the Technology Transfer Act of 1986, which opens federal research efforts to commercial applications. For the first time, federal laboratories have the statutory authority to enter into specific R&D agreements with private companies, universities, and nonprofit groups to transfer federal basic research advances to commercial ventures. Over 400 federal labs are funded at $55 to $60 billion per year, hold 20 percent of U.S. lab and equipment capabilities, and employ one of every six scientists. The labs can grant the patent to any invention made by federal employees to a collaborating party or parties. The law also encourages federal lab personnel to pursue research with commercial applications by allowing them to receive at least 15 percent of the royalties on their inventions.

Frequently, the U.S. wins the innovation battle, only to lose the commercialization war. Often there is a significant time lag in bringing research findings to market in tangible form. No single institution takes hold of the process and assembles all the critical elements. The burden for developing technology-transfer mechanisms requires the participation of all sectors, including state and local governments.

THE STATE ROLE IN PROMOTING INNOVATION

Many states are moving quickly into the high- and advanced-technology economic development sweepstakes. Governors from states with wide variances in economic composition, employment levels, and work force skills have put the prestige of their offices and considerable funding into projects aimed at capturing high-tech growth.

States seeking to develop ambitious programs without a solid record of industry-university achievements move forward at their peril. Universities hoping to collaborate successfully with industry must have well-defined institutional policies on shared research, a record of successful short-term applied research problem solving, patent policies that encourage innovation, and the proven capacity to coordinate research with other institutions. Two basic theses of this discussion cannot be ignored: first, the individual circumstances and peculiarities of both a university and a business fundamentally affect the evolution of their partnership. Second, this shared learning process is a prerequisite to larger-scale efforts, which inevitably generate complex problems.

The New York State Science and Technology Foundation relied heavily on records of prior successful relations with business in designating seven public and private university-based advanced technology centers. Following their selection, all the centers adopted policies to promote increased private-sector involvement. The State University of New York at Stony Brook medical biotechnology center has attracted more than fifty international corporations and small companies as sponsors. The center, created in 1982, organizes regular symposia, lectures, and workshops with speakers from the faculty and sponsor-industries on scientific subjects, product development, and financing. The success of these interactions has encouraged the university faculty and industrial scientists to help with new company start-ups. As a consequence, the center established incubator facilities in 1986.[39]

Innovation-based development has become a very important issue for federal and state policymakers. The 1986 Technology Transfer Act promises a major step forward for many state and local governments seeking to apply the benefits of technology to their economies. The act also allows "special consideration" for agreements with small businesses and small business consortia and firms—creators of a large percentage of new jobs.[40]

State policymakers have recognized the need for a better competitive posture for their industries, and significant state action has occurred during the past few years. Strategies include both the attraction of high-technology businesses and the development of new or expansion of existing firms through lished state-chartered programs dedicated to high-technology development. At least forty-four states also have established university-based centers. Arizona, California, Michigan, Missouri, New York, Ohio, Pennsylvania, Virginia, and West Virginia have committed substantial resources to develop such centers. Many have sought to coordinate the other major development tools at their disposal to complement innovation-based growth strategies: specialized training; technical assistance; R&D tax credits; tax-exempt financing; and grant, loan, and venture capital programs.[41]

State-Supported Research Centers

Many states support technical-assistance centers for small businesses. Often they emphasize technological innovation and new business incubation. Policymakers should consider linking these efforts to state-aided university-business cooperative research programs to leverage fully federal technical-assistance funding. This kind of structure is well suited to generate the nonfederal match required for the Small Business Development Center program (see the earlier discussion).

In addition, state participation in cooperative technical assistance programs helps entrepreneurs and inventors seeking assistance through the SBA's Small Business Innovation Research (SBIR) program, which was established by the Small Business Development Act of 1982. This legislation mandated those agencies of the federal government with the largest research and development budgets to set aside a standardized per centum each year for competitive SBIR awards to qualified small business concerns.

The SBA monitors and reviews the agencies' reports to Congress. Between fiscal 1984 and 1986, awards to small business increased from $110 million to $300 million. In fiscal 1986, federal agencies received 13,560 proposals and made 2,509 awards. SBIR is a three-phase process of awards to small businesses: project feasibility, product or technology development, and commercialization.

This program is relatively young but has received good response from the private sector primarily because it provides a simplified, efficient mechanism for small business to participate in federal R&D work. SBIR was established partly on the principle that small businesses produce two and one-half times as many technological innovations as large firms, but were not obtaining a fair share of awards, both contracts and grants, under the previous allocation system.[42]

Evidence that university-connected research centers are cost-effective economic development tools is highly persuasive. The research centers around Boston have helped fuel the high-technology boom that has turned the economy of the entire state around. University and state officials now believe that their investments in such centers will pay off.

State cooperative research centers should be evaluated closely to identify those factors most necessary for their success. The National Science Foundation has gained considerable experience in this area during the past decade through the operation of the Industry-University Cooperative Research Centers program (IUCRC). It provides one-year "seed" grants to get centers started, if they have raised at least $300,000 from industry, and whatever else they need from foundations and government. NSF then gives $50,000 per year for five years to help sustain their operations.[43] Forty centers are operational and several more are in the transition from planning to operations. Some centers, such as Ohio State University Center for Welding Research, Case Western Reserve University's Center for Applied Polymer Research, and Rensselaer Polytechnic Institute's Center for Interactive Computer Graphics have received solid support from business, the state, and the universities, and show good prospects for long-term self-financed operations.[44]

State and city policymakers have recognized more quickly than university administrators that centers of research and systems of higher education are critical resources for development. **Government officials at all levels should view research and educational funding as investments that show a return in heightened local business productivity, satisfy labor force requirements, and bring new business start-ups.** The federal government and the states share in the need to support programs that have potential, and to aid new programs in formation.

The establishement of cooperative research centers also parallels recent trends of business support for university research. Increasingly, businesses fund broad areas of academic research rather than targeting specific, short-term industry needs. Several recent university-industry agreements follow a pattern of multiyear funding with projects focused on both basic and applied research issues. The University of Washington's chemical analytical processing center and Georgia Tech's materials handling center, among many others, derive their success from carefully negotiated cooperative agreements.[45]

According to a recent article in *Fortune* magazine:

While universities are the more ardent partners, companies also have good reason to get cozy. Says Herbert I. Fusfeld, head of RPI's Center for Science and Technology Policy: "Many corporations are realizing they can no longer be self-sufficient technically." High-tech companies, for example, find that the time lag between pure research and product has shrunk so much that they need to be where the pure research is performed. "We need a window on innovation," says James P. Baughman, who supervises management development for General Electric. "When someone yells 'Eureka' at RPI or Stanford, we'll hear it."[46]

State government and university officials who wish to pursue high- or advanced-technology strategies should make a frank assessment of higher educational resources, the needs of the indigenous industrial base, and poli-

tical support for a sustained effort. Careful program definition is imperative. Participants must decide which goal is primary: the development of commercial technologies or returns to the state from the cooperative research. For example, imposition of restrictive patent licensing arrangements would enrich the state but would slow development.

The focus of the research center may be channeled into either a broad or narrow area—"niche filling." The University of Kansas adopted this latter strategy to exploit its expertise in biotechnology subspecialties. A state may want a more broad-based approach, such as Arizona State University's Center for Excellence in Engineering,[47] an ambitious five-year, $50-million project. These centers might serve primarily as business recruitment tools or concentrate on the development of new technologies for existing businesses. New business start-up also might be a major focus.

State policymakers must determine how closely to tie a center to its sponsor institution. The New York State Centers for Advanced Technologies (discussed earlier in this section) are university-based, operating as arms of the participating schools. This arrangement ensures close faculty cooperation and departmental involvement. Other centers, such as the Michigan Biotechnology Institute and the Industrial Technology Institute, operate with more autonomy. Officials at these institutes believe that a looser university connection increases their flexibility to meet industry research needs; it also helps their institutes set themselves apart from the university, which a number of potential clients still perceive as holding an antibusiness bias.[48] The resolution of these issues has clear implications for program design and evaluation.

Some question the capacity of a university or state government to measure the comparative stature of its university departments and leading faculty in the high-technology fields. The predominance of federal funding in academic research and the heavy skewing of federal contracts and grants to a small percentage of institutions underscore the importance of careful definition in areas of comparative excellence. There is a fast-track competition among a small, elite group of players, and even universities with national stature are not always successful in garnering significant federal funding. State backing of research enterprises that do not receive federal funds represents a major gamble of state resources.

Political and Private-Sector Support

The success of Texas in convincing the Microelectronics and Computer Technology Corporation (MCC) to locate near the University of Texas at Austin shows the importance of strong and visible political support. The university has been unflinching in its efforts to recruit a top-notch electrical engineering faculty and research program. Leaders in other states must realize that their efforts will not be self-sustaining from the start and must commit themselves to the long-term process.

One key measure of excellence is industry support. State and academic planners must cultivate industry participation. Business membership reflects the private-sector judgment that a cooperative research arrangement purchases more than could be accomplished in-house. Strong industry involvement at early stages will ensure that a center's goals and stucture are responsive to industry needs. It also will improve prospects for long-term industry support. Ultimately businesses will choose to remain members because of the quality of research output, the degree to which this output meets expectations, and the degree to which proprietary interests of the various industrial sponsors can be reconciled. **Unless policymakers and universities make businesses full partners in the development and operation of the center, the likelihood of failure is great.**[49]

Pennsylvania's Ben Franklin Partnership Program (BFP) and Ohio's similar Thomas Edison Program (TEP) are two of the more ambitious and comprehensive state-supported efforts to spur business-industry cooperative research. In the late 1970s, a number of Pennsylvanians recognized that a new response was needed to compensate for the decline in the steel industry. Industrial recruitment had not been particularly successful in the state. Surveys identified some important research strengths, but also poor business-university relations that were hindering high-tech development.

BFP features a decentralized approach that relies on local initiative to identify critical technologies. The central component of the BFP program is the distribution of challenge grants to four regional Advanced Technology Centers (ATCs) located throughout the state. These grants are matched with outside funds, preferably from businesses. To foster an entrepreneurial spirit, the ATCs compete among themselves for yearly funding. The state's $76.6 million appropriation has been matched with $281 million from program participants. This approach is intended to complement the strong base of industry and academic research already present in the state.

A key acheivement of the Ben Franklin Partnership has been the development of strong relationships among ATC consortia which include public and private academic institutions, business and industry, organized labor, economic development organizations, and private investors. The partnership has increased inter-university cooperation, for example, between Carnegie-Mellon University and the University of Pittsburgh.

Each advanced technology center gathers a large number of representatives of these groups. In contrast, each of Ohio's Edison Technology Centers is built with the participation of a couple of academic institutions, and a variable number of businesses. Like BFP, the Edison Program includes seed capital grants and incubator facilities. Both initiatives are supported by state organizations that perform technology transfer: the Ohio Technology Transfer Organization (OTTO), and PENNTAP in Pennsylvania.

The BFP has three goals: to maintain and create jobs in new advanced-technology enterprises, to improve productivity, especially among the state's existing businesses, and to diversify the state's economy. To ensure that development activities are retained by the state, restrictive patent policies are applied. Any new patent or technology produced through BFP-sponsored research must be commercially exploited by in-state manufacturers or the state funds must be fully repaid. The BFP or university retains patent ownership and may grant exclusive licenses; however, if the sponsoring firm does not exercise its license rights, an assignment protocol that includes state small businesses must be followed.

BFP has reached a $1.00 to $4.09 ratio of state to private funds. This high level of support has helped the program in creating over 5,600 jobs, retaining 4,700 jobs, and assisting in the start-up and expansion of more than 800 firms. Its ATCs reported the creation of over 1,180 new products, processes, or services and the issuance of more than 30 patents since its beginning.[50]

BFP has established a procedure to draw on the state's resources in a viable way. Its continued success rests in part on the sophistication of the university in responding to industry needs based on the kinds of interactions already described.

The BFP and TEP examples show that participating universities should have preexisting and sound relationships with business. They should have policies on shared research, a record of successful short-term applied problem-solving, patent policies that encourage innovation and the proven capacity to coordinate research with other institutions.

STIMULATING NEW BUSINESS START-UPS: INCUBATORS AND INNOVATION CENTERS

New business creation is a significant component of economic growth nationwide. Maintaining the financial viability of existing firms and promoting their expansion is also very important. About 8,400 new corporations are started each year, but only one-third will survive the first four years. New business start-ups are a primary goal of many of the programs in this discussion. Incubators and innovation centers are important components in bringing about the birth of new firms and helping businesses stay viable.

State policymakers should consider making available state funds to support the creation or expansion of incubators. States are involved extensively in the development of small-business incubators. Pennsylvania, with sixteen, is the preeminent state incubator operator. The Ben Franklin Partnership, the commonwealth's most visible program, coordinates resources among universities, development organizations, financial institutions, and education groups through four regional centers. (See previous section for details) Pennsylvania also uses funds from the Appalachian Regional Commission, the Pennsylvania Industrial Development Authority, and the U.S. Department of Housing and Urban Development's Small Communities program to support incubators. Most incubators have ties to at least one educational institution.

Although many incubators operate independently of university ties, such an arrangement has clear advantages. These firms are in much better positions to take advantage of technology-related university research, to tap into university resource networks, and benefit from the university's stature in the community. On the other hand, university incubators tend to be more bureaucratic and more dependent on in-house services than independent entities. It is sometimes difficult to circumvent technical or managerial shortcomings in the university community.

Several large and growing incubators are now in operation, including Science Park in New Haven (Connecticut), cofounded by Yale University, the Olin Corporation, and the city, and the University City Science Center, a multiuniversity consortium at the site of the Ben Franklin Partnership's regional advanced technology center in Philadelphia. RPI, the University of Pittsburgh, and Carnegie-Mellon University are among the most agressive promoters of incubators, research centers, and other business alliances.

University officials should identify financial and service resources as well as space that the university could contribute to an incubator facility. Start-up costs for some incubators have come from university endowments. Empty or underused university facilities provide an obvious home for incubators; some institutions also have made space available at low or no cost. Other universities absorb utilities and building maintenance costs and subsidize consulting services by university faculty and staff.

University administrators and state and local officials are motivated by more than improving the economic health of their communities. Some institutions have established incubators as a way of strengthening graduate programs, attracting nationally recognized faculty, and creating consulting opportunities for faculty and students. Rensselaer Polytechnic Institute set up an incubator and a research park to promote its reputation. RPI views its own success over the long term as linked inextricably to the success of its sponsoring of research-based development in the area.

University incubators may offer a great range of services to new businesses. Typically, services are provided and billed on an "as-used" basis. Rent may be subsidized, and space tailored to firm needs. The incubator may help in the preparation of business plans, in making contact with the venture capital network, and may even take equity positions in some firms. Incubators have synergistic benefits as well: the concentration of new companies can increase an individual firm's visibility, ease access to venture capital, and provide a mechanism for the exchange of information among business founders.

In 1982, Ohio University created the Innovation Center and Research Park to promote economic growth in southeastern Ohio and to expand student and faculty experience with industry and small business. Athens, Ohio, located in the depressed foothills of Appalachia, has no industrial base. A university study concluded that coal mining, subsistence farming, a few medium-sized businesses, and the university itself formed the region's economic core. In response to this study, Ohio University's president Charles Ping committed its resources to revitalize the region. Initial funding of $50,000 was contributed by the Ohio University Fund, Inc., a university endowment. The center is currently funded through a line item in the state budget.

The center negotiates lease arrangements with each client. A company needing minimum services can obtain space in the 40,000 square-foot incubator for as little as $4.50 per square foot per year. The incubator acquires an equity interest in the firm. A new business may acquire access to the university laboratories, equipment, faculty, and the machine and electronics shops through the center. Faculty or staff in charge of equipment are encouraged to negotiate directly with the center's clients to make available virtually all university apparatus during nonuse periods.

The center works aggressively with business to obtain financing. Center Director Dr. Wilfred Konneker uses his considerable contacts in the venture capital and business communities to identify potential investors. The center maintains files on all types of funding sources and helps write SBIR or state R&D funding proposals. The center has raised hundreds of thousands of dollars for phase I and II of SBIR financing, and more than $5.24 million through the state's Thomas Edison program.[51]

Universities must define the kinds of businesses they want to locate in their incubators and develop guidelines for continued tenancy in and relocation outside the incubators. The center imposes a number of selection criteria on potential clients: no retail, real estate, insurance, or consulting firms are allowed. Tenancy is limited to three years; the university operates the incubator as an interim arrangement for start-up businesses and not as a real estate operation for going concerns. Most clients come from spinoffs of university research. A new research park is available for business relocations. Its viability depends heavily on the incubator's success in developing "home-grown" businesses.

Universities must develop policies regarding faculty participation. One major concern of some Ohio University deans was that the incubator would siphon faculty from the university. In response, the Innovation Center promoted the use of release time, essentially encouraging faculty to work part-time. This arrangement allows entrepreneurial scientist to enjoy the benefits of faculty status while drawing part of their salary from the company. In addition, the center encouraged the university to bring in part-time adjunct professors and devise other arrangements that add diversity to the university community to benefit the faculty, students, and the center. This type of experimentation is critical to the success of incubators designed to draw extensively on university resources. Ohio University's model suggests a solution to a problem that hampers faculty participation in incubator projects at other universities: the lack of incentives for faculty to work outside their university teaching and research responsibilities.

Georgia's Advanced Technology Development Center (ATDC), located at the Georgia Institute of Technology, serves as a business incubator providing access to technology, management, capital, and facilities for start-up, high-tech companies. It also works to attract research and development divisions and new technology venture groups of large national and international corporations into Georgia.

The ATDC manages the operation of the Technology Business Center, a $6.1-million, 83,000-square foot facility that offers office, laboratory, and industrial research space to both entrepreneurs and corporate R&D divisions. Tenants represent the spectrum of high-technology in Georgia: biotechnology, telecommunications, computers, software development, electronics, aerospace, and engineering.

In 1987, three firms nurtured by the incubator program appeared on Atlanta's "Fast Tech 50" list, a ranking of the top fifty technology firms located in and around the city. The ATDC's recruiting efforts have resulted in the establishment in Georgia of sixteen high-tech companies, which have invested $170 million and employed 2,250 people from 1982 to 1986.[52]

Incubators are not significant job generators in the short term. By definition, incubating firms are at preproduction stages of development, cash-poor, and lean-staffed. Universities creating incubators must have the resolve, the resources, and the long-term view to produce substantial impact on the incubator's local economy.[53] Strong support from the top down is vital. **Without the absolute commitment of the chief university official, chances for success are slim.** Turf battles and red tape can paralyze efforts at the earliest stages.

There are caveats to this strategy. Direct university equity investment in incubated firms could jeopardize a university's tax status.[54] According to some venture capitalists, university endowment investments in faculty-headed enterprises should be discouraged. Thorny conflicts could arise as a company develops. For example, the university may attempt to protect its investment in a new business by forcing out tenured faculty whom it perceives as weak business managers. A weeding-out process is inevitable, and universities must try to avoid "protecting" incubated firms from venture capitalists or other market forces that play important roles in realizing a product's commercial potential.

One characteristic that distinguished some of the most successful incubators is the leadership that the program's architect brings to his or her work. George Low at RPI, Wilfred Konneker at Ohio University, and Joseph Pettit at the Georgia Institute of Technology's Advanced Technology Development Center are three outstanding examples of directors who made their universities full partners in the local economic development process.

8. Conclusion

Education and business are in the process of establishing a solid foundation for collaboration. A number of states, numerous communities, and a host of educational institutions already have discovered the benefits of partnership to promote economic growth and stability. These pioneers have established a track record, significant evidences of success, and a variety of models. The task is well begun but remains unfinished. Each sector of American society needs to examine its programs and priorities to determine which economic goals and tasks can be met by business-education collaboration.

The stakes are very high. The United States is engaged in a fierce economic competition with other nations. It has already lost a substantial portion of industries that feature low-skill jobs to foreign competition. It is being challenged in high-technology industries by Japan and other nations. The foreign competition and the economic restructuring at home presents a notable challenge to American institutions.

Business should examine its needs with an eye to the way educational institutions could serve those needs. Education needs to explore the resources and services it can offer to business. Government needs to find ways to focus its resources to maximize the benefits of the collaboration. Other sectors of society—labor, foundations, community organizations, nonprofit groups—should determine how they can help foster this important initiative.

Education is an enormous and not fully tapped resource. In developing and using this resource, the basic educational mission of imparting basic skills and developing intellectual capacities should not be short-changed. However, the basic task of education also makes it the ideal institution for developing the further resources that business and industry need to grow, flourish, and compete.

Notes

CHAPTER 2

1. U.S. Department of Education, National Center for Education Statistics, *Digest of Education Statistics 1983-84* (Washington, D.C.: U.S. Government Printing Office, 1983), pp. 45, 83.

2. U.S. Department of Labor, Bureau of Labor Statistics, *Occupations in Demand*, 1984 edition (Washington, D.C.: U.S. Government Printing Office, 1984), passim.

3. Ronald E. Everett, "Economic Development: Policy Implications for Education," *Educational Digest* (March 1983), p. 45.

4. National Education Association, *Estimates of School Statistics 1984-85* (West Haven, Conn., 1985), p. 20.

5. "Cost of U.S. Schools Is Estimated at $240 Billion," *New York Times*, August 19, 1984, p. 25.

6. State of Florida, Division of Public Schools, *Profiles of Florida School Districts, 1982-83*, Vol. II (Tallahassee, Fla., 1984), pp. 182-83.

7. Robert Haveman, *Economics of the Public Sector* (Santa Barbara, Cal.: John Wiley and Sons, 1976), p. 154.

8. Southwest/West Central Educational Cooperative Service Units and Office of Planning and Policy Research, Minnesota Department of Education, *Minnesota Educational Cooperative Service Units 1984-85* (Marshall, Minn.: Minnesota ECSU Directors, December 1984), pp. 1-4.

9. Preservation League of New York State, "Solutions for Surplus Schools," Technical Series No. 6 (Albany, N.Y., 1978), p. 1.

10. National Education Association, *Estimates of School Statistics 1984-85*, p. 11.

11. Tennessee Valley Authority and Sizemore Floyd Architects and Energy Planners, *Energy Design Guidelines for Schools* (Chattanooga, Tenn.: Tennessee Valley Authority, March 1985), p. 58.

12. Tennessee Valley Authority and Sizemore Floyd Architects and Energy Planners, "Case Study of Fort Stewart Dependents' Elementary School" (Chattanooga, Tenn.: Tennessee Valley Authority, 1980), p. 2.

13. Jack A. Myers, "Using Energy to Save School Dollars," *The School Administrator* (June 1985), pp. 27-28.

14. Leonard Lund, "Factors in Corporate Locational Decisions," *The Conference Board Information Bulletin No. 66* (New York, N.Y.: The Conference Board, 1979), p. 6.

15. Joint Economic Committee of the U.S. Congress, "Central City Businesses—Plans and Problems," No. 37-4210 (Washington, D.C.: U.S. Government Printing Office, January 14, 1979), p. 6.

16. Judith N. Getzels, "Recycling Public Buildings," Planning Advisory Service Report No. 319 (Chicago, Ill.: American Society of Planning Officials, August 1976), p. 3.

17. Ibid., p. 5.

18. Ibid., p. 4

19. Downriver Community Conference, *Annual Report, FY 1983-84* (Southgate, Mich., October 11, 1984), passim.

20. Joan Butterworth Grady, "Expanding the Use of the School Building to Improve Community Support," *NASSP Bulletin*, vol. 69, no. 478 (February 1985), pp. 89-92.

21. Getzels, "Recycling Public Buildings," p. 7.

22. Ibid.

23. Barbara H. Moore, *The Entrepreneur in Local Government* (Washington, D.C.: International City Management Association, 1983), p. 141.

24. Telephone interview with Dr. Howard Koenig, superintendent of schools, East Meadow Public Schools, East Meadow, N.Y., September 1985.

25. Interview with Margaret Seufert-Bosc, instructional program specialist, Arlington County Refugee Education and Employment Program, Arlington, Va., April 15, 1985.

26. Grady, "Expanding the Use of the School Building to Improve Community Support," pp. 89-92.

27. Telephone interview with Elizabeth Brothereau, director of community education, St. Louis Schools, St. Louis Park, Minn., September 10, 1985.

28. Ibid.

29. Interview with Terry Turner, director, Technology for Literacy Center, St. Paul, Minn., April 3, 1985.

30. Interview with Frank Carricato, director, Career and Vocational Education, Montgomery County School System, Rockville, Md., September 5, 1985.

31. Stuart Rosenfeld, "Something Old, Something New: The Wedding of Rural Education and Rural Development," *Phi Delta Kappan*, vol. 65 (December 1983), pp. 270-73.

32. Don Colburn, "Beyond the School Nurse," *Washington Post*, March 20, 1985, p. 7.

33. Interview with John Urman, staff associate, Maternal and Infant Care Projects, St. Paul-Ramsey Medical Center, St. Paul, Minn., April 9, 1985.

34. Jay Mathews, "School Health-Clinic Movement is Spreading Across the Nation," *Washington Post*, December 7, 1985, p. 4.

35. Linus Wright, "Public Relations," *The School Administrator* (June 1985), p. 30.

36. "South Orange-Maplewood Ponders School Image," *Star Ledger*, August 27, 1985, p. 24.

37. Wright, "Public Relations," p. 31.

38. Public Education Fund, "The First Two Years, 1983-1985" (Pittsburgh, Penn., 1985), p. 20.

39. Nancy Scannell, "Yuppie Boom Balance Sought for Arlington," *Washington Post*, July 7, 1985, p. C9.

40. G. Donald Jud, "Public Schools and Urban Development," *Journal of the American Planning Association* (Winter 1985), p. 80.

41. Getzels, "Recycling Public Buildings," p. 4.

42. Quoted in William S. Woodside, "Business in Education: How Good a Grade," Speech presented to the New Business Initiatives in Education Conference, New York, N.Y., March 27, 1985.

43. Letter from Dr. Leslie Duffy, administrative assistant, School-Business Programs, Columbus Public Schools, Columbus, Ohio, March 25, 1985.

44. Interview with Dr. Leslie Duffy, Columbus, Ohio, March 4, 1985.

45. Ibid.

46. Ibid.

CHAPTER 3

1. Committee for Economic Development, *Investing in Our Children* (Washington, D.C., 1985).

2. National Commission on Excellence in Education, *A Nation at Risk* (Washington, D.C.: U.S. Government Printing Office, 1983).

3. National Alliance of Business, *Employment Policies: Looking to the Year 2000* (Washington, D.C., February 1986), p. i.

4. U.S. Department of Labor, Bureau of Labor Statistics, *Employment and Earnings, January 1986* (Washington, D.C.: U.S. Government Printing Office, 1986), Table 38.

5. U.S. Department of Education, National Center for Education Statistics, *The Condition of Education, 1984 Edition* (Washington, D.C.: U.S. Government Printing Office, 1984), p. 154.

6. National Commission on Secondary Education for Hispanics, "Make Something Happen": Hispanics and Urban High School Reform, 2 volumes (New York: Hispanic Policy Development Project, 1984), p. 23.

7. Denis P. Doyle and Terry W. Hartle, *Excellence in Education: The States Take Charge* (Washington, D.C.: American Enterprise Institute, 1985).

8. U.S. Department of Labor, Bureau of Labor Statistics, *Employment and Earnings*, various issues.

9. Robert Taggart, *A Fisherman's Guide: An Assessment of Training and Remediation Strategies* (Kalamazoo, Mich.: W.E. Upjohn Institute, 1981). For reporting purposes, the U.S. Department of Labor has merged the categories of pre-employment competency and work maturity.

10. In the 1970s, 17 percent of the new jobs went to youth. In 1979, teenagers held 3.66 million full-time jobs, but this number had fallen to 2.4 million by 1984. Of the 4.18 million new jobs created since the beginning of the late 1982 recovery, less than 102,000—or 2.4 percent—went to teenagers. Testimony of Gordon Berlin before the House Committee on Education and Labor.

11. Andrew Hahn and Robert Lerman, *What Works in Youth Employment Policy?* (Washington, D.C.: National Planning Association, 1985) p. x.

12. National Commission on Excellence in Education, *A Nation at Risk*, p. 8.

13. American Council of Life Insurance, *Functional Literacy and the Workplace: Proceedings of a National Invitation Conference* (Washington, D.C., May 6, 1983) p. 22.

14. Committee for Economic Development, *Investing in Our Children*.

15. American Council of Life Insurance, *Functional Literacy and the Workplace*, p. 23.

16. Bernard Lefkowitz, *Jobs for Youth: A Report from the Field* (New York, N.Y.: The Edna McConnell Clark Foundation, 1982) p. 13.

17. American Council of Life Insurance, *Functional Literacy and the Workplace*, p. 22.

18. Task Force on Education for Economic Growth, *Action for Excellence: A Comprehensive Plan to Improve Our Nation's Schools* (Washington, D.C.: Education Commission of the States, June 1983) p. 30.

19. Henry M. Levin, *The Educationally Disadvantaged: A National Crisis* (Philadelphia, Penn. Public/Private Ventures, July 1985), p. 17.

20. Gordon Berlin, "Towards a System of Youth Development: Replacing Work, Service, and Learning Deficits with Opportunities," Statement before the U.S. House of Representatives, Committee on Education and Labor, Subcommittee on Employment Opportunities (Washington, D.C., March 26, 1984) p. 15.

21. Hahn and Lerman, *What Works in Youth Employment Policy?* p. 62.

22. Interview with Ivan Charner, project director, Institute for Work and Learning, Washington, D.C., June 10, 1985.

23. Martha Woodall, "Class Helps Students Make Their Job Searches Successful," *Philadelphia Inquirer*, April 22, 1985, p. 18.

24. "Youth Unemployment: One Company's Response," testimony by Richard V. Lawson, Polaroid Corporation, to the Northeast-Midwest Congressional Coalition, New York City, June 1983.

25. Henrietta Schilit and Richard Lacey, *The Private Sector Youth Connection*, volume 1 (New York, N.Y.: Vocational Foundation, 1985), p. 22.

26. J. Anthony Kline, quoted in Douglass Lea, editor, *Youth Can: Reporting on the Youth Conservation and Service Corps Conference*, May 7-9, 1985, Chevy Chase, Md., p. 4., available from Human Environment Center.

27. Anthony Patrick Carnevale, *Jobs for the Nation: Challenges for a Society Based on Work* (Washington, D.C.: American Society for Training and Development, 1984), p. 38.

28. Ibid., p. 32.

29. American Council of Life Insurance, *Functional Literacy in the Workplace*, p. 23.

30. Interview with Peter Comart, JTPA program planner, Department of Employment and Training, Montpelier, Vt., September 4, 1985.

31. Schilit and Lacey, *The Private Sector Youth Connection*, p. 22.

CHAPTER 4

1. Training program brochure, Oakland, California, June 1983.

2. Ellen Cole, *The Experience of Illiteracy* (Yellow Springs, Ohio: Union Graduate School, 1976), p. 123.

3. Jonathon Kozol, "The Crippling Inheritance," *New York Times Book Review*, March 3, 1985, p. 27.

4. Ibid., p. 28.

5. Ibid.

6. Daniel Gottlieb, "High Technology Training Surges," *High Technology* (October 1983), p. 71.

7. James F. Henry, "Expectations of the Workplace: *Basic Skills in the U.S. Workforce,*" in *Functional Literacy and the Workplace* (Washington, D.C.: American Council of Life Insurance, 1984), p. 23.

8. Robert W. Feagles, "Some Responses to the Literacy Problem: The Travelers Insurance Company" in *Functional Literacy in the Workplace*, pp. 42-43.

9. Mary L. Tenopyr, "Realities of Adult Literacy in Work Settings," American Telephone and Telegraph Company unpublished report, undated, p. 16.

10. Ibid., p. 12.

11. Commission on Higher Education and the Adult Learner, "Adult Learners: Key to the Nation's Future" (Columbia, Md., November 1984), p. 5.

12. Tenopyr, "Realities of Adult Literacy in Work Settings," p. 17.

13. Task Force on Education for Economic Growth, *Action for Excellence*: *A Comprehensive Plan to Improve Our Nation's Schools* (Washington, D.C., Education Commission of the States, June 1983), p. 30.

14. Paul Simon, "Perspectives on Literacy: Illiteracy—The Cost to the Nation" in *Functional Literacy and the Workplace*, p. 15.

15. John E. Roueche, "Literacy Needs and Developments in American Community Colleges, " Austin, Tex., unpublished paper, undated, p. 4.

16. Commission on Higher Education and the Adult Learner, "Adult Learners," p. 4.

17. Telephone interview with Larry Simpson, director, Career Development Institute, Cleveland, Ohio, November 1984.

18. Robert Orr, quoted in the newsletter of the Business Council for Effective Literacy, vol. 2 (January 1985), p. 4.

CHAPTER 5

1. American Association of Community and Junior Colleges (AACJC), *Shoulders to the Wheel*: *Energy-Related College/Business Cooperative Agreements* (Washington, D.C., February 1982), p. 8.

2. Ellen Anderson, "Two Community Colleges in a Period of Expansion," *Connection*, volume 3, no. 1 (Spring 1985), p. 6.

3. American Association of Community and Junior Colleges, *In Search of Community College Partnerships* (Washington, D.C., 1985) pp. 5-6.

4. Interview with James McKenney, associate director, American Association of Community and Junior Colleges (AACJC), Washington, D.C., March 13, 1986.

5. Telephone interview with Richard Weeks, Quad City Development Group, Cedar Rapids, Iowa, March 14, 1986.

6. National Postsecondary Alliance, *Economic Development and the Community College* (Columbus, Ohio, June 1984), p. 8.

7. Ibid., p. 13.

8. Ibid., p. 14.

9. Telephone interview with Evelyn Fine, director, Mid-Florida Research and Business Center, Daytona Beach Community College, March 13, 1986.

10. Wisconsin Board of Vocational, Technical and Adult Education, *Annual Report of Economic Development Activities in Wisconsin's Vocational, Technical and Adult Education Districts* (Madison, Wis., October 1985), p. 25.

11. Telephone interview with Rose Ninni, director of continuing education, Mercer County Community College, Trenton, N.J., March 18, 1986.

12. Illinois Community College Board, *Fiscal Year 1985 Economic Development Grant Report* (Springfield, Ill., January 1986), p. 3.

13. Telephone interview with Evelyn Fine, March 13, 1986.

14. Illinois Community College Board, *Fiscal Year 1985 Economic Development Grant Report*, p. 5.

15. Ibid., p. 3.

16. *Nation's Business*, "Small Business Survival Courses," July 1982, p. 8391.

17. Illinois Community College Board, *Fiscal Year 1985 Economic Development Grant Report*, p. 12.

18. National Alliance of Business, *Bulletin* No. N4-386 (October 1982), p. 1.

19. Telephone interview with Carol Eliason, education analyst, National Governors' Association, Washington, D.C., April 1986.

20. Telephone interview with Rose Ninni, March 3, 1986.

21. James McKenney, "Community Colleges, 'Land Grant Colleges for an Information Age,' " address to Work in American, Inc., New York, N.Y., March 14, 1986.

22. Donald J. Donato, president, Niagara County Community College, "Rural Economic Development," Supplement to AACJC Letter No. 174, June 24, 1986.

23. National Small Business Training Network (NSBTN), "College Helps Boost Economic Growth in Rural Communities," *AACJC/NSBTN Newsletter* (Fall 1983), p. 1.

24. Telephone interview with Rose Ninni, March 18, 1986.

25. Illinois Community College Board, *Fiscal Year 1985 Economic Development Grant Report*, p. 5.

26. U.S. Congress, Office of Technology Assessment, *Technology, Innovation, and Regional Economic Development* OTA-STI-238 (Washington, D.C., July 1984), p. 5.

27. Ibid.

28. Ibid.

29. Interview with James McKenney, March 13, 1986.

30. American Association of Community and Junior Colleges, *Ohio's First Advanced Technology Center, AACJC Journal* (March 1985), pp. 6-8.

31. AmeriTrust Corporation, "Community Colleges Taking Major Role in Shaping Region's Economic Renewal," *MidAmerica Outlook*, Vol. VIII, No. 1 (Spring 1985), p. 2.

32. Ibid., p. 3.

33. Ibid., p. 4.

34. National Postsecondary Alliance, *Economic Development and the Community Colleges*, p. 28.

35. Ibid.

36. Fox Valley Technical Institute, "High Tech Business, Industry Economic Development Complex," undated brochure, Appleton, Wis.

37. Wisonsin Board of Vocational, Technical and Adult Education, *Annual Report of Economic Development Activities in Wisconsin's Vocational, Technical and Adult Education Districts*, p. 21.

38. Telephone interview with Ronald Schubert, economic development coordinator, North Central Technical Institute, Wausau, Wis., March 1986.

39. Telephone interview with Joe E. Sturdivant, director, Industry Service Division, Department of Community Colleges, Raleigh, N.C., April 18, 1986.

40. American Association of Community and Junior Colleges, *In Search of Community College Partnerships*, pp. 15-18.

41. National Postsecondary Alliance, *Economic Development and the Community College*, p. 26.

42. Telephone interview with Richard Weeks, March 4, 1986.

43. National Postsecondary Alliance, *Economic Development and the Community College*, p. 25.

44. Telephone interview with Joe E. Sturdivant, April 18, 1986.

45. Ibid.

46. Ibid.

47. National Postsecondary Alliance, *Economic Development and the Community College*, p. 26.

48. Ibid.

49. Ibid.

50. Iowa Development Commission, "Industries Quick to Sign Up for Iowa's New Training Program, *Digest* (November-December 1983), p. 7.

51. Bay State Skills Corporation, undated brochure, Boston, Mass.

52. McKenney, "Community Colleges, 'Land Grant Colleges for an Information Age.' "

53. Ibid.

54. Ibid.

55. Ibid.

56. Telephone interview with David Bedford, assistant commissioner, Tennessee Department of Labor, Nashville, Tenn., May 29, 1986.

57. National Alliance of Business, *Bulletin* No. N4-386 (August 1982)

CHAPTER 6

1. Commonwealth of Massachusetts, Division of Employment Security (DES), *Bulletin*, Series: DES Training Opportunities (Boston, Mass., July 1985), pp. 2-3.

2. State of California, Health and Welfare Agency, Employment Development Department, *California Training Benefits Program*: *Second Annual Report to the Legislature* (Sacramento, Cal., December 1982), p. 6.

3. Commonwealth of Massachusetts, Division of Employment Security, *Bulletin*, p. 2.

4. Ibid., p. 1.

5. State of California, Health and Welfare Agency, Employment Development Department, *California Shared Work Unemployment Insurance Evaluation* (Sacramento, Cal., December 1982), pp. ES-3 and 1.15.

6. Paula Duggan and Virginia Mayer, *The New American Unemployment*: *Appropriate Government Responses to Structural Dislocation* (Washington, D.C.: Northeast-Midwest Institute, 1984), p. 29.

7. Robert Friedman, *The Self-Employment Opportunity Act of 1985* (Washington, D.C.: Corporation for Enterprise Development), p. 2.

8. U.S. Department of Labor, *Alternative Uses of Unemployment Insurance*, Washington, D.C., 1986, p. 53.

9. Marc Bendick, Jr., and Mary Lou Egan, *Transfer Payment Diversion for Small Business Development: British and French Experience* (Washington, D.C.: Bendick and Egan Economic Consultants, Inc., 1986), p. 4.

10. Ibid.

11. Ibid., p. 16.

12. U.S. Department of Labor, *Alternative Uses of Unemployment Insurance*, p. 59.

13. Great Britain, Manpower Services Commission, unpublished data (Sheffield, England, 1986).

14. Bendick and Egan, *Transfer Payment Diversion for Small Business Development*: *British and French Experience*, p. 15.

15. Ibid., p. 4.

16. U.S. Department of Labor, *Alternative Uses of Unemployment Insurance*, p. 60.

17. Ibid.

18. Ibid.

19. Bendick and Egan, *Transfer Payment Diversion for Small Business Development*: *British and French Experience*, p. 15.

20. Manpower Services Commission, unpublished data.

21. Bendick and Egan, *Transfer Payment Diversion for Small Business Development*: *British and French Experience*, p. 16.

22. Ibid., p. 10.

23. Center for the Study of Social Policy, *Restructuring Unemployment Insurance* (Washington, D.C., 1985), p. 58.

CHAPTER 7

1. Donald R. Fowler, "University-Industry Research Relationships: The Research Agreement," *Journal of College and University Law*, vol. 9 (1982-83), p. 515.

2. Jeremy Main, "Business Goes to College for a Brain Gain," *Fortune*, March 16, 1987, p. 80.

3. Interview with Olin Sansbury, Chancellor, University of South Carolina, Spartanburg, S.C., October 17, 1984.

4. Interview with Louis R. Pondy, Head of the Department of Business Administration, University of Illinois, Urbana, Ill., October 1984.

5. Interview with Edward Hunter, Minnesota Wellspring, Minneapolis, Minn., October 1, 1984, and July 28, 1987.

6. Herman Koenig, et al., "Industry-University Cooperation in Michigan: Final Report to NSF," unpublished manuscript, 1986: interview with Louis F. Tornatzky, Director, Center for Social and Economic Issues, Industrial Technology Institute, Ann Arbor, Mich., July 30, 1987.

7. For different models of interaction, see Arnold B. Grobman and Janet S. Sanders, *Interactions Between Public Urban Universities and Their Cities* (Washington, D.C.: National Association of State Universities and Land-Grant Colleges, 1984), pp. 3-13.

8. Interviews with Malcolm Portera, Vice President for External Affairs, University of Alabama, Tuscaloosa, Ala., October 16, 1984, and Lewis Campbell, Manufacturing Manager, General Motors Corporation, Tuscaloosa, Ala., October 26, 1984.

9. Interview with Richard Lorentz, School of Business, University of Wisconsin at Eau Claire, October 30, 1984, and July 28, 1987.

10. Information supplied by Johnnie L. Albertson, Deputy Associate Administrator, Business Development Office, SBDC program, Washington, D.C., July 24, 1987.

11. Ibid.

12. Interview with Bernard Tennebaum, Assistant Director, Wharton Entrepreneurial Center, Philadelphia, Pa., October 17, 1984.

13. Interview with Charles M. Estes, Associate Division Chief, Industrial Extension Division, Georgia Institute of Technology, Atlanta, Ga., August 14, 1987.

14. Interview with Marvin Sparks, Industrial Extension Service, North Carolina State University, Raleigh, N.C., August 3, 1987.

15. Douglas Ross, Paul Courant, et al., *The Path to Prosperity: Findings and Recommendations of the Task Force for a Long-Term Economic Strategy for Michigan* (Lansing, Mich.: Governors' Cabinet Council on Jobs and Economic Development, November 1984), p. 83.

16. Interview with Dr. Marietta Baba, Provost, Wayne State University, Detroit, Mich., August 1987: information from Michigan Modernization Service, Lansing, Mich., August 1987.

17. General Accounting Office, *The Federal Role in Fostering University-Industry Cooperation*, PAD-83-22 (Washington, D.C., May 1983), pp. 45-46.

18. National Academy of Sciences, Government-University-Industry Research Roundtable and Academy Industry Program, *New Alliances and Partnerships in American Science and Engineering* (Washington, D.C.: National Academy Press, 1986), p. 1.

19. Eric Holtzman, "A Perspective on the Biological Sciences," p. 53; Howard Mettee, "Federal Research Founding," p. 107; Howard Ehrlich, "The University-Military Research Connection," pp. 117-124, all in National Education Association, *Thought & Action*, vol. 1, no. 1 (Fall 1984).

20. U.S. Congress, House of Representatives, Committee on Science, Research, and Technology, Hearings on the role and balance of federal support for research and development (100th Congress, 1st Session), June 18, 1987.

21. See General Accounting Office, *The Federal Role in Fostering University-Industry Cooperation*, pp. 27-32.

22. Fowler, "University-Industry Research Relationships: The Research Agreement," pp. 523-25. Also see Irwin Stark, "The University Goes to Market," in National Education Association, *Thought & Action*, vol. 1, no. 1 (Fall 1984), pp. 15-17.

23. Main, "Business Goes to College for a Brain Gain," p. 89.

24. National Academy of Sciences, *New Alliances and Partnerships in American Science and Engineering*, p. 1.

25. The Association of American Universities Clearinghouse on University-Industry Relations issued two reports before ceasing operation in 1986: *University Policies on Conflict of Interest and Delay of Publication* in 1985, and *Trends in Technology Transfer at Universities* in 1986. Also, interview with Casey Kiernen, program officer with the Government-University-Industry Research Roundtable, Washington, D.C., July 22, 1987.

26. National Science Board, *University-Industry Research Relationships—Selected Studies* (Washington, D.C.: National Science Foundation, 1982), pp. 24-25.

27. Information provided by the officers at Illinois Resource Network, Urbana, Ill., July 1987.

28. See Chapter 9, National Science Board, *University-Industry Research Relationships*, for a complete typology of research interactions.

29. Information provided by MIT's Industrial Liaison Program officials, Cambridge, Mass., July 17, 1987: and by Stanford University's Office of Foundations and Corporate Relations, Palo Alto, Calif., July 14, 1987.

30. Information provided by Marc Barteau, Faculty Member of Chemical Engineering, Center of Catalytic Science and Technology, and Patricia Kraft, University-Industry Liaison, Center for Composite Materials, University of Delaware, Newark, Del., July 22, 1987.

31. Christine Winter, "U. of I. supercomputer center lures $3 million Amoco deal," *Chicago Tribune*, August 4, 1987.

32. " Avoiding Conflict of Interest: The Wisconsin Example," in *Thought & Action*, pp. 134-35.

33. Information provided by Niels Reimers, Director, Office of Technology Licensing, Stanford University, Palo Alto, Calif., July 14, 1987.

34. Main, "Business Goes to College for a Brain Gain," p. 88.

35. National Governors' Association, *State Initiatives in Technological Innovation* (Washington, D.C., February 1983), pp. 48-49.

36. Louis G. Tornatzky, "State-Level Manufacturing Technology Initiatives: Design Issues," in Jerry Dermer, ed., *Competitiveness Through Technology* (Lexington, Mass.: Lexington Books, 1986), pp. 191-93.

37. National Science Foundation, *Evaluation of the NSF Industry/University Cooperative Research Centers: Descriptive and Correlative Findings* (Washington, D.C., June 1986); Louis G. Tornatzky, Trudy Samantha Solomon, and J.D. Eveland, "Industrial Participant Survey-Final Report," submitted to the Office of Technology Assessment, United States Congress (Ann Arbor, Mich., February 1987).

38. Tornatzky, "State-Level Manufacturing Technology Initiatives," p. 192.

39. Information provided by the officers at the Medical Biotechnology Center at SUNY (State University of New York), Stony Brook, July 1987.

40. Joe Allen, "The Technology Transfer Act Will Help Economic Development," *The Economic Developer* (June 1987).

41. See National Governors' Association, *State Initiatives in Technological Innovation*, pp. 22-32.

42. Information provided by John J. Sweeney, Deputy Assistant Administrator, Office of Innovation, Research and Technology, SBA, Washington, D.C., July 22, 1987.

43. Interview with Alex Schwarzkopf, Program Manager, IUCRC Program, National Science Foundation, Washington, D.C., July 21, 1987.

44. National Science Foundation, *University-Industry Cooperative Research Centers—A* Practice Manual (Washington, D.C., May 1982), pp. 1-9.

45. Interview with Alex Schwarzkopf.

46. Main, "Business Goes to College for a Brain Gain," p. 81.

47. Interview with Kenneth Smith, Dean, College of Business and Public Administration, Arizona State University, Tucson, Ariz., October 1984.

48. Charles Bartsch, *Reaching for Recovery: New Economic Initiative in Michigan* (Washington, D.C.: Northeast-Midwest Institute, 1985), p. 27.

49. National Governors' Association, *State Initiatives in Technological Innovation*, pp. 16-17; Southern Regional Education Board, *Universities and High Technology Development* (Atlanta, Ga., June 1983), p. 6.

50. Ben Franklin Partnership Board, *Ben Franklin Partnership Challenge Grant Program for Technological Innovation* (Harrisburg, Penn., May 1987).

51. Information provided by Dinah Adkinf, Associate Director, Innovation Center and Research Park, Athens, Ohio, July 14, 1987.

52. Information supplied by Dr. Richard Meyer, Advanced Technology Development Center, Georgia Institute of Technology, Athens, Ga., August, 1987.

53. David N. Allen, Judith E. Ginsberg, and Susan A. Meiburger, *Homegrown Entrepreneurship: Pennsylvania Small Business Incubators* (University Park, Penn.: Institute of Public Administration, Pennsylvania State University, August 1984), p. 28.

54. See Stark, "The University Goes to Market," pp. 19-20.

Selected Bibliography

Allen, David N., Judith E. Ginsberg, and Susan A. Meiburger. *Homegrown Entrepreneurship*: *Pennsylvania Small Business Incubators*. University Park, Penn.: Institute of Public Administration, The Pennsylvania State University, August 1984.

Allen, Joe. "The Technology Transfer Act Will Help Economic Development." *The Economic Developer*, June 1987.

American Association of Community and Junior Colleges (AACJC). *In Search of Community College Partnerships*. Washington, D.C., 1985.

_____. *Ohio's First Advanced Technology Center*. Washington, D.C., March 1985.

_____. *Putting America Back to Work*: *The Kellogg Leadership Initiative—A Report and Guidebook*. Washington, D.C.: March 1984.

_____. *Shoulders to the Wheel*: *Energy-Related College/Business Cooperative Agreements*. Washington, D.C., February 1982.

American Council of Life Insurance. *Functional Literacy and the Workplace, Proceedings of a National Invitational Conference*. Washington, D.C., May 6, 1983.

AmeriTrust Corporation, "Community Colleges Taking Major Role in Shaping Region's Economic Renewal." *MidAmerica Outlook*, vol. VIII, no. 1, Spring 1985.

Anderson, Ellen, "Two Community Colleges in a Period of Expansion." *Connection*, vol. 3, no. 1, Spring 1985.

Bartsch, Charles. *Reaching for Recovery*: *New Economic Initiative in Michigan*. Washington, D.C.: Northeast-Midwest Institute, 1985.

Bay State Skills Corporation, undated brochure, Boston, Mass.

Ben Franklin Partnership Board. *Ben Franklin Partnership Challenge Grant Program for Technological Innovation*. Harrisburg, Penn., May 1987.

Bendick, Marc, Jr., and Mary Lou Egan. *Transfer Payment Diversion for Small Business Development*: *British and French Experience*. Washington, D.C.: Bendick and Egan Economic Consultants, Inc., 1986.

Berlin, Gordon. "Towards a System of Youth Development: Replacing Work, Service, and Learning Deficits with Opportunities." Statement before the

U.S. House of Representatives, Committee on Education and Labor, Sub-committee on Employment Opportunities. Washington, D.C., March 26, 1984.

California, State of, Health and Welfare Agency, Employment Development Department. *California Shared Work Unemployment Insurance Evaluation.* Sacramento, Cal., December 1982.

Carnevale, Anthony Patrick. *Jobs for the Nation: Challenges for a Society Based on Work.* Washington, D.C.: American Society for Training and Development, 1984.

Center for the Study of Social Policy. *Restructuring Unemployment Insurance.* Washington, D.C., 1985.

Chall, Jeanne S. "New Views on Developing Basic Skills with Adults." Paper prepared for the National Conference on Adult Literacy. Washington, D.C., January 19-20, 1984.

Chamber of Commerce of the United States. *Business and Education: Partners for the Future.* Washington, D.C., December 1984.

Colburn, Don. "Beyond the School Nurse." *Washington Post,* March 20, 1985.

Cole, Ellen. *The Experience of Illiteracy.* Yellow Springs, Ohio: Union Graduate School, 1976.

Commission on Higher Education and the Adult Learner. "Adult Learners: Key to the Nation's Future." Columbia, Md.: November 1984.

Committee for Economic Development. *Investing in Our Children.* Washington, D.C., 1985.

Cornell University. Office of the Vice President for Research and Advanced Studies. *Examples of University-Industry (Government) Collaborations.* Ithaca, N.Y.: August 1, 1984.

"Cost of U.S. School Is Estimated at $240 Billion." *New York Times,* August 19, 1984.

Donato, Donald J. "Rural Economic Development." Supplement to AACJC Letter No. 174. Washington, D.C., June 24, 1986.

Downriver Community Conference. *Annual Report, FY 1983-84.* Southgate, Mich., October 11, 1984.

Doyle, Denis P., and Terry W. Hartle. *Excellence in Education: The States Take Charge.* Washington, D.C.: American Enterprise Institute, 1985.

Duggan, Paula, and Virginia Mayer. *The New American Unemployment: Appropriate Government Responses to Structural Dislocation.* Washington, D.C.: Northeast-Midwest Institute, 1984.

Eberle, Anne, and Sandra Robinson. *The Adult Illiterate Speaks Out: Personal Perspectives on Learning to Read and Write.* Washington, D.C: U.S. Department of Education, National Institute of Education, September 1980.

Employment Development Department. *California Training Benefits Program: Second Annual Report to the Legislature.* Sacramento, Cal., December 1982.

Everett, Ronald E. "Economic Development: Policy Implications for Education." *Educational Digest,* March 1983.

Fowler, David R. "University-Industry Research Relationships: The Research Agreement." *Journal of College and University Law,* vol. 9, 1982-83.

Fox Valley Technical Institute. "High Tech Business, Industry Economic Development Complex." Undated brochure. Appleton, Wis.

Friedman, Robert. *The Self-Employment Opportunity Act of 1985.* Washington, D.C.: Corporation for Enterprise Development, 1985.

General Accounting Office. *The Federal Role in Fostering University-Industry Cooperation,* PAD-83-22. Washington, D.C., May 1983.

Getzels, Judith N. "Recycling Public Buildings." Planning Advisory Service Report No. 319. Chicago, Ill. American Society of Planning Officials, August 1976.

Gottlieb, Daniel. "High Technology Training Surges." *High Technology,* October 1983.

Grady, Joan Butterworth. "Expanding the Use of the School Building To Improve Community Support." National Association of Secondary School Principals *NASSP* Bulletin, vol. 69, no. 478, February 1985.

Grant, W. Vance, and Thomas D. Snyder. *Digest of Education Statistics 1983-84.* Washington, D.C.: National Center for Education Statistics, 1984.

Great Britain, Manpower Services Commission. Unpublished data. Sheffield, England, 1986.

Grobman, Arnold B., and Janet S. Sanders. *Interactions Between Public Urban Universities and Their Cities.* Washington, D.C.: National Association of State Universities and Land-Grant Colleges, 1984.

Hahn, Andrew, and Robert Lerman. *What Works in Youth Employment Policy?* Washington, D.C: National Planning Association, 1985.

Haveman, Robert. *Economics of the Public Sector.* Santa Barbara, Cal.: John Wiley and Sons, 1976.

"How Business Is Joining the Fight Against Functional Illiteracy." *Business Week,* April 16, 1984.

Illinois Community College Board. *Fiscal Year 1985 Economic Development Grant Report.* Springfield, Ill., January 1986.

Iowa Development Commission. "Industries Quick to Sign Up for Iowa's New Training Program. *Digest,* November-December 1983.

Jud, G. Donald. "Public Schools and Urban Development." *Journal of the American Planning Association,* Winter 1985.

Koenig, Herman, et al. "Industry-University Cooperation in Michigan: Final Report to NSF." Unpublished manuscript, 1986.

Kozol, Jonathan. "The Crippling Inheritance." *New York Times Book Review,* March 3, 1985.

Lawson, Richard V. "Youth Unemployment: One Company's Response." Statement to the Northeast-Midwest Congressional Coalition, New York City, June 1983.

Lea, Douglass, ed. *Youth Can: Reporting on the Youth Conservation and Service Corps Conference,* May 7-9, 1985. Washington, D.C.: Human Environment Center, 1985.

Lefkowitz, Bernard. *Jobs for Youth: A Report from the Field.* New York, N.Y.: The Edna McConnell Clark Foundation, 1982.

Levin, Henry M. *The Educationally Disadvantaged*: *A National Crisis*. Philadelphia, Penn.: Public/Private Ventures, July 1985.

Lund, Leonard. "Factors in Corporate Locational Decisions." *The Conference Board Information Bulletin No. 66*. New York, N.Y.: The Conference Board, 1979.

Main, Jeremy. "Business Goes to College for a Brain Gain." *Fortune*, March 16, 1987.

Massachusetts, Commonwealth of. Division of Employment Security. *Bulletin*, Series: DES Training Opportunities. Boston, Mass., July 1985.

Mathews, Jay. "School Health-Clinic Movement Is Spreading Across the Nation." *Washington Post*, December 7, 1985.

Matthews, Jana B., and Rolf Norgaard. *Managing the Partnership Between Higher Education and Industry*. Boulder, Colo.: National Center for Higher Education Management Systems, 1984.

McKenney, James. "Community Colleges, 'Land Grant Colleges for an Information Age.' " Speech to Work in America, Inc. New York, N.Y.: March 14, 1986.

Moore, Barbara H. *The Entrepreneur in Local Government*. Washington, D.C.: International City Management Association, 1983.

Myers, Jack A. "Using Energy to Save School Dollars." *The School Administrator*, June 1985.

National Academy of Sciences. Government-University-Industry Research Roundtable and Academy Industry Program. *New Alliances and Partnerships in American Science and Engineering*. Washington, D.C.: National Academy Press, 1986.

National Advisory Council on Vocational Education. *A Nation at Work*: *Education and the Private Sector*. Washington, D.C.: National Alliance of Business, April 1984.

National Alliance of Business. *Bulletin*, No. N4-386. August 1982.

_____. *Bulletin*, No. N4-386. Washington, D.C.: October 1982.

_____. *Employment Policies*: *Looking to the Year 2000*. Washington, D.C., February 1986.

National Commission on Excellence in Education. *A Nation at Risk*. Washington, D.C.: U.S. Government Printing Office, 1983.

National Commission on Secondary Education for Hispanics. *"Make Something Happen"*: *Hispanics and Urban High School Reform*, 2 volumes. New York, N.Y.: Hispanic Policy Development Project, 1984.

National Education Association. *Estimates of School Statistics 1984-1985*. West Haven, Conn., 1985.

_____. "Research and the Academy." *Thought & Action*, vol. 1, no. 1, Fall 1984.

National Governors' Association. *State Initiatives in Technological Innovation*. Washington, D.C., February 1983.

National Postsecondary Alliance. *Economic Development and the Community College*. Columbus, Ohio, June 1984.

National Science Board. *Selected Studies in University-Industry Research Relationships*. Washington, D.C., 1982.

National Science Foundation (NSF). *Cooperative Science*: *A National Study of Univeristy and Industry Researchers, Assessment of the Industry/University Cooperative Research Projects Program*. Washington, D.C., June 1984.

_____. *Development of University-Industry Cooperative Research Centers*: Historical Profiles. NSF 84-29. Washington, D.C., November 1984.

_____. *Evaluation of the NSF Industry/University Cooperative Research Centers*: Descriptive and Correlative Findings. Washington, D.C., June 1986.

_____. *University-Industry Cooperative Research Centers—A Practical Manual*. Washington, D.C., May 1982.

National Small Business Training Network (NSBTN). "College Helps Boost Economic Growth in Rural Communities." *AACJC/NSBTN Newsletter,* Fall 1983.

Nation's Business. "Small Business Survival Courses." July 1982.

Northeast-Midwest Institute. *The Guide to Federal Policy and the Region.* Washington, D.C., 1986.

Park, Rosemarie J. "Overcoming the Illiteracy Barrier." *Training and Development Journal*, volume 38, number 3, March 1984.

_____. "Preventing Adult Illiteracy: The Social, Cultural and Educational Barriers to Improving Literacy in the School-Age Population." Paper commissioned by the Far West Regional Laboratory for the Government White Paper on Adult Illiteracy. Minneapolis, Minn., unpublished paper, May 25, 1984.

Preservation League of New York State. "Solutions for Surplus Schools." Technical Series No. 6. Albany, N.Y., 1978.

Public Education Fund. "The First Two Years, 1983-1985." Pittsburgh, Penn., 1985.

Quayle, Dan. Speech delivered to Congress. *Congressional Record*, volume 130, number 77, June 8, 1984.

Robertson, Gregg E., and David N. Allen. "From Kites to Computers: Pennsylvania's Ben Franklin Partnership." Harrisburg, Penn.: Pennsylvania MILRITE Council, 1984.

Rosenfeld, Stuart. "Something Old, Something New: The Wedding of Rural Education and Rural Development." *Phi Delta Kappan*, vol. 65, December 1983.

Ross, Douglas, Paul Courant, et al. *The Path to Prosperity*: Findings and Recommendations of the Task Force for a Long-Term Economic Strategy for Michigan. Lansing, Mich.: Governor's Cabinet Council on Jobs and Economic Development, November 1984.

Roueche, John E. "Literacy Needs and Developments in American Community Colleges." Austin, Tex., unpublished paper, undated.

Scannell, Nancy. "Yuppie Boom Balance Sought for Arlington." *Washington Post,* July 7, 1985.

Schilit, Henrietta, and Richard Lacey. *The Private Sector Youth Connection*, vol. 1. New York, N.Y.: Vocational Foundation Inc., 1985.

Sheridan, Richard G. *Ohio Tomorrow*: State Economic Growth and Development and the Role of Higher Education. Cleveland, Ohio: College of Urban Affairs, Cleveland State University, 1984.

Southern Regional Education Board. "Sites for High Technology Activities." Atlanta, Ga., June 1983.

"South Orange-Maplewood Ponders School Image." *Star Ledger*, August 27, 1985.

Southwest/West Central Educational Cooperative Service Units and Office of Planning and Policy Research, Minnesota Department of Education. *Minnesota Educational Cooperative Service Units 1984-85*. Marshall, Minn.: Minnesota ECSU Directors, December 1984.

State of Florida. Division of Public Schools. *Profiles of Florida School Districts,* *1982-83*, vol. 2. Tallahassee, Fla., 1984.

Taggart, Robert. *A Fisherman's Guide*: *An Assessment of Training and Remediation Strategies.* Kalamazoo, Mich.: W.E. Upjohn Institute, 1981.

Task Force on Education for Economic Growth. *Action for Excellence*: *A Comprehensive Plan to Improve Our Nation's Schools.* Washington, D.C.: Education Commission of the States, June 1983.

Tennessee Valley Authority and Sizemore Floyd Architects and Energy Planners. "Case Study of Fort Stewart Dependents' Elementary School." Chattanooga, Tenn., Tennessee Valley Authority, 1980.

_____. *Energy Design Guidelines for Schools.* Chattanooga, Tenn.: Tennessee Valley Authority, March 1985.

Tenopyr, Mary L. "Realities of Adult Literacy in Work Settings." American Telephone and Telegraph Company unpublished paper, undated.

Tornatzky, Louis G. "State-Level Manufacturing Initiatives: Design Issues," in Jerry Dermer, ed. *Competitiveness Through Technology.* Lexington, Mass., Lexington Books, 1986.

Tornatzky, Louis G., Trudy Samantha Solomon, and J.D. Eveland. "Industrial Participant Survey-Final Report." Ann Arbor, Mich., February 1987.

U.S. Congress, House of Representatives, Committee on Science, Research, and Technology. Hearings on the role and balance of federal support for research and development (100th Congress, 1st Session) June 18, 1987.

U.S. Congress, Joint Economic Committee. "Central City Businesses—Plans and Problems." No. 37-4210. Washington, D.C.: U.S. Government Printing Office, January 14, 1979.

U.S. Congress, Office of Technology Assessment. *Technology, Innovation and Regional Economic Development.* OTA-STI-238. Washington, D.C., July 1984.

U.S. Department of Education, National Center for Education Statistics. *Digest of Education Statistics 1983-84.* Washington, D.C.: U.S. Goverment Printing Office, 1983.

_____. *The Condition of Education,* 1984 edition. Washington, D.C.: U.S. Government Printing Office, 1984.

U.S. Department of Labor, Bureau of Labor Statistics. *Displaced Workers, 1979-83.* Washington, D.C., July 1985.

_____. *Employment and Earnings,* January 1986. Washington, D.C.: U.S. Government Printing Office, 1986.

_____. *Occupations in Demand*, 1984 edition. Washington, D.C.: U.S. Government Printing Office, 1984.

U.S. Department of Labor, Employment and Training Administration. *Alternative Uses of Unemployment Insurance.* Washington, D.C., 1986.

"Wanted: Workers for the U.S. Job Machine." *Coopers and Lybrand Executive Alert,* September 1984.

Winter, Christine. "U. of I. supercomputer center lures $3 million Amoco deal." *Chicago Tribune*, August 4, 1987.

Wisconsin Board of Vocational, Technical and Adult Education. *Annual Report of Economic Development Activities in Wisconsin's Vocational, Technical and Adult Education Districts*. Madison, Wis., October 1985.

Woodhall, Martha. "Class Helps Students Make Their Job Searches Successful." *Philadelphia Inquirer*, April 22, 1985.

Wright, Linus. "Public Relations." *The School Administrator*, June 1985.

Index

About the Contributors

CHARLES W. BARTSCH is a senior policy analyst at the Northeast-Midwest Institute, specializing in economic development and education issues. He also advises the Institute's private-sector Leadership Council Task Force on Education and Economic Development, and directs a six-city technical assistance project on the same subject. Bartsch is the author of *Reaching for Recovery: New Economic Initiative in Michigan* and executive editor of *Guide to State and Federal Resources for Economic Development*.

CANDICE BRISSON is a staff associate for research and programs with the Southern Growth Policies Board. She was an educational policy analyst at the Northeast-Midwest Institute.

PAULA DUGGAN is a senior policy analyst at the Northeast-Midwest Institute, where she specializes in employment and training policy. She is the author of *The New American Unemployment* and *Schools and Jobs: A Guide for State Legislators*. Previously, she was a senior staff associate at the National Governors' Association, and a legislative analyst for the Massachusetts Department of Manpower Development. Ms. Duggan is also a former lecturer in political science at Suffolk University and the University of Massachusetts.

PETER H. DOYLE was a senior policy analyst at the Northeast-Midwest Institute, where the first several monographs in this series were published. He specialized in housing and economic development policy issues. Doyle now practices communications law at Dow, Lohnes and Albertson in Washington, D.C.

JACQUELINE MAZZA is a legislative analyst in economics and foreign affairs with the Democratic Study Group. She was an international economist with the Institute for International Economics, and a former staff member of the Northeast-Midwest Institute.

IAN McNETT is an independent, Washington-based writer and editor, who specializes in education and public policy. He has performed editorial work for such national efforts as the Commission of Excellence in Education and the President's Commission on Industrial Competitiveness. He has also written for *Congressional Quarterly, The Chronicle of Higher Education,* and *Change* magazine.

Artificial Intelligence
for Computer Games

Artificial Intelligence for Computer Games

An Introduction

John David Funge

A K Peters

Wellesley, Massachusetts

Editorial, Sales, and Customer Service Office

A K Peters, Ltd.
888 Worcester Street, Suite 230
Wellesey, MA 02482
www.akpeters.com

Library of Congress Cataloging-in-Publication Data

Funge, John David, 1968-
  Artificial intelligence for computer games : an introduction / John Funge.
    p. cm.
  Includes bibliographical references and index.
  ISBN 1-56881-208-6
  1. Computer games--Programming. 2. Artificial intelligence. I. Title.

  QA76.76.C672F88 2004
  794.8'1526--dc22

                                    2004048651

'Fluffy the Orc' model and textures by Joe Maruschak of BraveTree Productions
(joe@bravetree.com)

Torque Shader Engine rendering code was written by Brian Ramage
of GarageGames (bramage@garagegames.com)

Printed in Canada
08 07 06 05 04   10 9 8 7 6 5 4 3 2 1

Dedicated to David and Patricia.

Contents

Listings

Preface

This is the second book I have written about Artificial Intelligence (AI) and computer games. My first book was closely based on my PhD thesis and although it was therefore quite specialized it was well received. I was pleased by the compliments I received from some well-known game developers who told me they had enjoyed reading it and found it helpful. This new book is more accessible than the last one and should appeal to an even wider audience. I believe it should be useful to anyone looking to become a game AI programmer, as well as those already working in the field.

I also hope that this book will spark new interest among academics in AI research for computer games. There is a tendency to assume that games are just another application area for AI and as such they deserve no special attention. While it is true that many general purpose AI algorithms are applicable to games, there is also a wealth of opportunity for more specialized study.

There are already several interesting books available that are either solely or partially dedicated to AI and games. Those other books tend to take the form of compendiums of articles by different authors about a wide range of AI-related topics. Instead of trying to compete, in this book I take a complementary approach that presents a more unified overview of AI in games. In particular, the unifying theme of this book is of a Non-Player Character (NPC) and the capabilities that can be built into it.

There are also an enormous number of books on the subject of AI in general. The wonderful thing about the existence of all these books is that

it provides such a firm foundation to build upon. There is no need for subsequent books on AI (like this one) to rehash all the same ideas and algorithms. Instead, this book is free to concentrate solely on the application of AI to games and to give references for introductory material that is readily available elsewhere. At the other end of the spectrum, this book also provides a jumping-off point to many advanced topics in AI that are relevant to games.

In this day and age there are also many game- and AI-related resources online that provide lots of detailed information about algorithms and techniques. This book does, of course, contain a comprehensive bibliography that includes some web sites, but a traditional bibliography is limited and soon becomes out of date. There is therefore a companion web site for this book at www.ai4games.org that you will be referred to throughout the text for additional resources and information.

Since my first book, I have been working in the games industry developing AI technology. The experience has given me a much clearer understanding of game AI, and a perspective that I think many academics lack. For example, many academics will make efficiency arguments for why their AI is good for games. But AI programming is not usually such a significant part of the cost of a game that, from a business point of view, it would justify the risk of using a new technique. What the business people in the games industry do care about, however, is new effects that can help differentiate their game from the competition.

Typically new effects have come from the graphics industry, for example, the move to three-dimensions, texture maps, and lately, real-time procedural shading languages. That is why new games are constantly pushing the envelope for graphics while they often languish in the past with their AI. Until AI has some new exciting effects to offer the mainstream game player, this will continue to be the case.

Sooner or later graphics is going to run out of steam as a driving force behind games. Already the law of diminishing returns makes it hard for the casual gamer to tell the difference between this year and last year's graphics. AI has the potential to become the new driving force behind computer game innovation. With the right technology, whole exciting new game genres could be developed. I hope this book will help you think about new AI effects for your games that will generate enthusiasm for AI among game designers and players.

Acknowledgments

I am currently working at a startup which I cofounded that develops AI technology for the entertainment industry. It is one of my hopes that this book, by promoting a common framework and terminology, will make it easier for game developers to interact with AI middleware companies. At the time of writing, we are still being secretive about the technology we have developed so I have been careful not to include any confidential information in the writing of this book. Nevertheless many of my ideas about the general topic of game AI have been shaped and heavily influenced by my experiences at work and by the people with whom I work. I am therefore indebted to many of my current and former colleagues: Brian Cabral, Wolff Dobson, Nigel Duffy, Michael McNally, Ron Musick, Stuart Reynolds, Xiaoyuan Tu (cofounder), Ian Wright, and Wei Yen (CEO and cofounder).

Wei Yen is a remarkable person to whom I am grateful for giving me the opportunity to work for him in such an educational and interesting environment. Ian, Michael, and Wolff have all developed successful commercial games and their experience has been invaluable to me in understanding how AI is applied in the real world of game programming. Ian also proofread the book and provided numerous suggestions on style and content throughout the writing process that have significantly improved the book. Michael has taught me a great deal about programming and about good ways to organize a game's architecture. Ian and Brian have also improved my knowledge of programming. Nigel and Ron have taught me an enormous amount about AI, and Stuart has taught me a lot about reinforcement learning in particular. Xiaoyuan has been at the heart of developing our core technology and has helped me develop a deeper understanding of AI. Dale Schuurmans and Stuart Russell also deserve special mention for it was they who helped provide me with a more modern perspective on AI. Thanks also to Benjamin Funge who helped out with some proofreading.

I have also benefited from numerous conversations with people in the games industry over the years, too many to list, but I am thankful to them too. While much of the credit for the ideas in this book therefore lies with other people, the responsibility for any errors or omissions is obviously my own.

Xiaoyuan is my colleague and also my wife. At home, I am grateful for her love, kindness, and support. On the subject of home, I would also like to express my appreciation to Pung Pung and Willow for their companionship.

Finally, I would like to thank Alice Peters and all the staff at A K Peters for their support, understanding, and encouragement throughout the writing of this book. Special thanks to Jonathan Peters and the people at Garage Games for contributing their time and artwork to produce such a wonderful front cover.

John Funge
Sunnyvale, CA
USA

Chapter 1

Introduction

Computer games, or perhaps more accurately, video games, began with the invention of "Tennis for Two" in 1958. It was not until the 1970s that Atari introduced a wider audience to computer games with the successful console game Pong. Since then computer games have become a multibillion-dollar industry with countless titles published every year. Despite the large number of individual game titles, there is a relatively small set of different game genres. The exact list of genres is debatable, and just like with movies, people argue about which genre(s) a particular game belongs to. This book's companion web site (**www.ai4games.org**) has links to sites that provide a comprehensive list of genres and example games from each. There are also additional links to interesting information on the history and status of computer games.

1.1 Computer Game Characters

Lara Croft, Mario, and Pac-Man are all well-known computer game characters. Each of them is an example of a *player character*. A player character is a character whose behavior is controlled by a human player through some input device like a joystick. For example, the player presses the A button and the character jumps, presses the B button and it punches, pushes up on the thumb pad and it walks forward, and so on. Player characters often play the hero in a game and *Non-Player Characters* (NPCs) play the other roles such as villains, side-kicks, and cannon-fodder. Wario (Mario's

evil brother), Blinky, Pinky, Inky, and Clyde (the four ghosts in Pac-Man)
are some rare examples of characters who originally became famous as
NPCs.

The distinction between player characters and NPCs is not always
straightforward. For example, some games allow the player to control
different characters at different times. In such cases, which characters are
player characters and which are NPCs is constantly changing. In games
where the player controls a party of characters (a team or squad) the switch
between player character and NPC can be so fluid that the distinction becomes blurred. That is, the NPCs behave autonomously until the player
intercedes to give them a direct order. They then carry out the order, after
which they revert to behaving autonomously.

Within a game, NPCs also take on the role of camera person, lighting
technician, commentator, and even director. Of course, there is (usually)
no little person rendered into the scene who is holding a camera, moving
lights around, providing commentary, or directing the other NPCs. There
is, however, a piece of code that is controlling the camera, lighting, commentary, direction, etc. It is convenient to think of these pieces of code
as NPCs as they share many properties with their on-screen counterparts.
Most of techniques in this book therefore apply equally well to NPCs behind the camera as to those in front.

1.2   Behavior

Every character in a game has at least one *controller* associated with it and
controllers can be shared between different characters. A controller acts as
the character's brain, its inputs are information about the state of the game
world, and the outputs are the action choices that affect the game world
and produce the associated NPC's behavior.[1]

In other publications, the term "controller" is sometimes used to refer
to the player's input device. In this book, "controller" is used exclusively
in the sense of the character's brain. The term "joystick" is used for the
player's input device.

---

[1]When it is obvious from the context, the term "NPC's associated controller" is often
just replaced with "NPC". For example, "the NPC chooses to jump" is understood to mean
"the NPC's associated controller chooses to jump".

For player characters the controller consists of a mechanism for interpreting the player's various joystick presses. Of course, the human player's brain is also technically part of the player character's controller because that is where decisions about how to behave originate.

For NPCs the controller can take many forms and have various capabilities. The possible forms and capabilities of an NPC's controller is specifically what this book is all about.

Most players do not care what underlying mechanism is being used to create the appearance, movement, or behavior of the NPCs. The player is simply concerned about the end result. For behavior that means whether the NPCs are behaving "rationally". Rationality has to be defined with respect to what the NPC is trying to achieve because, from a wider perspective, its goals can be irrational. For example, it is not really rational for an NPC to run out from its hiding place and attack the player character who is usually much stronger and has just wiped out all of the NPC's comrades.

An NPC's ultimate goal is to be entertaining, but that goal is usually implicit. Instead, the NPC's controller will have been given lower-level tasks, such as trying to stop the player character at all costs. The tasks are those that the game designer hopes will lead to exciting game play.

What specifically counts as rational depends on the game, the difficulty level the game is being played at, the context within the game, and even the the player's expectations. Nevertheless, there are many common and easily-recognized examples of irrational behavior caused by bugs in a controller, for example, two NPCs continuously butting heads as they both try and go up a ladder at the same time or a battalion of NPCs charging across a battlefield in single file so that they can be easily mowed down by a single machine gunner.

Compared to the capabilities of humans, there are presently a huge number of technical limitations on an NPC's possible capabilities. But since it is only the behavior that counts, the game developer has a great deal of flexibility in choosing which of the possible capabilities a controller, and by extension the associated NPC, should have. Often two similar looking behaviors can be created in completely different ways. For example, consider the problem of getting an NPC to figure out how to get from one location to another. This is called *path planning*. One way to implement path planning is to use a controller that includes a map and a

path planning algorithm. This approach is described in detail in Chapter 6. Another approach is to simply have someone (often a level designer) go through and annotate the game world with "signposts". The signposts are not visible to the human player, but the NPC can use them. Whenever an NPC wants to get somewhere its underlying controller simply follows the corresponding signposts. From the player's perspective the behavior of the NPC can seem more or less identical in both cases.

Adding signposts to a map can (depending on the size and complexity of the map) be laborious, time-consuming, and error-prone. Moreover, if the map ever changes, or there are new maps, some or all of the map annotation must be re-generated. In contrast, the path planning approach is general across different maps. It should even work on maps created by the player, for example, a "mod". Nevertheless, the signpost approach is appealing in its simplicity and the high degree of fine-grained control it affords over behavior. It is also less demanding of hardware requirements and programming skills. Both methods are therefore legitimate and each has relative pros and cons that are a microcosm of the often lively debate about which capabilities an NPC really needs.

In general, the answer to the question about what capabilities an NPC's controller must, should, or could have will be determined on a case by case basis. The decision will depend on the capabilities of the underlying hardware, availability of software, level of expertise, familiarity with techniques, and personal preferences.

1.3   Overview

Figure 1.1 is a system architecture diagram for a typical game that shows the major components and their interactions. The architecture is just one possible software architecture. Alternatives will, however, all share roughly the same components. Briefly, the role of each component is:

Game-state. The game-state represents the current state of the world. It knows about all the objects in the world and provides access to them so that they can be queried by all the other components for information about their current state.

Simulator. The simulator encodes the rules of how the game-state changes, i.e. the game's "physics". Together with a set of animations it is the

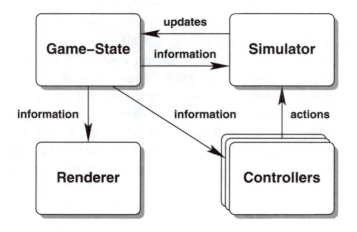

Figure 1.1. Architecture overview.

simulator that is therefore responsible for generating a character's movement in response to the actions chosen by the associated controller.

Renderer. Together with a game's geometry and texture maps, the renderer is responsible for rendering a depiction of the game-state. The output usually consists of images and sounds.

Controllers. Each character in the game has at least one controller associated with it. The controller is responsible for selecting actions. For player characters the controller interprets joystick presses. For NPCs the controller is the AI and low-level control that make up the character's brain.

To be able to influence the game world through its action choices an NPC needs to be embodied in the game. Chapter 2 therefore describes how the the game-state, the simulator, and the controllers work together to enable an NPC to act within the game world.

Just as fundamental as the capability to act in the game, is the ability for an NPC to perceive its world. Otherwise the associated controller cannot know which action is appropriate, or what effect its actions have, and the character is just stumbling around in the dark. For the player character, for which the human is an integral part of the controller, the renderer

provides the necessary feedback on what is happening in the game world. NPCs can instead just query the game-state directly to find out the information they need. It is easier, however, to write controllers if the unimportant details (from an AI perspective) can be abstracted away. A more abstract representation emphasizes the crucial similarities between game-states and allows controllers to be written in a more general fashion. Chapter 3 therefore describes some common and useful transformations of information from the game-state, and explains how to limit access to the game-state so an NPC perceives its world in a way that matches the intuitive expectations of the human player more closely.

Once an NPC can perceive its world, it needs to be able to make decisions about how to act. These decisions are contingent on the information it receives. Therefore, Chapter 4 describes how to write *reactive controllers* that can pick actions in reaction to the current perceived state of the game world.

Reactive controllers can be used to create a wide range of useful behavior. But without the ability to remember, controllers can end up going around in circles (literally and figuratively) as they are unable to realize when they have been in a similar situation before. Chapter 5 therefore describes how to add internal state to an NPC's controller that can be used to remember the past. NPCs thus have the capability to make decisions that depend not only on what is currently occurring, but on what occured before. An NPC with a controller that has the capability to remember (an arbitrary amount of) the past and act accordingly can be programmed to perform any computable behavior.[2]

Effective and powerful controllers can be written to achieve their goals by blindly following a set of preprogrammed rules. However, Chapter 6 explains that if a controller is given explicit goals, it can instead automatically search for actions that achieve these goals. To do so, a controller needs access to a model of its world that it can use to predict the outcome of action sequences before it executes them. The model of its world can be provided by giving the controller access to the game simulator. However, it is often sufficient, and faster, just to give a controller an approximate model of its world. Although searching is a powerful technique, it is also one that can consume a lot of CPU and memory resources.

---

[2]This is because it is Turing complete. That is, it is theoretically equivalent to a Turing machine, which is a mathematical model of what it means for something to be computable.

Beyond the simple capability to remember past events, an NPC's controller can also be given the capability to learn from past events. The idea of learning something implies some ability to generalize from past experience to new unseen cases. This is different from simply remembering what happened in the past and regurgitating it. There are many possible ways learning can be used inside controllers; Chapter 7 focuses on how a controller can be automatically learned by trial and error.

By the end of the book you should be able to recognize which techniques might have been used to generate the behavior you see in the computer games you play. You will also be able to decide which capabilities are appropriate for the NPCs in your game. Together with the references, and online resources available from this book's companion web site, you should also be able to implement controllers for NPCs with the capabilities you choose.

There are many other capabilities, not covered in this book, that an NPC's controller could be given. For example, if an NPC had access to a camera that looked out upon a game player's world it could be given the capability to see. With a microphone, the capability to understand and generate speech also becomes important. Cameras and microphones are an as yet small but growing part of computer games (see [Mar01, LDG03]).

1.4 Artificial Intelligence

Many of the potential capabilities of an NPC's controller are made possible thanks to the academic field of AI. AI began as a research field in the 1940s. There were some early successes and this led to great optimism about how quickly computers could become as intelligent as humans. Researchers, however, soon realized that many AI problems were much harder than they first appeared. In the 1980s expert systems emerged as a knowledge based approach to solving AI problems. The idea behind an expert system is that the knowledge of human experts is encoded into a Knowledge Base (KB). The KB can then be used to answer questions and solve problems.

Expert systems have had many well-known successes both in the academic and commercial world. They do, however, suffer from the serious drawback of having to create a KB that can cover all possible cases in advance. The problem with creating a KB is that the amount of knowledge

required to solve even simple problems can be enormous. Creating the KB can therefore be time-consuming, expensive, and error-prone. This has led to the criticism that expert systems are brittle and only applicable to so-called "toy problems".

To reduce the size of the required KB, logical reasoning (and the closely related subject of planning) have been widely studied throughout the history of AI. The idea is that logical consequences of the KB can be inferred rather than represented explicitly. For example, a KB might contain "All plumbers have mustaches" and that "Mario is a plumber", but not explicitly "Mario has a mustache". Instead, a reasoning engine can use logical deduction to answer "yes" to the question: "Does Mario have a mustache?" There are two criticisms that are commonly leveled at logical reasoning: first, for propositional logic there are problems that require an exponential amount of time to solve and for first-order logic there are problems that are uncomputable; and second, that the real world contains much uncertainty but logical inference is better suited to dealing with precise mathematical concepts.

A breakthrough in expert systems that addresses the uncertainty present in the real world has been the development of so called *graphical models*. Bayes nets and Hidden Markov Models (HMMs) are two well-known examples of graphical models. Efficient algorithms for probabilistic reasoning have been developed for graphical models and they have been successfully applied to many real-world problems like medical diagnosis and spam filtering. They are a manifestation of an important and well-established trend in modern AI research to use mathematical probability as the correct way to handle uncertainty.

When many labeled examples of a problem exist (or can be generated), an alternative to manually creating a KB is to create one automatically. Automatically acquiring knowledge is the domain of machine learning. Machine learning has a long tradition in AI, but many of the early approaches lacked firm theoretical underpinnings and neglected the importance of real-world empirical results. In contrast, a great anecdote that demonstrates the promise of modern statistical machine learning to automatically create useful KBs is provided by the FlipDog™ story. FlipDog was founded in 2000 as a spin-off from WhizBang! Labs™. FlipDog used machine learning techniques to allow their webbot to learn to recognize job postings on the Internet. The webbot then trawled the Web and in less

than a year acquired over 600,000 jobs from more than 50,000 employers in more than 3,500 locations. FlipDog was set to quickly eclipse the older and more established Monster.com™ as the market leader. Monster.com had been relying on more conventional means to build a KB of job postings. Monster.com quickly realized that FlipDog represented the future and acquired the company for an undisclosed sum.

The standard reference on AI is [RN02]; it has clear, incisive, and in-depth coverage on most of the important areas of AI. What that book does not cover, and what this book therefore focuses on, is the application of AI to games. Nevertheless, it is inevitable that this book must frequently venture into AI topics not specific to games. On those occasions (unless there is something specific to add) this book provides references, but does not attempt to go over the same material.

1.5 Game AI

The term "game AI" is sometimes used to distinguish AI used in computer games from academic AI. In particular, AI used in computer games does not have to be general purpose. The goal is not (necessarily) to advance human understanding by writing a technical paper. Often a solution is acceptable as long as a character's behavior appears to be plausible over some narrow range of situations. There are, however, clear economic advantages to generating solutions that are as general as possible.

The ease with which some problems could be solved in unconventional ways led to some initial misplaced optimism about the prospects of AI in games. For example, some people were led to make bold claims that AI techniques derived from games would soon surpass the capabilities of academic AI. It is interesting to note that in the early days of AI research similar enthusiasm was expressed by academics who were buoyed by their early successes on toy problems.

Aside from the degree of required generality, another disconnect between game AI and academic AI is the scope of what is considered AI. In particular, academic AI often has a different focus than game AI and there is an adage that once an AI problem is solved, it is no longer considered AI. Game AI is often used to refer to any kind of control problem in a game, some of which are more traditionally in the domain of control theory. For

example, trying to figure out the joint angles so that a character's hand moves to a specified point is sometimes thought to be a game AI problem. Outside of games it would be recognized as an inverse kinematics problem that has been well studied in robotics and control theory. This book emphasizes the problem of generating higher-level behavior, more in line with the traditional academic use of the term AI. There are numerous books on control theory that the interested reader can consult. A classic reference is [DB04]. There are also many papers on the application of control theory and AI techniques to low-level control problems in game-like worlds; see [GT95, HP97, LvdPF00, FvdPT01, LCR03].

The typical approach to creating high-level behavior in games can be largely characterized as the brute force approach of creating a controller that contains lots of knowledge about how to behave. This corresponds to building a controller that is an expert system; a game-specific expert system for deciding what the NPC should do next. As an expert system, the controller will suffer from all the scalability problems that plague expert systems in general, which often manifests itself as brittle AI. In particular, the enormous task of trying to anticipate all the situations that might arise inevitably means that some (possibly many) possibilities get overlooked. When one of the unanticipated situations does arise the NPC behaves inappropriately and can end up looking stupid.

If an AI bug is noticed in time it can be fixed by adding a new bit of knowledge to tell the controller what to do in the previously unanticipated situation. This gets to the heart of why expert systems can be problematic. The real world is so complicated that this process of adding new knowledge is potentially neverending. Only in toy problems is there any reasonable hope of finishing the task. That is why the expert system approach can be, and has been, successful in games. Many game worlds are, by definition, toy problems. If the game world is simple enough an expert system might therefore be appropriate. Games also have the advantage that the AI does not have to be perfect. The game can probably ship when the process of adding more knowledge offers diminishing returns. If there are still a few infrequent AI bugs then, provided they are not too glaring and it does not affect the overall enjoyment of the game, no one will mind. The same cannot be said of an AI medical diagnosis program!

Nevertheless, as game worlds become ever more sophisticated and less toy-like, the expert system approach will struggle to keep pace. To date,

machine learning has only been used sporadically in computer games. But as games become more complex, machine learning techniques will enable the AI to scale up and will inevitably become more commonplace.

In contrast to learning, search is often used in existing computer games. The special case of searching for a path to a given location (i.e., path planning) is particularly widespread, but as explained in Chapter 6, the same basic technology can also be employed to achieve a wide range of behaviors.

There are (usually) no inherently noisy sensors in a game world, but there are other sources of uncertainty. For example, uncertainty can be artificially added to increase realism (see Section 3.4 in Chapter 3) and there is inherent uncertainty about future states of the game world (see Section 3.5 in Chapter 3). Therefore some of the techniques, like graphical models, that were developed to deal with real-world uncertainty are potentially applicable to computer games. In particular, graphical models could be used to create expert systems that are less brittle and better able to handle uncertainty. Graphical models are also an important representation used for some learning algorithms. However, if the graphical model is only effectively removing uncertainty artificially added to increase realism, then there is clearly no net benefit.

There are some existing books about AI for games; see [Fun99, Cha03]. There are also a number of compendiums of articles by various authors that (among other subjects) cover a wide range of game AI-related topics: [DeL00, DeL01, TD02, Kir04, Rab02, Rab03a]. There is even a web site that attempts to catalog every game AI-related article [Rab03b]. Whenever there is a potential overlap, and there is nothing to add, this book avoids repeating information found in these other sources by providing references.

1.5.1 Game Design

The underlying technology is only one factor that influences the quality of the AI in a game; in some games the AI task is simply harder. Games can, however, sometimes be designed or modified to make life easier for the AI component. For example, the camera can be brought closer to the player character so that fewer NPCs are on screen at any one time.

Often in games a relatively simple controller can still yield complex behavior. For example, Section 4.2 in Chapter 4 explains how if each NPC follows just a few simple rules it can give rise to sophisticated flocking

behavior among a group of NPCs. This phenomenon of a few local rules giving rise to interesting global behavior is known as *emergence* and many games take advantage of it.[3] Typically the possibility space is so large that it is hard to control or anticipate exactly what behavior will emerge. In some games this is a big bonus as the game experience continues to evolve in ways the game designer might never have imagined. In other more tightly scripted games it can be viewed as a problem and game designers might shy away from using controllers with a large possibility space. But from an AI perspective restricting the possibility space can be a challenge and the resulting code is usually full of special cases, which make it buggy and hard to maintain.

By way of analogy, a good anecdote about the trade-off between controller simplicity and the level of control over the resulting behavior is nicely illustrated by a story from the computer animation industry. The director in an animation wanted a scene with raindrops rolling down a window, so the animators built an elegant program that generated the desired animation procedurally. The director was initially delighted when he saw the realistic-looking results that had been produced so quickly. But he was a perfectionist and on close examination he became unhappy with the precise movement of some of the raindrops. Of course, the programmers had no control over the animation at that level of detail, they simply set the initial conditions and let the simulation run autonomously. They could generate realistic-looking animations, but they could not generate (except by trial and error) the precise realistic-looking animation the director was after. The program was scrapped and the raindrop animation was created instead by hours of painstaking work animating the scene by hand. The connection with games is that in some games it is desirable to have realistic-looking behavior emerge from an elegant controller, but in some games the game designer might require more control.

In terms of the player's perception of a game's AI, appropriate animations can also make an enormous difference. For example, consider an NPC who is surrounded by hostile monsters and cannot think of anything intelligent to do. The NPC could simply stand there looking dumb, or the animation system can be triggered to play an animation of the NPC running around screaming. It is surprising how an appropriate animation can

---

[3] See [Wol02] for a fascinating look at the properties of emergence in an abstract mathematical setting.

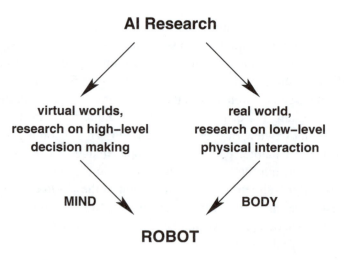

Figure 1.2. Different research tracks within AI.

make all the difference in the player's perception of the AI.

In summary, extensive play testing often shows up situations that were not anticipated by the AI programmer. If the AI bug is something simple it can be fixed by changing the controller. This section makes it clear that changing the game design, or simply playing an appropriate animation, can also sometimes provide a work-around.

1.5.2 Computer Games and AI Research

One of the major goals of AI research is to produce intelligent robots. Figure 1.2 shows that creating a robot is (at least) a two-pronged effort. For a time, there was a push in AI not to work on the high-level decision-making aspect until the low-level physical interaction research program was further along [Bro90]. But as pointed out in [Etz93] the two endeavors can obviously be worked on in parallel. Computer games therefore make a wonderful medium for carrying out research into abstract thinking. Of course, simulated worlds have been used before in AI, but computer games offer a commercial application with a degree of visual feedback in an intuitive real-time environment that is hard to match.

Until the physical interaction research program is further along, doing research on abstract thinking in the real world can mean a lot of wasted time dealing with problems like faulty actuators and uncalibrated sensors.

That is why AI research in robotics often ends up with applications like a robot trundling around picking up soda cans. As mechanical engineering improves more exciting applications are opening up, but computer games still offer an exciting and easily accessible platform for AI research.

Computer games even have something to offer the physical interaction research program. For example, in [TR97] a game-like world is rendered from the point of view of each eye of an NPC and vision algorithms are applied to the resulting pair of stereoscopic images. The end result of the vision algorithms could be obtained more quickly and easily by using the original three-dimensional representation of the world before it is rendered. However, the point of the exercise is not the end result, but to use the convenience of a game world to test and develop algorithms that could be used in the real world.

Chapter 2

Acting

This chapter describes how the AI in a character's controller interacts with the rest of the game. Although not specifically about AI, it is nonetheless important as it introduces an underlying game architecture that embodies a character's controller within the game. The controller can then perform actions to influence its world, which, along with the ability to perceive its world (covered in the next chapter), is one of the most basic capabilities it needs.

Recall from Chapter 1 that the game architecture is broken down into the game-state, the simulator, and the controllers. Each of these components is described in turn, but first this chapter introduces a simple game that is used as a motivating example throughout the rest of the book.

2.1 Tag Game

Since the game-state and simulator are different for each game it is difficult to describe them in completely general terms. Therefore they are introduced in the context of a specific example game: a simple game of tag.

Figure 2.1 depicts a scene from the tag game. The scene is depicted in three dimensions but all the important movement in the tag game takes place on a two-dimensional plane. This is often referred to as $2\frac{1}{2}D$.

The tag game begins with one character chosen at random to be the tagged character. The tagged character then chases the other characters until it touches one. Once a new character has been touched it takes over the role of the tagged character and the game continues. Either NPCs or

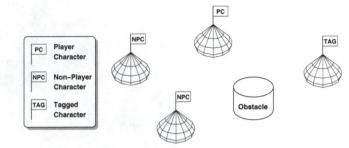

Figure 2.1. Scene from the tag game.

player characters can take on the role of the tagged character. To make the game a little more interesting there are some obstacles placed randomly within the game world.

By the standards of modern computer games, the tag game is hopelessly simple. Nevertheless, from an AI perspective it possesses many of the important characteristics of a more complicated game. The basic architecture should therefore apply to other games, while the simplicity makes it free of unimportant and distracting details that might encumber a more realistic example.

To help make the details of code organization within the tag game clearer, C++ is used to provide declarations for some of the important classes. Appendix B contains a few notes about the use of C++ within this book, and about game programming in general. You might therefore want to look at the relevant pages before proceeding.

2.2 Game-State

The game-state is the object that provides access to a complete description of the current state of the game world. Listing 2.1 shows part of the declaration of the tgGameState class. Only a few sample methods and class members are shown, but hopefully they show how the game-state provides access to a complete description of the state of the game world. That is, there are accessors for all game objects the game-state manages and those in turn provide accessors to their state information. For example, to find

```
class tgGameState
{
public:
    tgGameState();
    ~tgGameState();
    // Get the number of objects
    inline int getNumObjects() const;
    // Get a pointer to ith object
    inline tgObject* getObject(int i);
    // Get the number of characters
    inline int getNumCharacters() const;
    // Get a pointer to the ith character
    // NOTE: not necessarily the same as the ith object
    inline tgCharacter* getCharacter(int i);
    // Get the current time
    inline tgReal getTime() const;
    // Adopt an object
    void addObject(tgObject* o);
private:
    // List of all game objects
    vector<tgObject*> objects;
    // The current time
    tgReal time;
}; // tgGameState
```

Listing 2.1. Part of the game-state class declaration.

out from the game-state the current velocity of the *i* th character use:

```
// gs is the game-state object
tgRealVec const& v = gs.getCharacter(i)->getVelocity();
```

The base class for all the objects in the game is the tgObject class. Listing 2.2 contains part of the class declaration. Once again only a small representative sample of the available methods and member variables is shown.

NPCs and player characters are both instances of the tgCharacter class, a part of which is shown in Listing 2.3. The tgCharacter is a subclass of a tgObstacle class (not shown) that defines the physical extent of an object used in collision detection. The tgObstacle class is itself a subclass of the tgObject class.

Instances of NPCs and players are created as part of the program initialization:

```
// Shared perception object (see Chapter 3)
tgPerception perception(&gs);
for (int i = 0; i < numCharacters; i++)
{
    tgCharacter* c = NULL;
    if (0 == i)
    { // make character 0 the player character
        c = new tgCharacter(&gs, new tgControllerPC(&perception));
    }
    else
    {
        c = new tgCharacter(&gs, new tgControllerNPC(&perception));
    }
    gs.addObject(c);
}
```

As you can see, the only difference between NPCs and player characters is they have different types of controller. By swapping in different types of controllers a character can be either a player character or an NPC. The ability to swap controllers is useful for games where players can flip between characters to control. It is also important for testing because the game can be played without human intervention for hours on end to try and find bugs that might not show up during regular play testing.

2.3 Simulator

The simulator is responsible for making changes to the game-state. Ideally, the simulator is the *only* component of the game that can modify the game-state. All other components can only query the game-state.

```
class tgObject
{
public:
    tgObject(tgGameState* gs);
    virtual ~tgObject();
    // Get this object's position
    inline tgRealVec const& getPosition() const;
    // Set this object's position
    inline void setPosition(tgRealVec const& pos);
    // Get this object's mass
    inline tgReal const& getMass() const;
    // Set this object's mass
    inline void setMass(tgReal const& mass);
protected:
    // Local pointer to the game−state used in various methods
    // to access information about other objects in the game
    tgGameState* gs;
private:
    // This object's position
    tgRealVec pos;
    // This object's mass
    tgReal mass;
}; // tgObject
```

Listing 2.2. Part of the declaration of the base class for all objects in the game.

Action choices, the passage of time, and game world events like collisions are common causes of modifications to the game-state. The rules contained in the simulator that determine how to modify the game-state represent the game world's physics. Game physics obviously do not have to obey the same physical laws as the real world.

Note that, the separation of the simulator from the renderer is important if, as in Chapter 6, the simulator is used by an NPC as a world model to think about the consequences of its actions. Otherwise an NPC just thinking ahead would change what the player sees on the screen.

```
class tgCharacter : public tgObstacleCircle
{
public:
    tgCharacter(tgGameState* gs, tgController* controller);
    ~tgCharacter();
    // Get this character's controller
    inline tgController* getConstroller();
    // Set this character's controller
    inline void setController(tgController* controller);
    // Get this character's velocity
    inline tgRealVec const& getVelocity();
    // Set this character's velocity
    inline void setVelocity(tgRealVec const& vel);
private:
    // Pointer to this character's (possibly shared) controller
    tgController* controller;
    // This character's velocity
    tgRealVec vel;
};
```

Listing 2.3. Part of the class declaration for characters in the game.

2.3.1 Actions

A character's controller is responsible for selecting actions, but it is the simulator's job to resolve the effects of actions on the game-state. Often the immediate effects of an action are followed by additional ramifications. For example, activating an explosive device might be instantaneous, but the subsequent explosion could cause all sorts of ripple effects. Fortunately, the simulator can be written to deal with the effects one at a time. For instance, in the example of an explosion, the initial act of activating the explosive device causes the simulator to set the explosive device to "on". After some amount of predefined time the explosive device controller generates an explode action. This causes the simulator to play animations of explosions and characters being flung around. This might result in the death of a character that was some NPC's friend. This in turn causes the

corresponding NPC's controller to, say, choose a shoot action aimed at the character who set the explosion. The shoot action is then resolved by the simulator, and so on.

Although the simulator processes events one at a time, it can of course alternate between different tasks. Since it all happens so fast, events often appear to be happening simultaneously and in parallel.

Action Representation

One of the first steps in creating a game is to decide what actions are available and how they are represented. The decision can depend upon the complexity of the game world's physics. For example, in a simple world a "drop" action could just mean an object is deleted from the character's inventory and placed back into the world at a nearby location. At the other end of the spectrum, a game might simulate some of the laws of physics found in the real world. In such a world a character could have an action to relax its muscles. This then sets in motion a chain of events such as the force that was previously holding the object in place disappearing. The force of gravity then automatically starts accelerating the object toward the floor. This in turn causes a collision event between the object and the floor to be generated, and so on. In most games, the physics are somewhere in between these two extremes. But deciding on the correct level of abstraction, particularly between controllers and motion-captured animations, is a difficult problem.

The representation of actions is also complicated by the fact that actions can sometimes be parameterized. For example, a punch action might have a parameter indicating how hard to punch.

2.3.2   Animations

Animations are sometimes thought of as the renderer's responsibility. This might be because they are often created by the same artists who create the texture maps and three-dimensional models that are used by the renderer. Motion capture is another common source of animations. Regardless of an animation's genesis, while it is playing it is providing rules for how the associated object should move. In general, it is the simulator that encodes the rules on how an object should move. It makes sense therefore to think of

animations as implicitly encoding part of the game's physics as animation data and for them to be managed by the simulator.

Animations are triggered by actions and events that occur in the game world. When an animation is triggered the simulator proceeds to step through the animation. This continues until the animation is interrupted or completed. The current animation often needs to be interrupted by events, such as collisions, or new actions selected by a controller. When an animation is interrupted a new animation often needs to take its place. Blending between the current and the requested animation can require the simulator to modify one or both of the animations on the fly. Modification of an animation can consist of dropping frames to speed it up, or rescaling to make a smoother blend (see [KGP02]). Section 2.5.1 describes subtle interactions that can arise between the simulator and a controller when trying to smoothly blend between animations.

Note that, creating motion capture data requires careful planning to make sure a full and complete set of animations is obtained [Kin00]. But no matter how many animations are captured they will usually still need to be modified at runtime. The reason is that control generally needs to be exerted at a higher frequency than can be provided by a discrete fixed set of available animations.

2.3.3   Newtonian Physics

Except at speeds approaching the velocity of light, Newtonian physics provides an accurate model for movement in the real world. It is not surprising therefore that many games incorporate some aspect of Newtonian physics into the simulator in order to generate realistic-looking motions.

One of the biggest challenges with incorporating Newtonian physics into a game is that for active objects (like NPCs) locomotion can become a difficult control problem. Therefore Newtonian physics is most commonly applied to passive objects (ones with no internal source of energy). Some good references for Newtonian physics and games are [Bou01, WB01]. A few representative papers on tackling the control problem associated with the use of Newtonian physics for active objects are [GT95, HP97, LvdPF00, FvdPT01, LCR03].

In some popular cartoons an interesting version of Newtonian physics is used in which the law of gravity fails to apply until the character realizes

it has run off the edge of a cliff. As suggested in [Fal95], there is no reason why simulators in games could not incorporate such imaginative variations on Newtonian physics for the purposes of entertainment.

2.3.4   Tag Game Physics

The physics in the tag game uses a two-dimensional version of the *simple vehicle model* described in [Rey99] and originally inspired by [Bra84]. The vehicle model approximates the Newtonian physics of a vehicle with a point mass. The term "vehicle" is used loosely to apply to a wide variety of objects, to quote from [Rey99]:

> . . . from wheeled devices to horses, from aircraft to submarines, and (while certainly stretching the terminology) to include locomotion by a character's own legs.

In the case of the tag game, the vehicle refers to a character in the game.

Actions in the tag game are specified in terms of some new desired velocity. The desired velocity is then used to calculate a character's new velocity as follows:

```
// get character c's desired velocity
tgRealVec acceleration(c->getAction().getDesiredVelocity());
acceleration.clamp(c->getMaxForce());
// acceleration = force/mass
acceleration.scale(1.0/c->getMass());
// v = character c's current velocity
tgRealVec v(c->getVelocity());
v.add(acceleration);
v.clamp(c->getMaxSpeed());
c->setVelocity(v);
v.normalize();
c->setOrientation(v);
```

Once a character's new velocity has been determined, its new position is (assuming there are no collisions) just the new velocity added to the previous position:

```
tgCharacter* c = gs->getCharacter(i);
tgRealVec p(c->getPosition());
p.add(c->getVelocity());
c->setPosition(p);
```

One of the most visually obvious defects with the simple vehicle model is that there is no constraint on the rate of turning. In a Newtonian physics simulation this corresponds to moments of inertia. You can approximate the effect of moments of inertia by placing a constraint on rate of turning. But note that this constraint represents an upper bound and it should always be possible to turn less than the maximum turn rate. Otherwise unsightly oscillations can occur when the orientation gets close to the desired one.

2.3.5 Passage of Time

The simulator works by updating the game-state at discrete time intervals. The update frequency can either be a fixed constant as in Section 2.3.7, or allowed to vary as in Section 2.3.8. Regardless of whether the update frequency is allowed to vary, it should be greater than or equal to the frame rate, where the *frame rate* of a game is how many times a second the current state of the world is rendered as an image that is displayed on the screen for the player to see.

Some reasons the update frequency might need to be higher than the frame rate is to avoid missing collisions, or numerically solve stiff differential equations in a complex physical simulation. The frame rate, in turn, needs to be high enough and have low enough variance that motion does not appear jerky and discontinuous. The human eye usually starts to perceive motion as smooth at around 15–20 frames per second. But games that run at 60 Hz still appear a lot smoother than those that run at 30 Hz. Updates to the game-state also need to coincide with frame boundaries or the game will be out of sync.

The simulator still needs to modify the game-state even when no other actions are generated from any of the characters in the game. For example, any active animations still need to continue playing; simulated forces like gravity can cause objects to start or continue accelerating; other objects might have momentum that keeps them moving forward from previous frames; and simulated friction could cause objects to slow down.

2.3.6 Collisions

As objects move around according to the game world's physics they may bump into each other. Bumping into things can be accidental or deliberate. For example, in the tag game the goal of the tagged character is to "bump into" another character. The simulator therefore needs to be able to detect when collisions have occurred. It might also need to be able to detect when objects are on a collision course even if they have not yet collided. Collision detection is a widely studied problem in many different research communities. For collision detection in games, see [vdB03] or any of the other references and resources available on this book's companion web site.

Once a collision has been detected it needs to be resolved. For collisions stemming from deliberate actions, like the tagged character tagging another character, this usually involves playing a suitable animation. In addition, the game-state needs to be updated with important information like the identity of the newly tagged character.

In general, a game's realism is greatly enhanced if the laws of physics for collisions in the real world can be simulated. This is called *collision resolution* and there are two common approaches: impulse methods and penalty methods. See [WB01] and [Bou01] for an in-depth look at collision resolution.

In some games, characters can "collide" with permeable substances like water, in which case the result of the collision could be that a character is moving in a different medium. This would presumably require a new set of appropriate physics rules to be used.

2.3.7 Fixed Time-Step Simulation

In a fixed time-step simulation the game-state is updated at some constant fixed time interval. Every n time-steps the simulator polls each character's associated controller to see if there are any actions to execute. In the simplest case $n = 1$ and new actions can be generated every time-step but, depending on the game, it is usually sufficient to set $n > 1$. The simulator can also implement time slicing by varying n on a per controller basis. The order of polling controllers always needs to be randomized or else some characters are consistently able to act first, while others always act with the knowledge of the preceding character's choices.

The simulator creates the game-state according to rules that often specify change in a continuous way. Fixed time-step simulation corresponds to sampling the continuously changing state of the game world at fixed intervals. With any fixed sampling technique, events that occur in between samples will go unnoticed. For example, it is quite easy for the simulator to miss collisions and joystick presses. The player, however, may well notice that two objects just seemed to pass through each other in a completely unrealistic fashion, or that their presses are being ignored.

Even when a collision is detected at a particular time-step, it is unlikely the collision occurred at just that instant. Therefore the collision resolution strategy will have to be able to deal with the objects already interpenetrating. This is not such a problem for penalty methods, but could be an issue for impulse methods. In particular, the simulation might need to back up to find the exact time of collision.

It is always possible to construct pathological examples when using a fixed time-step simulation. But in practice, if the update frequency is high enough, then missed events are (probably) rare and (probably) hardly noticeable. A fixed time-step simulator might not be suitable for engineering applications that require a high degree of precision, but for games their simplicity makes them appealing.

2.3.8 Discrete Event Simulation

Discrete event simulation formalizes the notion of an *event*. There are different types of events and each event object has a time associated with it. Events also contain any other relevant information, such as the participants in a collision. Events are stored in a priority queue called the *event queue*, which is sorted by the time of the events. The simulator works by continually popping events off the front of the queue and processing them.

When an event is processed, the game world is simulated up to the time associated with the event. To ensure that an up-to-date version of the game-state is available for the renderer at frame boundaries, special tick events are inserted into the event queue. In particular, when the game starts, the tick event that corresponds to the first frame is placed in the event queue. Subsequently, whenever a tick event is popped from the event queue with associated time t, another tick event is immediately inserted into the event queue with associated time $t' = t + \Delta t$. Note that, to avoid the accumulation

of rounding errors the new time t' should not be calculated directly from the previous time. Instead, $t' = n\Delta t$, where n is the (integer) number of tick events so far.

Actions are handled by querying controllers in response to "get action" events that are placed in the queue at appropriate times. Again the query order needs to be randomized and this can be done by shuffling "get action" events that occur at the same time. Instead of just polling each controller at regular intervals, a controller can provide an estimate for how long it needs to calculate an action and insert an appropriate "get action" event in the event queue. Time-slicing for controllers can also be handled easily by scheduling start and stop thinking events that get sent to the respective controllers at appropriate times.

Discrete event simulation provides an elegant way to avoid missing collisions. After each change to the game-state there is a potential for new collisions. A collision detection algorithm is used to find such events and the time at which they occur. The information is then placed in the event queue. When a collision event is popped from the event queue a check is made to see if it is still valid and, if necessary, the collision is then resolved. The validity check is needed because other preceding events (for example, a character changed direction to avoid a collision) may have caused a predicted collision not to occur after all.

2.4   Controllers

Controllers are responsible for selecting the actions that get sent to the simulator. Listing 2.4 shows the tgController class that is the abstract base class for all controllers in the tag game. New controllers are subclasses of tgController and they must implement the calcAction method. As explained in the previous section, the simulator intermittently requests actions from characters' associated controllers. More specifically, the simulator calls a controller's calcAction method and a new action is computed and stored in the action class variable. The computed action can then be retrieved at any point by a call to the getAction method. Ideally, the action class variable should always contain a valid action, if not necessarily a sensible one. Therefore, if a controller cannot, or does not want to compute a new action, it should leave the lastAction variable unchanged, or overwrite it with some valid default value.

```
class tgController
{
public:
    tgController(tgPerception* perception);
    virtual ~tgController();
    // Calculate action for character[myIndex]
    virtual void calcAction(int const myIndex) = 0;
    // Get the last computed action
    inline tgAction const& getAction() { return this->action; }
protected:
    // The controller's perception object (see Chapter 3)
    tgPerception* perception;
    // The last calculated action
    tgAction action;
}; // tgController
```

Listing 2.4. Part of the controller base class declaration.

Every character will have at least one controller associated with it. One reason that a character would have more than one controller associated with it is if it alternates between being an NPC and a player character. Controllers can also be shared among several characters. The myIndex argument passed to the calcAction is the game-state index of the character for which the controller is currently computing an action. This information is also important for the perception object described in the next chapter.

Of course, if a controller is shared it does not mean that all the associated characters will behave in lock step with one another. At any given moment two characters with the same controller will generally be in different situations, so even if their controllers are the same, their behavior can be different. For example, in the tag game one character might be being chased by the tagged character and so is running away, while a different character is standing still hiding behind an obstacle. If the hidden character is spotted and the tagged player comes too close, it too will run away (although from a different starting point and most likely in a different direction).

Even if characters do not share the same controller instance, they can still share the same type of controller. This is often the case with parameterized controllers. For example, a "braveness" parameter could be used as a threshold in a test to decide whether to run away or not. The same controller type can then yield different behavior by instantiating it with different parameter values.

2.4.1 Hierarchical Control

A controller class will often provide other methods that implement what can be thought of as subcontrollers. The calcAction method then acts as the master controller that knows how and when to call the other subcontroller methods to compute an action. The subcontroller methods are usually in the protected section so that they are not publicly available, but can still be used and overridden by subclasses. This allows controllers to be conveniently layered to form hierarchies. At the low-level there are controllers to perform basic tasks like collision avoidance and path following. At the next level could be controllers to plan paths, and higher up still might be controllers that determine NPC motivations and intentions.

A common example of hierarchical control is when the player clicks on a point in the world where the player character should go. The decision on where to go has been made by the player, but getting there is achieved autonomously. The controller that gets a character to a given goal position can be shared by NPCs and player characters. For player characters the goal is provided by the player, but the NPC has the additional task of figuring out where to go and so there must be another controller for this task.

The camera character in many games is an interesting hybrid between a player character and an NPC. For example, some games feature automatic camera control, but it is not fully automatic because what the camera is pointing at has to depend on properties of the world like the player character's position and orientation. Other games allow tighter control over the camera, but usually only over some subset of the camera's degrees of freedom with the remaining ones determined automatically.

2.4.2 Hierarchical Actions

If there is a hierarchy of controllers, there will usually also be a hierarchy of actions. The actions that finally get sent to the simulator are called

the *game actions*. Actions that are not game actions, which are generated by high-level controllers, provide part of the input (along with relevant information about the game world) to low-level controllers. The low-level controllers translate the high-level actions into lower-level actions and eventually into game actions. Thus some of the controllers take actions output from other controllers as input. Of course, an "action" output from some controller might just be a numerical parameter input into another controller. Conversely, it could also be a complex behavior that generates a whole sequence of lower-level actions.

Some of the controllers described in Chapter 6 can use the simulator to search for an action to pick by trying out prospective candidates before selecting one. To speed up the search, other controllers might only perform an internal approximate simulation. For example, humans use a simple naive physics model all the time in their everyday lives.

An approximate simulator can even be defined as a separate distinct object that can then be used by any controllers that quickly want to try out actions in advance. The approximate simulator will normally not take game actions as input, but some higher level approximation. For example, in the tag game, the game actions are two-dimensional direction vectors. These could be approximated by discrete compass directions for input into an approximate simulator that represented the world as a two-dimensional grid. Or a discrete graph could be overlaid onto the map as in Section 6.4 in Chapter 6.

Figure 2.2 shows a possible hierarchy of controllers, simulators, and actions for a simple path planning example. The high-level controller decides on some high-level intention such as moving to a far-away location. It then generates a high-level action that consists of a goal location consistent with the intention. A path-planner then generates a sequence of grid locations that form a collision-free path to the goal location. To do this it takes advantage of an approximate simulator that implements movement on a grid as a simplified version of movement in the game. Finally, a path-follower translates the discrete path into a smooth one and sends the game-level actions to the simulator to be executed.

In general, so-called *hybrid controllers* can have highly sophisticated architectures with interrupts and many levels of subcontrollers. There may even need to be an overarching controller that acts as a miniature operating system allocating resources and scheduling other controllers. The *agent*

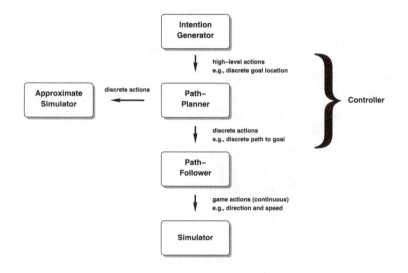

Figure 2.2. Example of a hierarchy of controllers and actions.

architecture literature studies many of these issues in detail. Other sources of inspiration on complex controller architectures are animal and human psychology.

2.4.3 Level of Detail

In computer graphics it is common to use lower resolution textures and simpler geometry when objects are far away from the camera. An analogous idea can be applied to controllers. In particular, an NPC can have a hierarchy of associated controllers that all perform the same task. This is different from the hierarchy of controllers described before because previously each controller performed a different subtask. Although all the controllers perform the same task, controllers higher up the hierarchy are more sophisticated. Some reasons to prefer using simpler controllers lower down in the hierarchy are as follows.

Failure. A more sophisticated controller might occasionally fail to pick an action. This might happen if the algorithm that it uses is specialized to apply only in a narrow range of circumstances. Or it might simply run out of time, or anticipate in advance that there is not enough

time. Whatever the reason, a simpler, more reliable controller can be used as a backup.

Distance. If an NPC is far away from the camera, it might be possible to use a simpler controller so that closer NPCs have extra time to use more sophisticated controllers. Unlike the level of detail used in graphics, distance is not always a good measure of the importance of behavior. For example, a general might be far away but could still be in close communciation with her troops. In which case, even though the troops might be closer, it might be sensible to devote more of the available CPU resources to the general's decision making.

Groups. If an NPC is part of a group, then the group itself can be treated as a single entity. For example, if the group's controller decides the group as a whole should move to a particular location, then the individual NPCs within the group need only decide how to get there. If the group later disbands, then the individual NPCs may need to use a more sophisticated controller to determine not just how to get there but where to go in the first place.

2.4.4   Game Action Compatibility

Controllers for player characters have to select game actions according to the player's button presses and joystick pushes. Sometimes this is quite easy and can be accomplished by a simple look-up table. For example, when the player presses the A button the player character controller generates a "punch" action, say. Other times the mapping can be more complicated. For example, generating combos usually requires monitoring the time and frequency of button pushes. Pressure-sensitive input can also be used to provide parameters to actions like how hard to punch.

If an NPC's controller generates actions at the level of button presses and joystick pushes, then its output needs to be filtered through the player character's controller to turn it into game actions. The advantage of having the NPC's controller work this way is that it can greatly simplify the task of swapping controllers and creating automatic tests for debugging the game.

2.5 Possible Actions

Not all the actions that are defined in a game are always possible. For example, a "shoot" action is not possible if a character does not have a gun. If a controller does select an action that is not possible, then executing it could cause the game to crash, or the game-state might become corrupt, leading to bugs and a possible crash later on. Therefore the simulator needs to check if an action is possible and ignore the illegal ones. It also wastes time when an NPC's controller spends time trying to decide whether to select an action that is not even possible. It is therefore a good idea if a controller can have access to information contained within the simulator about which actions are currently possible.

In simple games, where the list of actions is discrete and small, the information about possible actions can be given as an explicit list of actions. In games where actions take parameters, the list of possible actions needs to also include allowable ranges for parameter values. If the list of possible actions (along with allowable parameter ranges) is too long, a shorter list can be created by sampling possible actions and parameter values. To calculate the list of possible actions the simulator has a method calcPossibleActions. The getPossibleActions accessor is then used to obtain the most recently computed list.

If it is not feasible for the simulator to generate any kind of explicit list, there can simply be a method for a controller to test if a given action is possible or not. This approach corresponds to having the controller sample for possible actions instead of the simulator. The advantage of the simulator creating a list of possible actions is that it has a better idea of where best to sample for possible actions. Conversely, a controller probably has a better idea for where to sample for desirable actions. The choice of where to do the sampling therefore depends on the game and the particular implementation.

Often in games there is no method to generate possible actions or even test if a given action is possible. Instead, a controller simply pushes actions it would like to execute onto a stack such that the top of the stack is the most desired action. When it comes time for the simulator to execute an action, it simply keeps popping actions off the stack until it finds one that is possible, at which point it clears the stack and the process repeats. The bottom of the stack is usually some fail-safe action that the controller is sure will always be possible.

2.5.1   Animations and Controllers

Often an action is not possible because its associated animation is incompatible with the currently playing animation. Typically an animation is defined with certain blend points where it can be interrupted and blended into one of some set of alternative animations. If the current animation is not at a blend point, or the blend point is incompatible with the new requested animation, then the given action is not possible. Of course, when deciding if an action is possible the simulator needs to take into account any runtime modifications (such as dropping frames and rescaling) it could employ to make animations compatible.

What if the current animation is not at a compatible blend point (and cannot be modified to make it compatible), but will be in the next couple of frames? Then the action a, associated with the newly requested animation, will not appear in the list of currently possible actions. However, given the choice, a controller might want to pick a, but thinking it is not possible selects some other action b. If the controller had known that a would be available in a few frames it might have waited or chosen some other action c that could execute quickly. If b takes a long time to play its associated animation, then when it is time for the controller to select another action, b's animation could also be at a point incompatible with a. The controller might keep having to select suboptimal actions simply because it is starved of the information it needs to make a proper decision.

A solution could be to define a method that returns a list of soon to be possible actions. Unfortunately, there are likely to be a lot more of these than the list of currently possible actions. Another solution could be to provide a method that returns (approximately in some cases) how many frames (up to some limit) to go before a given action is possible.

To make matters worse, many animations will require the participation of more than one NPC. For example, sports games often require passing the ball from one NPC to another. This requires two different animations to be coordinated with one another and one NPC to end up in the right location and pose to receive the ball. It is therefore easy to see why having controllers simply push actions onto a stack (as described earlier) for the simulator to deal with is so commonplace. For example, if the NPC with the ball wants to pass, the simulator simply needs to find a suitable NPC offering to receive the ball somewhere in their stack of desirable actions.

Chapter 3

Perceiving

To act effectively controllers need to know what is happening in the game world. For player characters, the human can be thought of as a central component of the associated controller and the human primarily gets information about the game world through the renderer. For NPCs, access to information about the game world is through simulated perception.

3.1 Renderer

The renderer produces images and sounds that provide the human player with feedback about the game world.[1] Of course, the renderer's sole purpose is not just to provide adequate feedback for control purposes. In particular, stunning graphics and sound are a big part of the enjoyment of a game. High-quality graphics also contribute heavily to the desire to play the game in the first place; although it is often said that the AI and game-play are what keep the player's attention.

Aside from promoting game sales, the visceral and exciting nature of real-time computer graphics has led to widespread interest in the subject which has led to many books. Books on rendering sound are less commonplace, but some sources of information are included in the section on rendering on this book's companion web site.

---

[1]There have been popular games (especially in the early days) that just used textual descriptions to "render" the world. For example, NetHack is a popular text-based game.

From an AI perspective, one of the interesting features of the renderer is how it is used to simulate some of the limitations of real-world perception. For example, just as in reality, players are usually not allowed to see through walls. A fun exception to this rule, used in many games, are weapons with "X-ray" or thermal imaging capabilities.

Some techniques implemented in the renderer are so basic that their role in simulating real-world perception could easily go unnoticed. For example, the use of a perspective projection makes things that are farther away appear smaller when rendered (at least until zooming in with a sniper scope). It is therefore harder to tell an object's identity when it is in the distance. A few more examples of simulated perception that renderers have implemented in various games include heat haze, blurriness of vision after being hit on the head, and even the adjustment of the iris after entering a dark room. You might like to think of some additional examples that you have either seen in games or could imagine being used.

Another important point about the renderer worth mentioning from an AI perspective is its importance for debugging. During debugging it is usually extremely helpful to be able to visually depict an NPC's state of mind, for example, drawing an arrow toward where an NPC thinks the player character is, or drawing a character that an NPC thinks is the biggest danger in a bright color. The ability to somehow visualize an NPC's internal thought processes can often instantly transform a difficult bug into something obvious.

3.1.1   Computer Vision for NPCs

Perception for player characters is handled by the renderer. Therefore, why not use the same renderer to create an image of the world from each NPC's point of view? An NPC's controller could then use the image to figure out the state of the world from its point of view. This would put NPCs and player characters on a level playing field in terms of access to information about the world.

The big disadvantage to using the renderer to implement perception for NPCs is that interpreting an image is hard. Except for additional problems like noisy sensors and calibrating cameras, it is more or less the task that computer vision research tries to solve. In a virtual world various tricks can be used to make the image recognition task easier. For example, an image

could be rendered with the enemy in red and everything else in black. Then if there are any red pixels in the resulting image a character can infer that the enemy is visible. Nevertheless, compared to getting information from the game-state directly, computer vision in virtual worlds is still relatively slow and unreliable.[2] In addition, there is the extra cost of rendering extra images: one per NPC, instead of just one per player character.

Even if computer vision worked perfectly, the best it could produce would be a representation of the game world equivalent to the one already in the game-state. It is clearly pointless to go unnecessarily from one representation to another, and then back to the original, especially so if some of the transformations are slow and unreliable.

3.2 Simulated Perception

Instead of rendering an image from an NPC's point of view, an NPC's controller gets information from the world directly from the game-state. However, unless access to the game-state is restricted in some way, NPCs will be able to know too much about the game world. For example, NPCs will be able to see through walls, giving them an unfair advantage over player characters that cannot. In particular, the player character can never hide from NPCs but NPCs can easily hide from the player character. Since hiding can be a fun part of a game, this kind of imbalance can spoil the enjoyment.

To restrict an NPC's access to the game-state, a game will often introduce the idea of a *percept*. A percept is any transformation of information in the game-state, or another percept, into a form suitable for use by an NPC's controller. Not all percepts are used to filter out information, some (as in Section 3.3) just re-express the same information in a more convenient form. Such percepts, that represent values from the game-state without any processing or manipulation, are called *game percepts*. You will recall that Section 2.4.1 in the previous chapter makes an analogous distinction between game actions and higher-level actions.

Section 3.4 describes some higher-level percepts that do filter out information from the game-state. On occasions, percepts can even attempt

---

[2]As pointed out in Section 1.5.2 in Chapter 1, for computer vision research there are many advantages to using virtual worlds.

```
class tgPerception
{
public:
    tgPerception(tgGameState* gs);
    ~tgPerception();
    // Set character from whose point of view percepts are to be calculated
    inline void setMyIndex(int myIndex);
    // Get character from whose point of view percepts are being calculated
    inline int getMyIndex() const;
    // Some example percepts
    inline tgRealVec const& getMyPosition() const;
    inline tgRealVec const& getMyVelocity() const;
    inline tgRealVec const& getTaggedPosition() const;
    inline tgRealVec const& getTaggedVelocity() const;
    tgReal calcMyDistanceToCharacter(int who) const;
    tgReal calcMyDistanceToNearestCharacter() const;
private:
    // Pointer to the game-state object
    tgGameState* gs;
    // Index (from game-state) of "me" character
    int myIndex;
};
```

Listing 3.1. Part of the declaration of the perception class for the tag game.

to reconstruct information that has been filtered out by other percepts (see Section 3.5).

A simple way to implement percepts is as methods of the character's controller class. In general, there will be multiple controllers and each might use a different set of percepts. Inheritance can be used to factor out common percepts into base classes to avoid unnecessary code duplication.

Another possibility is for each controller to have a separate perception object associated with it. The perception object is still conceptually part of the controller, but each controller can then have a different type of perception object; or a different instance of a perception object of the same type; or even (if there is no controller specific state needed) a single shared

instance of a perception object. Of course, any combination of these three possibilities can occur across a set of controllers. To avoid duplicating shared percepts, the different perception classes can be arranged in some appropriate inheritance hierarchy.

A big advantage of having a separate perception object is that different perception objects can (potentially) be swapped in and out. For example, there could be one perception object type for when a character is in good health and a subclass for when the character has been hit over the head. The subclass used for concussed controllers could override some methods with versions that deliberately introduce errors into the values returned.

A portion of a simple perception class for a controller in the tag game is shown in Listing 3.1. Some of the methods are defined as virtual so that they can be overridden by subclasses if required. The use of virtual methods incurs a small penalty because inlining virtual methods has no effect. If your game does not need to swap perception objects in and out of controllers, then there is obviously no need to make any of the methods virtual.

Which methods a perception class provides will vary across controllers and games. Nevertheless, there are some common kinds of percepts that recur across games and the remainder of this chapter describes some examples.

3.3 Character-Specific Percepts

One basic type of transformation of information in the game-state is to make it character-specific. This can range from the simple relabeling of pre-existing information, to more complicated calculations such as the computation of relative coordinates.

3.3.1 My Values

At any given instant a controller is selecting actions for a particular NPC. As far as the controller is concerned the NPC in question can be thought of as "me" and it is probably going to make extensive use of various properties associated with "me". It is therefore useful to have a convenient shorthand for these variables. For example, the following definition of the

getMyPosition method calculates the position of the NPC that is currently
"me":

---

tgRealVec **const**& tgPerception::getMyPosition() **const**
{
    return getMyCharacter()−>getPosition();
}

Similar methods can be written for getMyVelocity, getMyOrientation,
getAmITagged, etc. All of these methods just wrap simple accesses to the
game-state.

For convenience, the index (from the game-state) of the character that
is currently "me" is stored in the class variable myIndex. The value of
myIndex is set by the controller prior to deciding which action to pick.
That way all the values it requests for "me" will be computed for the correct character. The controller, in turn, knows which character it is picking an action for because it is told by the simulator (see Section 2.4 in
Chapter 2).

3.3.2 Other Important Characters

There are often other characters (aside from "me") that are important for
a controller. Depending on the game, it could be the "boss monster", or a
companion, say, that are important in a controller's decision making. In the
tag game, properties of the tagged character (like its position) are likely to
figure heavily in the decisions of nontagged characters. For example, the
getTaggedPosition method is analogous to the getMyPosition method, but
returns the position of the tagged character. Since running away from the
tagged character is a central theme of the tag game, there are likely to be
many percepts related to the tagged character.

3.3.3 Affordances

Many games add affordances [Gib87] to the environment in the form of
labels that are only visible to NPCs. In the context of computer games, an
affordance is a piece of information that tells an NPC about actions it can
perform at a given location. For example, a doorway might have a label
"exit" and a ledge might have a label "jump here". If an NPC decides to

leave a room, say, it can access a percept like getPositionNearestExit to look up the nearest "exit" affordance, and then head toward that location.

3.3.4 Relative Values

Relative values, such as relative positions, relative directions, and relative distances, are another common type of percept. For example, the method to calculate the distance of the i th character relative to "me" is calcMyDistanceToCharacter. An example of a slightly more complicated method is calcMyDistanceToNearestCharacter, which is written in terms of calcMyNearestCharacter, which is itself written in terms of calcMyDistanceToCharacter (see Listing 3.2).

Relative values are often combined with percepts related to other named characters. For example, the relative position of the tagged character (to "me") is likely to be an important input to many controllers in the tag game.

Many percepts depend on each other so that calculating one involves calculating its dependents. For example, calcMyDistanceToNearest Character depends on calcMyDistanceToCharacter which in turn depends on calcMyDistanceToCharacter. If some of a percept's dependents have already been calculated, it is wasteful to recompute them. Therefore, percepts should be cached to avoid unnecessary recomputation. If caching is used, care needs to be taken to correctly clear the caches in response to clock ticks, or changing the character from whose point of view percepts are being calculated.

3.4   Partial Observability

If a controller is given full and direct access to the game-state, it has complete access to all the information about the game world and the game world is said to be *fully observable* by the controller. In contrast, if access to the game-state is restricted, then the game world is said to be only *partially observable*. This section introduces some percepts that make the world only partially observable from an NPC controller's perspective.

When the world is only partially observable, then many different game-states are indistinguishable. This is often a good thing as it means controllers can be made more general. That is, many percepts are defined so as to hide unimportant details and emphasize the crucial similarities be-

```
tgCharacter* tgPerception::calcMyNearestCharacter() const
{
    int which = tgGameState::nobody;
    tgReal dMin = Inf;
    for (int i = 0; i < gs->getNumCharacters(); i++)
    {
        if (i == myIndex) { continue; } // Don't include me!

        tgReal d = calcMyDistanceToCharacter(i);
        if (d < dMin)
        {
            dMin = d;
            which = i;
        }
    }
    assert(tgGameState::nobody != which);
    return gs->getCharacter(which);
}

tgReal tgPerception::calcMyDistanceToNearestCharacter() const
{
    tgRealVec p(getMyPosition());
    p.subtract(calcMyNearestCharacter()->getPosition());
    return p.norm();
}
```

Listing 3.2. Definition of percept to calculate the distance to my nearest character.

tween game-states. But as explained earlier, there are occasions when information is deliberately hidden to avoid giving NPCs an unfair advantage. For example, if the tagged character is hidden behind an obstacle, then an NPC is generally not allowed to know its position. From the NPC's point of view, the tagged character could potentially be in any position that is obscured by the obstacle. The set of game-states in which the character is in one of the possible hidden positions it could occupy is referred to as a *belief state*.

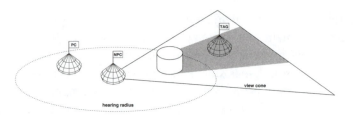

Figure 3.1. Simulated visibility and audibility.

Section 5.3 in Chapter 5 explores how an NPC can maintain its belief state so that it is useful for making decisions. In the meantime, the next few subsections describe some specific ways for simulating some of the limitations of perception that put NPCs and player characters on a more level footing.

3.4.1 Visibility

The image produced by the renderer is often from the direction the player character is looking. Therefore, unless the player character turns her head, she cannot see what is behind her. Many games mitigate this limitation by augmenting the display with an overhead map view. Proper rendering of sound also lets a player hear something sneaking up behind them. Nevertheless, in many games the renderer makes it possible for NPCs to hide from player characters behind opaque objects. To be fair, the converse should also be true: player characters should be able to use objects like walls to hide from NPCs.

For NPCs, instead of using the renderer to implement visibility, a getIsVisible percept can be defined. As the name suggests, the getIsVisible method can be used to determine if a character is visible from another character's point of view. Figure 3.1 shows some simple situations involving visibility in the tag game. In particular, the tagged character is not visible for although it is within the NPC's view cone, it is hidden by an obstacle. In contrast, the player character is outside the view cone, but within the hearing radius and so is visible (or at least audible). See [Leo03] for a good article about building a perception system for a game.

Visibility calculations are commonplace in computer graphics and similar code can be used for calculating visibility percepts. Coherency be-

tween frames can allow calculations on previous frames to be reused, which can make a dramatic improvement in the total cost of visibility calculations. In addition, fast approximate visibility tests using bounding boxes and spheres are sometimes sufficient for controllers' purposes. Good references on visibility testing are available from any graphics textbook that describes ray tracing and BSP trees; for example, see [FvDFH95, Shi02].

3.4.2 Simulated Noisy Sensors

The human player will not in general be able to precisely judge object properties like location and speed. Instead, the human will be (implicitly) using values that contain a certain amount of noise. NPCs can be given similar noisy sensor readings by randomly perturbing the true values of various percepts. For example, in the tag game suppose $\mathbf{p} = (x, y)$ is the true position of the tagged character. Then the virtual method getTagged Position could be overridden in a subclass that returns the position $(x + \Delta x, y + \Delta y)$, where Δx and Δy are chosen randomly according to some probability distribution. For example, standard distributions from probability theory can be used, such as a uniform distribution, or a normal distribution with the mean centered on the true position.

3.4.3 Discretization

A percept like getMyDistanceToTagged returns a floating-point number. However, it might be more useful for a controller to predicate its decisions on a more abstract notion of whether the tagged character is close or not. For example, if the distance to the tagged object is d, then the getIsTaggedCloseToMe method computes the predicate: $d < k$, where k is some fixed threshold.

Converting a value (like distance) into a predicate that is either true or false is just one example of *discretization*. In general, a value can be discretized (or bucketed) into more than simply two values. For example, instead of an angle or a unit vector, a direction could be discretized into one of eight compass directions.

Although discretization does hide information about precisely where an object is, it is often done more as a convenience than as a hindrance. For example, in Chapter 6, discretizing positions into a grid is important in

order to apply certain types of search algorithms. To show how to define a grid, assume a two-dimensional world bounded by a box with the origin as the lower left hand-corner and (x_{max}, y_{max}) as the upper right-hand corner. Then a grid of $m \times n$ rectangular cells (hexagons or triangles can also be used to tessellate the plane) can be laid over the world, such that the width s and height t of each cell is, respectively, $s = x_{max}/m$ and $t = y_{max}/n$. The grid coordinate (i, j) of a position $\mathbf{p} = (x, y)$ is thus

$$\begin{pmatrix} i \\ j \end{pmatrix} = \begin{pmatrix} \lfloor \frac{x}{s} \rfloor \\ \lfloor \frac{y}{t} \rfloor \end{pmatrix}.$$

3.5 Predictor Percepts

Space Invaders was one of the earliest successful computer games. A key part of the game challenge was being able to accurately anticipate where the invaders would be in the future. This was because the invaders were moving and the bullets took some time to travel. So (unless you got lucky) the bullets would miss if you aimed at the invader's location at the time of firing. Instead, you had to time your shot to end up where the invader would be by the time the bullet arrived. In modern computer games, NPCs sometimes need to use similar kinds of anticipation to shoot back at you. It is convenient therefore to define *predictor percepts* that predict future values. Predictor percepts are also useful for predicting any hidden values. For example, Section 5.3 in Chapter 5 explores how predictor percepts are used to represent a belief state.

In the tag game, a specific example of a predictor percept is calcPosition Tagged Future that predicts the position of the tagged character at some specified time in the future. If the tagged character is currently the player character, then its future position is uncertain because it depends on the future action choices of the human player.

Of course, an NPC can sometimes cheat and know what a player character will do before the appropriate animation is played, but an NPC cannot know for certain (unless the player character is confined somehow) where the player character will be in five minutes. However, if it is important for an NPC to independently show up in the player character's neighborhood in five minutes there are alternatives to trying to predict the location. In particular, if the NPC in question could have plausibly gotten to the

player character's destination in time, then it can just be magically teleported there (or at least moved extra quickly). This will work so long as
the player character does not see the NPC being teleported (unless the ability to teleport is part of the game). It will also appear odd to the player if
an NPC she saw some time ago heading in the opposite direction suddenly
manages to show up later on nearby.

Predicting future values associated with another NPC can be calculated
with more certainty and without resorting to teleporting. This is because
one NPC can, in principle, ask another NPC what it will do in a given
situation. There are, however, reasons why this is not always possible or
desirable:

Influence of the player character. An NPC will react to the player character and so the NPC's future behavior is contingent upon the player
character's future behavior. Since the human player's behavior is
uncertain, then so is the NPC's behavior. Of course, if the player
character is unable to influence an NPC (for example, if it is too far
away), then it may be possible, for a time, to calculate some future
values with certainty.

Random number generators. Random number generators are often used
in games to randomize action choices inside controllers, and other
decisions inside the simulator. Random number generators typically
(unless they have access to specialized hardware) generate pseudorandom numbers. Pseudorandom numbers are not really random
because they are generated by a deterministic computer program,
but they (ideally) share many statistical properties with true random
numbers. If an NPC knew the algorithm by which the pseudorandom
numbers were being generated, it could, in theory, remove the uncertainty they introduce. This would be complicated and (as explained
in the upcoming realistic perception explanation) undesirable.

Game world complexity. Many game world simulators are so complex
that it is hard to accurately approximate their functionality. Consequently, the only certain way of knowing what will happen in the
future is to use the real simulator to look forward in time. In Chapter 6 this is exactly what is described as one way of picking actions.
The problem with going too far into the future is that simulation is

usually CPU-intensive and there is still the problem of predicting what the player character will do.

Approximate simulator. In Chapter 6 an NPC needs to predict both where it and other NPCs will be in the future using a discrete representation of the game world. One way to do this accurately would be to temporarily discard the discrete representation, simulate forward using the continuous representation and the game simulator, and then rediscretize the answer. In practice, this would be slow and cumbersome so the game world's physics are usually also approximated inside the discrete representation directly. To be fast, the approximate game world physics ignores many details but it can still be accurate enough to be useful. Nevertheless the resulting prediction of the NPC's future position is not certain.

Realistic perception. Even if an NPC has access to information that would reduce uncertainty about the game world, it is often undesirable to take advantage of it. A classic example of unrealistic behavior generated from giving a character too much information about the game is given in [Fun99]. In the example, a character uses the simulator to precompute trajectories of falling bricks and then nonchalantly walks through them without any fear of being hit.

Therefore, regardless of whether some future value is really random or not, from the NPC's point of view, it can make sense to think it is. Thus in the tag game, calcPositionTaggedFuture corresponds to the value of a random variable $\mathbf{p}' = (p'_x, p'_y)$ that ranges over possible future positions. Notice that the possible future positions represent a belief state about the future, hence there is a close connection with belief maintenance described in Section 5.3 in Chapter 5.[3]

Before proceeding, you should realize that just because probability is being used to describe predictor percepts, it does not mean that probability

---

[3]In the real world, predictions often have to be made based on noisy sensor readings. In these cases a Kalman filter (see [RN02]) is sometimes used to estimate future (and current) values. In a game world, a similar effect to predicting from noisy sensors can, if required, often be achieved more easily by slightly randomizing the output (as in section 3.4.2) of a simpler prediction method that takes advantage of the availablity of non-noisy sensor values.

has to be used in the implementation of a predictor percept. For example, an implementation of a predictor percept that does not explicitly use probability at all is given toward the end of this section. The implementation falls out as a special case from the more general theoretical framework based on probability. Therefore, regardless of the final implementation, it is still worth exploring the theory behind predictor percepts in a little more detail. To do so, consider just the subproblem of determining the probability that the tagged character's future x-coordinate p'_x, at some fixed time in the future, is in some given interval (a, b). The probability could depend on the current and past values of any number of percepts, but assume the NPC makes the reasonable approximation that it only depends on the current x-position p_x and velocity v_x. Then the NPC needs to calculate the conditional probability $P(a < p'_x < b \mid p_x, v_x)$ that, given the current position and velocity, p'_x will be in the interval (a, b).

Usually the conditional probability distribution is unknown and one possibility is to try and learn it. In particular, learning a conditional probability distribution for the player character can lead to some powerful AI effects. It is, however, complicated and CPU-intensive. In addition, the game designer may not want the NPCs to be too good at predicting the player. As pointed out earlier, even if more accurate or longer term predications are required, it is often easier to cheat. An alternative to learning, or cheating, is to simply define a probability distribution as part of the definition of the behavior of the NPC. That is, the NPC is simply defined to be a character that computes the conditional probability in a certain way. For example, Figure 3.2 defines a possible underlying conditional probability density function from which the conditional probability can be calculated as the area under the curve, as indicated by the shaded region.

However the probability is determined, the final value of the predictor percept needs to be determined for use in a controller. A controller could be defined to take a probability distribution directly as input, but a controller usually expects a single value for the value of a percept. There are numerous ways to generate a single value from a distribution and two of the most common, picking the most likely and picking randomly from the distribution, are described in Appendix A.

In many cases, defining a distribution for a predictor percept at all is overkill. Instead, a percept can just directly compute a single value. You can think of it as a short-circuited version of defining a distribution in terms

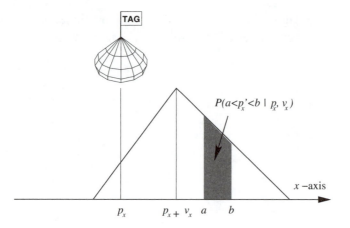

Figure 3.2. Example conditional probability density function.

of the most likely value and then picking the most likely value. As an example, the following code defines the tagged character's future position directly using the current velocity to perform a simple linear extrapolation of the current position:

```
tgRealVec tgPerception::calcTaggedPositionFuture() const
{
    tgRealVec p(getTaggedPosition());
    return p.add(getTaggedVelocity());
}
```

Extrapolating from the current position is also sometimes referred to as *dead reckoning*, and is often used to reduce communication between machines in networked games. The idea is that if two networked instances of a game world use the same dead reckoning algorithm to predict uncertain future values, then communication over the network only has to take place when the difference between the predictions and what subsequently happens exceeds some margin of error.

Note that, predictor percepts that predict the output of a controller blur the distinction between percepts and controllers. For example, if the calcPositionTagged Future is particularly good at predicting the tag character's behavior, then, in theory, its predictions could be used as the con-

troller for the tagged character. Similarily, as mentioned in Section 6.6.1 in Chapter 6, a controller can be used as a predictor percept.

Chapter 4

Reacting

A controller is a function from percepts to actions, and a reactive controller is the special case that has no memory and therefore uses only the current value of the percepts. Because only the current percepts are used, from one call of the calcAction method to the next, a reactive controller (or its associated perception object) is not allowed to store information about the percepts, or action chosen, from the previous invocation. Therefore, if a reactive controller receives identical values for its percepts over and over again, it will select the same action every time, i.e., it is idempotent. Of course, during one invocation of the calcAction method a reactive controller is free to use internal state to store intermediate results. It is just not allowed to use those intermediate results to influence its behavior from one invocation to the next.

Because a reactive controller is idempotent you never have to worry about what state it was left in last time it was used. For example, the same instance of a reactive controller can easily be shared between NPCs. In addition, no state needs to be saved out when the game is turned off or otherwise interrupted. This can result in simpler code and less memory usage. The downside of a reactive controller is that because it is not allowed to remember past situations it can, literally and figuratively, end up going around in circles. Nevertheless, reactive controllers are useful, versatile, and powerful. For example, some insects appear to use primarily reac-

51

tive controllers and there are some classic publications in the AI literature that used computer games to argue for reactive systems as a basis for AI [AC87, Cha91].

4.1 Definition of a Reactive Controller

A reactive controller (or policy) is a function ϕ from percepts $\mathbf{x} = (x_0, \ldots, x_{m-1})$ to actions $a(\mathbf{y})$ such that

$$\phi(\mathbf{x}) = a(\mathbf{y}), \tag{4.1}$$

where x_i is the current value[1] of percept i and $\mathbf{y} = (y_0, \ldots, y_{k-1})$ are the k action parameters. Note that, in general, $\mathbf{x}$ represents a belief state as described in Section 3.4 in Chapter 3.

In the tag game there is only one game action, the move action. But it takes two parameters that indicate the direction to move, and it is the controller's job to determine them. More realistic games will require the controller to choose from many possible actions, some or all of which may have parameters. If some of the actions do have parameters, then selecting an action is a two-step process: step one is to select the action and step two is, given the selected action, to choose desirable parameters. If desirable parameters cannot be found, then step one needs to be repeated until a different action is selected for which suitable parameters can be found.

Providing a definition of a reactive controller does not answer the more interesting question: where do controllers come from? The answer is that they are either defined by the game developer, or learned. The focus of Chapter 7 is on the topic of learning controllers, while this and the next two chapters concentrate on defining them directly.

4.1.1 Stochastic Version of a Reactive Controller

Ignoring the problem of picking parameters for now, assume that the controller's sole task is to pick one of n possible actions: $a_0, \ldots, a_{n-1}$. The stochastic version of a reactive controller does not pick an action directly. Instead, it defines a conditional probability distribution over the possible

---

[1]The "value" of a percept need not be a numerical value, it can be a Boolean value (true or false), a label, a set of label, a string, a set of strings, etc.

actions and uses one of the methods described in Appendix A to pick an action. The conditional distribution $P(a_i|\mathbf{x})$ specifies the probability of picking each a_i, given the current values of the percepts.

An interesting special case is when, regardless of the value of the percepts $\mathbf{x}$, the probability $1/n$ is unconditionally assigned to each action (i.e., the probability distribution is the uniform distribution). Then picking randomly from the distribution gives an equal chance of selecting any of the actions. The resulting controller is called the *random controller* and is useful for stress-testing a game.

In general, the probability assigned to each action should represent the probability that it is the action you want the NPC to pick in the current situation. For example, if an NPC is far away from a dangerous enemy, then perhaps it is better for the NPC to run away, but you'd also be happy if it stays where it is for a while. Then you would assign a 70% chance, say, to the run-away action, and a 30% chance to the stay action. If you are sure which action you want the NPC to do in every situation, then there is obviously no need to use a stochastic controller.

Note that, since a stochastic reactive controller is still reactive, if it receives identical values for its percepts over and over again, it will select the same probability distribution every time. Although, if one of the methods used in Appendix A is then used to pick an action randomly from the distribtion, then the final action that gets sent to the simulator will of course vary.[2]

As for a deterministic controller, picking parameters in a stochastic controller can be done as a separate step. For example, suppose an action a has been chosen and that it can take one of k parameter values: $y_0, \ldots, y_{k-1}$. Then another conditional probability distribution $P(y_i|a, \mathbf{x})$ gives the probability of picking y_i, given the action choice a and the current value of the percepts.

If the parameter is continuous, then there is some underlying conditional probability density function. If there is more than one parameter and they are not independent, or cannot be treated (as an approximation) as if they are independent, then the situation gets complicated and is beyond

---

[2]To avoid violating the definition of a reactive controller as idempotent, the seed to the random number generator must be included in the percepts, in which case identical percepts will yield an identical action choice. Alternatively, the picking randomly part can be considered as a separate process.

the scope of this book. Similarly, complications arise if picking actions and parameters cannot be done independently.

Now that you know what a stochastic controller is, it is worth quickly pointing out why you might want to use one:

- it is often more exciting to play against NPCs who are not completely predictable.

- as pointed out in Section 3.4.2 and Section 3.5 in the previous chapter, the inputs to a controller can contain uncertainty, so it makes sense that the outputs can, too. That is, it is hard to know in advance precisely what the best action is, so randomizing allows the AI programmer to hedge.

- randomness can break symmetries to avoid, for example, an NPC getting stuck in a corner forever.

- in the real world actuators (like sensors) can be noisy. For example, holding an object completely still is difficult and the object usually wobbles slightly. In games where there is a sniper mode this wobbling is sometimes modeled for the player character by randomly moving the displayed image around in the sniper mode. For NPCs a similar effect can be achieved by slightly randomizing the output of its aiming controller.

- from the NPC's point of view, the player character is somewhat enigmatic. Even if an NPC tries to learn to predict the player character's actions, there will be hidden variables that (given the available percepts) make aspects of the player's behavior impenetrable. For example, the player might behave differently when she is hungry, but there is no realistic way to define a percept to say how hungry the player is. For the purposes of learning, the hidden variables can be modeled as random variables whose distribution must be determined from the data. A crude way to make the NPC's behavior also appear (to the player) somewhat enigmatic is, therefore, to add randomness to the NPC's controller output.

- humans often see patterns in, and ascribe meaning to, random events. Somewhat like seeing patterns in the clouds, players often mistake

blind luck for intelligence. This can obviously work both ways and NPCs could end up looking stupid by not picking the most obvious action.

4.2 Simple Functions of Percepts

Even relatively uncomplicated functions from percepts to actions can yield interesting behavior. For example, the controller in Listing 4.1 causes a character to pursue the nearest character if it is tagged, and run away otherwise.

```
void tgControllerNPC::calcAction(int whoami)
{
    perception->setMyIndex( whoami );
    tgRealVec v( perception->getMyPosition() );

    if ( perception->getAmITagged() )
    { // Pursuit
        v.subtract( perception->getMyNearestCharacterPosition() );
        v.scale( -1.0 ); // run towards
    }
    else
    { // Evasion
        v.subtract( perception->getTaggedPosition() );
    }
    v.normalize();
    v.scale( perception->getMyMaxSpeed() );
    v.subtract( perception->getMyVelocity() );
    action.setDesiredVelocity( v );
}
```

Listing 4.1. Simple pursuit and evasion controller for the tag game.

Pursuit and evasion are two examples of *steering behaviors*. A more complex example of a steering behavior is the *boids* model of flocks, herds, and schools. The boids model was first published in [Rey87], and since then it has been widely used in games and movies. Boids flocking be-

havior is obtained by adding together three weighted steering components *alignment* $\mathbf{v}_a$, *cohesion* $\mathbf{v}_c$, and *separation* $\mathbf{v}_s$ to obtain the overall desired velocity $\mathbf{v}_d$.

$$\mathbf{v}_d = w_0 \hat{\mathbf{v}}_a + w_1 \hat{\mathbf{v}}_c + w_2 \hat{\mathbf{v}}_s$$

Different relative weights w_0, w_1 and w_2 give rise to different kind of flocks. For example, a lower weight for cohesion gives rise to a more loosely knit flock. Note that, if the weights sum to one, then $\mathbf{v}_d$ will be automatically normalized.

The individual steering components are all computed with respect to nearby characters. A percept calcCharactersNearMe is therefore used to compute the list of characters within some threshold. The threshold itself is another one of the boid flocking model parameters.

The alignment steering component $\mathbf{v}_a$ is the average orientation of the nearby characters. Similarly, cohesion $\mathbf{v}_c$ is a vector that points toward the nearby characters' average position. Separation is slightly more complicated. Intuitively, if there were only two characters, the separation component would be a vector pointing in the opposite direction to the other character. With multiple characters nearby, separation is defined as the sum of all the normalized vectors pointing away from each character, scaled by the inverse of the distance:

$$\mathbf{v}_s = \sum_i \frac{\hat{\mathbf{q}}_i}{|\mathbf{q}_i|},$$

where $\mathbf{q}_i = \mathbf{p}_i - \mathbf{p}$, $\mathbf{p}$ is "my" position and $\mathbf{p}_i$ is the position of nearby character i.

Obviously, because each flock member is in a slightly different situation, the steering vector $\mathbf{v}_d$ needs to be computed separately for each individual. But since flocking can be implemented as an idempotent reactive controller, the same identical instance of the controller can be used for an entire flock.

A good source of further details on the boid flocking model, its variations, and a wide range of additional steering behaviors is [Rey99]. There is also an open source library called OpenSteer that implements a wide variety of important steering behaviors (see this book's companion web site for a pointer to the code).

```
void tgControllerNPC::calcAction(int myIndex)
{
    perception->setMyIndex(myIndex);

    tgObstacle* obj = perception->calcMyNearestObstacle();
    if ( perception->calcAmICollidingSoonWith(obj) )
    {
        avoidCollision(obj);
    }
    else
    {
        flock();
    }
}
```

Listing 4.2. Controller that gives priority to avoiding collisions.

4.3 Reactive Production Rules

One common steering behavior is collision avoidance. Avoiding collisions is usually a high priority, higher than maintaining a flock formation, for example. It is convenient therefore to be able to write conditional rules to express the different priorities. For example, suppose the
tgControllerNPC class has methods avoidCollision and flock that, respectively, produce steering vectors to avoid collisions and maintain the boid
flocking model. In addition, suppose there is a percept calcIsCollsionsIm-
mininent, then Listing 4.2 shows a conditional controller that gives priority
to avoiding collisions.

In general, conditional rules have the form of *if-then* rules and are referred to as *production rules*.[3] The *if* part contains a test, or firing condition, and the *then* part executes some action or subcontroller. When the test
is true the rule is said to have fired or activated. Production rules can be
nested and arranged in hierarchies to create elaborate behaviors. Production rules are also important for implementing more general, nonreactive,
controllers as explained in Section 5.4.3 of the next chapter.

---

[3]Production rule systems consist only of pattern matching rules, rather than procedural
code as in Listing 4.2.

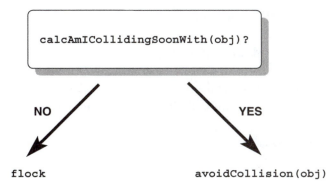

Figure 4.1. Example of a decision stump.

4.4 Decision Trees

Figure 4.1 shows the same conditional rule as in Listing 4.2, but represented as a decision tree. More specifically, it is a tree with only one internal node, which is commonly referred to as a *decision stump*. In general, a
decision tree consists of a number of nodes and branches. The leaf nodes
represent decisions, i.e. action choices. The internal (nonleaf) nodes represent tests and each node has as many branches as there are possible answers to the test. A controller uses a decision tree to pick an action by
evaluating tests and taking the branch that corresponds to the result. When
the controller gets to a leaf, then that is the action to choose. For example,
Figure 4.2 shows a decision tree that might be used by a high-level controller in the tag game. The controller is not meant to be taken seriously as
a legitimate controller, but there are a couple of things to note:

- not all tests in a decision tree have to be binary. For example, in
  the diagram the percept calcDistanceToTagged returns a Boolean.
  In general, a test can also return an integer or even a float. If a test
  does return a number over a wide possible range, then usually each
  branch represents a bucket of values.

- not all the leaf nodes have to be game actions. For example, in
  the figure only one leaf node sets the desired velocity. The others
  call other methods of the controller class, which implement subcontrollers, and may be decision trees themselves.

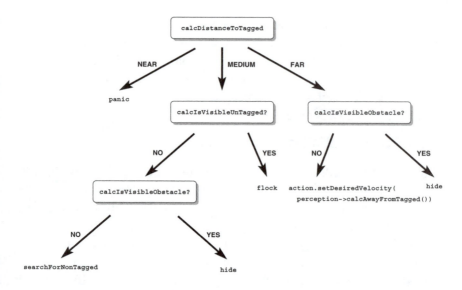

Figure 4.2. Example of a decision tree.

- the same test in a different part of the tree can yield different action choices. For example, in the figure an NPC that is far from the tagged character will run even farther away if it cannot see an obstacle to hide behind. But an NPC that is only a medium distance to the tagged character, and cannot see another untagged character, will search for a fellow untagged character.

Decision trees are easy to program (see this book's companion web site for pointers) and have been used as a representation for controllers in computer games. One important reason they are suitable representation is that, with a suitable Graphical User Interface (GUI), they can be created and maintained by nonprogrammers.

Decision trees are closely related to production rules in that a decision tree can easily be converted into a set of rules. In particular, there is a rule for each leaf such that the *if*-part is the conjunction of each of the tests on the way from the root to the leaf; and the *then*-part is just the action at the leaf node.

Trees and production rules are also both popular representations for the output of machine learning algorithms. CART and C4.5 are two classic machine learning programs that can output decision trees or produc-

tion rules (see [HTF01]). More recent machine learning algorithms use weighted forests of decision trees (or stumps) and new decision tree-like data structures like AD-trees. The big advantage decision trees and production rules have as a representation of a learned function is that, unlike neural network weights for instance, they can be inspected to see if they make sense intuitively (see [WF99]).

4.4.1 Stochastic Decision Trees

If instead of a single action choice at each leaf node there is a probability distribution defined over all possible actions, then a decision tree can be used to represent a stochastic controller. The deterministic version of a decision tree can be thought of as the special case of a stochastic one in which all the probability is assigned to a single action. Specifying probabilities for all the possible actions is obviously more work. When selecting continuous parameter values, the leaf node will typically specify *sufficient statistics* that completely specify some standard distribution. For example, a leaf node could specify the mean and standard deviation that is then used to define a normal distribution.

Note that, in the stochastic version of a decision tree, there is no randomness in selecting a probability distribution at a leaf node. That is, given the current values of the percepts the leaf node is selected deterministically using the tests at the internal nodes. The stochastic nature of the controller is in the fact that it outputs a probability distribution instead of a single action. As described earlier, one of the methods described in Appendix A can then be used to (if desired) add randomness when picking an action according to the distribution.

If, as is usually the case, an NPC can choose a new action every few frames, then you have to be careful when picking randomly from a distribution to not get an NPC that flip-flops between decisions. For example, an NPC might randomly pick a different action each time and never get far executing either one. The effect the human sees on the screen in such cases is often of an NPC having a violent twitching fit! The solution is to make the controller take into account previous action choices, but that would require remembering, which is covered in the next chapter. The reason twitching is not such a concern with a deterministic controller (although it can happen at decision boundaries) is because, in a similar situation, the controller is likely to choose a similar action.

4.5 Logical Inference

An *if-then* rule, like those in Section 4.3, is an example of a simple inference rule. In academic AI many other more sophisticated types of inference rules have been studied, and it is conceivable that these other inference rules could be used in games to pick actions. One particularly important set of inference rules is known as first-order logic. First-order logic
was created as a formal language for mathematics, but it is sufficiently expressive that it has been widely used in AI for representing various problem
domains.

Here is an example of an inference rule that could be used by a controller:

$$\forall x \; P(x) \Rightarrow Q(x), P(a) \vdash Q(a).$$

What it says is that if every x that is a P is also a Q, and a is a P, then
a must also be Q. P and Q can be any predicates (i.e., Boolean valued
functions) so if x can range over all NPCs in a game, $P(x)$ represents "x
is a plumber", $Q(x)$ represents "x has a mustache", and a is Mario, then
the inference rule allows the controller to infer that Mario has a mustache.
This could be useful if an NPC had the task of choosing a gift for his
friend Mario the plumber, but was never explicitly told that Mario had a
mustache. Note that, with the same interpretation of P and Q, the rule does
not allow the controller to infer that an NPC is a plumber just because he
has a mustache.

Aside from its expressive power, the big advantage of using first-order
logic is that it has a proof system with some reassuring properties:

Sound. The proof system is sound. This means that if you start out with a
set of assumptions, then any sentence that you prove is (with respect
to the initial assumptions) true. Note that, this says nothing about
whether the initial assumptions are true, and indeed if they contain
a contradiction, then you will be able to prove anything!

Complete. The proof system is complete, i.e., any true sentence can be
proved.

Importantly for computer games, the proof system for first-order logic
can be embodied in a computer program known as a *theorem prover*. Prolog is a well-known example of a programming language that contains a

built-in theorem prover [Lin98, RN02]. Using a theorem prover inside a controller is therefore potentially powerful, as an NPC could infer all sorts of consequences of what it knows and appear highly intelligent. Unfortunately, using a theorem prover in games faces a number of obstacles:

1. if a sentence is true, it can potentially take an exponential amount of time for the theorem prover to prove it. Researchers have proposed more restricted proof systems for first-order logic that are sound, but not complete. The advantage of these limited systems is that they are guaranteed to succeed in polynomial time if the sentence is true.

2. first-order logic is only *semidecidable*. This means that if a sentence is false, the theorem prover might never be able to prove it. That is, the theorem prover might go into an infinite loop, but there is no way to tell (in general) that it has gone into an infinite loop, or that it is just about to return the answer. This makes it difficult to know when the theorem prover should be set to time out.

3. theorem provers potentially use an enormous amounts of memory.

4. in general, to prove anything useful, a character needs a lot of commonsense knowledge. The Cyc project is attempting to alleviate this problem by creating a vast KB of commonsense knowledge [Len95].

5. theorem provers typically do not have much support for representing uncertainty. There have been attempts to combine first-order logic and probability theory, but the work is presently largely of theoretical interest.

Because of the obstacles to using first-order logic in games, a more reasonable alternative is to use propositional logic. Propositional logic is a subset of first-order logic that does not include any variables. Propositional logic is fully decidable, but testing the validity of a proposition can still take an exponential amount of time in the worst case. However, there are sound but incomplete "SAT" solvers that use stochastic methods to quickly solve many nontrivial problems [KS03].

One downside of propositional logic is that because it does not have variables, to express the fact that all NPCs in the game are green, say, you cannot write $\forall x$ Green(x). Instead, you have to write out a separate

proposition for each NPC. For example, if there are three NPCs called Fred, Mary, and Bill, you'd have to write out

$$FredGreen \land MaryGreen \land BillGreen.$$

If there are a lot of NPCs this can get tiresome, and if there are a lot of properties each NPC can possess, then there are an exponential number of potential propositions. There are tools for automatically converting first-order logic style expressions to propositions, but the end result can still consume a lot of memory.

Aside from any technical difficulties, logical reasoning would require a game design that justified its inclusion, for example, if the game needed to simulate human logical reasoning, or if the game world was a complex domain that required runtime logical inference. The behavior rules that game developers normally write can be thought of as the result of their own logical inference. That is, they think in advance about which rules an NPC needs to operate effectively in their world, given the game physics and the NPC's capabilities.

Chapter 5

Remembering

Because reactive controllers are idempotent they are simple to use, but they also have serious drawbacks. For example, because a reactive controller cannot remember previous percepts and actions, it cannot remember which action it picked last time it was in the same situation. When it finds itself in the same situation as before, it cannot therefore decide to pick a different action from before. If last time the choice turned out to be a bad one, then a reactive controller will carry on making the same mistake over and over again, just like a fly repeatedly hitting a window pane. Since there is no way for it to distinguish seeing a situation once to seeing it a thousand times, it cannot even count how many times it has been in the same situation before.

Coupled with a way to randomly pick from the resulting distribution, a stochastic reactive controller can output different actions in the same situation. But this does not fundamentally alter the limitations of a reactive controller because, on average, the frequency with which it picks different actions will, in identical situations, be the same.[1]

---

[1] If the percepts include a value that is always different (like the current time), then no two situations are ever the same. If no two situations are the same, then obviously the problem of not being able to recognize being in the same situation never arises. But normally percepts are chosen so as to emphasize the similarity between game-states, as this makes controllers more general.

The only way to address the inherent limitations of a reactive controller is to permit the controller, and associated perception object, to remember the past values of percepts. Such controllers have no inherent limitations and can be programmed to compute any computable function from percepts to actions.

5.1   Definition of a Controller

Except that it can use previous values of percepts, the definition of a controller is similar to the definition of a reactive controller given in Equation 4.1 in the previous chapter. In particular, if the percepts at time t are denoted $\mathbf{x}^t = (x_0^t, \ldots, x_{m-1}^t)$, then a controller ϕ is a function from percepts to actions such that

$$\phi(\mathbf{x}^0, \ldots, \mathbf{x}^t) = a(\mathbf{y}), \tag{5.1}$$

where $\mathbf{y}$ are the action parameters.

For the case where there are no parameters and the sole task is to pick one of n actions, $a_0, \ldots, a_{n-1}$, the stochastic version of a controller is defined by a conditional probability distribution over the possible actions. Similar to the definition in 4.1.1 in the last chapter, the conditional probability distribution $P(a_i | \mathbf{x}^0, \ldots, \mathbf{x}^t)$ specifies the probability of picking each a_i, given the values of the percepts. Once again, one of the methods described in Appendix A can be used to pick a single action from the distribution.

5.2   Memory Percepts

Equation 5.1 expresses a controller's ability to use any of the past percepts in its calculations. That does not mean a controller has to use all the past percepts, and in practice a controller would quickly run out of memory if it had to remember the value of every single percept it has ever seen. Instead, a controller remembers certain key percepts, like the last place it saw the tagged character, or summary percepts, like the number of times it has been chased around a particular obstacle. These percepts are called *memory percepts*.

Note that although the state used to store memory percepts is typically part of the perception object, any controller that makes use of a memory

percept is automatically stateful, and no longer reactive. That is because the function the controller is computing can depend on some previous percepts' values, and not just on the current ones. Depending on what those previous values are, the controller can thus behave differently in two otherwise identical situations. Conceptually, where the state used to remember the previous percepts' values happens to be located is an irrelevant detail. However, from an implementation perspective, it does keep the code simpler if the state can all be added in the perception object, but as explained in Section 5.4 this is not always desirable. The advantage to keeping the state in the perception object is that NPCs can share a controller instance. The perception object is then responsible for managing the state associated with each character. This can be done by having a separate perception object instance for each character, but a simpler alternative is used in what follows.

Memory percepts are often stored on a per character basis, but information can also be remembered on a per level basis, or a per location basis, etc. As an example of a memory percept, consider getWhoLastTaggedMe that remembers which character was the last one who tagged "me". This information might be useful to a controller for an NPC that likes to get revenge. Remember that which character is "me" is indicated by the myIndex class variable and changes according to whose turn it is to select an action.

Because the information is not needed by the simulator, the game-state does not store information about who last tagged who and the getWhoLast TaggedMe method cannot therefore be a function of the game-state. Of course, it is possible to imagine a version of the tag game where it is important for the simulator to record who last tagged who, for example, if a rule was added that prevented a character tagging back the character who just tagged them. But even then the game-state would only need to store the information for the currently tagged character. The point is that as the game stands, the information is not needed by the simulator and is therefore not (and should not be) stored in the game-state.

Since the game-state does not know which character last tagged "me", the information needs to be stored in the perception object. There are a variety of ways to do this, but a simple solution is to add a new private class variable to the perception object (or a subclass): lastTaggedByList. The lastTaggedbyList is a list (e.g., an array) with an entry for each character, such that the i th entry is the index of the last character who tagged

character i. The percept getWhoLastTaggedMe then simply looks up the
corresponding entry in lastTaggedByList:

```
int tgPerception::getWhoLastTaggedMe() const
{
    return lastTaggedByList[myIndex];
}
```

For the getWhoLastTaggedMe method to return the correct answer
lastTagged ByList had better be kept up-to-date, and this is where adding
state to controllers gets tricky. The problem is that, unless the simulator polls every controller every time the game-state changes, events can
happen in the game world without the controllers ever becoming aware
of them. To illustrate the problem, suppose the perception object has
a method updateLastTagged that checks if the tagged character changed
since it was last called and updates the lastTagged variable accordingly:

```
void tgPerception::updateLastTagged()
{
    int const taggedIndex = getTaggedIndex();
    // Note: lastTaggedIndex is a class varaible
    if ( taggedIndex != lastTaggedIndex )
    { // A new character has been tagged since last update
        // Assume lastTaggedIndex tagged taggedIndex
        lastTaggedByList[ taggedIndex ] = lastTaggedIndex;
        lastTaggedIndex = taggedIndex;
    }
}
```

The potential problem is with the assumption that the character with
index lastTaggedIndex was the one who tagged the character with index
taggedIndex. For example, suppose character i was tagged by character j
who then tagged character k all before the updateLastTagged was called.
This might happen if time-slicing meant that controllers were not always
invoked and the tag events were just a consequence of collisions handled
by the simulator. When a controller was finally called and the perception
object updated, the lastTaggedByList would be updated with the wrong

information! In particular, it would incorrectly assert that character k was tagged directly by character i. Character i might then unfairly receive the wrath of character k that should have been directed at character j. To the human watching all this take place, character k's behavior would seem puzzling indeed. Obviously this example is somewhat contrived but the problem is a genuine one.

There are a number of solutions to the problem. For example, an event-based message passing system could be used, such that if a tagging event occurs, then an appropriate update message gets sent. Alternatively, all perception objects could share a common instance of another perception object that contains all the state information. The common instance has an update method that needs to be called whenever the game-state changes, that way there is no danger of missing important events. Having to call the update method so often can cause difficulties if the CPU budget is tight. Depending on the game and if you are willing to tolerate the odd mistake, it may therefore be possible to call it less often. However, once the controller's state is allowed to get out-of-date, bugs that are difficult to track down can crop up unexpectedly.

5.2.1 Using Memory Percepts

Memory percepts can be used to make an NPC's behavior depend on what has happened in the past. For example, in role-playing games NPCs typically choose what to say based on what the player character has already achieved.

Fortunately, the mechanics of using memory percepts is trivial. In particular, they can be used wherever regular percepts are used. For example, looking back at the previous chapter, memory percepts can be used in controllers that are simple functions of percepts (see Section 4.2), production rules (see Section 4.3 and also Section 5.4.3 later on in this chapter), and decision trees (see Section 4.4).

Listing 5.1 shows a possible method of a controller class in the tag game that uses the getWhoLastTaggedMe memory percept to determine who the tagged character should chase. The calcWhoToChase method will be called from the calcAction method whenever the tagged character (assuming it is not currently also the player character) needs to compute an action.

```
tgCharacter* tgControllerNPC::calcWhoToChase()
{
    tgCharacter* const c = perception->calcMyNearestCharacter();
    tgCharacter* const t = perception->getTaggedCharacter();

    // Sometimes it is obvious who to chase
    if (c == t) { return c; }

    tgReal const dc = perception->calcMyDistanceToNearestCharacter();
    // If a character is really close, chase them no matter what
    // Note: minChaseDist is part of the character definition passed in
    // to the controller's constructor
    if (dc < minChaseDist) { return c; }

    tgReal const dt = perception->calcMyDistanceToTaggedCharacter();
    // If the character who last tagged me is a lot farther away forget it
    // Note: minChaseRatio is also part of the character definition
    if (dt/dc < minChaseRatio) { return c; }

    // OK, it's reasonable to chase the character who last tagged me
    return t;
}
```

Listing 5.1. Decide who to chase.

5.3 Belief Maintenance

Recall from Section 3.4 in Chapter 3 that a belief state is the set of possible game-states that is consistent with the current percept values. So, for example, if the tagged character is not visible it could potentially be in any obscured location. Based on the values of its memory percepts, an NPC could attempt to predict where the tagged character is. The simplest prediction an NPC can make is to predict that the tagged character is exactly where it last saw it.

Figure 5.1 illustrates an example of a common problem that arises with predicting that hidden state remains unchanged. On the left is the situation

Figure 5.1. An NPC's beliefs can become out-of-date.

when an NPC last saw the tagged character. Later on, the NPC has turned away and the tagged character has sneaked up behind it. But on the right the NPC foolishly believes the tagged character is still where it was. The problem is that the memory percept taggedLastKnownPosition is no longer an accurate representation of the game-state. But the NPC is still using it to predict that the unseen portions of the game world have not changed. If the NPC picks actions based on incorrect beliefs it will make bad choices. It is therefore important for an NPC to try and realize when its beliefs are unreliable and, if possible, to maintain them in a useful state. This is called belief (or truth) maintenance.

5.3.1 Invalidating Memory Percepts

Typically, the longer it was since the memory percept was refreshed, the more unreliable it is. A simple mechanism to model this is to represent the memory percept as an interval (see [Fun99]). When the memory percept is refreshed the interval is of width zero, then widens over time. If at any point an NPC wants to use the memory percept to make a prediction about the current game-state, it checks how wide it has become. If the width is above some acceptable threshold, then it is either not used, or if the value is important, an *information gathering* action is selected.

As the name suggests, an information gathering action is one whose purpose is to gather information. The player character also often chooses information gathering actions, for example, by running out to look where an enemy is. Many games include a stealth mode in which there are special information gathering actions such as "lean" that allow the player character to peek around corners without being seen.

Uniformly widening the interval representing a memory percept is simple and effective, but there are also more sophisticated approaches. For example, the interval could be widened more in some directions than others. In the case of the taggedLastKnownPosn percept, it could be widened more in the direction the tagged character was last seen to be traveling.

A still more sophisticated approach is to represent a memory percept as a probability distribution, similar to the approach described in Section 3.5 in Chapter 3. For example, for taggedLastKnownPosn the distribution represents the probability of the tagged character being in a certain area of the map. When the memory percept is refreshed all the probability is on the region where the tagged character is perceived to be. The entropy of the probability distribution then gradually increases over time, possibly at different rates in different directions. So long as the tagged character is not visible, the probability it is in a visible area needs to be (assuming there are no cloaking devices in the game) set to zero. These ideas are explored more fully in [IB02]. More recently, in [Ber04], a related and popular AI technique called *particle filtering* is applied to games. See [RN02] for more on sophisticated probabilistic reasoning in the context of general AI. Also see Section 6.6 in Chapter 6 for some additional ideas on how NPCs can model adversaries.

The full power of being able to predict the current game-state from past information is illustrated by the prowess of the well-known cyber-athlete Thresh. When Thresh played Doom or Quake he used a tactic that whenever he saw a player enter a room with a single exit he would not follow them inside. Instead, he would wait patiently outside to ambush them when they came out. If he remembered the contents of the room, he would even simulate them in his mind's eye going to pick up the rocket launcher, say, and then heading out. He was so precise that on occasions he could time firing a rocket at the entrance so that the rocket exploded just as the player emerged.

It is possible that players would assume NPCs with the same ability to predict hidden state as well as Thresh were cheating! Such NPCs might also not be much fun for some players, especially beginners, to play against (which is something to bear in mind before expending a lot of effort on an NPC's belief maintenance abilites).

5.3.2 Cheating

If an NPC really needs to know the location of a character obscured from view, then it can just cheat by looking it up in the game-state.[2] The downside of this kind of cheating is that human players can often tell. This can be frustrating and contribute to making playing against NPCs less fun than playing against other humans over a network. But by using simulated noisy sensors (see Section 3.4.2 in Chapter 3) to look up values in the game-state, humans players can often be fooled for much longer as to whether the NPCs are cheating or just being smart. This is because the noisy sensors will only return the correct (or near correct) answer some of the time.

Cheating can also be used in a more subtle way to check on the validity of memory percepts. In particular, by checking the degree of divergence between a memory percept and the corresponding value in the game-state, an NPC can realize when a memory percept is stale. If necessary it can then generate an information gathering action to discover the new value by legitimate means. Within reason, it is unlikely a player could quickly spot this kind of cheating, especially if randomness was introduced, for example, the NPC could be forced to use a noisy sensor to look up the true value of a memory percept. That way it would sometimes make the wrong decision about whether or not it needed to do any information gathering. To the player, this should look like highly realistic behavior.

NPCs can also use the ability to cheat to help player characters. For example, an NPC in a game might be able to throw hand grenades that damage all players within some blast radius. If the NPC's controller does not know where the player is (for example, the player character is hiding behind a rock), it might randomly throw a grenade nearby the player character. If the player character and NPC are supposed to be enemies, then, on the face of it, damaging the player character seems desirable. The "real" goal of the NPC is, however, to make the game fun. The game designer might therefore have mandated that the probability of throwing a grenade that will damage the player character should go down if the player character is nearly dead. That way the player might enjoy the game more as she survives long enough to get to the next health pack while grenades

---

[2]Note that, when predictor percepts are predicting future vales, this kind of cheating is obviously not possible because the future game-state does not yet exist.

"luckily" explode off in the distance. Sometimes such "cheating" (even with good intentions) can backfire and the feeling of danger is spoiled, but game designers need the option of making such choices.

5.4   Mental State Variables

The calcWhoToChase method in Listing 5.1 will decide to chase the character who last tagged "me", unless it is too far away relative to the nearest character. On successive calls to the calcWhoToChase method it is quite possible that a different character will be chosen to chase. This would happen, for example, if the tagged character was chasing the one who last tagged it and a different character wandered too close. In that case, the tagged character would break off the current chase and begin chasing the nearest character. If the nearest character got far enough away, it would return to chasing the character who last tagged it. There is nothing wrong with this behavior and given the continuous nature of movement in the tag game it would all look smooth and natural. But suppose that (for the sake of argument) once the tagged character has started chasing a character, the game developer wants to make it exhibit more goal commitment and continue chasing that character no matter what.

If there was a memory percept like getWhoLastChasing, then changing the controller as desired would be easy. To implement getWhoLastChasing there would have to be a list that stored, for each character, who it last chased. But how could the information about who a character is currently chasing be calculated from the game-state? It could not. You can imagine writing code to make a reasonable guess at who is being chased, but if there are two characters nearby (or even roughly in the same direction from the tagged character) it would be hard to be certain. The reason is that the notion of chasing a character really relates to a character's internal mental state. Such quantities are referred to as *mental state variables*.

The same reasons it is inappropriate to store memory percepts in the game-state, mentioned earlier in Section 5.2, also apply to mental state variables. Mental state variables could be stored as memory percepts, but unlike other percepts they are not just functions of the game-state or other percepts. In particular, they are also functions of a controller's internal state. Thus if they were memory percepts, then they would be part of the

output of a controller, which breaks the rule that controllers only output actions. As with all good programming practice, there is nothing to stop you breaking the rules but it is likely to quickly lead to confusing and hard-to-maintain code. It therefore reinforces their internal hidden nature if mental state variables are represented as private member variables within the controller class. In the tag game, that means in the tgController class or one of its subclasses. Explicitly adding state to the controller class means that there has to a be a separate controller instance for each character.

Like the state in the perception objects, the state in controllers needs to be kept up-to-date. However, it is not quite so important for controllers because the mental states are not simple functions of the game-state and it is therefore harder for an outside observer (like the player) to say for sure that a character is behaving wrongly. That is, if you are lucky, unusual behavior might be attributed to an NPC's personality. However, you should obviously not rely on being afforded such a kind interpretation of your bugs.

5.4.1 Emotions

NPC's emotions act as a sort of rough summary of past events. This makes sense if you think for a moment about the real world. For example, if a sequence of bad events happens to you, you might well end up feeling angry without necessarily being able to recall all the specific events that made you so. The same would apply to feeling happy, or bored, etc. This is not the place to get into a philosophical debate about the true nature of emotions (see [Wri97] if you are interested). But having mental state variables like angerLevel, isHappy, etc. is common, useful, and powerful.

For example, every time an NPC is tagged its anger level could go up and then slowly subside over time when it was not tagged. If it got tagged when it was really angry it would feverishly chase the character who tagged it, otherwise it would go for the nearest character. The anger level toward each individual character could also be maintained. That way if a character got tagged by another character one too many times it would go after the character, but if instead it was tagged by a character that it felt ambivalent toward it might instead go after another character that it was annoyed with.

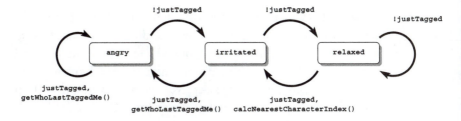

Figure 5.2. Simple FSM for the tag game.

If another character got tagged and instead of going after the nearest character it went for someone else, the spared character might reduce its anger toward that character. Or it might instead increase its feeling of friendliness toward that character and reciprocate the favor later on. Clearly the possibilities are endless.

From a game design perspective, mental state variables representing emotions usually have a pervasive influence on action selection. They are widely used in games to give an NPC moods, especially in games where you must look after the NPC's needs, for example, any game with some kind of virtual pet.

5.4.2 Finite-State Machines

A popular and convenient way to represent mental state variables is as Finite-State Machines (FSMs). Figure 5.2 shows a simple example FSM for the tag game. The nodes represent states and the arcs represent state-transitions. The event that triggers the transition is written on the arc, and following it is the output (if any) that occurs when the transition occurs. The start state is also an important part of the specification.

Just like decision trees, FSMs are intuitive and, with a suitable GUI, FSMs can be built and maintained by nonprogrammers. FSMs can easily be arranged in hierarchies in which each node can itself be a (hierarchical) FSM. FSMs can be augmented with timers to enable state transitions after a preprogrammed amount of time.

FSMs are also a convenient way to represent controllers that depend on any memory percept's value, not just mental state variables. For example, FSMs with states like "in attack mode" or "in following mode" are common. The states do not even have to be explicitly labeled as repre-

senting anything particular at all. FSMs are one of the most popular and well-documented techniques in game AI and this book's companion web site has links to some relevant articles (see also [HF03] and [Sam02]).

One of the key reasons FSMs are so useful is that an NPC can often be designed to have a single state variable whose value can be represented by the current node of the FSM. The inputs and outputs to the node then drive the character's behavior in that state. The downside of FSMs is that they can often get very complicated with a huge number of transitions and a proliferation of states.

5.4.3 Production Rules

Reactive production rules were introduced in Section 4.3 in the previous chapter. More generally, production rules are an important and convenient mechanism for creating general purpose controllers. In particular, they are well suited to implementing expert systems in which the game developer writes a Knowledge Base (KB) for how the character should behave. The KB can also be used to store, access, and manipulate a character's mental state using the convenient and powerful general purpose language of production rules.

When implementing production rule style systems using regular programming languages (like C/C++) *if*-statements, problems can arise when the number of rules becomes large. In particular, it can take a long time to test all the rules to see which ones fired. Therefore, special purpose production rule systems have been developed that use a fast algorithm (such as RETE) for matching the rules' firing conditions. They also have built-in support for conflict resolution when multiple rules match.

The first production rule system was called OPS5 and was invented in the early 1980s. Since then a number of other production rule systems have been created of varying degrees of sophistication [LNR87, SP96]. More recently, a language called RC++ was designed specifically for use in computer games. RC++ is a superset of C++ that adds the ability to specify production rules to control character behavior (or anything else for that matter). RC++ also provides a reactive subset for use with reactive controllers; more details and references can be found in [WM03].

5.4.4 Logical Inference

As a generalization of production rules, logical inference can obviously also be used to manage controller state. In particular, first-order logic can also be used to reason directly about the effects of actions, but the task is complicated by the fact that there is no inherent notion of change. One solution is to define a formal language within first-order logic called the *situation calculus* that includes a built-in notion of change. If you are interested in learning more about this approach see [Fun99, Rei01].

5.5 Communicating

Communicating between characters is useful and important for cooperating on tasks and formulating joint plans.[3] Communication also adds realism and highlights the AI by illustrating an NPC's internal mental state and thought processes.

In the simplest case, communication does not have to be verbal. For example, if a character is embarrassed, then the renderer can have access to this information so that its cheeks can be drawn in red. A player will see this and realize something about the NPC's internal state. Other NPCs should also be able to realize the NPC in question is embarrassed, but they cannot see and analyze the rendered image that the player sees. Therefore, the embarrassed NPC should directly broadcast how it is feeling to NPCs that are close enough and for whom it is otherwise reasonable, within the context of the game world, to expect them to know how the NPC is feeling.

Because of the current state of natural language processing, communicating from the player to the NPC is obviously hard. Typically the player communicates with NPCs through some simple (possibly voice-activated) menu system, or through button presses or gestures that have predefined meanings.

NPCs often communicate with players by using scripted dialog and cut scenes. A phrase of prescripted dialog can be treated as a speech action. Selecting which speech action to pick (if any) based on events in the game

---

[3]Although, unless NPCs have the ability and desire (i.e., they are on the team) to communicate, it is also unrealistic to assume that they would tell each other about their future plans.

world and an NPC's internal state can be performed using any of the techniques for building controllers described in this book. For example, in the tag game if an NPC starts being pursued it could say "Oh no, I'm being chased". If the NPC has a memory percept that records how many times it has been chased recently, the dialog could be more elaborate. For instance, if it has been chased a lot recently it could say something like "How come I'm the one who keeps getting chased?". While if it has not been chased much it could instead remark "Oh I thought you'd forgotten about me". More elaborate still is the case when an NPC has mental state variables like anger. An NPC can then utter phrases like "you're making me angry by keep chasing me", or "OK, that's it I'm going to get you back for this". Such comments can later make it clear to the player that the NPC they just tagged is not just chasing them by accident but is pursuing them to exact revenge. In contrast, without any dialog, all your hard AI programming work might go unnoticed and, more importantly, the player will not get the same immersive sense of the NPCs being alive.

From a game design perspective, care needs to be taken to avoid the dialog becoming boring or repetitive. This is often especially a problem when designing the controller for the NPC who plays the role of the commentator in a sports game. Typically, for any given situation, the commentator will randomly select one of several different appropriate pieces of dialog.

To generate more free-form dialog, you can use a text-to-speech engine, and the technology is getting to the point where it can be effective. In some games, the NPCs speak gibberish, but the tone is modulated according to how they are feeling.

For verbal communication between NPCs the ability to communicate does not have to be a literal one. It just means that it is plausible that they could communicate, for example, if they are nearby or if they are rendered to look like they are carrying some kind of communication device. For the sake of window dressing, you might like to have them appear to be speaking, but underneath the mechanism can be simpler. For example, NPCs can call the appropriate accessors on a controller class to return the value of various mental state variables. A more flexible approach is to use an explicit formal language. XML is a well-known example of a standard that is used to build formal language so that computers in the real world can communicate with each other in a flexible way.

In games, formal languages are also used for communicating among NPCs. To date, formal languages in games are often simpler than their XML-based real-world counterparts. The advantage of using even a simple formal language is that the game content does not have to be fixed in advance. Later on (even after the game ships), if new characters (or even inanimate objects) are added to the world they can communicate information about themselves to the existing NPCs. Provided the existing NPCs understand the same formal language they will know how to interact with the new object. The formal language can (as in [WW04]) even drive a text-to-speech engine to add the necessary window dressing to make it seem like they are talking.

5.6   Stochastic Controllers

As explained in Section 4.4.1 in the previous chapter, reactive stochastic controllers have no hysteresis and can result in NPCs who keep changing their minds. Adding state can therefore help enormously to make stochastic controllers more practical. In particular, if a controller is still in the middle of an action it can lower the probability that it will pick another action until it is finished. Once the action is finished it is free to pick randomly again. To avoid creating NPCs that are subject to rapid and violent mood swings the same idea can be used when selecting emotions. As a simple example, Listing 5.2 shows the calculation of an anger mental state variable such that there is an element of chance for whether the NPC gets angry when tagged, but once angry it stays angry until it tags someone else.

5.6.1   Hidden Markov Model

A Hidden Markov Model (HMM) is like an FSM with probabilities attached to the transition arcs and outputs. HMMs are so named because the states are hidden from the external observer and the transitions only depend on the current state (i.e., the Markov property). An HMM where the transitions depend on the state and the inputs is called an input-output HMM. If an arc corresponding to some input i leads from some state s to some new state s' and is labeled with probability p, then this means that

```
void tgControllerNPC::calcIsAngry()
{
    if (!perception−>getAmITagged())
    { // If I'm not tagged then don't be angry
        isAngry = false;
        return;
    }

    // If I'm tagged and angry then stay angry
    if (isAngry) { return; }

    // If I'm tagged and not angry then there's a small chance I'll get angry
    tgReal probAngry = 0.1;

    // But if I just got tagged, then I get angry in proportion
    // to how often I've been tagged recently
    if (perception−>getWasIJustTagged())
    {
        int const n = max(9, perception−>getMyRecentTaggedCount());
        probAngry = tgReal(n)/10.0;
    }

    // Pick a random number uniformly between 0 and 1
    tgReal const r = tgMath::getRandom();
    if (r < probAngry) { isAngry = true; }
    else { isAngry = false; }
}
```

Listing 5.2. Stochastically calculate if NPC is angry.

the probability of making the transition given the input i is p:

$$P(s'|i, s) = p.$$

When the new state becomes s' there is also some probability q of outputting an action a:

$$P(a|s') = q.$$

Representing HMMs visually can be a bit confusing compared to a regular FSM because for each transition event there are multiple arcs (representing the different probabilities) going to multiple states. Writing a useful GUI is therefore more of a challenge, but see [aiS00] for an example of a tool for visualizing HMMs (and other graphical models).

An input-output HMM can be represented as a three-dimensional table, where the entry in table i, row j, column k corresponds to the probability of transitioning from state j to state k given the input i. If the HMM is in state j when an input i is received, then the k entries in table i, row j provide a probability distribution over possible next states. One of the methods in Appendix A is then used to pick the new state. To be complete, tables also need to be given for the probabilities of outputting actions in each state. As usual, one of the methods from Appendix A is used to pick an action from the probability distribution over actions associated with the new state.

HMMs are widely used as a representation in machine learning applications. Usually the structure of the HMM is given and the learning algorithm must determine the state-transition and action output probabilities that result in an output that matches the training examples. It is also possible to learn the structure of an HMM, but finding effective means for doing so is still an open research problem. To read more about HMMs, see [MS99].

Chapter 6

Searching

Despite their best efforts, controllers will sometimes pick actions that turn out to be a poor choice. Often it will only become apparent that an action was not the best choice after several more actions have been selected and executed. In such cases, it would be ideal if the game world could be set back to how it was before the (what turned out to be) undesirable action was selected. That way a different action could be picked and the whole process repeated until the best action choice was made. This chapter explains that, with certain caveats relating to speed, memory, and the extra knowledge a controller needs about the game world, it is possible for a controller to speculatively try out different action sequences until it finds a suitable one. In such cases, the controller is said to be searching for an action.

6.1 Discrete Tag Game

Section 2.1 in Chapter 2 introduced the tag game as a game that, from an AI perspective, was free of unimportant and distracting details. This chapter will (starting from Section 6.4) also use the tag game to explain how controllers can use search. But to explain the basic idea of search the tag game is too complicated to initially fulfill its pedagogical role. The problem is that search algorithms view change as a discrete phenomena so additional work is required to apply them to the continuous world of the tag game.

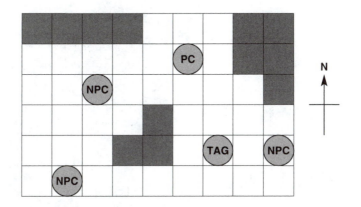

Figure 6.1. Scene from the discrete tag game.

The tag game can be turned into a simpler discrete version by assuming that all movement takes place on a discrete grid. The new game is referred to as the *discrete tag game* and Figure 6.1 shows a scene from the game. Assume each character can move up to one square at a time in any nondiagonal compass direction. Including staying still (denoted U), that gives five possible actions:

$$U : (0,0), N : (0,1), E : (1,0), S : (0,-1), W : (-1,0).$$

Adding the diagonals as directions to move or using a hexagonal is straightforward, and is left as an exercise to the reader. Removing the grid assumption is altogether more interesting and is covered later in Section 6.4. Note that there can be only one character in a cell at a time, and that a character is tagged if the tagged character is in a directly adjacent cell (i.e., diagonals do not count).

6.2   Controllers that Use Search

A controller that uses search to pick actions can simply try each possible action in turn and see which one turns out to be best. Figure 6.2 depicts the neighborhood around the tagged character in each of the five possible future game-states that arise from everyone else staying still while the tagged character is trying out each of its available actions. The assumption

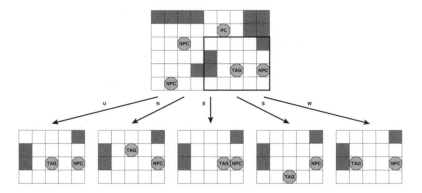

Figure 6.2. Five possible future game-states.

that everyone else stays still is a simplification that makes it easier to explain how search algorithms work. Later, in Section 6.6, the assumption is removed.

The maximum possible number of actions available to an NPC in any state is called the *branching factor*, so in the figure the branching facto is five.

The tagged character wants to end up in a cell next to an untagged character. Of the possible actions, the best one to pick is therefore E because, from the tagged character's point of view, it leads to a desirable outcome. A desirable game-state is referred to as a *goal* and is calculated by the percept calcIsGoal:

```
bool dtgPerception::calcIsGoal() const
{
    return 1 == getMyManhattanDistanceToNearestCharacter();
}
```

where the Manhattan distance d between two grid cells (p_x, p_y) and (q_x, q_y) is defined as

$$d = |p_x - q_x| + |p_y - q_y|.$$

The controller shown in Listing 6.1 searches for a goal one move ahead. To perform the search the controller needs access to the simulator, which is therefore passed in as a reference to itself when it calls the

```
void dtgControllerNPC::calcAction(int whoami, dtgSimulator& sim)
{
    perception->setMyIndex( whoami );
    // See Chapter 2 for a description of calcPossibleActions
    // Note: includes the null action (i.e., U in the text)
    sim.calcPossibleActions();
    vector<dtgAction> const& actions = sim.getPossibleActions();
    bool foundGoal = false;

    for (unsigned int i = 0; i < actions.size(); i++)
    {
        dtgSearchContext searchContext(&sim);
        searchContext.doAction(actions[i], whoami);
        if (perception->calcIsGoal())
        {
            foundGoal = true;
            action = actions[i];
            break;
        }
    }

    if (!foundGoal && !actions.empty())
    {
        action = actions[dtgMath::getRandomInt(actions.size())];
    }
}
```

Listing 6.1. Example of a simple one-step search.

controller's calcAction method. If the search fails, then the controller just picks an action randomly. A better alternative when a search fails is to use a heuristic to pick the "best" action; Section 6.4.1 describes the use of heuristics in more detail.

The dtgSearchContext object in Listing 6.1 is responsible for executing actions and then resetting the game-state back to how it was. Listing 6.2 shows the doAction method that records which actions are performed

```
void dtgSearchContext::doAction(dtgAction const& a, int const i)
{
    sim->doAction(a, i);
    actionList.push_back(a);
    identityList.push_back(i);
}

dtgSearchContext::~dtgSearchContext()
{
    while ( !actionList.empty() )
    {
        sim->undoAction(actionList.back(), identityList.back());
        actionList.pop_back();
        identityList.pop_back();
    }
}
```

Listing 6.2. Setting the game-state back to how it was.

and calls a corresponding method in the simulator. In particular, the simulator's doAction method provides a mechanism for performing speculative forward simulations outside the normal execution path. Executing an action with the doAction method alters the game-state, which can then be queried (through the perception object) to see if it is a goal.

The destructor of the dtgSearchContext class, also shown in Listing 6.2, is what resets the game-state back to how it was when the dtgSearch Context object was constructed. The simplest way for it to work is to make a copy of the game-state in its constructor and restore the copy in its destructor. An alternative solution, shown in the figure, requires no copying of the game-state object, uses no extra memory, and is therefore usually much faster. The idea is that the simulator has an undo method that gets called the required number of times in the dtgSearchContext's destructor. For the discretized tag game, writing an undo method is trivial, but for more complex games it can be time-consuming and error-prone. If you get it wrong, then a controller just thinking about what it wants to do can end up altering the actual state of the game world!

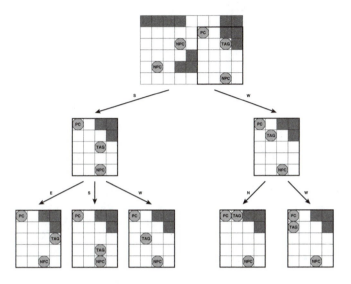

Figure 6.3. Doing and undoing actions.

Using the simulator to perform a search in the way just described is such a clever and powerful technique that it is important to appreciate its significance. In particular, the actual simulator for the game is being used as a proxy for the NPC's model of its world without affecting the real game-state.

If the perception object has internal state, then there also needs to be a mechanism to restore the original state after a search is finished. Otherwise a character thinking about what it wants to do can again lead to subtle AI bugs caused by the corruption of memory percepts.

6.3 Searching Further Ahead

The root of the tree in Figure 6.3 shows a different possible configuration of the discrete tag game in which no single action can result in a goal. The tagged character's controller therefore needs to search for a *sequence* of actions that lead to a goal. The search tree in the figure shows all future possible game-states that could arise from the tagged character moving two steps and (until Section 6.6) everyone else staying still. The search tree is a tool for thinking about search algorithms; practical algorithms do not

explicitly build a search tree but simply explore it implicitly during their execution. There are some interesting points to observe about the search tree:

- only possible actions are shown. For example, in the initial configuration it is not possible to move N or E because there is an obstacle in the way; there are therefore no paths corresponding to moving N or E originating from the root node.

- no child nodes of a node x are shown if the child is the same node as x's parent. For example, the path S followed by N brings the tagged character back to where it just was. For the same reason no paths corresponding to the U action appear, since by staying still a character will, by definition, end up in the same grid cell. However, longer cycles are not removed, for example, the path W, S is shown even though it results in the same state as S, W on the other branch. At the possible cost of some extra memory required to remember some of the previously visited states, it is usually straightforward to detect and remove all repeated states.

- because repeated states are disallowed and the search space is finite, the search tree is finite. If repeated states are allowed, then the search tree would contain infinite branches such as $U, U, U, \ldots$ or $S, N, S, N, S, N, \ldots$. The search tree does nevertheless continue on much further than is shown in the figure.

- the search tree grows exponentially. Therefore, in the worst case, when there is no goal in the entire tree, a search can take an exponential amount of time because every single node has to be examined.

A sequence of actions that leads to a goal is called a *plan*. In the specific case where the goal is a location and a plan corresponds to a path to the goal, searching for a plan is called *path planning*. Since any game-state in which the tagged character is adjacent to any untagged character qualifies, there are many possible goals in Figure 6.3. For each goal, there are also many possible paths to reach it. For example, the path W, W leads to a goal and the path W, N leads to the same goal. There is only one plan

of length two that leads to the goal along the path S, S, but there are many other longer plans that lead to the goal (not shown in the figure) such as W, W, S, S, S, E.

6.3.1 Uninformed Search Algorithms

Uninformed search algorithms are simple search algorithms that, unlike those described later in Section 6.4.1, do not use a heuristic to potentially speed up the search. The algorithms can be used to search a tree like the one in Figure 6.3 and are described in all introductory AI textbooks, in many introductory computer science books, and on numerous web sites. The section on search algorithms in [RN02] provides a particularly good presentation.

The two basic uninformed search algorithms are breadth-first search and depth-first search. Breadth-first search is guaranteed to find the shortest path to a goal but potentially uses an exponential (in the depth of the tree) amount of memory to store instances of the game-state. Depth-first search can be implemented using a simulator's undo mechanism to backtrack when it fails to find a goal and thus avoids storing (or copying) any additional instances of the game-state. Even without an undo mechanism, depth-first search can be implemented using only a linear (in the depth of the tree) number of stored instances of the game-state. The downside of depth-first search is that it is not guaranteed to find the shortest path. Moreover, on search trees that have infinite branches depth-first search can get stuck in an infinite loop, but this can be remedied by placing an artificial limit on the maximum depth of a search. Iterative deepening depth-first search works by successively increasing the maximum search depth by one each time until it finds a goal. For example, first it performs a depth-first search on plans of length one, then (assuming it did not find a goal) a depth-first search on plans of length two, then length three, and so on. At the negligible cost, at least compared to the overall cost, of researching the tree at previous depths, iterative deepening depth-first search is guaranteed to find an optimal plan and does not require an exponential amount of memory.

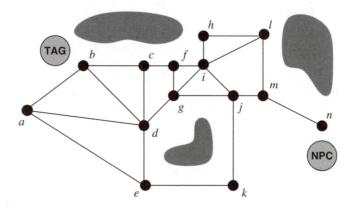

Figure 6.4. Waypoints for the original tag game.

6.4 Searching in Continuous Domains

Figure 6.4 shows a top-down view of a map from the original tag game (i.e., the one before the discrete version was introduced) overlaid with a collection of connected nodes, or a graph. The graph nodes are called *waypoints* and the lines indicate the ability of an NPC to move from one waypoint to another in a straight line without getting stuck on any obstacles. The waypoint graph provides a discrete representation, of the underlying continuous map,[1] which is suitable to apply search algorithms to. Of course, the absence of a connection between two nodes does not necessarily imply that an NPC cannot travel between them. If an NPC has another controller that does not employ path planning it can use that and completely ignore the waypoints. The waypoints simply represent the option to use path planning in a continuous domain, for example, to plan a path to a faraway goal that is hidden from view.

Figure 6.4 also shows the tagged character and an NPC. If the tagged character wants to move toward the current NPC's position, it first needs to compute the closest waypoint to its current position (i.e., node *b*) and the closest waypoint to its goal position (i.e., node *n*). It can then use any search algorithm it pleases to search the graph to find a path from *b* to

---

[1]The map is continuous in the sense that it is meant to represent a continuous domain. Obviously it is still ultimately implemented on a digital computer using floating-point numbers.

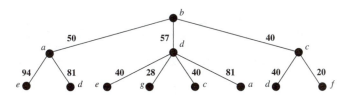

Figure 6.5. Searching the waypoint graph.

n. For example, it might find the path b, c, f, i, j, m, n. Once it has computed a path, the tagged character can use a path-following subcontroller
to smoothly reach its destination. Path following is another example of a
simple steering behavior like those described in Section 4.2 in Chapter 4,
and can be implemented easily using the pursue/seek controller.

The two separate levels of, first, path planing using the discrete waypoint representation, and second, path following using the underlying continuous representation, can be implemented in a variety of ways. For example, looking back at Figure 2.2 in Chapter 2 there are possibly multiple
levels of simulators and controllers. For path planning in the tag game the
simulator mentioned in the figure is obviously the regular tag game simulator, and the approximate simulator is for the waypoint grid. For example,
if the search is currently considering node a, then the approximate simulator is responsible for generating the possible successor nodes b, d, and
e. The approximate simulator is so simple that it might be overkill to refer
to it as a simulator at all. It certainly need not be implemented with the
formality of defining an approximate simulator class, approximate game-
state, etc. In particular, the approximate simulator can just be represented
as the method in the search algorithm that is responsible for generating,
from a given waypoint node, successor nodes to search.

6.4.1 Informed Search

In the discrete tag game each grid cell can be thought of as a waypoint,
where each waypoint is connected to its four neighbors and itself. Therefore, searching the waypoint graph is similar to searching in the discrete
tag game, and Figure 6.5 shows the first two steps in the corresponding
search tree. The numbers on the arcs correspond to the distances (rounded
to the nearest integer) between nodes and in general are referred to as *costs*.

The total cost of a path to the current node x is denoted $g(x)$; for example, the cost to get to node e along the path b, d, e is

$$g(e) = 57 + 40 = 97.$$

Note that, because the NPC is no longer searching on a regular grid, the optimal path to the goal is not necessarily coincident with the path with the shortest number of steps. For example, the path b, c, f, i, j, m, n is clearly shorter than the path b, d, e, k, m, n even though it contains more steps. This means that breadth-first search is no longer guaranteed to find the optimal path, but a simple generalization called uniform cost search will.

Informed search methods are characterized by the use of a heuristic function h that attempts to estimate the cost of the cheapest path to the goal from any given node x. Combined with the known cost to reach the current node x, this gives an estimate for the cheapest cost to reach the goal through the node x as

$$f(x) = g(x) + h(x). \tag{6.1}$$

If the heuristic function makes a reasonable guess at the true remaining cost to the goal it is useful during the search because the most promising paths can be explored first. As a special case, if the heuristic function was always exactly right (i.e., it was an oracle), then following it would result in taking the optimal path to the goal without any need to search alternatives paths.

The most well-known and widely used informed search algorithm is called A⋆. If the heuristic function used with A⋆ is always optimistic about the expected cost to the goal, then A⋆ is guaranteed to find the optimal path. An optimistic heuristic function is said to be admissible, and the Euclidean distance between two nodes qualifies as an admissible heuristic in the tag game.

For any given admissible heuristic, no other algorithm will explore less of the search tree than A⋆ and still be guaranteed to find the optimal path. A⋆ is thus as good an optimal search algorithm as there is, which explains why it is so popular. You can read more about the theoretical properties of A⋆ in [Pea84, RN02]; there are also a great many articles about how to implement A⋆ to be found in the game AI literature. One interesting article

[Rab00] examines the practical consequences of relaxing the requirement that the heuristic function be admissible. There are many online resources, including source code, devoted to search algorithms in general, and A⋆ in particular. This book's companion web site has pointers to such resources.

A problem with using the standard A⋆ algorithm for games is that in the worst case it requires an exponential amount of memory. A simple modification called iterative-deepening A⋆ reduces the memory requirements at the cost of potentially reexploring parts of the search tree. Other more recent and complicated algorithms like memory-bounded A⋆ and simplified memory-bounded A⋆ are described in [RN02]. See [AL98] for an article about using A⋆ with partially ordered "soft" constraints.

6.4.2 Replanning

When an NPC starts following a path that was computed by applying a search algorithm to the waypoint graph, unexpected events will inevitably occur. That is because the waypoint graph is just a discrete approximation to the real underlying continuous game world. The game world could have all sorts of complicated physics that are not captured in the waypoint graph. For example, an object not even represented in the waypoint graph could fall over or explode and debris could block the preplanned path. The preplanned path also does not take into consideration low-level behaviors, like collision avoidance routines, that can override other behaviors and could easily become activated to cause the path to deviate from the anticipated one.

The consequence of all this uncertainty is that a plan cannot be followed blindly. Lower-level controllers, like collision avoidance behaviors, constantly need to be active. The world can diverge so quickly from how it was when a plan was computed that in practice a plan is almost never executed to completion. Instead, it is periodically discarded and a new plan that takes into account the updated state of the game world is computed. This is called replanning and how often it needs to be done depends on how accurate an approximation the waypoint graph is to the real underlying game world. Although replanning has to be done regularly it does not usually have to be done so regularly that the search calculation cannot be spread across several frames.

Later, in Section 6.6.1, replanning is explored in more detail in the context of the additional uncertainty that arises from taking into account the possible future actions of other characters.

6.5 Waypoints

Waypoints are usually added to a map by a level designer. There are also automatic procedures to generate waypoints, for example, the Area Awareness System (AAS) described in [vW01].[2] The AAS also supports fast computation of the nearest waypoint to a given position, which can otherwise be a significant time cost. One of the disadvantages of automatic waypoint placement is that waypoints do not always end up in the ideal location. That is, waypoint placement is something of an art and a good level designer will take care to place waypoints near interesting features in the game world that an automatic system might not be able to recognize as important.

Waypoints can also be annotated with additional information like the affordances described in Section 3.3.3 in Chapter 3. For example, a waypoint can be annotated with whether it is a good sniping location, so that an NPC that wants to do some sniping can then calculate the nearest suitable waypoint and plan a path to get there. In the tag game, waypoints could be annotated to state if they make a good hiding position. Hiding information depends on the current location of the tagged character, so a waypoint would have to be annotated with a list of waypoints from which it is hidden. To determine a hiding spot an NPC could then pick the nearest waypoint that is hidden from the nearest waypoint to the tagged character. For example, in Figure 6.4, node b is the nearest node to the tagged character and node k is the closest to the NPC that is hidden from b.

Using annotations to place knowledge in the environment at design time, versus having NPCs figure it out at runtime, represents a trade-off between flexibility and speed [Doy02]. In particular, with a lot of knowledge embedded in the environment, NPCs themselves do not need the flexibility afforded to them by sophisticated AI algorithms. At runtime they can thus make decisions much faster. With AI routines usually given no more than

---

[2]See [KL00] for a different approach to the path planning problem, from robotics research, that skips the need for waypoints.

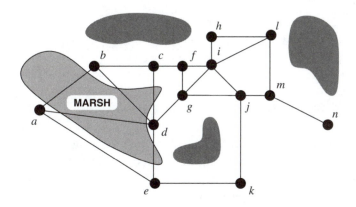

Figure 6.6. Marsh land is expensive to cross.

10% of the CPU per cycle (and often less), game designers therefore usually spend a lot of time and effort on annotating the game world. But, as computers get faster, more of the work can reasonably be done at runtime by the AI algorithms.

Some information that a game can use to annotate waypoints is only available at runtime. For example, if there was enough time and memory, a memory percept could record for each waypoint a list of characters that had been within visual range of the waypoint. That way an NPC would only be permitted to use the portion of the waypoint network consistent with its past experiences.

6.5.1   Tactical Path Planning

Not only can waypoints themselves be annotated, but so can the arcs between them. For example, in Figure 6.6 some marshland has been added to the tag game world. Unlike an obstacle, marsh land is traversable but suppose it multiplies the usual time cost due to distance ten-fold. The result is that if an NPC wanted to go from node a to node d it would be cheaper to take the path a, e, k, j, g, d rather than go directly and have to venture through the marsh.

In general, annotations on waypoint arcs can be computed automatically provided a rule is given for how terrain and nearby objects affect the cost. Common causes of increased cost are nearby guard towers or regions vulnerable to snipers. Arc costs can also be computed dynamically in real-

time depending on the location of enemies and allies. In [RG03] arc costs are increased along paths with fallen comrades since they clearly represent undesirable routes. If the arc costs do vary significantly it will obviously invalidate any plan computed with the old costs and a replanning step will be necessary. The arc costs can also vary according to character type. For example, some characters might travel through water more easily than across dry land and so should associate different costs with submerged arcs to characters that do not like to get their feet wet. You can read more about tactical path planning in [vdS02].

Increasing arc costs to influence behavior must be done with care because in practice the efficient operation of A⋆ depends on the heuristic function not being too optimistic. For example, if the heuristic function is always zero (maximally optimistic), then A⋆ reduces to uniform cost search, which is slow and uses a lot of memory. So the higher the arc costs, the more relatively optimistic the heuristic becomes and the longer the search algorithm takes. Of course, a controller can also modify the heuristic to reduce its optimism but if it goes too far, so that it becomes pessimistic, you can end up with stupid NPCs that take noticeably suboptimal paths.

6.6 Adversarial Search

The examples used up until now in this chapter, of the tagged character using search to plan a path to the nearest untagged character, have a serious flaw: they all assume that the other characters being chased stay still! Clearly, if a character saw the tagged character heading toward it, it would run away. If the tagged character blindly followed the path it had planned based on the original position, by the time it reached its destination the untagged character would be long gone.

However, if the tagged character does not wait until it has finished executing its plan, but replans part way through, the situation is slightly improved. Now, provided replanning is frequent enough, the tagged character will always (more or less) be heading toward the untagged character. If the tagged character is a lot faster it should eventually catch the untagged character, but if they are about the same speed, then it will just chase the untagged character around and not necessarily get any closer. A better solution would be if the tagged character could anticipate the untagged

character's future position and plan a path to arrive at where it thinks it will be instead of where it is right now. That way it could plan to cut the untagged character off, as shown later in Figure 6.8.

One way to anticipate the untagged character's future behavior is to use adversarial search techniques that come from the academic field of game theory [Osb03, RN02]. The idea is that there is some notion of a score that one character is trying to maximize and the other character is trying to minimize. In the tag game example, the distance between the tagged character and a given character can be used as the "score", in which case, the tagged character is trying to minimize the score and the untagged character to maximize it.

When the tagged character is deciding where to move it assumes the untagged character is rational (see Section 6.6.1 for some other possibilities) and will always pick its move to maximize the score (i.e., the separation distance). Given the move that represents the untagged character's rational choice, the tagged character then picks a move to minimize the score. Figure 6.7 shows the first layer (or ply) in the adversarial search tree that corresponds to the discrete tagged game shown in Figure 6.1. In the figure only one other character's moves are shown, but in general it should include all the possible moves of all the other characters. Clearly, with all the additional possibilities provided by the other player's moves, the adversarial search tree expands faster than that in Figure 6.2.

In Figure 6.1, the NPC shown cannot move E because it is already at the Eastern edge of the grid. The reason it cannot also move W after the tagged character has moved E is due to the assumption of only one character per grid cell. Since characters move simultaneously the choice to let the tagged character occupy the disputed cell is arbitrary and up to the simulator to decide. Notice the U move, to move nowhere, is important in an adversarial search because if the tagged character decides an untagged character's best move is to move next to it, then it obviously wants to stay where it is.

Ideally the adversarial search tree would be expanded out until all the leaves have been resolved and one or another character has won. In the tag game the tagged character wins if it catches the untagged character. The cases when the untagged character has not been caught could potentially go on forever, but there may be cycles that it can stick to without ever being caught. Or the game could dictate that the tagged character loses if

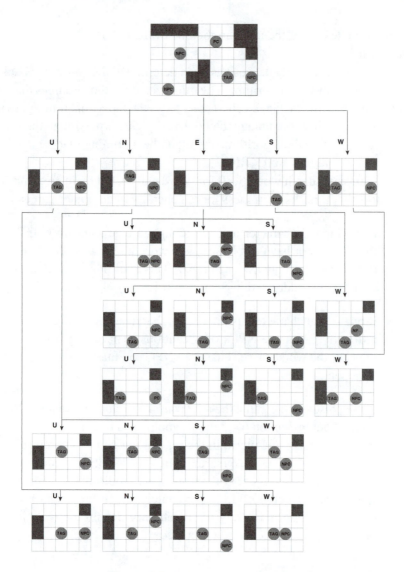

Figure 6.7. Adversarial search tree.

it has not caught a character in a certain number of moves. Regardless, it is usually infeasible to search all the way to resolution for all but the simplest games. In particular, the adversarial search tree is usually so large that an NPC must artificially restrict the number of ply it can look ahead. The

value of the leaves of the tree can then be evaluated based on the score at that point.[3]

Once the score at the leaves has been determined the values are backed up using the min-max algorithm. The min-max algorithm assumes that one player (in this case the tagged character) picks the move that minimizes the score and the other (the untagged character) picks to maximize the score. More details about the algorithm, and alpha-beta pruning that can speed it up, can be found in [Osb03, RN02].

Adversarial search works well for board games, but there are a number of factors that limit its usefulness more generally in computer games:

- if the tagged character and the untagged character are both NPCs there does not have to be any guesswork about what each one will do; they can simply ask each other. This does, however, raise a new set of issues addressed in Section 6.6.1.

- if one of the characters is the player character, assuming it will play rationally can make NPCs over-cautious. That is, by always planning for the worst case scenario an NPC can make for a very boring opponent.

- for the discrete tag game the adversarial search is reasonable. But as pointed out in Section 6.4.2 the waypoint grid is just a rough approximation to the game world in the regular tag game. Therefore, after a couple of plays, an adversarial search's view of the game world is likely to have diverged so far from what would really happen that it is unlikely to be useful. Unfortunately, this is a difficult problem because if there is no way to search very deeply the technique is probably not reliable in the first place.

6.6.1   Treating Adversaries as Part of the Environment

An alternative to adversarial search is to treat other characters as part of the environment. This means that when searching forward an adversary's

---

[3]Some games do not have a score until the end when someone wins or loses. But it is usually straightforward to invent a heuristic that measures how well each player is doing that can act as the "score" before the game is finished.

action choices are determined by some other mechanism. For example, a controller could be used as a predictor percept to predict an action.

Section 3.5 in Chapter 3 already explained why it is sometimes not possible, or desirable, to use an NPC's actual controller as a predictor percept for how it will behave in future. But in light of Section 6.4.2, the point about the use of an approximate simulator should be clearer. In particular, if the adversarial search is using an approximate simulator, then an adversary's actual controller cannot be used directly because it is only compatible with the real game simulator. However, if the adversary has a high-level controller that can interact with the approximate simulator, then that could be used instead. But the results will not be completely reliable because it is still only the approximate simulator that is being used.

A more sophisticated alternative (also alluded to in Section 3.5) is to simulate forward the whole game loop, i.e., pick a high-level discrete action, translate the high-level action down to appropriate game actions, and execute the game actions up to the point where the adversary's action choice is required. At that point the adversary's real controller is used to provide a prediction about which action it will pick that is (subject to the influence of the player character) guaranteed to be correct. To find the best action choice, the process can be repeated for all the high-level actions the controller is considering. The process can also obviously be applied repeatedly to search further into the future. Of course, if the adversary is also using a similar search as part of its decision-making process, then care must be taken to avoid getting stuck in an infinite loop.

By using a suitable controller as a stand-in for the player, the player character can also be treated as part of the environment during a search. Creating a controller that is accurate enough to be a useful stand-in can require online learning (see Section 7.2 in the next chapter), but an existing NPC's controller might suffice.

Before proceeding with an example, it is important to fully appreciate that treating an adversary as part of the environment means the search only considers one possible action that an adversary might choose. In contrast, an adversarial search explicitly considers all the adversaries' possible actions. Note that, even if a predictor percept is written to return a probability distribution over possible actions as an answer to which action a character will pick, this still qualifies as treating the character as part of the environment. That is because in the adversarial search nothing is assumed about

which action the character will pick, indeed it is part of the min-max algorithm's job to figure it out. But if the probabilities are supplied, then the information is already fixed and there is nothing for the adversarial search to calculate.[4] In fact, the case where a single action is chosen as a character's future action is just a special case in which all the probability is assigned to one action.

In [Fun99] there is an example of using search (limited to looking only six moves ahead), in which the adversaries are treated as part of the environment, to implement herding behavior. The example can easily be recast in the context of the tag game as the problem of getting the tagged character to herd the untagged characters into some corner of the game world. Presumably this would be a good tactic for increasing the odds of tagging someone.

Figure 6.8 illustrates how intermittent replanning, with the goal of getting more untagged characters heading in the desired direction (in this case the upper left corner), leads to herding behavior. In particular, the desired effect of the tagged character getting in and around the untagged characters to frighten them in the right direction emerges automatically. The tagged character uses a simple model of how the untagged characters will move to anticipate their future positions. In particular, it knows the untagged characters are afraid of it and will run in the opposite direction if it gets too close. It does not model their collision avoidance behavior and thus an unanticipated near-collision between the two untagged characters results in what actually happens when the plan is executed diverging from what the tagged character planned.

6.7   Rendering a Search

Search is being presented as a tool that can be used by a controller to pick actions. In this context, the only visible part of the search is the end re-

---

[4]In games that include an element of chance the min-max algorithm can be modified to use expected score. But this is still not the same as supplying a probability distribution for the character's action choices. The difference is that the probability used to calculate the expected score is the probability of different outcomes due to uncertain game world physics and not uncertainty about which action the character will choose. Once the expected score of each move has been calculated the rational character modeled in the adversarial search will, with absolute certainty, pick the move with the best expected outcome.

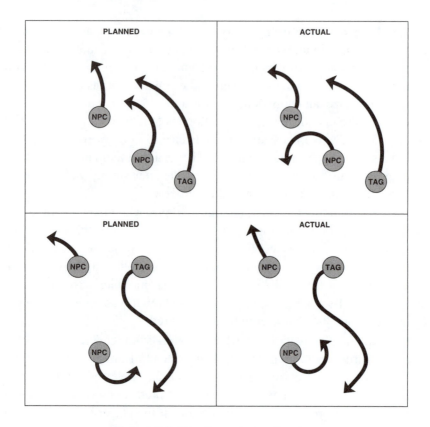

Figure 6.8. Herding using replanning.

sult: the action that the character decides to perform. The search process itself takes place inside the character's head and an external observer has no way to tell that search is being to used to pick actions or not. Of course, if the search takes a long time, then there may be a visible pause while the character thinks about what to do. If a character takes a particularly long time to search, an animation of it scratching its head might be appropriate.[5] While this might hint at the internal mechanism being used by the controller, the search itself is still hidden.

There are, however, occasions when the search process itself is rendered. This can be because the game designer wants to explicitly dramatize an NPC trying to figure something out, or simply as the by-product

---

[5]As pointed out earlier, the search cost can usually be spread across several frames.

of the player character trying to solve a problem. For example, consider a character stuck in a maze and trying to get out. The character could be the player character (in which case the human is directing the search) or an NPC. By rendering the game-state as the character tries different paths through the maze, an animation of the search process is created. The case when the search is not rendered is analogous to a character having a map of the maze. The map is searched in advance to find a way out, and only then does the character start to move. The resulting animation would (assuming the map was accurate) be of the character simply walking out of the maze without making any mistakes or detours.

When a search is rendered, undoing actions (when they do not lead to goals) means performing in-game actions that get the world back to how it was. For example, if a character in a maze finds a dead end, then it has to walk back to some previous point in the search. Note that, the game-state may represent quantities like time and fatigue, in which case, the game-state can only be put back to approximately how it was because time will have passed and the character will be more tired.

As explained in Section 6.2, when a search is not rendered, if an action sequence turns out to be no good, then, instead of undoing it with more in-game actions, the current game-state is either reversed with a special undo action or discarded and a saved one restored. For a rendered search, NPCs cannot revert to a previous game-state if the player has already seen or felt the consequences of subsequent actions. At least, it would make for a frustrating (although perhaps fairer) game-play experience if the world kept popping back to how it was for the convenience of an NPC.

For human players there are less restrictions on resetting the game-state. Human players can usually save games in some kind of permanent storage, which leads to a crude, but widely used, form of search in which the player can revert to a save point whenever something disastrous happens. Upon resuming the game the player will choose some alternative course of action that hopefully has more desirable consequences. Many games automatically save at key points; there are also often restrictions placed on the number and location of save points. Although it is interesting to imagine if it were otherwise, usually games do not model the frustration NPCs might feel about having the world reset whenever the player character is doing badly. On the contrary, NPCs are invariably kept blissfully ignorant that the world has been reset at all.

6.8 General Goal Action Planning

This chapter has emphasized path planning as an application of search. This is because path planning is widely used in games, and simple extensions like tactical path planning can yield a wide variety of impressive behaviors. Because it is clear which actions and percepts are relevant, path planning problems are relatively simple.

In the real world, there are much more complex planning problems where the relevant actions and percepts are not at all obvious. For example, even something seemingly simple like trying to catch a bus involves figuring out the solution to many subproblems at many different levels of abstraction. There can also be trade-offs that need to be resolved between multiple competing goals, such as the goal to eat versus the goal to catch the bus.

To describe planning problems, languages such as the Planning Domain Definition Language (PDDL), have been invented. They help the problem to be carefully specified, heuristics to be automatically generated, and the problem to be automatically broken down into subtasks and (hopefully) solved.

In computer games there are also complex planning problems that are often presented in the form of puzzles for the player to figure out. For example, a common scenario in a game is a locked door. The player might be expected to infer (using commonsense knowledge about locks and keys) that they need to find a key. They then formulate a high-level plan to go and find the key, come back, and open the door. Each of the steps in the plan is a planning problem in and of itself. Finding the key involves formulating a plan to search some portion of the game world. Subtactical path planning problems like walking across a room unnoticed, say, and staying close to cover might present themselves. Once the key is found a plan to get back to the locked door is needed.

Although computer games contain complex planning problems it is often the player's job to figure them out. NPCs usually only need to solve simpler path planning problems that might arise during the execution of the player's high-level plan. Even if the player needs some help, it is easier to simply give them prescribed hints, which is possible because the game designer who thought up the puzzle in the first place also thought of how it would be solved.

In the tag game the problem of deciding which waypoint is the goal is a high-level control problem. But it does not really require planning, instead controllers like the ones described in Section 5.4 in the previous chapter would be appropriate. For example, if the tagged character is angry with a particular character, then its goal should be the waypoint closest to that character. Or better still, the goal should be to head toward the waypoint that it believes will end up being the closest to the object of its anger a couple of moves in the future. If the tagged character is not angry, then its goal is the waypoint that gets it closest to any untagged character. Selecting goals for the untagged characters is equally as straightforward. There simply needs to be a controller to decide whether to run away, or whether to hide.

If the tag game was extended so that, for example, characters could move obstacles around to build and dismantle barricades of different shapes and forms, then it could be made equivalent to the classic blocks world planning domain. The addition of weapons that require ammunition can result in planning problems that are analogous to the problem (mentioned earlier) of finding a key for a lock. If there are a lot of objects that require various resources to make them work, and getting those resources entails finding resources for other objects, then it might be reasonable to consider using a planner. But if there are only a few resource-driven objects, it is better to just write simple *if-then* rules such as "if the gun is empty, then look for ammunition". The NPC then blindly follows the rules without any understanding of what it is trying to achieve. But the resulting behavior obviously looks no different than the case where a sophisticated planner figured out from first principles that in order to kill its enemy it needed a loaded gun.

There is a lot of interesting literature on planning, for example, the work done on real-time planning for NASA's Deep Space One mission [MNPW98]. There is also some exciting work that has been done using stochastic search to quickly (on average) solve complex planning problems [KS96, KS03]. Once again, see [RN02] for a thorough overview of the subject.

Chapter 7

Learning

Machine learning promises to play a prominent role in helping game AI scale up to more complex game worlds. But to date machine learning has only been used sporadically in computer games, so this chapter is therefore more speculative than the others. It is also more technically challenging, but by the end you should at least have gained some important intuitions. As usual, plenty of references are provided to help you follow up on any topics of interest.

There are a lot of potential applications of machine learning to games, but in any industry there is a natural resistance to using new technology, so this chapter takes a conservative approach. In particular, the emphasis is on machine learning techniques that do not necessarily have a major impact on game design, and that a game developer can easily experiment with by themselves. As such, this chapter only skims the surface of what is possible, but will hopefully whet your appetitive for this exciting and important subject.

7.1   Simulated Learning

Although machine learning has not been used widely in games, there are numerous games in which characters appear to learn. The effect is typically achieved by having a character slowly reveal information that they already possessed when the game shipped. The order, or nature, of the information revealed sometimes depends on interaction with the player. A related trick is to impair a character in some way (as is done with different difficulty

settings) and have the character slowly improve over time by reducing the level of impairment.

Players also often associate stateful controllers that simply remember past information with learning. For example, an NPC in a game might ask a player her name. When the NPC later refers to the player by name you might say the NPC has "learned" her name.

None of these simulated learning techniques would qualify as machine learning in the academic sense, but they are simple and can be surprisingly effective from the player's point of view. Before embarking on applying machine learning to your game it is therefore important to consider whether simulated learning could be used instead. The main reason why "real" learning might be required is if it would produce a better quality solution than hand coding, or if a character has to learn something at runtime from a source of information (such as the person who bought the game) that is unavailable at development time.

7.2   Definitions

The controllers that have been described in earlier chapters are all intended to be defined by the game developer according to some internal notion of how they think an NPC should behave. In contrast, learning a controller requires a developer to be much more explicit about how an NPC should behave. This usually involves giving the NPC examples of how to behave, or giving it rewards when it does the right thing. Giving an NPC examples of how to behave is called *supervised learning*, while providing rewards is referred to as *unsupervised learning*. Unsupervised learning is so named because an NPC must largely figure out for itself how to behave in order to receive the rewards.

Another important distinction is whether the learning takes place *online* or *offline*.[1] Online learning takes place in real-time while the game is being played, while offline learning takes place as a batch processing step that occurs when the game is not being played.

---

[1]In the context of machine learning, the terms "online" and "offline" should not be confused with their more conventional meanings in terms of networks. The two uses of the words are unrelated; online and offline learning can take place regardless of whether the player is online (in the network sense) or not.

A common misconception about machine learning is that most of the effort goes into the machine learning algorithms. Although the algorithms are obviously important, the real effort usually goes into crafting the percepts that act as the data for the machine learning algorithm. Unfortunately, getting the percepts right is a difficult subject to write about. The problem is that each learning problem usually requires its own unique set of percepts. There are, however, some common patterns and it turns out that many of these have already been covered in Chapter 3 and Chapter 5. That is, the percepts that would be useful for you to write a controller are often the same ones that would be useful to a machine learning algorithm. For example, your controller code will usually be a lot simpler if you use percepts that calculate relative coordinates instead of global coordinates. Similarly, for a machine learning algorithm, the learning problem will usually be a lot simpler (i.e., you will need less data) if it has access to relative coordinates. Think of the machine learning algorithm as trying to write the controller code instead of you. If you imagine you would have to write an extremely complicated controller to figure out the correct action, given the available percepts, then chances are the learning algorithm will fail dismally. Any percept you define to make the problem simpler is therefore a good thing. There are many good books about machine learning; for example, see [Mit97, DHS00, HTF01, RN02]. For a less technical introduction, see [WF99]. There are also a number of articles that have specifically addressed learning in games and game-like worlds, for example see [BDI+02, Ale02, Man03, DEdGD04].

7.2.1 Offline Unsupervised Learning

From a technical perspective, the attractive property of online learning is that the player can be involved in the process, which can lead to some exciting AI effects. But because the learning directly impacts the player's experience of the game the decision to use online learning has ramifications for game design. Shipping a game that includes online learning also requires confidence that the algorithms are robust enough to provide a quality experience no matter what (within reason) a player does. Finally, the learning has to be shoehorned into the often tight CPU and memory budgets available for the game AI. Online learning is therefore a challenging way to introduce learning into games, requiring many advanced tricks

from machine learning that are still proprietary and beyond the scope of an introductory book like this one.

That leaves offline learning. The advantage of offline learning is that it can be applied before the game ships and so fits in with a game's standard quality assurance process. If the learned controllers are not good enough they can be relearned, or if necessary dropped entirely and (at the expense of all the wasted effort on learning) replaced by hand-coded ones. The CPU and memory constraints are also more lax as all the hard work is done before the game ships. The downside of offline learning is that there is no way for a player to necessarily be able to tell whether a controller for an NPC was learned or written by hand. The NPCs the player encounters in the game have no ability to learn, it is just that learning was possibly used to create their controllers. The learning is simply being used as a means to an end, as an alternative method for creating controllers.

Offline learning's apparent major benefit is therefore that it can act as a labor-saving device for developers. Instead of needing to hand-craft a controller for an NPC, the NPC can learn how to behave on its own. In reality, the process is far from as magical as it sounds and involves hours of hard work to get the learning to produce an acceptable controller. It is probably better to think of offline learning as a tool for mass producing (at least in the long term) higher quality AI that can better interact with more complex game worlds. When learning works correctly, the jump in quality can be by orders of magnitude. The reason is that, by automating the process of producing controllers, the scale of problems that can be tackled, the generality, and the robustness all improve. In that sense it is similar to other forms of automation. The first time an automated assembly plant for making cars (or anything else) was created it probably took more time and effort than it would have to simply make the object by hand. The benefits come much later when the manufacturing process has been refined. Once machine learning techniques become established in the games industry, the quality and range of AI in games should see a similar transformation. In all likelihood, machine learning will come to dominate game AI in much the same way as it has come to dominate academic AI.

Having established offline learning as worthy of further interest, the question remains about whether to use supervised learning or unsupervised learning. Aside from the technical differences, the biggest practical impediment to using supervised learning in game development is that it requires

a data set to learn from. Where will this data set come from? Academic researchers stumble across the same problem when developing new machine learning algorithms. They have therefore set up a machine learning repository [BM98] that includes a number of data sets that can be used for comparing and evaluating algorithms. But there is no such repository of data sets for your game, so you would have to create one! That can be a tremendous amount of work, especially if you are inexperienced at doing it. You have to decide what data to collect, who is going to generate it, how much data you need, how to store it, how to clean it up, and much much more. In addition, every time the game's physics changes (which it is likely to do all the time during production) you might have to regenerate all the data. To have even a chance success, a supervised learning project would therefore probably require coordination between the whole development team.

In contrast, unsupervised learning only requires access to standard computing resources and the programming resources of an individual or small team. When the game physics changes, a controller might still need to be relearned but, if everything is set up right, it should be just a matter of rerunning the learning.

There are also some strong precedents for the successful application of unsupervised offline learning to games, one of the most well-known of which is in traditional board games where the TD-Gammon program used a version of *reinforcement learning* to learn to play backgammon [Tes95]. The program learned to play at the level of the world's best human experts simply by playing millions of games against itself. Previous attempts to hand-code solutions had failed to produce anything more than programs that were mediocre players. Reinforcement learning has also been successfully used in video games like Ratbag games' "Dirt Track Racing". Reinforcement learning is therefore the focus of this chapter.

7.3 Rewards

In what follows, a controller that can learn is referred to as a *learner*. Once a learner has finished learning it reverts to a being regular controller. A learner may also be referred to as a controller when (often as part of the learning algorithm) it is being used in its role as a controller. The difference

between a learner and a controller is that a learner can modify the function it computes between percepts and actions. In order to modify the function so that the learner improves it needs some kind of feedback on how it is doing. There also has to be some initial unlearned controller to bootstrap the process; for example, the random controller introduced in Section 4.1.1 in Chapter 4 could be used.

In the previous chapter on searching, goals and costs can be thought of as providing a type of feedback. Cost is negative feedback and reaching a goal is positive feedback. In this chapter, rewards are introduced as a unifying concept that is used to provide explicit feedback to a controller. Negative rewards correspond to punishment and positive rewards to encouragement. Rewards can come from a variety of sources, such as the game itself, or from another player. Like goals, rewards are implemented as percepts. For example, in the tag game, a positive reward would be granted to the tagged character upon tagging another character. At every step when the tagged character fails to tag another character it would receive no reward, or possibly even a negative reward.

Since the reward percept is defined by the game developer it provides a lot of control, albeit somewhat indirect, over the NPC's personality. That is, the conditions of the reward are like high-level goals or the "ends". The reinforcement learning algorithm must then work out the best "means" to receive the rewards. For example, to make an NPC that likes to get revenge, the associated learner could receive an extra reward for tagging a character with whom the NPC is angry. However, depending on the relative weighting assigned to different rewards and punishments, this scheme could backfire. For example, an NPC might learn to deliberately make itself angry by letting itself be tagged repeatedly by the same character just so it can get angry, and receive the extra reward from tagging it back. It might even chase the tagged character around trying to get itself tagged! Since the learning algorithm has no way to know the underlying intent behind the reward function, it will simply try to exploit the environment in any way it can to receive the reward.

Clearly coming up with a reward that yields the desired behavior can require some ingenuity. For example, researchers have struggled for a long time with how to use rewards and learning to automatically generate realistic-looking motion. Initial attempts rewarded the distance traveled in a fixed time period which led to some realistic motions and a lot of

comical-looking ones. Modifying the reward function to include terms for smoothness and symmetry helped tilt the scales more toward aesthetically pleasing motion. But it was only recently, in [LCR03], that the insightful discovery was made that rewarding motion that is resilient to noisy sensors is one of the most effective strategies.

If tweaking the reward to get the desired behavior starts to become a painstaking and frustrating experience it is worth questioning whether the behavior you want is so specific that it might be easier to hand-code it.

7.3.1 Utility

Whenever an NPC has to make a decision, there are a number of possible actions it can take, some of which may result in positive rewards and some in negative rewards. What makes the problem of choosing actions interesting is that some of the actions that result in an immediate negative reward may ultimately lead to a large positive reward. The task of the NPC is to learn which actions are most likely to lead to large rewards in the long run. This is somewhat similar to the case of searching, where the action that takes an NPC closer to its goal (in terms of Euclidean distance) may ultimately lead to a dead end. That is, the optimal path may sometimes momentarily appear to lead away from the goal.

The idea of long-term reward is captured in the notion of utility. Utility is defined as the reward from the current game-state plus a measure of the long-term future reward a controller expects to receive. Notice that, because the long term future reward depends on how the controller behaves in the future, the utility of a game-state depends on the controller.

To formalize the definition of utility, this section needs to introduce some additional notation taken from [RN02]. First, recall that percepts are a function of the game-state and that a controller is a function ϕ from percepts $\mathbf{x}$ to actions. The simulator is a function from the current game-state s and the controller's action choice $\phi(\mathbf{x})$ to a new game-state s'. More generally, a simulator can be thought of as a function T (called the transition model) that assigns probabilities to the possibility of ending up in a state s': $T(s, \phi(\mathbf{x}), s')$. The generalization might not be needed for the game simulator because it is typically deterministic. But, as seen from Section 6.4.2 in the previous chapter, the generalization is clearly needed for an approximate simulator.

Using the transition model, here is the formal recursive definition of the utility of a controller ϕ in a game-state s:

$$U^\phi(s) = R(s) + \gamma \sum_{s'} T(s, \phi(\mathbf{x}), s')\, U^\phi(s'), \qquad (7.1)$$

where $R(s)$ is the percept representing the current reward and γ is called the *discount factor*. The discount factor is a number between 0 and 1 where smaller numbers give more weight to short-term reward versus longer-term reward. Notice how the transition model is used to calculate the expected future utility over all the possible (as dictated by the possible actions) subsequent game-states s'.

If an NPC knows the utility of all states, it can behave optimally by picking actions that lead to states with the highest utility. Instead of a heuristic, it would be like having an oracle. A controller with access to an oracle does not need to search more than one step ahead. The next possible future game-state that the oracle says is best would necessarily be the optimal choice. Therefore, automatically learning a utility function would amount to learning to behave optimally.

7.4 Remembering

Normally, the idea of learning something implies some ability to generalize from past experience to new unseen cases. This is different from simply remembering what happened in the past and regurgitating it. Nevertheless, simple recall of past actions is a good place to start.

For example, consider the discrete tag game described at the start of the previous chapter. For now, assume that, except for the initial position of the tagged player, the game always starts in the same configuration and none of the other characters can move! If the tagged character has a path-planner like one described in the previous chapter, then when the tagged character plans a path to the nearest untagged character it ends up implicitly calculating the path cost. Suppose it also gets a reward for tagging a character, then the utility of the grid cell in which it started is set to the reward minus the path cost. The utility for each cell can be calculated in a similar manner. Notice, that by starting from the goal node and working outward, previous calculations can be re-used. That is, the utility of a path is always the utility of the current cell minus the cost to get there. This is,

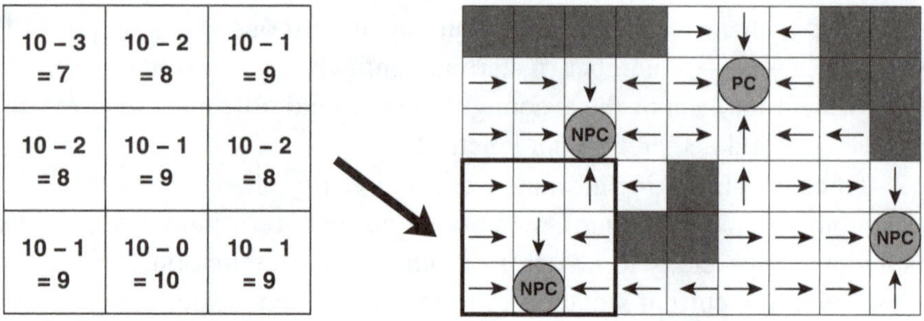

10 – 3 = 7	10 – 2 = 8	10 – 1 = 9
10 – 2 = 8	10 – 1 = 9	10 – 2 = 8
10 – 1 = 9	10 – 0 = 10	10 – 1 = 9

Figure 7.1. Induced vector field.

more or less, the intuition behind an algorithm called *dynamic programming* [SB98, RN02].

Once the utility of each cell has been calculated, the resulting values implicitly define a vector field. Figure 7.1 shows the vector field that results for one particular configuration. The inset on the left shows how the utility of each cell might be calculated. For example, the tagged character receives a reward of 10 whenever it gets to a cell containing an untagged character.[2] The utility of a cell is the reward available from the cell minus the least possible cost (using the Manhattan distance) of getting to the reward. The vector field is therefore induced by the direction of the adjacent cell with the highest utility. When there is a tie for the best utility among the adjacent cells, the figure arbitrarily shows just one of the optimal directions. At runtime, wherever the tagged character is placed, it can take the optimal route to the nearest untagged character by mindlessly following the vector field.

7.4.1 Function Approximation

Dropping the assumption that the game always starts in the same configuration leads to problems.[3] In the discrete tag game, with $m \times n$ grid

---

[2]Notice that the tagged character receives a reward for landing on the *same* cell as an untagged character. Previously the goal of the tagged character was stated as ending up in a cell *adjacent* to an untagged character. The only reason for the change is that the numbers in the figure are a bit more varied with the new rule.

[3]Note that this is also equivalent to letting the other characters move, since each subsequent board position will be equivalent to one of the initial configurations.

cells and k characters, there are (assuming at most one character per cell) a possible $\frac{(mn)!}{k!(mn-k)!}$ number of starting configurations. Storing a separate vector field for each of those configurations would obviously require a lot of memory and is therefore not practical.

Of course, by taking advantage of rotational symmetry, and other loss-less compression techniques, memory usage could be minimized. A better solution, however, is to switch to a different representation. Instead of describing the current situation in terms of the game-state, use percepts. Percepts have been used throughout the book as a convenient and parsi-monious representation for the game-state. As explained in Section 3.4 in Chapter 3, percepts hide unimportant details and emphasize crucial simi-larities between game-states. That is, they effectively act as a lossy way of compressing the game-state to leave only the information that is important to the AI algorithms.

Once a suitable collection of percepts has been defined an approxi-mation to the table of vector fields can be learned. There are numerous possibilities for representing the approximation; popular choices are deci-sion trees and neural networks. Depending on the chosen representation, various learning algorithms can be used to create a learned instance. The input to the learning would be a table of percept values, each line labeled with the corresponding average utility. Average utility is used because the percept values represent a set of possible game-states (i.e., a belief state) and so the calculated utility will vary depending on which (hidden) actual game-state the NPC is in. Of course, the table need never be explicitly computed; a planner is simply used to label examples, one at a time, from which the learner will learn. This is an example of a supervised learning *regression* problem. Unfortunately, the approach is unlikely to be suc-cessful because it ignores the fact that rewards in different states are not independent.

Instead of immediately considering alternatives, the next section drops the unrealistic assumption about movement taking place on a grid.

7.5 Reinforcement Learning

Reinforcement learning works by exploring the space of possible con-trollers to find ones that lead to high rewards. In particular, it looks for which actions, in which situations, lead to rewards. In the tag game, game

level actions consist of two-dimensional direction vectors, which means that a controller is a mapping from percepts to $(R)^2$. That is a lot of possible different actions, so the space of possible controllers is enormous. It would therefore clearly be absurd to try and store the controller as a big table from percepts to actions. Without even having to go into details about how it might work, it should be clear that with so many possible actions, learning an approximation to the table would be hard. The problem is that, with so many actions, it would require too much data to explore the space well enough to spot any patterns that might occur. For example, the learner might notice that in some given situation it is a good idea to go in the direction $(0.6, 0.8)$. But without a lot more data it would not realize that in the same given situation any similar direction is probably also good.

It is therefore naive to expect to apply reinforcement learning directly to the problem of learning a controller in the tag game, or most other games. In the tag game, the actions used by the learned controller therefore need to be simplified and then fed into another subcontroller that will convert them into game actions. The next few subsections explore some possibilities for high-level actions that could be learned.

7.5.1 Compass Directions

Instead of a two-dimensional direction vector, a controller could learn in which of eight compass directions to move. The compass directions could then easily be somehow translated into a direction vector by a subcontroller.

Solely from a problem representation point of view, using compass directions makes the application of reinforcement learning feasible. However, the problem representation for the learner is still not nearly as simple as it could be. For example, suppose the tagged character has already learned to chase the nearest untagged character but that there is now an obstacle between it and its target. It will have to learn to go around the obstacle first, which may involve (in part) unlearning what it previously learned about heading directly toward its target. This will require a lot more data for it to figure out precisely under what circumstances it needs to take a detour before heading for its target. If a complicated maze was introduced into the tag game world, the situation becomes hopeless; the controller is never realistically going to learn to solve mazes and to reach the nearest character.

7.5.2 Waypoints

The waypoint graph introduced in Section 6.4 in the previous chapter can also be used for learning. In particular, the problem is to learn which waypoint to select as a goal. Once a waypoint is selected then control is handed over to a subcontroller that plans a path to the goal and follows the path. There would be some additional details to decide, such as how long the subcontroller should follow the path before it asks for a new goal; what it should do when it arrives at the goal; what it should do if it sees a nearby untagged character *en route*; etc. But assuming these details could be worked out the learning problem is now a lot easier. In particular, the path planning problem has been factored out of the equation.

The percepts that would be needed by the learner would be information about each of the waypoints, for example, whether there is an untagged character nearby, which direction the nearby character is heading, whether there is a large group of untagged characters nearby, etc. If the reward function is defined to give an extra reward to an NPC for tagging a character with whom it was angry, then there would also need to be percepts to provide information about whether there was a character with whom the NPC is angry near a waypoint.

To make the learning even easier the list of waypoints could be pre-filtered to just include a few promising ones. For example, the choice could just be between the waypoint with the nearest untagged character, or the waypoint with the nearest character with whom the tagged character is angry. Depending on how far each waypoint is, the directions the characters are traveling, and how the reward function is defined, a different waypoint could be the optimal one in different circumstances. The learning would figure out the trade-off on its own. Of course, if the problem is made simple enough, a different learning algorithm might be more appropriate.

The downside of simplifying the problem is that there will be less variety in the NPC's learned behavior. That is, if it has more action choices, then it has the potential to discover quirks about special situations that warrant a different response. By simplifying a problem you are biasing the learning to produce a certain kind of solution and there is less room for surprises. But if there are no surprises left at all, then you might have restricted the problem so tightly that it would be better off to just hand-code the one remaining solution that is left.

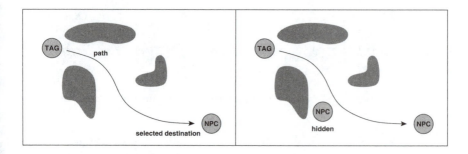

Figure 7.2. Two indistinguishable scenarios.

7.5.3 Transition Model

Another important consequence of simplifying the learning problem is that
it introduces uncertainty. For example, Figure 7.2 shows two different scenarios in the tag game. In the scenario on the right-hand side, an NPC is
hiding from the tagged character behind an obstacle. Assume that the percepts are correctly modeling the fact that the hidden NPC and the tagged
character cannot see each other. Then from the learner's point of view both
scenarios are indistinguishable.[4] In both cases the same waypoint will be
selected and the tagged character will follow a path to that same waypoint.
But in the scenario on the right, the tagged character may well stumble
across the hidden NPC, who will be unable to see the tagged character
coming. In the scenario on the left, no such good fortune will greet the
tagged character and it is quite likely the NPC will see the tagged character coming and run away.

From the learner's point of view, the same action in two identical situations resulted in two different outcomes. The same ambiguity will also
happen due to other sources of hidden information. Some of the information will be hidden deliberately; a lot more is simply not represented in
the simplified model of the game-state represented in the percepts. The
end result is that the learner sees the game world as noisy and full of
uncertainty.

---

[4]This assumes there is no memory percept that records the last place a character was
seen, as if there was, then the two situations in the figure are distinguishable. In such cases,
an NPC could learn to explore areas near to where it last saw a character. But if in one case
the hidden character had moved far away, but in another it had stayed near to where it was
last seen, there would still be different outcomes. In general, partial observability always
leads to uncertainty due to indistinguishable game-states.

x_0	x_1	x_2	x_3	...	a	x'_0	x'_1	x'_2	x_3	...	$T(\mathbf{x}, a, \mathbf{x}')$
f	N	b	E	...	b	f	S	c	E	...	0.02
f	N	b	W	...	g	b	S	f	W	...	0.04

Table 7.1. Two lines of an approximated transition model.

To make sense of its uncertain world, a learner can use its past experience to approximate the probabilities for the transition model that appears in Equation 7.1. That is, the learner uses a snapshot of itself so far as the controller and the associated NPC proceeds to interact with the game world. As the NPC moves around, performing actions in the game world, it can calculate the probability it will end up in some belief state $\mathbf{x}'$ given it performs an action a in belief state $\mathbf{x}$ as follows:

$$T(\mathbf{x}, a, \mathbf{x}') = \frac{\text{number of times performing } a \text{ in } \mathbf{x} \text{ resulted in } \mathbf{x}'}{\text{number of times performed } a \text{ in } \mathbf{x}}.$$

For example, suppose in the approach described in Section 7.5.2 that there are (among many others) the following four percepts:

$$x_0 = \text{The tagged character's current nearest waypoint,}$$
$$x_1 = \text{The tagged character's heading,}$$
$$x_2 = \text{The nearest untagged character's nearest waypoint,}$$
$$x_3 = \text{The nearest untagged character's heading.}$$

Then probabilities in the approximate transition model table would look something like those in Table 7.1. Only two lines of the table are shown, and there is no significance meant to be attached to the values shown other than that they are of the right type. If the whole table was to be all written out explicitly it would have an enormous number of lines. But in principle, once the table has been determined, it can be used to calculate the expected utility of a belief state, and the action which leads to the belief state with the highest expected utility can be chosen. Therefore, once the transition model has been determined an NPC can use dynamic programming to calculate an optimal controller for that model.

But the NPC also does not have to wait until the transition model is fully acquired. At any point it can apply dynamic programming to the current transition model to get the best controller so far. This is called adaptive

dynamic programming. It works because the transition model is a model of the environment and so is independent of the particular controller that has been learned so far. Unfortunately, for all but the simplest problems, it is often impractical to solve dynamic programming problems of the size that get generated in the adaptive dynamic programming approach.

To avoid solving large dynamic programming problems there are different methods of reinforcement learning. One particularly popular approach is called Q-learning. It has the advantage that, in a version called temporal difference Q-learning, the transition model probabilities are not explicitly required at all. The Q values represent the utility of performing an action a in game-state s, i.e., $Q(a, s)$. Q values can be learned with a relatively simple-looking update rule that is applied iteratively until the Q values converge:

$$Q(a, s) = Q(a, s) + \alpha(R(s) + \gamma \max_{a'} Q(a', s') - Q(a, s)),$$

where R is the reward, α is the learning rate, and γ is the discount factor.

7.5.4 Convergence

One reason reinforcement learning is popular is that if the world is fully observable it is guaranteed to converge to the optimal solution provided every action is performed an infinite number of times in every state. In practice, it often converges to a good solution after a long time of autonomously running millions of game simulations. Care also needs to be taken in practice that a wide variety of possible actions are tried in each state. Otherwise, if during learning the controller is too greedy to exploit what it has already learned, the learning can get stuck in a local minima. One way to ensure the learner properly explores the state space is to introduce some randomness by forcing the learning to not always pick the action that leads to the greatest expected utility. Instead, the learner only picks the best action with some probability. As the learner discovers more about its environment, the expected utility becomes more accurate and the learner can therefore explore less and exploit more. This can be done by gradually increasing the probability of picking the action with the greatest expected utility. Alternatively, the learner can be made to always be optimistic about the utility of actions it has not taken before in a given state.

When the game-state is only partially observable (through the percepts **x**) the theory underlying reinforcement learning is more complex. But in practice, it also often works provided the algorithm is run long enough and percepts are sufficiently well engineered to give the algorithm all the important information it needs. This is where games once again have an advantage over other AI application areas. In games, the percepts could (if necessary, and subject to concerns about realistic perception) be expanded to make the game-state fully observable. In other applications, the true underlying state of the world is often genuinely inaccessible and so optimism about percept engineering ultimately yielding success is less warranted.

In some nongame AI applications, running all the simulations required for reinforcement learning can take a long time and is risky. For example, if a robot makes a mistake and falls over a cliff it is a disaster. In games, simulation is cheap and the game world can easily be reset. In addition, if the renderer is decoupled from the rest of the game code, then running millions of simulations can be sped up by orders of magnitude.

You can read more about the topics of reinforcement learning, Q-learning, and learning in general in [Mit97, SB98, DHS00, HTF01, RN02].

7.5.5   Function Approximation

For any practical problem the state space is too large to explicitly store the Q-function (or transition model, if required) as a table. The table can therefore be represented by a function approximator like those described in Section 7.4.1. Unfortunately, the convergence guarantees also no longer apply if the Q-function is only approximated. But, as usual, it can often be made to work by changing percepts, adding percepts, or changing the problem representation.

There are articles in the games AI literature that suggest using a neural network as a function approximator. Neural networks can be used successfully, especially when (as in [Tes95]) there is an enormous amount of training data. But in general they are susceptible to problems because of the nature of the training samples. In particular, remember the learner is also the controller, so the training samples are not independent because they are generated by the learner itself. There is therefore potential for a harmful feedback loop: a learner generates experience that is used as input to a neural network that is used as the representation of the learner.

The neural network is, in effect, responsible for generating its own training data.

Other function approximators, like decision trees, do not suffer so much from the problem with feedback loops. The reason is that decision tree learning algorithms generalize training examples by interpolating, whereas neural networks can also extrapolate. Decision trees also have the desirable property that the output can be inspected to see if it looks somewhat reasonable. This is especially important if the algorithm is failing to converge as some important clues can be found by inspecting the decision trees being learned. In contrast, it is unlikely that staring at the weights of a neural network will reveal much useful information. For more about advanced research work on reinforcement learning, see [SJJ94, JSJ95, KLM96, Lit96, WS97, Per02].

Appendix A

Picking

The stochastic version of a controller described in Section 4.1.1 in Chapter 4 defines a probability distribution over possible actions. In this appendix, two common ways of picking a single action from a probability distribution are described: picking the most likely and picking randomly.

The descriptions assume some familiarity with basic mathematical probability. If you need a refresher course there are a huge number of references available on the underlying theory of mathematical probability. For example, a good standard textbook on the subject is [MMF04]. For a less formal presentation on some of the underlying intuitions, see [Isa96]. Also [RN02] and [KN03] include a lot of probability theory and references applicable to AI. Additional references, including to freely available resources on the Internet, are included on this book's companion web site.

There are, of course, other ways of measuring uncertainty besides probability, but probability is the optimal choice. It is optimal in the following sense: if you were playing a game that involved gambling and uncertainty, anyone using the laws of probability would do better (over the long haul) than a person using some other set of laws.

A.1 Picking the Most Likely

The simplest way to pick an action from a probability distribution is to pick the most likely one. For example, suppose there are five actions: $a_0, \ldots, a_4$ with probabilities as shown in Table A.1. Then the most likely action is a_1 because it has the largest associated probability.

a_i	a_0	a_1	a_2	a_3	a_4
$P(a_i|\mathbf{x})$	0.2	0.3125	0.25	0.0375	0.2

Table A.1. Example probability distribution.

If the probability distribution a controller is picking from is generated by some genuine real-world source of uncertainty, then picking the most likely action is a reasonable thing to do. However, in games, there are occasions when it can lead to unintended consequences. For example, suppose the probability distribution is fixed by the developer before the game ships as part of the character definition because the developer is presumably hoping that the probability distribution will introduce a bit of variety into the controller's decisions. However, the most likely action will always be the same one. There is no nondeterminism.

Even if the probability distribution is computed at runtime based on some inputs from the game world there can be problems. For example, in a simulated world it is common to find many examples of perfect symmetry. This can result in a probability distribution that assigns the same maximum probability to a set of actions, in which case, depending on the indexing order, the first action in the list will always be chosen. Two special cases of the problem are when all possible actions get the same probability, and when one single action is always given slightly more probability than any of the others. In the first case, picking the most likely is equivalent to picking the first action; and in the second, to always picking the same action.

A.2 Picking Randomly

Unless all the probabilities are the same, picking randomly according to a probability distribution does not mean that all actions have an equal chance of being selected. In particular, each action has the chance of being selected equal to its probability. For example, if a controller picked 50 actions using the probabilities in Table A.1, then you would expect it to pick action a_4 ten times. Of course, there is a small chance ($0.8^{50} \approx 0.0000143$) it would not pick a_4 at all, and an even smaller chance ($0.2^{50} \approx 0.11259 \times 10^{-34}$) it would pick a_4 every time.

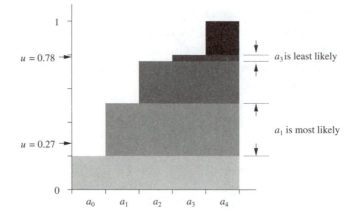

Figure A.1. Cumulative distribution.

Implementing a random pick according to a probability distribution is straightforward: use a random number generator to generate a (pseudo) random number u from the uniform distribution between 0 and 1. Then, add up the probabilities of each action one at a time until they equal or exceed u. The action whose probability caused the running total to equal or exceed u is the choice. For example, using the probability distribution in Table A.1, if the random number generator picks $u = 0.27$, then action a_1 (the most likely) is chosen. Figure A.1 shows the cumulative distribution and how it is used to pick an action given the value of u.

Notice that if the random number generator had picked $u = 0.78$, say, then the least likely action a_3 would have been picked. Depending on the game, having the (even remote) possibility of picking such low-probability actions might be undesirable. If so, it is straightforward to filter out the low-probability events, renormalize, and then pick according to the new distribution.

Be careful to have only one instance of a random number generator in your game and seed it just once at the start. That way, for a given seed, you will always get the same sequence of random numbers. If the inputs are kept the same, you will therefore get the same number of calls to the single random number generator, which will, in turn, produce the same simulation every time. This will help you track down the source of errors when you are debugging because the bug will be easily reproducible.

Obviously if the input changes, such as when a player is playing the game, the random sequence will quickly diverge. That is a good thing as, once the game ships, players do not want to see the same simulation every time. To be extra careful, the shipped version of the game can alternate between different initial seeds.

Appendix B

Programming

C++ code snippets are used throughout this book to make concepts clearer and more concrete. To understand the C++ code you obviously need to have some degree of familiarity with programming in an object-oriented programming language like C++. As software engineering practices become more refined, C++ is displacing C as the most popular language for game development. All the major game development platforms have a choice of C++ compilers available and provided the programmer is careful to avoid some common pitfalls (see [Ise04]), it is at least as efficient as C.

Like C++, Java is another popular object-oriented programming language. For games that appear within web pages and on mobile devices it might make a good choice, but at the time of writing it is not well supported on the major console platforms. Among AI researchers in academia, LISP has traditionally been widely used and it has also enjoyed some popularity among game developers. The company Naughty Dog used Allegro CL to create GOOL (Game Object-Oriented Language) for use in programming their successful Crash Bandicoot series. Since being acquired by Sony, the same team plans to use LISP even more extensively in future titles. Nevertheless, LISP is not widely known in the game development community, so C++ remains the most reasonable choice for code given in this book. It should be straightforward for an experienced programmer to translate the code (or at least the underlying ideas) to other programming languages.

Games development used to be notorious for bad software engineering practices. Some of this was justified by the fact that games were often written as one-off, throw-away, applications. Companies also like to

rewrite their games from release to release to give them a fresh feel. But so many games are now building on previous codebases, or using game engines across projects, that good software engineering is becoming a necessity. Even within a single project, games are becoming so complex that sloppy coding practices can cause development times to grow needlessly. Numerous good references and pointers to online resources about software engineering are therefore available on this book's companion web site.

Here are a few miscellaneous notes about the code in this book:

- the code has been written to make it as easy to understand as possible, and it is often therefore not particularly efficient. In particular, there is little or no caching of previous results as that would add complexity to the code. For example, in the tgGameState class introduced in Chapter 2 it would make sense to have a private class variable characterIndices to store the list of indices of those objects that are characters. This would make it faster to iterate through the characters and return a pointer to a requested character. As the code stands, many simple operations would require searching through the whole list of game objects to find the desired one(s). Another place where caching is important is in the calculation of percepts, but care has to be taken to correctly purge and manage the caches as the myIndex variable changes.

- class methods in this book often use the "get" prefix for accessors to class member variables and "calc" methods that actually need to do some work. However, the convention is only followed laxly as, depending on the underlying implementation, some methods could be defined either way around.

- the code given in this book makes limited use of the Standard Template Library (STL) (see www.sgi.com/tech/stl) as it is convenient and greatly simplifies some of the code. However, to use STL in your own games you might need to write your own custom memory allocation routines (see [Ise02]).

- AI code often depends on a number of geometric calculations. These calculations resolve various geometric relationships between entities in the game world. A simple example is determining the distance between an NPC and its nearest enemy. A more complex example is

determining whether an NPC can be seen from its current location. Some kind of linear algebra package is required to perform the relevant calculations. The code in this book assumes the existence of a class tgVec for performing linear algebra calculations. Operator overloading is *not* used as it can easily lead to confusing code. This book's companion web site has some links to some freely available linear algebra packages that could be used in games. For the simple linear algebra used in most games it is also not hard to write your own package from scratch.

- aside from methods for geometric calculations, there are some other methods that are referenced but never defined. In such cases the semantics of the method should hopefully be obvious from the name.

- the code given in this book does not contain much error checking. Error checking is important in debug releases of code and there are many books on software engineering that cover the topic.

- the code in this book is not console-compliant. For example, the code creates objects whenever it needs to, which can lead to memory fragmentation. To avoid this, consoles typically use a pool or a stack memory manager that preallocates space when the game first starts up.

- all the objects in the tag game are declared in the tagGame namespace. The "tg" prefix is therefore not strictly necessary, but serves to avoid ending up with variable names that clash with reserved words (similarly for the "dtg" prefix used in the discrete tag game).

- the code in this book might not be formatted to your taste. For example, you might prefer to write your if-statements with the curly bracket on the same line, or put the **const** designator before the type, or use sophisticated naming schemes for variables, etc. There is not much to write about such issues, except that most of the choices in this book have some rationale behind them, but ultimately it comes down to a matter of personal taste.

Bibliography

[AC87]   Philip E. Agre and David Chapman. Pengi: A Theory of Activity. In *Proceedings of AAAI 87*, 1987.

[aiS00]   aiSee. Graph Visualization. Available from World Wide Web (www.aisee.com), 2000.

[AL98]   Natasha Alechina and Brian Logan. State space Search with Prioritised Soft Constraints. In *Proceedings of the ECAI 98 Workshop: Decision Theory meets Artificial Intelligence*, 1998.

[Ale02]   Thor Alexander. GoCap: Game Observation Capture. In Steve Rabin, editor, *AI Game Programming Wisdom*. Charles River Media, Hingham, MA, 2002.

[BDI$^+$02]   Bruce Blumberg, Marc Downie, Yuri Ivanov, Matt Berlin, Michael Patrick Johnson, and Bill Tomlinson. Integrated Learning for Interactive Synthetic Characters. In *Proceedings of ACM SIGGRAPH 2002*, Computer Graphics Proceedings, Annual Conference Series, 2002.

[Ber04]   Curt Bererton. State Estimation for Game AI Using Particle Filters. In *AAAI Workshop on Challenges in Game AI*, 2004.

[BM98]   C.L. Blake and C.J. Merz. UCI Repository of Machine Learning Databases. Available from World Wide Web (www.ics.uci.edu/~mlearn/MLRepository.html), 1998.

[Bou01]   David M. Bourg. *Physics for Game Developers*. O'Reilly & Associates, Sebastopol, CA, 2001.

[Bra84]   Valentino Braitenberg. *Vehicles: Experiments in Synthetic Psychology*. MIT Press, Cambridge, MA, 1984.

[Bro90]   Rodney A. Brooks. Elephants Don't Play Chess. *Robotics and Autonomous Systems*, 6(1&2), 1990.

[Cha91]   David Chapman. *Vision, Instruction, and Action*. MIT Press, Cambridge, MA, 1991.

[Cha03]   Alex J. Champandard. *AI Game Development*. New Riders, Indianapolis, IN, 2003.

[DB04]   Richard C. Dorf and Robert H. Bishop. *Modern Control Systems*. Prentice Hall, Upper Saddle River, NJ, tenth edition, 2004.

[DEdGD04]   Jonathan Dinerstein, Parris K Egbert, Hugo de Garis, and Nelson Dinerstein. Fast and Learnable Behavioral and Cognitive Modeling for Virtual Character Animation. *Computer Animation and Virtual Worlds*, 15(2), 2004.

[DeL00]   Mark DeLoura, editor. *Game Programming Gems*. Charles River Media, Hingham, MA, 2000.

[DeL01]   Mark DeLoura, editor. *Game Programming Gems 2*. Charles River Media, Hingham, MA, 2001.

[DHS00]   Richard O. Duda, Peter E. Hart, and David G. Stork. *Pattern Classification*. Wiley, New York, NY, 2000.

[Doy02]   Patrick Doyle. Believability through Context: Using Knowledge in the World to Create Intelligent Characters. In *Proceedings of the International Joint Conference on Autonomous Agents and Multi-Agent Systems (AAMAS 2002)*, 2002.

[Etz93]   Oren Etzioni. Intelligence without Robots (A Reply to Brooks). *AI Magazine*, 14(4), 1993.

[Fal95]   Petros Faloutsos. Physics-based animation and control of flexible characters. Master's thesis, University of Toronto, 1995.

[Fun99]   John D. Funge. *AI for Animation and Games: A Cognitive Modeling Approach*. A K Peters, Wellesley, MA, 1999.

[FvDFH95]   James D. Foley, Andries van Dam, Steven K. Feiner, and John F. Hughes. *Computer Graphics: Principles and Practice in C*. Addison-Wesley, Reading, MA, second edition, 1995.

[FvdPT01]   Petros Faloutsos, Michiel van de Panne, and Demetri Terzopoulos. Composable Controllers for Physics-Based Character Animation. In *Proceedings of ACM SIGGRAPH 2001*, Computer Graphics Proceedings, Annual Conference Series, 2001.

[Gib87]   James J. Gibson. *The Ecological Approach to Visual Perception*. Lawrence Erlbaum Associates, Mahwah, NJ, 1987.

[GT95]   Radek Grzeszczuk and Demetri Terzopoulos. Automated Learning of Muscle-Actuated Locomotion Through Control Abstraction. In *Proceedings of SIGGRAPH 95*, Computer Graphics Proceedings, Annual Conference Series, 1995.

[HF03]   Ryan Houlette and Dan Fu. The Ultimate Guide to FSMs in Games. In Steve Rabin, editor, *AI Game Programming Wisdom 2*. Charles River Media, Hingham, MA, 2003.

[HP97]   Jessica K. Hodgins and Nancy S. Pollard. Adapting Simulated Behaviors for New Characters. In *Proceedings of SIGGRAPH 97*, Computer Graphics Proceedings, Annual Conference Series, 1997.

[HTF01]   Trevor Hastie, Robert Tibshirani, and Jerome Friedman. *The Elements of Statistical Learning*. Springer-Verlag, New York, NY, 2001.

[IB02]   Damian Isla and Bruce Blumberg. Object Persistence for Synthetic Creatures. In *Proceedings of the International Joint Conference on Autonomous Agents and Multiagent Systems (AAMAS)*, 2002.

[Isa96]   Richard Isaac. *The Pleasures of Probability*. Springer-Verlag, New York, NY, 1996.

[Ise02]   Pete Isensee. Custom STL Allocators. In Dante Treglia and Mark DeLoura, editors, *Game Programming Gems 3*. Charles River Media, Hingham, MA, 2002.

[Ise04]   Pete Isensee. Common C++ Performance Mistakes in Games. In *Game Developer's Conference Proceedings*, 2004.

[JSJ95]   Tommi Jaakkola, Satinder P. Singh, and Michael I. Jordan. Reinforcement Learning Algorithms for Partially Observable Markov Problems. In *Advances in Neural Information Processing Systems 7, Proceedings of the 1994 Conference*, 1995.

[KGP02]   Lucas Kovar, Michael Gleicher, and Frédéric Pighin. Motion Graphs. *ACM Transactions on Graphics*, 21(3), 2002.

[Kin00]   Melianthe Kines. Planning and Directing Motion Capture for Games. *Gamasutra*, 2000.

[Kir04]   Andrew Kirmse, editor. *Game Programming Gems 4*. Charles River Media, Hingham, MA, 2004.

[KL00]   James Kuffner and Steven M. LaValle. RRT-Connect: An Efficient Approach to Single-Query Path Planning. In *Proceedings of the IEEE International Conference on Robotics and Automation (ICRA 2000)*, 2000.

[KLM96]   Leslie Pack Kaelbling, Michael L. Littman, and Andrew P. Moore. Reinforcement Learning: A Survey. *Journal of Artificial Intelligence Research*, 4, 1996.

[KN03]   Kevin B. Korb and Ann E. Nicholson. *Bayesian Artificial Intelligence*. CRC Press, Boca Raton, FL, 2003.

[KS96]   Henry Kautz and Bart Selman. Pushing the Envelope: Planning, Propositional Logic, and Stochastic Search. In *Proceedings of the Thirteenth National Conference on Artificial Intelligence*, 1996.

[KS03]   Henry Kautz and Bart Selman. Ten Challenges Redux: Recent Progress in Propositional Reasoning and Search. In *Proceedings of the Ninth International Conference on Principles and Practice of Constraint Programming (CP 2003)*, 2003.

[LCR03]   Greg Lawrence, Noah Cowan, and Stuart Russell. Efficient Gradient Estimation for Motor Control Learning. In *Proceedings of the Nineteenth Conference on Uncertainty in Artificial Intelligence*, 2003.

[LDG03]   Seth Luisi, Glenn Van Datta, and Bob Gutmann. SOCOM: Bringing a Console Game Online. In *Game Developer's Conference Proceedings*, 2003.

[Len95]   Douglas B. Lenat. CYC: A Large-Scale Investment in Knowledge Infrastructure. *Communications of the ACM*, 38(11), 1995.

[Leo03]   Tom Leonard. Building an ai Sensory System: Examining the Design of Thief: The Dark Project. In *Game Developer's Conference Proceedings*, 2003.

[Lin98]   Fangzhen Lin. Applications of the Situation Calculus to Formalizing Control and Strategic Information: The Prolog Cut Operator. *Artificial Intelligence*, 103(1&2), 1998.

[Lit96]   Michael Lederman Littman. *Algorithms for Sequential Decision Making*. PhD thesis, Brown University, 1996.

[LNR87]   John E. Laird, Allan Newell, and Paul S. Rosenbloom. SOAR: An Architecture of General Intelligence. *Artificial Intelligence*, 33(3), 1987.

[LvdPF00]   Joseph Laszlo, Michiel van de Panne, and Eugene L. Fiume. Interactive Control for Physically-Based Animation. In *Proceedings of ACM SIGGRAPH 2000*, Computer Graphics Proceedings, Annual Conference Series, 2000.

[Man03]   John Manslow. Using Reinforcement Learning to Solve AI Control Problems. In Steve Rabin, editor, *AI Game Programming Wisdom 2*. Charles River Media, Hingham, MA, 2003.

[Mar01]   Richard Marks. Using Video Input for Games. In *Game Developer's Conference Proceedings*, 2001.

[Mit97]   Tom M. Mitchell. *Machine Learning*. McGraw-Hill, New York, NY, 1997.

[MMF04]   Irwin Miller, Marylees Miller, and John E. Freund. *John E. Freund's Mathematical Statistics with Applications*. Prentice Hall, Upper Saddle River, NJ, seventh edition, 2004.

[MNPW98]   Nicola Muscettola, P. Pandurang Nayak, Barney Pell, and Brian C. Williams. Remote Agent: To Boldly Go Where No AI System Has Gone Before. *Artificial Intelligence*, 103(1&2), 1998.

[MS99]   Christopher D. Manning and Hinrich Schütze. *Foundations of Statistical Natural Language Processing*. MIT Press, Cambridge, MA, 1999.

[Osb03]   Martin J. Osborne. *An Introduction to Game Theory*. Oxford University Press, New York, NY, 2003.

[Pea84]   Judea Pearl. *Heuristics: Intelligent Search Strategies for Computer Problem Solving.* Addison-Wesley, Reading, MA, 1984.

[Per02]   Theodore J. Perkins. Reinforcement Learning for POMDPs Based on Action Values and Stochastic Optimization. In *Proceedings of the Eighteenth National Conference on Artificial Intelligence*, 2002.

[Rab00]   Steve Rabin. A* Aesthetic Optimizations. In Mark DeLoura, editor, *Game Programming Gems*. Charles River Media, Hingham, MA, 2000.

[Rab02]   Steve Rabin, editor. *AI Game Programming Wisdom*. Charles River Media, Hingham, MA, 2002.

[Rab03a]   Steve Rabin, editor. *AI Game Programming Wisdom 2*. Charles River Media, Hingham, MA, 2003.

[Rab03b]   Steve Rabin. Game AI Articles and Research. Available from World Wide Web (www.aiwisdom.com), 2003.

[Rei01]   Raymond Reiter. *Knowledge in Action: Logical Foundations for Specifying and Implementing Dynamical Systems*. MIT Press, Cambridge, MA, 2001.

[Rey87]   Craig W. Reynolds. Flocks, Herds, and Schools: A Distributed Behavioral Model. In *Computer Graphics (Proceedings of SIGGRAPH 87)*, Computer Graphics Proceedings, Annual Conference Series, 1987.

[Rey99]   Craig Reynolds. Steering Behaviors for Autonomous Characters. In *Game Developer's Conference Proceedings*, 1999.

[RG03]   Christopher Reed and Benjamin Geisler. Jumping, Climbing, and Tactical reasoning: How to Get More Out of a Navigation System. In Steve Rabin, editor, *AI Game Programming Wisdom 2*. Charles River Media, Hingham, MA, 2003.

[RN02]   Stuart Russell and Peter Norvig. *Artificial Intelligence: A Modern Approach*. Prentice Hall, Upper Saddle River, NJ, second edition, 2002.

[Sam02]   Miro Samek. *Practical Statecharts in C/C++*. CMP Books, Gilroy, CA, 2002.

[SB98]   Richard S. Sutton and Andrew G. Barto. *Reinforcement Learning: An Introduction*. MIT Press, Cambridge, MA, 1998.

[Shi02]   Peter Shirley. *Fundamentals of Computer Graphics*. A K Peters, Wellesley, MA, 2002.

[SJJ94]   Satinder P. Singh, Tommi Jaakkola, and Michael I. Jordan. Learning without State-Estimation in Partially Observable Markovian Decision Processes. In *Proceedings of the Eleventh International Conference on Machine Learning*, 1994.

[SP96]   Aaron Sloman and Riccardo Poli. SIM AGENT: A Toolkit
            for Exploring Agent Designs. In Mike Wooldridge, Joerg
            Mueller, and Milind Tambe, editors, *Intelligent Agents Vol II
            (ATAL-95)*. Springer-Verlag, New York, NY, 1996.

[TD02]   Dante Treglia and Mark DeLoura, editors. *Game Program-
            ming Gems 3*. Charles River Media, Hingham, MA, 2002.

[Tes95]   Gerald Tesauro. Temporal Difference Learning and TD-
            Gammon. *Communications of the ACM*, 38(3), 1995.

[TR97]   Demetri Terzopoulos and Tamer Rabie. Animat Vision: Ac-
            tive Vision in Artificial Animals. *Videre: Journal of Com-
            puter Vision Research*, 1(1), 1997.

[vdB03]   Gino van den Bergen. *Collision Detection in Interactive 3D
            Environments*. Morgan Kaufmann, San Francisco, CA, 2003.

[vdS02]   William van der Sterren. Tactical Path-Finding with A*. In
            Dante Treglia and Mark DeLoura, editors, *Game Program-
            ming Gems 3*. Charles River Media, Hingham, MA, 2002.

[vW01]   Jean Paul van Waveren. The quake III arena bot. Master's
            thesis, Delft University of Technology, 2001.

[WB01]   Andrew Witkin and David Baraff. Physically based model-
            ing. SIGGRAPH 2001 Course Notes, 2001.

[WF99]   Ian H. Witten and Eibe Frank. *Data Mining: Practical Ma-
            chine Learning Tools and Techniques with Java Implementa-
            tions*. Morgan Kaufmann, San Francisco, CA, 1999.

[WM03]   Ian Wright and James Marshall. The Execution Kernel of
            RC++: RETE*, a Faster RETE with TREAT as a Special
            Case. *International Journal of Intelligent Games and Simu-
            lation*, 2(1), 2003.

[Wol02]   Stephen Wolfram. *A New Kind of Science*. Wolfram Media,
            Champaign, IL, 2002.

[Wri97]   Ian Wright. Emotional agents. Master's thesis, University of
             Birmingham, 1997.

[WS97]   Marco Wiering and Jüurgen Schmidhuber.   HQ-Learning.
             Adaptive Behavior, 6(2), 1997.

[WW04]   Will Wright and Mike Winter. Stupid Fun Club. Available
             from World Wide Web (**www.stupidfunclub.com**), 2004.

Index